Grammar of Khuzestani Arabic

Studies in
Semitic Languages
and Linguistics

Editorial Board

Aaron D. Rubin (*Pennsylvania State University*)
Ahmad Al-Jallad (*The Ohio State University*)

VOLUME 108

The titles published in this series are listed at *brill.com/ssl*

Grammar of Khuzestani Arabic

A Spoken Variety of South-West Iran

By

Bettina Leitner

BRILL

LEIDEN | BOSTON

Cover illustration: Man on a canoe, Shadegan. Photo by Bettina Leitner.

The Library of Congress Cataloging-in-Publication Data is available online at http://catalog.loc.gov
LC record available at http://lccn.loc.gov/2022022261

Typeface for the Latin, Greek, and Cyrillic scripts: "Brill". See and download: brill.com/brill-typeface.

ISSN 0081-8461
ISBN 978-90-04-51023-4 (hardback)
ISBN 978-90-04-51024-1 (e-book)

Copyright 2022 by Bettina Leitner. Published by Koninklijke Brill NV, Leiden, The Netherlands.
Koninklijke Brill NV incorporates the imprints Brill, Brill Nijhoff, Brill Hotei, Brill Schöningh, Brill Fink, Brill mentis, Vandenhoeck & Ruprecht, Böhlau and V&R unipress.
Koninklijke Brill NV reserves the right to protect this publication against unauthorized use. Requests for re-use and/or translations must be addressed to Koninklijke Brill NV via brill.com or copyright.com.

This book is printed on acid-free paper and produced in a sustainable manner.

For Sebastian

وللشعب الأحوازي

كجل الناس تگعد سوا واتسولف مامن تلفزونات

*"In the past, people sat together and told stories;
there were no televisions."*
UMM SAAD

• • •

"I might be wrong."
RADIOHEAD

∴

Contents

Acknowledgements   IX
List of Tables, Maps and Figures   XI
Abbreviations   XIII

PART 1
Introduction and General Classification of Khuzestani Arabic

1 **Introduction**   3
- 1.1   Area   3
- 1.2   History of Arabs and Arab Tribes in Khuzestan   6
- 1.3   Current Situation of the Arabs and of Arabic in Iran   9
- 1.4   Khuzestani Arabic and Cognate *gələt*-Type Arabic Dialects   10
- 1.5   Data, Methodology, Organization   11

2 **General Classification and Internal Subdivisions of Khuzestani Arabic (KhA)**   17
- 2.1   Classification of KhA—The Position of KhA among the Mesopotamian Arabic Dialects   17
- 2.2   Internal Subdivisions of KhA   23
- 2.3   Conclusion   28
- 2.4   Illustrations   31

PART 2
Grammar

3 **Phonology**   43
- 3.1   Consonants   43
- 3.2   Vowels   57
- 3.3   Diphthongs   64
- 3.4   Emphasis   65
- 3.5   Syllable Structure   67
- 3.6   Stress   68
- 3.7   Phonotactics   69

VIII

4 Morphology 73
    4.1   Pronouns 73
    4.2   Quantifiers 114
    4.3   Adverbs 116
    4.4   Prepositions 152
    4.5   Paradigms of Prepositions with Pronominal Suffixes 174
    4.6   *māl* Constructions and the Analytic Genitive 176
    4.7   Conjunctions 189
    4.8   Particles 213
    4.9   Nouns 236
    4.10 Numerals 263
    4.11 Verbal Morphology 266

5 Texts 327
    5.1   Ahvaz, Abu Khazʕal [A1] 327
    5.2   Umm Saʕad [A10] 361
    5.3   ʕArab (ʕazīb) [A12], Semi-Nomads 372

References 383
Index of Subjects and Words 397

Acknowledgements

This monograph is based on my PhD thesis on the Arabic variety spoken in Khuzestan.

The basis for the linguistic descriptions found in this book was my fieldwork in Ahvaz in 2016 when I stayed with an Ahvazi family for one month—thanks to my dear friend Majed. This way I could immerse in the Khuzestani Arabic language and culture from the first until the final day of my stay. For one month, I had the honor to experience and get to know many important aspects of their culture, such as their incredible hospitality, their great sense of humor, their love for water buffalos, but also the problems they face due to their minority status in Iran.

Since I could not obtain another visa for Iran ever since this first field trip, this situation forced me to find other ways of additional data collection. Apart from additional fieldwork in Kuwait in 2018, where a considerable Khuzestani Arab minority lives, I had to rely on online elicitation, communication softwares for voice messages and video calls and of course, the help of my Ahvazi friends in Vienna.

There are many people whom I'd like to thank for their help and support during this project.

First and foremost I want to thank all my Ahvazi friends, without whom this book would not exist. Not only because I would obviously have no linguistic data without them, but also because of their admirable patience when helping me with my manifold questions regarding their dialect and my recordings.

I am especially thankful to my dear friend Majed for always being there for me, helping with enquiries of all sorts, explaining words not found in any dictionary, and building bridges between our cultures whenever needed.

I thank Majed's brother Nāṣər and his wife Amīna for hosting me in their house and treating me like their sister from the very first day of my arrival. I thank my friend Maryam and her family for all their help during and after my fieldwork in Ahvaz. I am also thankful to all the other Ahvazi friends who live in Vienna, especially Abu Khazʕal, Muḥammad, and Zahra, for always helping me during all this time and welcoming me into their houses.

I am very grateful to Prof. Peter Behnstedt, may his soul rest in peace, and Prof. Manfred Woidich for sending me their manuscript of the WAD IV, which was the basis for many comparative remarks in this book.

I also thank the faculty of Philological and Cultural Studies of the University of Vienna for its financial support, enabling my field trips to Iran and Kuwait. I am also very grateful to Craig for helping to improve the style and readability of my English writing, may you rest in peace.

I owe much gratitude to all my colleagues, fellow Arabic Dialectologists, and friends who supported me throughout this project and commented on draft versions of this book. Special mention should be made of Gisela Kitzler, my *abla*, Simone Bettega, and of course Stephan Procházka. His immense and most impressive knowledge not only of the Arabic Language in all its diversity but also about the culture and history of the Arab people has always been a major inspiration for me from the very beginning and one of the main reasons I became interested in the study of Arabic dialects. I am grateful and honored for having had the possibility of being his student, for I could not have wished for a more competent, patient, caring, and inspiring mentor.

I am grateful to my family, especially my parents Alfred and Edith, my brother Stefan and Anna, for their love and unconditional support. Thank you to all my friends for always being there to help, to listen, to give support, and to make me smile. Gisi, Kathi D. and Kathi T., and Anna, you rock!

And finally, I am of course infinitely thankful to Sebastian, my beloved partner—you are not only an immense emotional support but also my favourite intellectual inspiration and the best proofreader. Thank you for your love, your patience, your advice, and for being my personal jukebox, whose music adds additional colors to my life.

Bettina Leitner
Vienna

Tables, Maps and Figures

Tables

1 Consonant inventory of Khuzestani Arabic   43
2 Vowel inventory of KhA   57
3 Independent personal pronouns   73
4 Pronouns suffixed to nouns and prepositions   78
5 Pronouns suffixed to verbs   78
6 Indirect object suffixes complementing to a verb   80
7 Pseudoverb ʔǝl- plus pronoun for possession   80
8 Negative pronouns   83
9 Proximal demonstratives   87
10 Distal demonstratives   96
11 Total numbers of occurrences of *māl* without a pronominal suffix   177
12 Total numbers of occurrences of *māl* with a pronominal suffix   177
13 Inflectional affixes   269
14 *šāf* 'he saw' and *šāfat* 'she saw' with object suffixes   325

Maps

1 Fieldwork Locations, Rivers and Marshes in Khuzestan   4
2 Arab villages in Khuzestan (Hourcade et al. 2012)   9
3 Classification of Khuzestani Arabic   29

Figures

1 Woman at the market selling *bāmya* 'okra', Shadegan (photo taken by the author)   31
2 Date palm, Ahvaz (photo taken by the author)   31
3 Man climbing a palm tree with a *farwand* (photo taken by the author)   32
4 Date harvest, Shadegan (photo taken by the author)   33
5 Kids running in a palm yard, Shadegan (photo taken by the author)   34
6 Traditional *tannūr* 'clay oven' (photo taken by the author)   35
7 Shepherdess, Ahvaz (photo taken by the author)   35
8 Shepherd, Ahvaz (photo taken by the author)   36
9 Umm ʕAzīz in front of her house, Ahvaz (photo taken by the author)   36

10 Umm ʕAzīz baking *səyāḥ/ʕēš təmən* 'rice bread' (photo taken by the author) 37
11 Water buffalos and their owner, Ahvaz (photo taken by the author) 38
12 Water buffalos bathing in the river Karun, Ahvaz (photo taken by the author) 38
13 Elderly woman, Susangerd (photo taken by the author) 39

Abbreviations

ADJ	adjective
AP	active participle
Ar.	Arabic
COLL	collective (noun)
CONT	continuation marker
CS	construct state
DEF	definite (article)
DEM	demonstrative
DIM	diminutive
DIST	distal
DP	discourse particle
EL	elative
EMP	emphatic particle
EXIST	existential particle
F	feminine
FUT	future particle
GA	Gulf Arabic
GL	genitive linker
HORT	hortative particle
IMP	imperative
IND	indicative
INDEF	indefinite (article)
INTERJ	interjection
intr.	intransitive
IPFV	imperfective
KhA	Khuzestani Arabic
M	masculine
MSA	Modern Standard Arabic
NEG	negation
OA	Old Arabic
OBJ	object marker
OBL	oblique case
Pers.	Persian
PFV	perfective
PL	plural
POSS	possession
PP	passive participle

PRO	pronoun
PROX	proximal
PRST	presentative particle
REL	relative pronoun/particle
SG	singular
SGT	singulative
s.v.	sub voce
trans.	transitive
Tur.	Turkish
VOC	vocative particl

PART 1

Introduction and General Classification of Khuzestani Arabic

∵

CHAPTER 1

Introduction

This book is a descriptive account of the phonology and morphology of Khuzestani Arabic (KhA). The main point of reference for this description is the local dialect of the province's capital city of Ahvaz (Ar. Aḥwāz) because a major part of the data used for this book is from there (cf. 1.5.1). Also, many of my consultants in Vienna were originally from Ahvaz (from the tribe of the Nəwāṣər). However, recordings have also been collected from other parts (towns and villages) of the province. These places are listed below with a short description of the speakers (cf. 1.5.1).

This introductory chapter includes information on the region of Khuzestan, its history and Arab inhabitants (1.1–1.3), a discussion of the available sources on the Arabic dialect of Khuzestan and its cognate *gələt*-type dialects (1.4), and a presentation of the data used as a basis for the grammatical descriptions with information on the speakers interviewed (1.5). This chapter is followed by a chapter on the linguistic classification of KhA, with a comparison of my data with earlier research conducted on this dialect.

1.1   Area

Khuzestan is a province in southwest Iran. Its name goes back to that of an ancient folk named Khuz/Ḥūz/Hūz that inhabited this area (Oppenheim 1967: 4; Savory 1986b: 80).

On the northern and eastern borders of the province lie the Zagros Mountains, to the south and southeast the Gulf, and to the west the marshlands of Iraq and the Šaṭṭ al-ʕArab. The three main rivers of Khuzestan are the Kārūn, the Karxa, and the Ǧarrāḥi (cf. Map 1). A part of the province's cultural heritage is connected with the marshlands and the culture of the marsh-dwellers, the so-called *Maʕdān*,[1] who live from buffalo-breeding and rice cultivation. There are two main marsh areas in Khuzestan: one around Hoveyzeh (*Hōr əl-əḤwēza*), and that around Fəllāḥīya/Shadegan (*Hōr əl-Fəllāḥīya*) (cf. Map 1). The marshlands of al-Hoveyzeh in Iran and Iraq have suffered profound anthropogenic

---

1   Cf. Oppenheim (1952: 477–486) on the history, the tribes and the culture of the *Maʕdān*; and Westphal-Hellbusch (1962) on their culture and lifestyle.

© BETTINA LEITNER, 2022 | DOI:10.1163/9789004510241_002

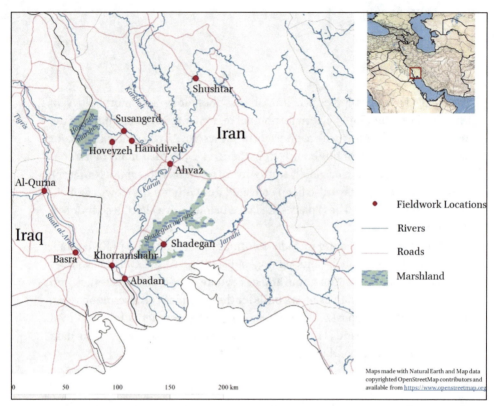

MAP 1   Fieldwork Locations, Rivers and Marshes in Khuzestan
MAPS MADE WITH NATURAL EARTH AND MAP DATA COPYRIGHTED OPENSTREETMAP CONTRIBUTORS AND AVAILABLE FROM HTTPS://WWW.OPENSTREETMAP.ORG

changes since the 1980s resulting in serious concerns that the Mesopotamian marshlands may be about to disappear (Albarakat, Lakshmi, and Tucker 2018: 19).

The province of Khuzestan has about 4.5 million inhabitants.[2] The province's capital city Ahvaz, called Sūq al-Ahwāz in medieval times, is situated at the river Kārūn and has now more than a million inhabitants.[3] Although no official numbers exist, it has been estimated that around 2 to 3 million people of the inhabitants of Khuzestan are Arabs (Matras and Shabibi 2007: 137; Gazsi 2011: 1020). Yet it is hard to determine, what percentage of this population uses Arabic actively. Estimates in the 1960s of the Arabic-speaking pop-

---

2   Statistical Center of Iran (Census 2016: 34, table 10).
3   https://iranicaonline.org/articles/ahvaz-04-population#prettyPhoto[content]/0/ [access 05.05.2021].

INTRODUCTION

ulation in Iran ranged from 200,000 to 650,000 (Oberling 1986: 216). Today, the usage and cross-generational transfer of Arabic has lowered in the recent decades, especially among the wealthier social classes and in multilingual cities and neighborhoods. In rural areas and neighborhoods (e.g. Shadegan and Hoveyzeh), where the majority of the residents are Arabs, this tendency is not felt.

For many centuries, the cultivation of rice, sugar cane and, in the southern parts, date palms, have played an important role in the province's agricultural production (cf. Oppenheim 1967: 5; Savory 1986b: 80, who states that in the 10th century, Khuzestan had the monopoly of the sale of cane-sugar throughout Iran, Iraq, and Arabia). Khuzestan has long been known for its very harsh climate: from May until October it is extremely hot and humid, and has frequent dust storms. In the winter months temperatures may occasionally fall below zero (cf. Oppenheim 1967: 6; Savory 1986b: 80).

Persian, because it is the official language in education and media, plays a crucial role for all people in the whole of Iran, including Khuzestan. The majority of the Khuzestani Arabs are bilingual, but there are still monolingual Arabic speakers, especially among the older generation. There are some Arab families who raise their children in Persian, but their number does not appear to be significant.

The Khuzestani Arabs themselves prefer to refer to the whole province as *Aḥwāz* (or *Ahwāz*) because many of them consider "Khuzestan" to be a Persian or non-Arabic name. In this book, however, we will stick to the term Khuzestan when referring to the whole province, and Ahvaz when referring to the province's capital—certainly not for any disrespect for the people of this region, but for the sake of clarity for the reader so the capital city and province will not be confused. Wherever possible, the English rendering of the towns' and cities' names will be given (cf. 1.5.1 for their KhA and Persian equivalents).

6   CHAPTER 1

1.2   History of Arabs and Arab Tribes in Khuzestan[4]

Arab settlement in southern and western Iran (i.e. Khuzestan and Fars) is
already documented for Sasanian times (226–651),[5] and thus precedes the
arrival of the Arab Muslim armies (Zarrinkūb 1975: 27). However, "the real Arab,
so to speak, dispersal into Iran began after the initial Islamic victories"[6] and
many tribes from the vicinities of Kufa and Basra entered Iranian soil following the conquest (Zarrinkūb 1975: 27; cf. Oppenheim 1967: 6, who states that in
the time after the Islamic conquest until the late 9th century Khuzestan was
too densely populated for nomadic tribes to settle there).

In 980, following the commencement of the Bedouinization of parts of Iraq,
the city of Hoveyzeh was founded by the Bedouin sheikh of the Asad, Dubays
ibn ʕAfīf (Oppenheim 1967: 6). Some centuries after the Islamic conquest, the
use of Arabic appears to have been replaced by the Persian language: Ibn Baṭ-
ṭūṭa noted, when he passed through Khuzestan in 1327, that not even the inhabitants of Hoveyzeh, a city founded by Arabs, spoke Arabic (Oppenheim 1967: 7).

1.2.1   *Settlement of Arab Tribes in Khuzestan*
Many of the Arab tribes who immigrated into Khuzestan had originated in
Arabia (cf. Savory 1986b: 81; cf. Nadjmabadi 2005: 122; Nadjmabadi 2009: 132,
fn. 28–29;Field 1939: 604) and first settled in southern Iraq. Their subsequent
immigration to Khuzestan led to an extensive Arabization of the province,
parts of which were officially called ʕArabistān from the 16th/17th century until
1923 (Oppenheim 1967: 3, 10; Savory 1986b: 80–81; cf. Ingham 1997: ix).

In the 16th century, a branch of the Banū Tamīm settled in Dōraq (later Fəl-
lāḥīya/Shadegan). In the 17th century, the Āl Katīr, who are relatives of the Banū
Lām, and the Āl Xamīs moved from Iraq to Khuzestan (Oppenheim 1967: 11).
In the 18th century, the Banū Kaʕab settled in Dōraq, founded the new city of
Fəllāḥīya, five miles to the south of Dōrag, and came to rule the whole south
of Khuzestan (Oppenheim 1967: 9–10, 13). The Muḥaysin, a subsection of the

---

4   For Arab tribes in other parts of Iran cf. Zarrinkūb: "In Sistan and eastern Khurasan, the
    Bakr and Tamim tribes predominated. In western Khurasan and round Qumis, the Qais were
    mainly to be found. The Azd tribe reached Khurasan a little later" (1975: 28–29). For literature
    on the Banū Kaʕab and the Qawāsim cf. the references cited in Nadjmabadi (2005: 113, fn. 5).
5   Among these were perhaps the Banū Tamīm (cf. Oppenheim 1967: 6).
6   After the Arabs' victory at Ǧalūlāʔ in 637 AD, they had secured the whole of Iraq and went on to
    conquer the plains of Khuzestan from Basra (Hinds 1984: 42). Tustar (Šuštar), then the main
    stronghold of Khuzestan, of strategic importance, and a site of great hydraulic works, was
    taken in 641 AD and with this victory the Arab conquest of Khuzestan was complete (Hinds
    1984: 42, fn. 67; 44; Zarrinkūb 1975: 15, 21; Savory 1986b: 80).

INTRODUCTION

Kaʕab, settled around Muḥammara (Pers. Khorramšahr; cf. Savory 1986a: 65–66 on the history of this town). The Kaʕab are said to have ruled in Khuzestan from the Šaṭṭ al-ʕArab on the west to Hendijan on the east, and from the Gulf coast on the south to Hoveyzeh on the north (Niebuhr 1772: 320).

According to Oppenheim (1967: 15), between 1789 and 1848 11,350 Arab families, many of whom were subject to or allies of the Banū Lām, immigrated to Khuzestan. Although some returned to southern Iraq, many stayed in Khuzestan for good (e.g. the Bāwiya) and joined the ruling tribes already in the area, e.g. the tribes of Hoveyzeh, the Āl Kaṯīr, and the Kaʕab (Oppenheim 1967: 15).

Between 1788 and 1846 almost 20,000 families from the Banū Lām moved to Khuzestan and gradually adopted a sedentary lifestyle (Savory 1986b: 81). At the turn of the 20th century, a significant part of the (then quite small) population of Khuzestan/ʕArabistān were Arab tribes leading a nomadic or at least semi-nomadic life; a lesser number were already sedentary living in villages and towns (Zagagi 2016: 61; Shahnavaz 2005: 46). The major economic activities in Khuzestan during that time were farming and animal husbandry (Shahnavaz 2005: 52). The members of the Muḥaysin tribe (a section of the Kaʕab) combined pastoral nomadism with agriculture, while the members of the Banū Ṭuruf tribe were strictly pastoral nomads (Shahnavaz 2005: 46).

Most Arab tribes, such as the Kaʕab, adopted Shiism after their settlement in Iran, but some remained Sunnis, e.g. the Muntafiq, who migrated to Hoveyzeh in 1812 (Savory 1986b: 81).

One of the most important characters in the recent history of Khuzestan was Shaykh Khazʕal (1863–1936) of Muḥammara (Pers. Khorramshahr), the greatest land owner in Khuzestan/ʕArabistān (Zagagi 2016: 62). He had significant influence during his time, when the Qajar central administration was rather weak and dependent on the cooperation of the tribes. And he had good relations with the British Empire (Zagagi 2016: 62–63; Oppenheim 1967: 19). Under his rule (1897–1924), he united the whole tribe of the Kaʕab, administrated Ahvaz/Nāṣiri[7], and later also subjected Hoveyzeh. In the early 1930s he publicly advocated his (never realized) plans for the separation of Khuzestan from Iran (Oppenheim 1967: 18–19) and may thus be considered an early figure of the separatist movement of the Khuzestani Arabs, which is still active today, although harshly suppressed by the Iranian government.

The British Empire had increased (vested) interest in the (stability of the) region after the discovery of oil fields in Khuzestan near Masjed Soleyman

---

7   The river-port Nāṣiri was built next to Ahvaz in the 19th century when the Lower Kārūn was opened for European seafarers. By then, Ahvaz was no more than a village. In 1933, Ahvaz had less than 50,000 inhabitants, and Muḥammara about 20,000 (Oppenheim 1967: 22, fn. 1).

(east of Šuštar) by the Anglo-Persian Oil Company in 1908 (Zagagi 2016: 63; Savory 1986b: 81; Oppenheim 1967: 19). Only a short time later, pipelines from this site to Ahvaz and Abadan were constructed as well as refineries on the Abadan islands, with settlements for the staff in what became the city of Abadan (Zagagi 2016: 63; Oppenheim 1967: 19, who states that in 1956 Abadan had 226,000 inhabitants).

The Iran-Iraq War (1980–1988), which began with the Iraqi invasion of Iranian territory,[8] destroyed numerous houses and forced many families to flee their hometowns. Many of these war refugees went to comparably safer cities such as Ahvaz or left the province of Khuzestan and went, for example, to Tehran. For this reason, during that time, the city of Ahvaz witnessed an immense population growth.[9] Contrary to the Iraqi authorities' expectations, the majority of the Arab population in Khuzestan did not support the invading Iraqi troops (Gieling 2006). Both the city of Muḥammara (and its port) and the city of Abadan (and its refineries) were completely destroyed in the course of the Iran-Iraq War by Iraqi artillery and aerial bombardments. The inhabitants had to evacuate these areas which, according to the 1986 National Census, became totally depopulated. After some years, the war refugees began to return to their homes and the population of the two towns increased again: in 2011, Muḥammara had 129,418 (Nejatian 2015b) and Abadan 212,744 inhabitants (Nejatian 2014).

1.2.2 Renaming of Places
The Arabic names of all towns had been changed into Persian ones in the early 20th century: Fǝllāḥīya became Shadegan, Xafaġīya became Susangerd, and Muḥammara was named Khorramšahr, etc. Some names were simply adapted phonologically to Persian pronunciation: Abadan and Hoveyzeh were renamed Ābādān and Howeyzeh, respectively. The Khuzestani Arabs mostly prefer the Arab and not the Persian toponyms.

---

8 One of the reasons for this war was the official support of Iraq of the separatist insurgents in Khuzestan and Iraq's promise to assist in their liberation from Iran, cf. (Gieling 2006).

9 According to (Nejatian 2015a: https://iranicaonline.org/articles/ahvaz-04-population#pretty Photo[content]/0/) the number of inhabitants in Ahvaz grew from 334,399 in 1976 to 724,653 in 1991, and to 1,112,021 in 2011.

INTRODUCTION 9

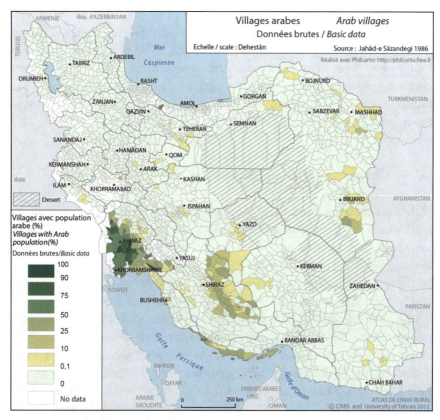

MAP 2   Arab villages in Khuzestan
         HOURCADE ET AL. 2012. HTTP://WWW.IRANCARTO.CNRS.FR/RECORD.PHP?Q=
         AR-040537&F=LOCAL&L=EN [ACCESS 25.03.2022].

1.3 Current Situation of the Arabs and of Arabic in Iran

The distribution of Arabic-speaking communities and of ethnic Arabs in Iran is shown in the maps of Irancarto (Hourcade et al. 2012, see Map 2). Outside of Khuzestan, Arab communities are found in the Iranian provinces of Fars, Bushehr, Hormozgān, and Khorasan.

Most Arabs outside Khuzestan and the southern coast are ethnically Arab but in many cases have shifted to Persian and other neighboring languages (Dahlgren 2002: 90; Seeger 2002: 631–632).

Within Khuzestan, many Arabs work in the sugar cane or oil industries, but few hold white-collar or managerial positions (de Planhol 1986: 55–56). This is one of the reasons why many Arabs in Khuzestan feel strongly disadvantaged in society and politics in comparison to their Persian neighbors.[10] There is a political movement aiming at a full separation of Khuzestan from Iran but also fighting for rights such as schooling in Arabic. Many members of these separatist groups live in exile or have been held captive in Iran. Due to their unfavorable economic status and the tense political situation, many Arab families in Khuzestan, especially young men, have moved to Kuwait or other Gulf countries in hope of finding jobs there, or have fled to Europe.

1.4   Khuzestani Arabic and Cognate *gələt*-Type Arabic Dialects

Hitherto there have been only a few in-depth descriptions of *gələt*-type dialects, and some date back more than 50 years (Meißner's grammar of Kwayriš/Babylon Arabic, published in 1903, even more than 100 years!). Among them are: Blanc (1964) and Erwin (1963) for Muslim Baghdadi Arabic;[11] Denz (1971) and Meißner (1903) for Kwayriš (Babylon) Arabic; Mahdi (1985) for Basra Arabic; and Salonen (1980) for al-Shirqat/Assur (Širqāṭ) Arabic.

The Arabic dialects of Khuzestan have been given some attention but hitherto we have no full description of its grammar. The main source of information on these dialects are the publications made by the British arabist and linguist Bruce Ingham (Ingham 2007; 1976; 1973) for which he gathered data during field trips in 1969 and 1971. There are two published articles that deal with contact induced changes in KhA: one is by Yaron Matras and Maryam Shabibi (2007), which is based on Shabibi's unpublished dissertation *Contact-induced grammatical changes in Khuzestani Arabic* (2006, University of Manchester), and one is by Leitner (2020). Finally, there is one recent publication by Nawal Bahrani, a Persian MA student, and Golnaz Modarresi Ghavami, her supervisor, on some aspects of the phonology of KhA (mainly based on speakers from Abadan; Bahrani and Modarresi Ghavami 2019).

This book aims to contribute to the field of Arabic dialectology a first comprehensive description of the phonology and morphology of KhA based on data from different towns and speakers, obtained through recordings and elicitation. Comparative features and references to existing or differing linguistic phenomena in cognate dialects will also be included. For comparison with

---

10   The KhA term for the Persian people and their language is *ʕaǧmi* PL *ʕaǧam* 'non-Arab; Persian (people and language)'.

11   Cf. Palva (2009: 18–29), who shows that Muslim Baghdadi Arabic is not a pure *gələt* dialect but has retained many *qəltu* features which show its original *qəltu*-type character.

INTRODUCTION

Iraqi and Bahraini Arabic and KhA's classification as a south-Mesopotamian *gələt* dialect, the main sources are Blanc (1964), Erwin (1963), Meißner (1903), Salonen (1980), Holes (2016), and Johnstone (1976). For comparison with other Arabic dialects in Iran, I have mainly consulted the work of Ulrich Seeger (2002; 2013). For general comparison of lexical items with other dialects of Arabic, the (for now) three-volume work *Wortatlas der arabischen Dialekte* (WAD) by Peter Behnstedt and Manfred Woidich was used wherever possible. Furthermore, the Bahraini-Arabic glossary of Holes (2001), the Iraqi-Arabic dictionary of Woodhead and Beene (WB), and especially the KhA dictionary by ʕAbd al-ʔAmīr Ḥassūnizadeh (LA) proved very helpful.

1.5 Data, Methodology, Organization

The descriptions of KhA phonology and morphology in this book are based on my own corpus and elicited data. The corpus consists of the transcription and translation of about 75 texts based on about 3 hours (200 minutes) of recorded speech (in total 75,000 words—defined as phonological units of one or more syllables, with one main stress, cf. Dixon and Aikhenvald 2002: 13–18 for a more detailed definition of a phonological word). The recordings were made during my own fieldwork in Khuzestan (September 2016), where I was lucky to stay with a Khuzestani Arab family (relatives of Khuzestani Arab friends of mine who live in Vienna), in Kuwait (September 2018), and with the Khuzestani minority group living in Vienna. Unfortunately, after my first field trip to Khuzestan, I was unable to obtain another visa to Iran, which was most likely because Iranian authorities try to prevent any media or other attention from being given to the (often highly underprivileged, cf. 1.2 and 1.3) situation of the Khuzestani Arabs.

For the collection of my material, I tried to communicate with the members of the KhA speech community in their colloquial variety, but usually I asked a friend (a native speaker) to conduct the interviews so my presence and non-nativeness would not, or as little as possible, affect the people's way of speaking. Consent was collected orally after explaining the purpose of my research and the interview.

The gathered data covers all major towns in the province of Khuzestan (cf. 1.5.1). Most texts are unmonitored conversations, some are narratives, and some are based on a set of questions I asked and which can be labeled as narrative interviews. The corpus thus includes various text types (folk tales, recipes, instructions, family conversations, accounts of every-day matters, memories of the past, etc.), which is important because each type brings forth different language data. For example, one finds significantly more discourse particles or imperatives in dialogues than in narratives of a traditional story.

The narratives and conversations cover a wide range of topics. Some were directed and initiated by my questions; others arose within the course of a conversation. Among the topics in the corpus are: marriage customs, handicrafts, food and traditional dishes, agricultural work and equipment, sheep breeding, buffalo breeding, fishing, (the Iran-Iraq) war, etc.

In addition to the corpus, I have elicited further data with questionnaires and via direct interviews about grammatical structures with consultants in Khuzestan and Vienna. The lexical questionnaires are based on the model of the word atlas of Behnstedt and Woidich (2011; 2012; 2014; 2021).

1.5.1 *Speakers*

This section gives some information on the towns, speakers and research partners, grouped together according to the town or village which they are from or in which the recording was made, and the tribes to which they belong. All speakers interviewed for the description of KhA agreed to make their paternal/maternal names (Ar. *kunya*, e.g. Abu/Umm Fulān 'father/mother of So-and-so') and the information on their background public. The abbreviations [xy] for the speakers/speaker groups are given below in the headline of each example and the texts.

Shushtar (KhA Tustar, Pers. Šuštar)

[T1]: Elderly man; about 70 years old; tribe: Banū Kaʕab; born in Šaʕībīya (at the outskirts of Tustar), used to work in the sugar cane factory; recorded at their house in Tustar.

[T2]: Wife of [T1]; about 70 years old.

Susangerd (KhA Xafağīya, Pers. Susangerd)

[X1]: Elderly woman and her husband recorded in their house.

[X2]: Middle-aged woman working as a vegetable farmer; recorded in her house.

[X3]: Fayyūra, female; Maryam's aunt; about 45 years old, tribe: Banī Hāšim, ʕašīra: Āl Bū Šōka.

Hamidiyeh (KhA Ḥamīdīya, Pers. Hamidiyyeh)

[Ḥa1]: Two elderly women sitting on the street in front of their houses.

Hoveyzeh (Ar. Ḥuwayza, Pers. Howeyzeh)

[Ḥ1]: Ḥağīyat Mōza; female; about 75 years old; mother of Umm ʕAzīz (her only child); tribe Ḥəyādər, ʕašīra: Al Bū Krēm; was married to a member

INTRODUCTION   13

of the ʕašīra əl-Məgādfa (also from the tribe Ḥəyādər), born in Hoveyzeh (district Ṭīna), but now lives in Ahvaz; knows very little Persian.

[Ḥ2]:   Umm ʕAzīz; female; about 63 years old; mother of 11 children (among
        them Abu Maher, Abu Amǧad, Abu ʕAdnān, Abu Ǧāsəm's wife, and, her
        youngest son, Majed); tribe: Ḥəyādər/ʕAčrəš (cf. Banī Ṭuruf, and Ǧābir
        1996: 71 on the history and geographical distribution of the ʕAčrəš),
        ʕašīra: əl-Məgādfa; her deceased husband was from the Āl Bū ʕĪd; born
        in Hoveyzeh, moved then to Ahvaz where she still lives (district əl-
        Ḥərša, Kūt ʕAbd-Alla) with her children and grandchildren (in the
        same house where Umm Amǧad and Abu Amǧad live, opposite Umm
        ʕAdnān and Abu ʕAdnān's house); knows very little Persian.

Ahvaz (KhA Aḥwāz; Pers. Ahvāz)

[A1]:   Abu Khazʕal; male; about 50 years old; actor and journalist; tribe:
        Nəwāṣər, ʕašīra: Āl Bū ʕĪd; born in Ahvaz, lived in Fəllāḥīya for sev-
        eral years during the Iran-Iraq War, returned then to Ahvaz where he
        lived until he fled to Vienna in 2015.

[A2]:   Abu Maher; male; 37 years old; employee; tribe: Nəwāṣər, ʕašīra: Āl Bū
        ʕĪd; born in Ahvaz, where he lived until he fled to Vienna in 2012 (his
        wife and two children came to Vienna a year after him).

[A3]:   Umm ʕAdnān; female; 34 years old; housewife; tribe: Nəwāṣər, ʕašīra:
        Āl Bū ʕĪd; born in Ahvaz, where she still lives (district əl-Ḥərša, Kūt
        ʕAbd-Alla) with her husband Abu ʕAdnān and their three children.

[A4]:   Abu ʕAdnān; male; about 35 years old; works in the sugar cane fac-
        tory; tribe: Nəwāṣər, ʕašīra: Āl Bū ʕĪd; married to Umm ʕAdnān; born
        in Ahvaz where he still lives (district əl-Ḥərša, Kūt ʕAbd-Alla).

[A6]:   Reḍa A.; male; 34 years old; goat and sheep herdsman; tribe: Salāmāt
        (cf. Oppenheim 1967: 35–36 and 1952: 478 on the Sālāmāt as one of the
        tribes of Hoveyzeh whose people are farmers and shepherds); lives in
        Ahvaz.

[A7]:   Abu Ǧāsəm; male; about 35 years old; buffalo farmer; tribe: Nəwāṣər,
        ʕašīra: Āl Bū ʕĪd; born in Ahvaz, where he still lives (district əl-Ḥərša,
        Kūt ʕAbd-Alla).

[A9]:   Palm tree cultivator; male; about 35 years old; tribe: Kaʕab, ʕašīra: Āl
        Bū Ġbēš (cf. Oppenheim 1967: 84; Banī Ṭuruf, and Ǧābir 1996: 73); born
        in Ahvaz, where he still lives.

[A10]: Umm Saʕad; female; about 45 years old; tribe: Kaʕab, ʕašīra: Rbēḥāt (cf.
        Oppenheim 1967: 85), born in Fəllāḥīya, now lives in Ahvaz (district
        əl-Ḥərša, Kūt ʕAbd-Alla); 4 children, no school education, little knowl-
        edge of Persian; all recordings with her are fairy tales and folk tales.

14   CHAPTER 1

[A11]: Umm ʕAli; female; about 40 years old; tribe: Nəwāṣər, ʕašīra: Āl Bū ʕĪd; sister of Abu Amǧad and Abu ʕAdnān; born in Ahvaz, where she still lives (district əl-Ḥərša, Kūt ʕAbd-Alla); recorded in her courtyard during breakfast.

[A12]: Semi-nomadic family; three women and one man, all between 45 and 60 years; shepherds; ʕašīra: Zhērīya (tribe Bdūr); live in the surroundings of Ahvaz; no school education; recording was made in front of their tent.

[A14]: Majed; male; 27 years old; tribe: Nəwāṣər, ʕašīra: Āl Bū ʕĪd; born in Ahvaz, moved to Vienna in 2015 and works there now as an architect and studies architecture at the University of Vienna; highly educated (studied architecture at the University of Ahvaz) and has a very good knowledge of Persian as well as Modern Standard Arabic, English, and German.

[A15]: Maryam; female; 26 years old; tribe: Banī Hāšim, ʕašīra: Āl Bū Šōka (she is a ʕalwīya, i.e. their ancestors are said to go back to the prophet Muhammad's family); highly educated (studied Psychology at the University of Ahvaz); has a very good knowledge of Persian as well as Modern Standard Arabic, and moderate knowledge of English; is now married and just had her first daughter.

[A16]: Umm Amǧad; female; 27 years old; tribe: Nəwāṣər, ʕašīra: Āl Bū ʕĪd; born in Ahvaz, where she still lives with her husband Abu Amǧad and their three children.

[A17]: Abu Amǧad; male; 31 years old; tribe: Nəwāṣər, ʕašīra: Āl Bū ʕĪd; born in Ahvaz, where he still lives with his wife Umm Amǧad and his children.

[A18]: Aḥmad; male; 28 years; tribe: Kaʕab, ʕašīra: Āl Bū ʕAbīd; he was born in Ahvaz, grew up in Ḥamīdīya, and now lives in Ahvaz; studied herbal medicine and law and is a writer and activist in the fields of history and cultural heritage of the Khuzestani Arabs.

[A19]: Farmer; male; around 60 years old; recorded with his son, who is about 35 years old; tribe Banū Tamīm, born in Fəllāḥīya, then worked some years in Kuwait, now lives in Ahvaz.

Shadegan (KhA Fəllāḥīya, Pers. Šādegān)

[F1]: Family from Fəllāḥīya living in Kuwait City, where I recorded them during my second fieldwork; their grandmother, who was about 75 years old and still lived in Fəllāḥīya, came for a visit during my stay; tribe: Banū Ṭuruf, ʕašīra: Məzrəʕa (cf. Oppenheim 1967: 42), she had 9 children (7 boys, 2 girls), no formal education and her family in Khuzestan lived from palm cultivation.

INTRODUCTION   15

Khorramshahr (KhA Muḥammara, Pers. Khorramšahr)

[M1]:   Three elderly people (2 male, 1 female); all about 65 years old; tribe:
        əHlālat, Muḥaysin/Kaʕab (cf. Oppenheim 1967: 85 and 88; cf. also Banī
        Ṭuruf, and Ğābir 1996: 107); were born in Muḥammara where they still
        live (a very modest life); recorded in their living room.

[M3]:   Five different people at the market of Muḥammara: four men, one
        woman; first one's tribe is unknown, the second one is from the tribe
        Āl bū Fərḥān (Muḥaysin/Kaʕab, cf. Oppenheim 1967: 85), the third one
        from the Banū Ṭuruf (family is originally from Xafağīya), and fourth
        one from the tribe al-Ḥalāf (cf. Oppenheim 1967: 35; his family is orig-
        inally from Ḥamīdīya/Xafağīya); and one woman, about 55 years old,
        from the Kaʕab, ʕašīra: Āl Bū Ġbēš (born in Abadan).

[M4]:   Abu Mehdi; male; 34 years old; tribe Āl bū Fərḥān (Muḥaysin/Kaʕab, cf.
        Oppenheim 1967: 85); was born and still lives in Muḥammara; knows
        Persian well; recorded while he spent the evening with his son and wife
        fishing in the river Kārūn.

Abadan (KhA ʕAbbādān, Pers. ʔAbbādān)

[AB1]: Woman, about 55 years old, and her son, who is about 25 years old;
        Mušaʕšaʕīn; were born and still live in Abadan; recorded in their liv-
        ing room.

1.5.2   *Main Objectives*

This book contains a description of the phonology and morphology of Khuzestani Arabic and aims to position it linguistically in the wider context of Mesopotamian and Gulf Arabic. This content of this book is largely based on my
dissertation (Leitner 2020b).

My data on the dialect's phonology and morphology can be the basis for
further research on syntax, which was not feasible in the framework of this
book. Several articles on selected syntactic and sociolinguistic topics of KhA
have already been published (Leitner 2020a; 2019; Leitner and Procházka 2021;
Leitner and Hasani 2021; Bettega and Leitner 2019) or are in preparation. Features shared with cognate and geographically close dialects, particularly southern Iraqi and northern Gulf Arabic, and features that distinguish KhA from
these dialects will be highlighted. The status of KhA a Bedouin[12] dialect of the
Mesopotamian *gələt*-group spoken in Iran will be supported with substantial

---

12   Arabic dialects are still commonly classified by the sociologically-based distinction seden-
     tary-type vs. Bedouin-type, which refer to different dialect types that reflect the history
     of settlement of a certain Arabic-speaking community, but do not necessarily reflect the

16   CHAPTER 1

phonological and morphological evidence. Mesopotamia is here defined as the area from Khuzestan in the south to eastern Anatolia in Turkey in the north, including the so-called Ǧazīra of north-eastern Syria (cf. Talay 2011: 909).

1.5.3   *Transcription, Glossing and Translation*

The transcription of the examples and texts is basically phonemic. The glottal onset *ʔ* is only clearly heard and therefore also transcribed between vowels and in initial position. All predictable phonological changes like assimilations or the raising of final -*a*, are described in the respective paragraphs in chapter 3 and not considered in the transcription of the examples and texts. Similarly, the secondary emphatics *ļ*, *ḅ*, *ṃ*, and *r̝* (3.4.3) are not considered in the transcription because their emphatic character can be predicted by their phonetic context.

Wherever two or more variant phonological or morphological variants exist, they are separated by the symbol ~, e.g. *gabəl* ~ *ġabəl* 'before'. The examples given to illustrate grammatical phenomena are either taken from the corpus or from elicited data (indicated by the word "elicited" in the headline of the example). Speakers' abbreviations are always given within square brackets in the headline of the example. Their corresponding full names as well as some information on their social and demographic background are found above in 1.5.1.

All numbered examples taken from my corpus that appear in the description of the grammar are glossed so they are useful for general linguists or all non-Arabists alike. The glossing system used in this book is a simplified version of the Leipzig Glossing Rules adapted to the needs of a Semitic language. Simplified, because verbs are not separated by morphemes. Most adaptations and added glosses follow the system used in the CorpAfroAs.[13] Persian loanwords are marked by two superscript ᴾ, e.g. ᴾ*sīm xārdār*ᴾ 'barbed-wire fence'.

I have tried to achieve an English translation as close to the KhA origin and as fluent as possible at the same time. Words or phrases in the translation that are within square brackets is context-giving information. Words or phrases in parentheses are not articulated in the Arabic original but added in this way in the translation for better understanding and/or a more fluent translation.

---

present-day lifestyle of these communities (Palva 2006: 605). For critical views on this dichotomy, cf. fn. 2 (in chapter 2 "General classification and internal subdivisions of KhA").

13   http://corpafroas.tge-adonis.fr/glosses.html.

CHAPTER 2

General Classification and Internal Subdivisions of Khuzestani Arabic (KhA)

2.1 Classification of KhA—The Position of KhA among the Mesopotamian Arabic dialects

Khuzestani Arabic is a South-Mesopotamian Bedouin-type dialect and generally classified among the *gələt*-type group of dialects. The term *gələt* is based on the 1SG PFV verb for 'to say': *gələt* versus *qəltu*—the latter being the other group of dialects spoken in Iraq and southern Anatolia. Blanc (1964: 7–8) provides some basic phonological and morphological characteristics of the *gələt* dialects based on Muslim Baghdadi Arabic[1] and compares these with the respective *qəltu* forms. Typologically closest to KhA are the *gələt* dialects spoken in southern Iraq, e.g. the dialects of Kwayriš and Basra. As will be shown in the discussion of the KhA grammatical phenomena, it also shares many features with certain Arabic dialects of the Northern Gulf, Central Asia (especially the dialect of Khorasan), and with the Šāwi-dialects of the middle Euphrates.

In many scientific contributions to the field of Arabic Dialectology, especially those that are dealing with the Mesopotamian linguistic area, the terms 'urban' and 'sedentary' as well as 'rural' and 'Bedouin' have been used interchangeably (cf. Leitner 2021) and KhA has hitherto usually been labelled a rural Bedouin *gələt* dialect. The synonymous use of these labels seems to partly result from the fact that the classification of the Mesopotamian dialects has primarily been based on a diachronic perspective. This approach was partly justified by the fact that, in this area, the features urban and sedentary as well as rural and Bedouin are historically indeed often closely linked. However, for a synchronic classification of the present-day *gələt* dialects, a synonymous use of these concepts would be misleading. Even though all *gələt* dialects (outside of Arabia) are originally thought to be Bedouin and rural in character (cf. Blanc 1964: 167–168), the vast majority of their speakers in present-day Khuzestan has given up the Bedouin-type lifestyle. Furthermore, the urban–rural distinction has not played a role for a long time in Khuzestan, as also most town or

---

1 KhA differs from these features in some points: compare e.g. Muslim Baghdadi Arabic *kull* 'all, every' and KhA *kəll* [kil:] (which Blanc 1964: 166 describes as a rural *gələt* feature), or Muslim Baghdadi Arabic *hīči* 'thus' and KhA *hēč* 'thus; like this; such'.

© BETTINA LEITNER, 2022 | DOI:10.1163/9789004510241_003

18 CHAPTER 2

city inhabitants are of rural origins. In Khuzestan, a subdivision of the KhA dialects can instead be made based on other socioeconomic factors closer to the sedentary/Bedouin split (cf. 2.2.1 on the *ḥaḍar* and *ʕarab* groups). However, modern-day Khuzestan is witnessing a rapid growth of urban centers, especially in the city of Ahvaz, for which reason the term 'urban' and its sociolinguistic and socio-economic implications (e.g., increase of contact and leveling tendencies) must at least be considered as an emerging category in the KhA context.

The usefulness of the label *Bedouin-type* or the distinction *sedentary* versus *Bedouin-type* has been recently criticized by scholars such as Janet Watson (2011: 859), who describes the sedentary/Bedouin split as "an oversimplification and of diminishing sociological appropriacy".[2] As this distinction continues to be used in most descriptions of Arabic dialects, reference will be made to it here, while keeping in mind the aforementioned critical points.

2.1.1 *KhA as a Bedouin-Type Dialect*

Bedouin-type dialects are characterized by a voiced velar pronunciation of the Old Arabic[3] (OA) sound /q/, which is the only feature shared by all dialects of this type. There are, however, also bundles of lexical, morphological, and phonological features that are shared by many but not all Bedouin-type dialects. Typical Bedouin-type features found in the KhA lexicon are for example the following items: *zēn* 'good', *bərṭəm* 'lip', *xašəm* 'nose', *bāčər* 'tomorrow', *nəšad* 'to ask', *ḥēl* 'much, a lot, very; with a loud voice', *xāf* 'maybe', *əyāwīd ~ ǧəyāwīd* 'good, fine men', *ganaṣ* 'to hunt', *zād* 'food for the journey', *šēn* 'bad', *ʕazam* 'to invite',[4] the opposition *əlbārḥa* 'last night' vs. *ʔaməs* 'yesterday' (cf. Johnstone 1967: 69, fn. 2), and *ʔanṭa* 'to give' (also *ʔəṭṭa ~ ʔəṭa*).[5] An example

---

2 Cf. also Clive Holes (2018: 144, fn. 54; 145), who points out that (especially concerning the Gulf Arabic dialects) geographic considerations also intersect with the Bedouin/sedentary dichotomy and shows that certain phonological and morphological isoglosses (e.g. reflexes of OA interdentals, and gender distinction in the plural) are valid for some parts of the present-day Gulf Arabic region but not for others.

3 The term Old Arabic as used in this book covers the Arabic varieties of the pre-Islamic period as reflected in early inscriptions, the language of the Quran, pre-Islamic poetry, and descriptions of Bedouin dialects by early Arab grammarians (see Eid et al. 2006: vi; and Macdonald 2008: 464–465).

4 Cf. Rosenhouse 2006: 267–268; and Palva 2009: 29 on a short list of Muslim Baghdadi Arabic items belonging to Bedouin-type vocabulary.

5 Cf. WAD III: 406–409, where *ʔanṭa, yinṭi* is described as typical of Bedouin dialects of the northern (Arabian) Peninsula. By contrast, in Bahraini Arabic this lexeme (*naṭa—yinṭi*) is used only in the sedentary-type dialects.

GENERAL CLASSIFICATION AND INTERNAL SUBDIVISIONS

of a morphological feature that KhA shares with the majority of (Eastern[6]) Bedouin-type dialects is the retention of the feminine plural forms of the 2nd and 3rd persons in verbs and pronouns. Gender distinction in the plural has in fact been retained in most other *gələt* dialects, except for Muslim Baghdadi Arabic, in which feminine plural forms may be used but are usually replaced by their masculine plural counterparts. Gender distinction in the plural is a feature often given up in urban contexts (cf. Procházka 2014: 129). However, in both the dialects of the cities of Basra and Ahvaz, it is still retained. Furthermore, the small-scale socio-linguistic study published in Leitner (2021) shows that urban *gələt* speakers from Southern Iraq do not seem to associate this feature with rural speech.

Examples of phonological features KhA shares with many other Eastern Bedouin-type dialects are the affrication of OA *$*k$* which in KhA becomes *č* in the environment of front vowels; the shift from OA *$*q$* > *g*, with affrication > *ǧ*, in the environment of front vowels (Palva 2006: 606); and the *g(a)hawa*-syndrome (cf. 3.7.2). These same features have also often been described as rural features with regard to the *gələt* group (see below).

IPFV endings on -*n* in 2SG.F (-*īn*) and 2/3PL.M (-*ūn*) are typical of the Mesopotamian dialect group[7] but also found in dialects spoken on the Arabian Peninsula (cf. Palva 2009: 29, 2006: 60; Johnstone 1967: 43).

2.1.2 Discussing the Validity of the Label "Rural gələt" for the Classification of KhA

As argued elsewhere (Leitner 2021), the usefulness of the urban–rural distinction as hitherto applied to the *gələt* dialect group should be reconsidered (its usefulness as categories within the KhA dialects is even more questionable cf. below 2.2.1). So far, this division has been based mainly on the comparisons of Muslim Baghdadi Arabic—a *gələt* dialect with a *qəltu* substrate—as the default urban *gələt* type with Kwayriš (Babylon) Arabic, which was described over a century ago, as the basic model of the rural *gələt* type. Aiming at a solid classification of the *gələt* dialect group by using the urban–rural dichotomy, it is significant to acknowledge the different nature of older or longer established urban communities, as found in Baghdad, and the communities of newly emerging urban contexts, such as Ahvaz. While in the former context a longer

---

6 Arabic dialects are broadly divided into an Eastern (*mašriqi*) and Western (*maġribi*) group, the boundary between them running through the western part of the Nile Delta and following the Nile Valley from Asyūṭ to Luxor (Palva 2006: 605).

7 Some Anatolian *qəltu*-dialects have lost the final -*n* but partly kept the original final stress, Fischer and Jastrow (1980: 153).

established (once *qəltu* speaking) urban community has witnessed rural immigration (for centuries and still ongoing), in the latter, virtually all inhabitants are of rural origin (cf. Leitner 2021: 18).

As discussed in more detail elsewhere (Leitner 2021), Muslim Baghdadi Arabic with its unique history and linguistic development (i.e. a *gələt* dialect with a *qəltu* substratum), does not constitute a good reference point for the description of a default urban *gələt* type against which rural type dialects can be defined. KhA, unlike Muslim Baghdadi Arabic, has never had a preexisting *qəltu*-type layer that was later "overwritten" by *gələt*-type features and had thus developed in a totally different environment.

From a synchronic perspective, in the modern context of Southern Iraq and Khuzestan, we cannot speak of urban groups that are clearly distinct from the rural population, since the current inhabitants of all urban centers are partly or completely descended from rural populations themselves. It appears more precise to define the (sociolinguistic) profile of the present-day urban *gələt* dialects in this area alongside the linguistic dynamics observable in such urban centers and around them, i.e. which (rural) features are readily given up in urban contexts or spread from such (prestigious) centers, instead of basing it solely on the features of Muslim Baghdadi Arabic as *the* default urban *gələt* dialect.

Future investigations on this topic should ideally include a socio-linguistic perspective that aims at discerning which features spread from prestigious urban centers and which features are marked as rural or "provincial" and therefore readily given up by rural speakers when moving to urban contexts.[8]

Bearing the criticism with which we approach the use of the labels *urban* and *rural* in mind, we discuss in the following paragraphs three of the criteria that have previously been used[9] for establishing an urban–rural distinction for the *gələt* dialect group.

1. OA PFV verbal forms CaCaC-v(C)

   Blanc described reflexes of the OA PFV verbal forms CaCaC-v(C), e.g. *katab-at* 'she wrote', with initial CC- as typically "rural"[10] *gələt* (1964: 166). In KhA, the most common reflex of such forms is CəCC-v(C) and not

---

8   Cf. Leitner (2021) for preliminary results and a small-scale sociolinguistic survey on these questions.

9   Blanc (1964: 165–166) compares some Muslim Baghdadi Arabic ("urban") features with their equivalents in the dialect of Kwayriš/Babylon, which he describes as a rural *gələt*-dialect; cf. Palva (2009: 21–29). Cf. Leitner 2021 for a lengthier discussion of possible rural *gələt* features in Southern Iraqi and Khuzestani Arabic.

10   Cf. Ingham 1982a: 48–49, 52 who described such forms as characteristic of the Mesopotamian *bādiya* dialects, in contrast to the Mesopotamian *ḥaḍar* dialects that have CiCCat (see also 2.2.1).

CCvC-v(C)—e.g. OA *katabat* > *kətbat* 'she wrote', not *ktəbat* (cf. 2.2.1). Although no forms such as *ktəbat* appear in my corpus data, they are used in some more remote areas in Khuzestan and were perceived by speakers from Ahvaz as of *ʕarab* type (cf. 2.2.1 on this subgroup of KhA dialects). Basra Arabic and Muslim Baghdadi Arabic also both have forms of the structure CəCC-v(C) as found in most KhA dialects. "Rural" CCvC-v(C)-forms, e.g., *ktibat*, are found in the *gələt* dialects of Kwayriš (Babylon) (Meißner 1903: LII) and al-Shirqat (Salonen 1980: 80), as well as in all Šāwi-dialects (Younes and Herin, 'Šāwi Arabic', *EALL*). To solidly define this type of resyllabification as a rural feature for the modern-day *gələt* dialects, we would need more and new data from more *gələt* dialects spoken in rural areas.

2. *g(a)hawa*-syndrome

Another feature described by Blanc as typical of rural *gələt* dialects is the reshuffling of syllables in guttural context, the so-called *g(a)hawa*-syndrome (Blanc 1964: 166; cf. 3.7.2 on this phonological rule). Although there are many traces of this resyllabification rule still found in contemporary KhA, it has ceased to be an active phonological process. In the case of Muslim Baghdadi Arabic, the incoming Bedouin tribes and the rural population that has settled in Baghdad apparently have fully given up this feature in the urban context due to its highly marked character (cf. Leitner 2021). Also for Basra Arabic and Kwayriš/Babylon Arabic we only find traces of its use (cf. Leitner 2021: 6 for examples). On the basis of the data on Mesopotamian dialects available to us, it seems that the *g(a)hawa*-syndrome has remained more of an Arabian than a Mesopotamian feature, and it does not appear to be a useful criterion for dividing the present-day Mesopotamian *gələt* dialects into a rural and an urban subgroup.

3. Conditioned affrication of (OA *$^*q$ >) *g* > *ǧ*

Finally, the phonetically conditioned affrication of (OA *$^*q$ >) *g* > *ǧ* in high-vowel environments (cf. 3.1.2.1) has usually also been labelled as a rural *gələt* feature as it was not found in Muslim Baghdadi Arabic (cf. Fischer and Jastrow 1980, pp. 142–143; Blanc 1964: 25–28; Palva 2009: 37, fn. 19). Palva writes of Muslim Baghdadi Arabic that "the contrast between urban and rural *gələt* is diminishing", because such features as the conditioned affrication of *g* or the use of feminine plural forms in the 3rd person are gaining ground in that dialect (Palva 2009: 37, fn. 19). In modern-day Ahvazi Arabic there appears to be variation regarding the realization of OA *$^*q$ as *g* or *ǧ* (e.g. *məḍayyəǧ* ~ *məḍayyəg* 'worried'; cf. 3.1.2.1 and Leitner 2021). Also for Basra Arabic, Mahdi (1985: 86–87, fn. 102) states that there is variation between the affricated and non-affricated realization of OA *q. In sum, this means that at present we do find this feature in certain urban *gələt* contexts, although apparently to a lesser degree than on the countryside which might indicate a certain tendency in urban or urbanizing contexts towards de-affrication or replacement of *ǧ* with the less marked or less "provincial" *g*. While it does seem to be the case that with the continuing influx of rural people to the city of Baghdad certain features as mentioned by Palva can be heard again, those features that are clearly marked as rural speech will most likely not persist but rather be dropped soon after people start to accommodate to the city's dialect (cf. Leitner 2021). Moreover, the affricated pronunciation of OA *q does seem to be still associated with rural speech, especially in Iraq.

Even though in Khuzestan many speakers have led a sedentary life in towns and villages for a considerable time, many KhA dialects have retained features such as conditioned affrication of *g* and all have retained gender distinction in the plural. Other features previously described as rural have been given up by most KhA speakers (especially in cities like Ahvaz), such as the 3SG.F PFV verbal pattern CCəCat (in favor of the pattern CəCCat) and the *g(a)hawa*-syndrome. This is probably due to their higher marked or stigmatized character as nomadic or rural features.

We can conclude that the use of the dichotomy "rural" versus "urban" is not at all as clearly demarcated as often claimed. Due to the overall scarcity of the data available on this group, the internal classification of the *gələt* dialect group is still not solidly established, and no bundle of features has been defined that clearly and validly differentiates all rural *gələt* dialects from the urban ones. For these reasons, I propose that the label "rural" (as it has been used until now) is inadequate for the (sub)classification of KhA as a *gələt* dialect and will therefore not be used in this book. Additionally, for the description of internal KhA divisions or subgroups, as discussed below (2.2), the terms *ʕarab* and *ḥaḍar* will be preferred over urban and rural.

2.1.3   *KhA as a Minority Dialect*

In Iran, Arabic is not the language of the majority population and is not used in education (outside of religious instruction) and administration. The majority language as well as the only official language and language of education and administration is Persian. KhA can be considered a "peripheral" dialect of Arabic (cf. Akkuş 2017: 454 and 456, who defines "peripheral" Arabic as a continuum spanning the northern periphery of Arabic from Anatolia to Central Asia). This implies that it is insulated from influence by MSA and instead influenced by a contact language, in this case Persian. Sharing a long geographi-

GENERAL CLASSIFICATION AND INTERNAL SUBDIVISIONS

cally open border with Iraq, Khuzestan is, however, not totally isolated from the Arabic-speaking world. The largely Shiite population of Khuzestan frequently visits religious places in South-Iraq (for example the shrine of Ḥusayn in Kerbala). These visits as well as tribal or family connections allow for some intra-Arabic contact. In addition, the Iran-Iraq War led to considerable demographic changes within Khuzestan and across borders. But since the dialects of South Iraq are linguistically very similar to KhA,[11] people feel less need for linguistic accommodation. In the course of the work migration of Khuzestani Arabs from Khuzestan to Kuwait or other Gulf countries, many speakers accommodated to the respective Gulf dialect. Many of those have, after working in the Gulf, returned to Khuzestan for good or regularly come back for holidays and family visits. The language of such speakers, who have adopted certain Gulf features, might have an influence on local KhA speakers, too. In addition to these influences, since around the year 2000 people in Khuzestan have had access to Arabic news, television shows (usually in Syrian Arabic), etc. via satellite TV. However, my data suggests that this influence is at most marginal.

The linguistic influence Persian has had on KhA is strongest in lexicon, but is also evident in some aspects of its phonology and syntax. Contact-induced changes in KhA will not be addressed in detail in this book. However, whenever a phenomenon described shows a clear influence from Persian, this will be indicated. For a more detailed evaluation of language contact phenomena in KhA, cf. Gazsi (2011), Ingham (2005), Shabibi (2006), Matras and Shabibi (2007),[12] and Leitner (2020).

2.2   Internal Subdivisions of KhA

Ingham divides the dialects of Khuzestan into three main subgroups according to geographical and social, and morpho-phonological aspects: *ḥaḍar* (urban) speech, *ʕarab* (rural) speech, and the speech of the people living in the marshes (*Maʕdān*).[13] This dialectal distinction is still perceived by speakers as such,

---

11   KhA is often differentiated from its neighboring Iraqi dialects by the number of Persian borrowings that are employed (Gazsi 2011: 1020).

12   The results presented in Shabibi's work (which is also the basis for Matras and Shabibi 2007) differ significantly from those presented in Leitner (2020) in that the evidence of language contact Shabibi found is in many regards significantly more far-reaching. I can only assume that the persons and families she interviewed have started to give up speaking Arabic at home and are exposed to Persian for a large part of their work- and private-lives.

13   Ingham (1976: 64–65) discerns a further group outside the *ḥaḍar* and *ʕarab* division: The speech of the Kawāwila, a group akin to the gypsies of Europe and with a nomadic type of

though many admit that there has been a lot of mixing and leveling of dialects in recent years due to population movement and the growth of cities like Ahvaz.

This chapter provides a general comparison of my data (collected from 2016–2020) with Ingham's division of KhA dialects based on data he collected in 1969 and 1971—which means that there is about a half-century between the data sets. The main result of this comparison is that in the city of Ahvaz, where speakers of many different areas came to live next to each other, we observe certain leveling tendencies of the dialectal subdivisions and therefore must question whether the once ʕarab character of this town is still maintained (cf. below for more details).

The following section will discuss several peculiarities that appear in the speech of some groups within Khuzestan, that can be defined either socio-economically (ḥaḍar versus ʕarab) or geographically (northern versus southern).

2.2.1 Division ḥaḍar and ʕarab—'Only the ḥaḍar-People Say laʕad'

In the introduction to his book *Arabian Diversions* (1997: ix–x), Ingham states that geographically and demographically both dialect groups, ḥaḍar and ʕarab, are really rural and actually rather differ regarding lifestyle: the ḥaḍar ('urban') group are riverine-palm-cultivating Arabs of mixed tribal descent, living along the banks of the Šaṭṭ al-ʕArab and the lower parts of the Kārūn (e.g. the tribal confederation of the Muḥaysin, Ingham 1976: 64); and the ʕarab ('rural') group are larger territorially-organized tribes living away from the river in the plain (*bādiya*)—sometimes as semi-nomads—involved in a variety of occupations, including cereal, rice, and date cultivation, sheep herding, and water buffalo breeding (for example the Kaʕab at Fəllāḥīya, Ingham 1976: 64). Based on this explanation, in the following only the terms ḥaḍar versus ʕarab (not urban versus rural) will be used.

Ingham made this division mainly according to morphological, morpho-phonological, and lexical distinctions (Ingham 1973: 534). He notes that the ʕarab dialect shows "considerably more resemblance to the dialects of Arabia than did the Urban" and that the ḥaḍar was "more strictly Mesopotamian than the Rural" (Ingham 1997: ix).

---

speech (with more nomadic elements than, for example, the marshland dialects). During my fieldwork, however, I was not able to get in touch with members of this group nor did people seem to know a lot about them in general apart from the fact that they used to be hired to dance at weddings.

GENERAL CLASSIFICATION AND INTERNAL SUBDIVISIONS 25

As stated before, the people of Khuzestan themselves still confirmed this distinction but could only mention a few distinguishing features. One repeatedly mentioned feature is the use of the discourse particles *laʕad* and *ča*, which appear to fulfill more or less the same functions. Whereas *ča* is considered a characteristic of the speech of the *ʕarab* people, or those living to the north of Fəllāḥīya in, for example, Ahvaz, Hoveyzeh, and Xafağīya, *laʕad* is said to be used by the *ḥaḍar* population living, for example, in the town of Fəllāḥīya (mostly palm cultivators). A woman [A12] from the outskirts of Ahvaz, who still leads a semi-nomadic life with her family, told me: *bass əl-ḥaḍar ygūlūn laʕad* 'only the *ḥaḍar*-people say *laʕad*'. In my corpus, however, the discourse particle *laʕad* does not occur at all.

According to Ingham's division, the dialect of Ahvaz belongs to the *ʕarab*-type (2007: 572). However, my data shows that while some features of the present-day dialect of Ahvaz correspond to what Ingham defined as typically *ʕarab*, others are instead typical of the *ḥaḍar* dialects. This indicates that in the city of Ahvaz—and probably also in other cities—we can note a certain leveling of these dialectal divisions and that the present-day dialect of Ahvaz is no longer a "pure" *ʕarab*-type dialect, but rather a mixed-type dialect. This development is probably linked to the immense population growth that the city of Ahvaz witnessed during and after the Iran-Iraq War (cf. above, fn. 7 and fn. 9)

In the following, I present some of the morphological and lexical features that demonstrate the mixed character of Ahvazi Arabic:

i. PFV.3SG.F form: CCvCat vs. CvCCat

    Ingham describes the syllabic structure CCvCat for the 3SG.F PFV—e.g. *ktəbat* 'she wrote'—as typically *ʕarab* (2007: 573). In my corpus data, the form with two initial consonants does not occur. Instead, we only find the form that Ingham lists for *ḥaḍar* dialects, CvCCat—e.g. *kətbat* 'she wrote', and *šəbgat* 'she hugged'. The *ʕarab* form is nowadays still typical of northwestern towns and villages, like Xafağīya (Pers. Susangerd) and Hoveyzeh.

ii. PFV.3SG.M: Ca- vs. Cə- in guttural contexts

    The form Ca- in the first syllable of 3SG.M PFV verbs in the contiguity of gutturals is classified as typically *ʕarab*-type, whereas the form Cə- is considered a *ḥaḍar* feature (cf. Ingham 1973: 539–540). The former type with a vowel *a* is the form used in present-day Ahvazi Arabic, e.g. *xaḍa* 'he took', not *xəḍa*; and *laʕab* 'he played', not *ləʕab*.

iii. Use of the *g(a)hawa*-syndrome

    Ingham (1973: 543–544) lists some nouns that show the *g(a)hawa*-syndrome as *ʕarab*-type, among them: *ʔahal-i* 'my family', *ghawa* 'coffee', and *nʕaya* 'ewe'. As explained in more detail in 3.7.2, in most present-day KhA dialects such forms are limited to certain lexemes and in the latter

26 CHAPTER 2

two of the above three examples the resyllabicated form is apparently no longer in use: present-day KhA uses *gahwa*, not *ghawa* 'coffee'; and *naʕya*, not *nʕaya* 'ewe'. On the other hand, the form *ʔahal-i* 'my family', does occur in my corpus but never *ʔahl-i*, the typical *ḥaḍar* form.

iv. Imperative singular masculine of final weak verbs

Ingham describes the imperative form of final weak verbs lacking the final vowel—e.g. *ʔəməš* 'go! (IMP.SG.M)', *ʔəḥač* 'speak! (IMP.SG.M)'—as *ʕarab*-type and, conversely, the form with the final vowel—e.g. *ʔəmši* 'go! (IMP.SG.M/SG.F)', *ʔəḥči* 'speak! (IMP.SG.M/SG.F)'—as *ḥaḍar*-type (2007: 577; 1973: 544). In the present-day dialect of Ahvaz, both variants are used.

v. Lexical features

Certain lexical features regularly used by my consultants from Ahvaz were classified as *ʕarab*-type by Ingham (1973: 538), e.g. *(le-)ǧād* for 'there'. However, its *ḥaḍar* equivalent *hnāk* 'there' is equally attested in Ahvaz. On the other hand, there are some lexical items found in Ahvaz that belong to the *ḥaḍar*-type, for instance *taʕadda* 'to pass on'. The *ʕarab* equivalent of this lexeme would be *mərag*, which occurs only once in my corpus, in a recording from the outskirts of Ahvaz (speakers [A12][14]). Some lexemes that Ingham mentions are not used by my consultants and sometimes were not even known anymore: the word for 'meal' today is neither *marag*[15] (which Ingham lists as *ḥaḍar*) nor *ydām* (which Ingham lists as *ʕarab*), but *ʔakəl*; and the most commonly heard word for 'mirror' in present-day Ahvazi Arabic is neither *mnədra* (*ḥaḍar*), nor *mrāya* (*ʕarab*), but *məšūfa* (PL *məšāwəf*) and *məšaffa* (PL *məšaffāt*).[16]

In some cases, items from both types are used in Ahvazi Arabic, leading to co-existent forms. For example, 'to look (at)' may be expressed by *əṣṭəba* (*ḥaḍar*), *bāwaʕ* (*ʕarab*), or *ʕāyan* (*ʕarab*) in present-day Ahvazi Arabic.

Thus we can conclude that the KhA subdialects described by Ingham have been subject to leveling since the times of his fieldwork in 1969 and 1971. This leveling is probably strongest in the present-day dialect of Ahvaz, which does not exactly correspond to one of these dialectal categories anymore and should

---

14 These speakers also used *ḥənna* instead of the otherwise common *ʔəḥna* for the 1PL independent pronoun.

15 *marag* in present-day Ahvazi Arabic means 'sauce'.

16 *mnədra* was not known to any of my informants. They all were familiar with the form *mrāya*, but gave various descriptions for where it was used: some attributed it to the speech of the southern towns such as Muḥammara, others to the speech of the people living east of the river Kārūn, and yet others thought that *mrāya* was a MSA form.

GENERAL CLASSIFICATION AND INTERNAL SUBDIVISIONS

rather be considered of mixed typology. The reasons for the observed mixture of dialectal features lie mainly in the demographic changes that have occurred during recent years due to the Iran-Iraq War, socio-economic factors like job opportunities and better access to educational institutions in bigger cities such as Ahvaz.

2.2.2 Marshland Dialects

Ingham describes the marshland dialects as the third dialect group of KhA spoken by people traditionally living in reed homes in the marshlands around ʕAmāra and Hōr al-Ḥammār in Iraq, and Hōr al-Ḥuwayza in Iraq and Iran (cf. Map 1; Ingham 1976: 65). These people, called Maʕdān, mostly live, or used to live, from buffalo breeding and the production of reed mats, called bārya PL bawāri[17] (cf. Ingham 1976: 65). He lists the main distinguishing characteristics of the marshland dialects as the following (most are supported, some contradicted by my data):

i.   The use of the particle ʕēb for the negation of verbs (Ingham 1976: 70)[18]
     This particle does not occur as a negation particle for verbs in my corpus, only as an interjection with the meaning 'don't do that, shame on you!' (as said, for example, when a child does something bad).

ii. ž as a reflex of *ǧ
     Ingham (1976: 67; 1982a: 30) describes this feature as characteristic of the marsh dwellers in the area of ʕAmāra and the surrounding marshlands. In the rest of Khuzestan, the reflex of OA *ǧ is either y or ǧ (cf. 3.1.2.3). In my corpus, this feature is attested for speakers from Hoveyzeh and Xafaǧīya. This feature is perceived as a hallmark of the speech of the Maʕdān and often mimicked by speakers who do not have ž as a reflex of *ǧ.

iii. Insertion of -ē- in PFV forms of all verbal types
     Ingham notes that this feature was typical of the ḥaḍar dialects (1974: 16; 1973: 544). In my corpus it is attested for speakers of Ahvaz, Hoveyzeh, Xafaǧīya, and Ḥamīdīya; but its use is most developed among speakers from Hoveyzeh, Xafaǧīya, and Ḥamīdīya. Examples from my corpus are: tarsēna 'we filled', instead of tarasna (more common in Ahvaz), and ṭalʕēna 'we went out, we took out', instead of ṭalaʕna.

iv. mūš for the negation of nouns
     This negation particle, described by Ingham as a typical marsh-dialect feature (1982a: 30), occurs in my corpus only in recordings of people from Hoveyzeh, Ḥamīdīya, and Tustar.

---

17   Cf. Holes (2016: 13) on Bahraini Arabic: "bari pl bawāri 'reeds (used as a building material)' < Aram būriyā 'reed mat', Akk burû 'reed mat'".

18   Cf. Hassan (2016: 304) on this marker in South Iraqi Arabic.

28   CHAPTER 2

v.   *lī-* 'to' instead of *l-*

The form *lī-* (instead of *l-*, as common in Ahvaz) for the preposition 'to' was used by speaker [Ḥ1] from Hoveyzeh, e.g. *waṣlat lī-ha* 'she reached her' instead of *waṣlat-əlha* (as heard in Ahvaz). Ingham mentions the use of the form *lī-* in the meaning 'towards' in the marshland dialects and dialects spoken in northern and eastern parts of Khuzestan, contrasting with *lē-* used in other parts of Khuzestan (1976: 68).

2.3   Conclusion

KhA has typical *gələt*-type features such as affrication of *k* and of *g* (< OA *q*) in front vowel environments (cf. Fischer and Jastrow 1980: 142–143) or the velarization of *l* (Fischer and Jastrow 1980: 143). On the other hand, it also shares a few features that have been classified as **qəltu** or **sedentary** type, e.g. the future marker *rāḥ* and the proclitic *d(ə)-* before imperatives.[19] KhA can also be classified as a **southern Mesopotamian** dialect, with features such as the development from OA *ǧ > y* (except for the *Maʕdān* dialects, which have *ž*) also found in the south of Iraq and in Kuwait (cf. Ingham 1982a: 26, 31, 35), whereas in all other Mesopotamian dialects OA *ǧ* is retained (Fischer and Jastrow 1980: 142). KhA can also be described as a **minority** dialect (in Iran), which has been influenced by the Persian language resulting in morphosyntactic and lexical borrowings. KhA can further be defined as a **peripheral** dialect, on the basis of such features as the temporal use of the prepositions *ǧəddām* 'in front of, before (temporal)' and *wara* 'behind, after (temporal)' (cf. 4.4.5 and 4.4.7), relative clauses with an indefinite head noun (cf. 4.1.9.2), and the combination of internal and external plural forms (cf. 4.9.2.4.6), e.g. *malək* 'king' PL *əmlūkīya*. In certain regards, KhA (and the Arabic dialects of southern Iraq) share some fea-

---

19   Palva states that in modern Muslim Baghdadi Arabic the future marker *raḥ* and the proclitic *d(i)-* before imperatives are evidence that this dialect is a "continuation of the pre-Abbasid sedentary dialect spoken by the Muslim population of Baghdad, and that its bedouinization is of relatively recent date" (2009: 35). That both features are also found in KhA is either the result of a (comparatively recent) adoption via contact with *gələt*-type Muslim Baghdadi Arabic (via spread of urban and prestigious features), or of an earlier migration of medieval (*qəltu*-type) Muslim Baghdadi Arabic speakers to the area of Khuzestan. In the 14th century, Muslim Baghdadi Arabic was still a *qəltu*-type dialect and probably undifferentiated from the non-Muslim dialects (Blanc 1964: 170; cf. Palva 2009: 36, fn. 18). Because we have no data on KhA from this time, this remains a merely speculative point.

GENERAL CLASSIFICATION AND INTERNAL SUBDIVISIONS

MAP 3   Classification of Khuzestani Arabic

tures with certain dialects of **northern Gulf Arabic**, e.g. the insertion of -ē- in PFV suffixes with verbs of all types (cf. 4.11.1.1), and the insertion of -ā- in geminated and medial weak SG.M PFV verbs before consonant-initial suffixes, as in *gāl-ā-lha* 'he told her' (cf. Ingham 1982a: 39; cf. 3.7.1 and 4.11.15). Finally, KhA shares many features with the **Šāwi-dialects** spoken in Syria and Anatolia—e.g. the use of *māmən* 'there is not' to express non-existence (cf. 4.8.1.7)—and with the Arabic dialect spoken in **Khorasan** (Iran), e.g. the forms of the 3rd person plural pronouns (cf. 4.1.1).

Map 3 illustrates the multi-faceted classification of KhA on the basis of the above-listed features: Its typological classification (basically Bedouin *gələt* with a few sedentary features) is shown in blue color; its areal characteristics are shown in red; and dialects with which KhA shares a significant number of features and that are thus called "cognate dialects of KhA" are presented in green bubbles.

It is often stated that Bedouin dialects have retained more morphophonemic categories than the sedentary dialects (cf. Palva 2006: 606) and are therefore more archaic. This is true for KhA in certain regards, for example the retention of the OA interdentals and the retention of feminine plural in all persons as a productive category. On the other hand, like many other Bedouin-type dialects too, KhA has suffered many reductional changes and given up, for example, the use of the internal passive or the verbal Pattern IV (cf. Ingham 1982a: 42–43, 51).

In the domain of morphosyntax, sedentary dialects are generally said to be more prone to use different verb modifiers and more analytic genitive structures, whereas Bedouin dialects more often make use of synthetic structures (Palva 2006: 606). KhA seems to have adopted such sedentary characteristics (cf. 4.8.3, 4.11.16, and 4.11.1.3.1 on the use of certain verb modifiers; and 4.6 on the use of analytic genitive structures).

All these points show the complexity of classifying a dialect in a selective way. This task becomes even more difficult with increased demographic dynamics and the growth of big cities where people from different geographical and social origins come to live next to each other. Hence, instead of a singular categorization of KhA a description as a multi-faceted linguistic construct appears to be epistemologically more meaningful at this point, cf. Map 3.

In my data, there are many more linguistic features than the above mentioned that show (phonological or morphological) variation and will need further investigation to comprehensively understand whether they might be socially and/or geographically determined (a combination of these influences seems probable). Among these features we find different forms of demonstrative pronouns, the retention or dropping of the vowel *a* following the prefix *t-* in the IPFV of Pattern V and VI verbs—e.g. *nətʕašša ~ nataʕašša* 'we have dinner' (cf. Leitner 2021: 7; Ingham 1976: 74–75)—and the retention or raising (and elision) of OA **a* in pre-tonic open syllables—e.g. *əmrākəb ~ marāčəb* 'boats' < OA **marākibᵘ*. The above analysis also shows that in KhA most intra-regional differences are in morphology and phonology.

Finally, more research specifically on *gələt* dialects spoken in northern Iraq is needed to determine if the features which several southern *gələt* dialects share with northern Gulf Arabic (e.g. the pronunciation of OA **q* as *ǧ*, cf. 3.1.2.1) are also found in these northern *gələt* dialects. Until more descriptions and data from other *gələt* dialects become available, we must conclude that "the classification of *gələt* dialects is still tentative" (Jastrow 2007: 415).

2.4 Figures

FIGURE 1 Woman at the market selling *bāmya* 'okra', Shadegan
PHOTO TAKEN BY THE AUTHOR

FIGURE 2 Date palm, Ahvaz
PHOTO TAKEN BY THE AUTHOR

FIGURE 3　Man climbing a palm tree with a *farwand*
(*Note*: Broad piece of cloth, used not to hurt one's back when climbing up the palm trees)
PHOTO TAKEN BY THE AUTHOR

FIGURE 4   Date harvest, Shadegan
PHOTO TAKEN BY THE AUTHOR

FIGURE 5 Kids running in a palm yard, Shadegan
PHOTO TAKEN BY THE AUTHOR

FIGURE 6   Traditional *tannūr* 'clay oven'
PHOTO TAKEN BY THE AUTHOR

FIGURE 7   Shepherdess, Ahvaz
PHOTO TAKEN BY THE AUTHOR

FIGURE 8   Shepherd, Ahvaz
PHOTO TAKEN BY THE AUTHOR

FIGURE 9   Umm ʕAzīz in front of her house, Ahvaz
PHOTO TAKEN BY THE AUTHOR

GENERAL CLASSIFICATION AND INTERNAL SUBDIVISIONS

FIGURE 10   Umm ʕAzīz baking *səyāḥ*/*ʕēš təmən* 'rice bread'
PHOTO TAKEN BY THE AUTHOR

FIGURE 11   Water buffalos and their owner, Ahvaz
PHOTO TAKEN BY THE AUTHOR

FIGURE 12   Water buffalos bathing in the river Karun, Ahvaz
PHOTO TAKEN BY THE AUTHOR

FIGURE 13 Elderly woman, Susangerd
PHOTO TAKEN BY THE AUTHOR

PART 2

Grammar

CHAPTER 3

Phonology

3.1 Consonants

3.1.1 Synchronic Description of the KhA Consonant Inventory

The basic consonant inventory (28 consonants[1]) of KhA may be schematized as follows (Table 1):

TABLE 1   Consonant Inventory of Khuzestani Arabic

	Labial	Alveolar	Alveolar alveolar	Palato-alveolar / palatal	Velar	Uvular	Pharyngeal	Glottal
voiceless stops	*p**	*t*	*ṭ*		*k*		*ʔ*	
voiced stops	*b, ḅ**	*d*			*g*			
voiceless affricates				*č*				
voiced affricates				*ǧ*				
voiceless fricatives	*f*	*s, ṯ*	*ṣ*	*š*		*x*	*ḥ*	*h*
voiced fricatives		*z, ḏ*	*ẓ*, *ḏ̣*	*ž***		*ġ*	*ʕ*	
nasals	*m, ṃ**	*n*						
laterals		*l*	*ḷ**					
rhotics		*r*	*ṛ**					
approximants	*w*			*y*				

* Marginal phonemes *p*, *ẓ*, *ḷ*, *ṃ*, *ḅ*, and *ṛ*

The marginal phoneme *p* occurs only in loan words (usually borrowed from Persian), e.g. *panǧara* 'window' < Pers. *panǧere*, *patu* 'blanket' < Pers. *patu*, and *panka* 'ventilator' < Pers. *pānke*. In KhA, *p* is often softened to *b*, especially among the older generation, e.g. *bebsi* < Pepsi, and *blēt* 'metal/iron (plates)' < Engl. *plate*.

ẓ is restricted to different forms of the lexeme *ẓġayyər*, *aẓġīr* PL *aẓġār* 'small' < OA *ṣaġīrᵘⁿ* and thus is only the result of assimilation (to an adjacent consonant).

ḷ, *ṃ*, *ḅ*, and *ṛ* have only been found in emphasis-spreading or emphasis-inducing conditions (cf. 3.4 below).

** Phoneme *ž*

The phoneme *ž* reflects OA **ǧ* (cf. 3.1.2.3) in some parts of Khuzestan, especially in the surroundings of Xafaǧīya and Hoveyzeh. In all dialects of Khuzestan *ž* is found in some loan words, e.g. *təknəlōžī-yāt* 'technologies'.

---

1   *ǧ* and *ž* are counted as just one phoneme since they are regional variants: either the one or

44   CHAPTER 3

3.1.2   *Historical Correspondences and Sound Shifts*

This chapter provides a short overview of the main historical sound shifts that occurred in KhA, accounting for the phonetic environments triggering or limiting/impeding such sound shifts, with some comparative remarks regarding similar shifts in other dialects.

3.1.2.1   Reflexes of *$*q$

OA *$*q$ has two main realizations in KhA: (1) the voiced velar phoneme /g/; and (2) its affricated variant /ǧ/, which occurs in front vowel environments. In very few lexemes, OA *$*q$ has shifted to /k/. Due to the influence of Persian, as will be explained in more detail below, a fourth realization of *$*q$ has emerged: /ġ/.

*$*q > g$

The main KhA reflex of OA *$*q$ is the voiced velar phoneme /g/ (this pronunciation of OA *$*q$ occurs about 2,000 times in my corpus), e.g. *galəb* < *qalb^{un}* 'heart', *gāʕəd* < *qāʕid^{un}* 'sitting (AP.SG.M)', *dagg* < *daqqa* 'he hit', *gēḏ̣* 'summer' < *qayḏ̣^{un}*. This reflex is typical of Bedouin dialects (Rosenhouse 2006: 260; Behnstedt and Woidich 2005: 42–43; cf. also Blanc 1969: 22). In some loans from Persian, English, and Ottoman Turkish, *g* does not derive from OA *$*q$, e.g. *glāṣ* with the meaning 'glass' < Engl. 'glass', and *glōb* 'light bulb' < Engl. 'globe'.

*$*q > ġ$

In some KhA lexemes, OA *$*q$ is reflected as *ġ* (cf. Ingham 1973: 537). In my texts, the OA *$*q$ is pronounced, *ġ* 241 times, i.e. about one-tenth the realization of OA *$*q$ as *g*.[2] According to Bahrani and Modarresi Ghavami (2019: 4), in the speech of Abadan, there is a full merger of OA *$*q$ and *$*ġ$ into one phoneme /q/. This is, however, not confirmed by my data from Abadan, in which the basic phoneme representing OA *$*q$ is /g/ as elsewhere in Khuzestan.

A fricative pronunciation of *$*q$ is elsewhere also attested for other dialects in Mesopotamia, some dialects in the Gulf region,[3] and also for a couple of Yemeni dialects: either as a free variant besides *q* (e.g. in Daṯīnah) or as its

---

the other is used for OA *$*ǧ$; compare Bahrani and Modarresi Ghavami (2019: 2–3), who claim 33 consonants, including *p*, *ḷ*, and *ṛ* as fully phonemic, as well as assuming a phoneme *v* and counting both *ǧ* and *ž*; in my data, *v* does not occur at all.

2   The preponderance of forms with *g* in my corpus can partly be explained by the fact that forms of *gāl* 'to say', in which *$*q$ is always pronounced *g*, are highly frequent.

3   Cf. Edzard (2009: 2) on the diachronic development; Mahdi (1985: 58–59) on Basra, the Šaṭṭ

PHONOLOGY   45

only reflex (Behnstedt 2016: map 1: 4–5). Although there are many references
that mention this phenomenon, only few have tried to explain the motivation behind this phonological change. Al-Ani (1976: 54) states on Iraqi Arabic
that this change is mainly observed for lexemes borrowed from literary Arabic;
Mahdi (1985: 58) states on Basra Arabic that he has observed this phenomenon
mainly among uneducated people; and Holes shows that in the dialects of
Kuwait and (Bedouin-type) Bahrain *q is realized as [ɣ], [q], or [ɢ] in MSA
neologisms (2007: 610; 2016: 53). In the Šāwi-dialects of Syria, OA *ǧ has generally shifted to q⁴ (Behnstedt 1997: 15, map 7); but in some words *q is realized
as [ɣ], e.g. ta[ɣ]ālīd 'traditions' (Talay 2008: 441). This has been explained as the
result of a hypercorrection among speakers, who are aware of the shift *ǧ > q in
their dialect but misinterpret MSA forms with etymological q (Behnstedt 2000:
431–432).

On KhA, Ingham states that "there is a degree of merger between Classical
Arabic /ǧ/ and /q/" (2007: 573). Whereas my data fully supports the pronunciation of OA *q as ǧ, the opposite development, i.e. *ǧ > q, is not attested to
the same extent. In most cases, *ǧ is retained as a voiced uvular fricative [ʁ]
(see below). Only among some speakers and in some words (especially when
in postvocalic positions), *ǧ was pronounced as a voiced uvular stop [ɢ], e.g.
ṣəbə[ɢ] 'dye (noun)', or as a voiceless uvular stop [q], e.g. lə[q]a 'language'.
Hence, we can only speak of a "degree of merger" as in Ingham's statement,
but definitely not of a full merger of OA *ǧ and *q. Hypercorrection is therefore also less likely an explanation for this change in most KhA dialects. As will
be argued below, from the analysis of my corpus, it appears that language contact with Persian, and contact with Khuzestani speakers who have stayed for a
significant time in Kuwait or Bahrain, may have played an essential role in the
development from OA *q to ǧ in KhA.

My corpus yields the following results regarding the distribution of ǧ < *q:

i.   As illustrated in the following table, ǧ < *q mostly occurs word initially
      and between two vowels (cf. Bahrani and Modarresi Ghavami 2019: 4;

---

al-ʕArab area, and Kuwait; Al-Ani (1976: 54) on Bedouin-type Iraqi dialects; and Johnstone
(1967: 20, 36) on Arabic dialects in Kuwait, Bahrain, and Qatar; cf. also Al-Nassir (1993: 40).

4   A process *ǧ > q is also attested in Basra Arabic (Mahdi 1985: 59), some Bedouin-type Iraqi
    dialects (Al-Ani 1976: 55), Arabic dialects in Central and Eastern Sudan (Reichmuth 1983: 46–
    47), and in pre-Hilalian and Hilalian dialects in (southern) Algeria (Bouhania 2011: 245–246;
    Cantineau 1941: 74, who says that in southern Algeria not only is a change from *ǧ to q found
    in some cases, but also the reverse change from *q to ǧ, cf. Fischer and Jastrow 1980: 52).
    In Bedouin-type Bahraini Arabic (Holes 2016: 53–54; fn. 5 and 6 for further references) and
    Kuwaiti Arabic (2007: 610; 2016: 53) *ǧ may be realized as [ɢ], [q] or [ɣ] (i.e. the same three
    allophones which OA *q has in these dialects in MSA neologisms).

Mustafawi 2017: 24 on the universal tendency of stops to turn into fricatives in intervocalic positions), but might occur in any other position, too:

Position	Occurrences of $\dot{g}$ < *q (in total: 241)	Example
initial: *qv-	89	*ġaṣd* 'intention'
intervocalic: v-*q-v	63	*baġar* 'cows'
C-*q-v-	30	*bərġi* 'electronic'
v-*q-C-	31	*taġrīban* 'approximately'
final: v-*q#	28	*yəfrəġ* 'it differs'

ii. The KhA lexemes in which $\dot{g}$ < *q occurs are either **Persian borrowings** (of Persian as well as of ultimately Arabic origin), words that have a **cognate lexeme in Persian**, or **loans from MSA**.

　23. Examples from my corpus are: *ġəsma* 'part, section' (cf. Pers. *ɢesmat* 'part, section'), *taṣdīġ* 'driving license' (cf. Pers. *taṣdīɢ* 'certificate, attestation'), *yifrəġ* 'it differs' (cf. Pers. *farɢ* 'difference'), *taġrīban* 'approximately' (cf. Pers. *taɢrīban* 'approximately'), *mangəla* 'coal pan' (cf. Pers. *manɢal* 'coal pan'), *bərġi* 'electronic' (cf. Pers. *barɢi* with the same meaning but ultimately going back to OA *barquⁿ* 'lightning'), *yġəṣdūn* 'they (PL.M) mean', *ġaṣd* 'intention' (cf. Pers. *ɢasd* 'intention'), *ġabəl ~ gabəl* 'in former times' and the homonymous preposition *ġabəl ~ gabəl* 'before, ... ago' (cf. Pers. *ɢabl (az)* and *ɢablan* 'before'), and *ġərʔān* 'Quran'. The few MSA loans found in my corpus are: *ġalīl* 'few, little' (cf. KhA *ġəlīl* 'few, little'), *masġaṭ rās* 'hometown', *baġar* 'cows' (cf. KhA *hōš* 'cows'), *aṣdəġā* 'friends' (but also KhA *ṣədġān* 'friends' with *ġ*).

iii. In most purely dialectal words, i.e. words which **do not have a corresponding lexeme** in Persian nor are **loans from MSA**, *q is usually realized as g in all positions, e.g. *gāl* 'he said', *gām* 'he got up, he started to', *gēḍ* 'summer', *gədar—yəgdar* 'to be able to', *marag* 'sauce', *təngəl* 'you (SG.M) move (sth.)'.

iv. In a few dialectal words, *q is still pronounced *ġ*, even though there is no cognate form in Persian. The only examples found in my corpus are: *brēġəš* 'small mosquito', *tġašmar* 'he joked',[5] and *yəġra* 'he reads'.

5　Cf. Holes (2001: 424) on *tgašmar, tkašmar*, and *tġašmar* (Bedouin-type) 'to joke, play a joke' in Bahraini-Arabic, cf. also Johnstone (1967: 96) on *ġašmar* 'to joke with, make a joke of (s.o.)' in Bahraini-Arabic.

PHONOLOGY

47

v. $*q$ is never $ǧ$ but consistently realized as g, whenever it is doubled, e.g. in *dagg* 'he hit', *bagg*[6] 'gnat, mosquitoes', and *səgga* 'butter hose'.

vi.   In some words, e.g. the adverb *ǧabəl ~ gabəl* 'in former times' and the homonymous preposition *ǧabəl ~ gabəl* 'before, ... ago', there appears to be variation regarding the pronunciation of $*q$ as $ǧ$ or g.

vii. In two lexemes for which a fricative realization of $*q$ was found, there is a variant form with $ǧ$: *ǧalīl ~ ǧəlīl* 'little, few', and *ṭarīǧ ~ ṭarīǧ* 'way'.

viii. There is one doublet which well shows the two developments of OA $*q$: the "dialectal" one $*q > g > ǧ$ in front-vowel environments vs. $*q > ǧ$ in loans from Persian (even though its ultimate might be Arabic): *bāǧi* 'rest, remaining' vs. *bāǧi* 'change (noun) [money]' both < OA *bāqī* 'remaining.'

In Persian, both $*q$ and $*ǧ$ are reflected by the phoneme /ɢ/, which can have various allophones, including [ʁ] and [ɣ].[7] We can assume that the pronunciation of $*q$ as /ɢ/ in Persian has had an impact on the pronunciation of KhA words. This pronunciation had probably first been borrowed together with loans from Persian (even though their ultimate origin might be Arabic, cf. Leitner 2020: 118–119), and then spread to loans from MSA and dialectal forms. As mentioned above, in the (Bedouin-type) dialects of Kuwait and Bahrain $*ǧ$ has an allophone [q] (besides [ɣ] and [ɢ] among educated speakers; uneducated speakers of Bedouin-type Bahraini Arabic generally have OA $*ǧ > q$, Holes 2016: 53–54), and $*q$ in MSA neologisms may be realized as [ɣ], [q], or [ɢ] (in non-MSA loans OA $*q$ is g, cf. Holes 2016: 52 on Bedouin-type Bahraini Arabic). The fact that many Khuzestani Arabs live or have lived in one of these two countries (usually for job opportunities), could have also fostered the development of the process $*q > ǧ$ in KhA. We might even consider the process of fricativization of q and the limited merger of the phonemes $ǧ$ and q to be areal phenomena typical of the northern and central Gulf region because it is found in Persian as well as in the Arabic dialects of Bahrain, Kuwait, South-Iraq, and Khuzestan.

---

6 Proto-Semitic *baqq- for a 'gnat' is reflected in Akk. *bakku*, Syr. *bāḳā*, CA *baqq-* (Kogan 2011: 212).

7 According to Modarresi Ghavami (2018: 95), the Modern Persian phoneme ɢ has the allophones, [ɢ, x, ʁ]; contrast Majidi (1986: 58–60), who states that the underlying phoneme is /ǧ/ with allophones [ɢ] and [ɣ]; cf. Bijankhan (2018: 113), who summarizes the positions on the debate on whether the underlying phoneme in Persian is a dorso-velar fricative or a dorso-uvular stop. Note that there are some varieties of Spoken Modern Persian or other Iranian languages spoken in Iran that do maintain a difference between $*q$ and $*ǧ$; for instance Persian dialects spoken in the province of Fārs (Paul 2018: 582), the Persian dialects of the cities

As shown in the table above, the total number of occurrences of $\acute{g}$ < *q in my corpus is 241. However, the number of different lexemes within these 241 instances is only 71. That this shift occurs in such a comparatively small number of different lexemes supports my hypothesis that the pronunciation of $\acute{g}$ in these lexemes is a consequence of the contact with Persian. Similarly, the three words for which variants with $\breve{g}$ exist also speak against an internal development, because the change $\breve{g}$ > $\acute{g}$ is extremely unlikely and thus can be ruled out.

The fact that other non-Persian languages spoken in Western Iran have adopted a fricative realization of q as a replication of the Persian model—e.g. Turkic varieties, or Neo-Mandaic (Khan 2018b: 387)—further supports the hypothesis that in KhA, too, this phenomenon is the result of language contact and not an internal sound change.

If this is correct, we can assume that the perception of a less "dialectal" pronunciation of *q as $\acute{g}$, instead of the more dialectal realizations of *q as g or $\breve{g}$, might have further supported the pronunciation of *q as $\acute{g}$ in MSA loans, though such are not very numerous in general due to the marginal influence of MSA in this region.

KhA examples that do not have a Persian cognate but in which *q is still realized as $\acute{g}$ (see above) might support the hypothesis that internal change has also played a role in this development.[8] However, such examples are few in number in comparison to those which do have a Persian cognate. Another support for this hypothesis is the fact that a shift *q > $\acute{g}$ is also found among Bedouin dialects of North-Africa (cf. Ritt-Benmimoun 2005: 281 and the references there on both shifts $\acute{g}$ > q and q > $\acute{g}$ in various dialects of the Maghreb; and Marçais 1944: 40 on the dialect of Bou-Saada in Algeria) and in Central and Eastern Sudan (Reichmuth 1983: 46–47). In these countries the factor of Persian influence can be definitely ruled out. Apart from the fact that in Central and Eastern Sudan this process is again only found in MSA loans, there OA *$\acute{g}$ also has an allophone [q] in word-final position (in non-final position it usually has an allophone [ɣ], and before voiceless consonants [x]), similar to Bahraini Arabic and other dialects (cf. above, fn. 4). This reverse process might have supported the pronunciation of *q as $\acute{g}$ in MSA loans and thus cannot be fully compared with the situation found in KhA.

---

of Dezfūl and Šuštar in Khuzestan province (MacKinnon 2019), and some Bakthiari varieties (Anonby and Asadi 2018: 40, 85–86).

8 Cf. for example Holes (2016: 53–54), who explains the $\acute{g}$–q merger among the Najd-descendent Bahraini Arabic speakers as an internal development.

PHONOLOGY

*q > x

The pronunciation of *q as [x], as in [ʔaxsa:m] 'types, kinds, groups' (cf. MSA *ʔaqsām* with the same meaning), and [taxsʕiːr] 'blame; fault' (cf. MSA *taqṣīr* 'failure'), is the result of a series of sound changes q (> g?) > ġ > x. The last step occurred because of assimilation: The voiced uvular fricative [ʁ] is devoiced due to the adjacent voiceless consonant.

*q > g > ǧ

As in many Eastern Bedouin-type dialects,[9] historical g is itself often further fronted and affricated to ǧ, especially in the environment of front vowels (cf. the affrication k > č described below, which is also restricted to front vowel environments). Historically, affrication of g > ǧ must have developed after both the voicing of q and the affrication of k (Holes 1991: 657, 665–667). Examples for this sound shift in KhA are *raǧǧi* 'watermelon' (cf. *raggi* in Iraq WAD I: 512), *bāǧi* 'change (noun) [money]' < OA *bāqī* 'remaining', *ǧərīb* < *girīb < qarīb^un 'close', *ḥaláǧ* (also *ḥaláġ*) < *ḥalq^un* 'mouth', *ǧəlīl* < *gilīl < qalīl^un* 'little', *ǧəla* < *qalā* 'to fry', and *ǧəddām* < *giddām < quddām^un* '(in) front (of)'. An exception to this process is KhA *ǧāʕad* (also *gāʕad*) 'sitting', in which g may be affricated even though it is not in the vicinity of front vowels. In some lexemes there is variation with g, e.g. *məḏ̣ayyəǧ ~ məḏ̣ayyəg* 'worried', *ṣədəǧ ~ ṣədəg < ṣidq^un* 'truth'.

*q > k

This change is attested only for the lexemes *wakət* 'time' < *waqt^un* (cf. WB: 502 *wakit* 'time' in Iraqi Arabic; and Holes 2001: 563 *waqt, wagt* and *wakt* 'time, season' in Bahraini Arabic), *kətal* 'to hit' < *qatala* 'to kill' (typically Bedouin, cf. Rosenhouse 2006: 267), and *wakəḥ* 'naughty'. In Iraqi-Arabic, this change is also limited to the same items (cf. Al-Ani 1976: 55 on the same items in Iraqi Arabic).

3.1.2.2   Reflexes of *ġ

*ġ is generally realized as a voiced uvular fricative [ʁ] in KhA, e.g. [ʁ]əda 'he became', [ʁ]əlab 'he won'. Among some speakers, *ġ might be pronounced as

---

9 Cf. Palva (2006: 606); cf. also the map in Johnstone (1963: 5); Holes (2018b: 139) on Gulf Arabic; Salonen (1980: 52–53), and Meißner (1903: IX) on the Iraqi *gələt* dialects of Širqāṭ, and Kwayriš/Babylon, respectively.

50   CHAPTER 3

a voiced uvular stop [ɢ], especially when in postvocalic positions, e.g. ṣəbə[ɢ] 'dye (noun)'. This, too, is very likely the result of contact with Persian (cf. above).

ġ is devoiced to [x] in some lexemes in the environment of certain voiceless sounds in syllable-final position (cf. Ingham 1974: 103–104), e.g. [təxsəl] 'she washes' < OA *taġsilu*, [ʔəxta:ðˤ] 'he became angry' < OA *ʔiġtāḏa*, and [ʔəstaxfar] 'he asked forgiveness' < OA *ʔistaġfara*.

*ġ > q

As mentioned above, this shift is only attested for some speakers, (one from Abadan, one from Fəllāḥīya living in Kuwait, and one in Ahvaz), and always with the same lexeme, *ləqa* 'language' < *luġa^{tun}*.

3.1.2.3   Reflexes of **ǧ*

*ǧ > y

In KhA, the OA phoneme *ǧ* is generally reflected by the approximant *y*,[10] so that, on a synchronic level, it has merged with *y* < **y*.[11] Occasionally *ǧ* is maintained, e.g. *tərǧaʕ* 'you (SG.M) return', *bərəǧ* 'watchtower; month' *bəri* in Dōḥa Arabic, Johnstone 1965: 240), and *ǧās* 'he touched', but in most cases this shift is stable, e.g. *yāb* < **ǧāba* 'he brought', *ʕaray* F *ʕarya* PL *ʕaryān* 'to have a lame leg' (cf. CA *ʔaʕraǧ^u*), *yōʕān* < *ǧawʕān^{un}* 'hungry', and *ḥanyūr* < **ḥanǧūr^{un}* 'throat' (cf. CA *ḥanǧara* 'head of the windpipe; consisting of a part or the whole of the larynx ...', WAD I: 132). In some cases, however, both sounds are attested, e.g. *rayyāl ~ raǧǧāl* 'man'. The shift **ǧ > y* is often blocked in geminates, e.g. *ətraǧǧaʕ* 'she brings back', *ḥaǧǧ* 'Hajj, pilgrimage, go on a pilgrimage', and *ətwaǧǧahat* 'she showed'.

Word-initially *y < ǧ* tends to be elided, e.g. *ǧīrān > yīrān > ʔīrān* 'neighbors'. In intervocalic position *y < ǧ* may shift to *ʔ*, e.g. *Xafaǧīya > Xafaʔīya* (Pers. Susangerd), but is often retained, e.g. *ʕayīn* 'dough'.

---

10   Cf. Holes (2018: 141, 2016: 62, fn. 18) and Johnstone (1967: 2, 9–11) on this shift in Gulf Arabic and on the south coast of the Arabian Peninsula; cf. also Ingham (1976: 67) on its regional distribution, and Mustafawi (2017: 23) on further references for the discussion of this process among the Banū Tamīm in medieval texts as well as for phonological investigations of this process and its constrains in Qatari Arabic.

11   Bahrani and Modarresi Ghavami (2019: 5–6, fn. 5) state that in Muḥammara OA **ǧ* is traditionally preserved, but that some speakers also show a shift *ǧ > y* due to contact with speakers from Ahvaz and Abadan.

PHONOLOGY

*ǧ > ž

In the dialects of some tribes of the Maʕdān (i.e. the marsh dwellers, of which many are members of the Banū Ṭuruf tribe[12]) living, for example, in Xafaǧīya (Susangerd) or Hoveyzeh, OA *ǧ is consistently realized as a voiced fricative ž [ʒ], e.g. aždād-i 'my ancestors' < ʔaǧdād-i, žēna 'we came' < ǧiʔnā (cf. yēna in Ahvaz), and manžal 'sickle' < minǧalᵘⁿ (cf. manyal in Ahvaz). The pronunciation of OA *ǧ as ž can be considered a hallmark of Maʕdāni-speech. Among the non-Maʕdāni speakers, the Maʕdāni pronunciation of *ǧ as ž is perceived as a deviation from their "standard dialect rules" and as one of the biggest differences from their own their dialect: they tend to make fun of this Maʕdāni feature, inventing jokes with it or imitating Maʕdāni-speech.

3.1.2.4 Reflexes of *ṯ, ḏ, ḍ, (ẓ)

In general, interdentals are consistently retained, which is common in many Bedouin-type dialects in general (Rosenhouse 2006: 260; Behnstedt and Woidich 2005: 42–43; Holes 2013: 94; Palva 2006: 606), e.g. maṯal 'like' (OA *miṯlᵘⁿ), xaḏa 'he took' (OA *ʔaxaḏa), and naḏḏaf 'he cleaned' (OA *naḏḏafa).

As in almost all dialects of Arabic, ḍ has merged with ḏ > ḍ, e.g. ḍalla 'shadow' < OA ḏallaᵗᵘⁿ, and abyaḍ 'white' < OA ʔabyaḍᵘ.

However, in a number of cases, especially often with demonstratives, interdentals are pronounced as alveolar stops: e.g. hāda ~ hāḏa 'this (M)', dāk ~ ḏāk 'that (M)', and dahab ~ ḏahab 'gold'.

ẓ [dˤ] appears only as an allophone of ḍ, e.g. [dˤ]ammar 'to destroy', glā[dˤ]a 'necklace'.

3.1.2.5 Reflexes of *k

In most Bedouin-type dialects across the wider Eastern Arabic dialect zone, the OA phoneme k has been fronted and affricated in the environment of front vowels (Rosenhouse 2006: 260; cf. the map in Johnstone 1963: 5). In KhA, OA *k has shifted to č in front vowel environments (including ā in some words, if not word-final).[13] Holes (2016: 60) describes this historical process as "historically conditioned" (i.e. categorical) for the Bedouin-type dialects of Bahrain. Although, as will be shown below, there are a few exceptions, this shift is fairly regular in KhA, i.e. categorical.

---

12 Bahrani and Modarresi Ghavami (2019: 4–5) mention tribes from Xafaǧīya and Ḥamīdīya (the Sawāri, Ḥaydari, and Sāʕadi).

13 Compare Najdi Arabic, where OA *k has shifted to [ts] in front vowel environments (Ingham 1994: 14).

52   CHAPTER 3

Examples from KhA are *səmač* [sɪmɛtʃ] < OA *samak^{un}* 'fish', *čaləb* [tʃɛlɪb] <
OA *kalb^{un}* 'dog', *bāčər* [baːtʃɪr] 'tomorrow' < OA *bākir^{un}* 'early', and *čān* [tʃaːn]
< OA *kāna* 'he was'. Affrication did not always occur, wherever **k* is next to
[u] or [uː]—e.g. *məknāsa* [muknaːsɛ] 'broom', and *ykūn* [ɪkuːn] 'he is', but
yḥūčan 'they (PL.F) weave'—or in the syllable *-āk#*: e.g. *ḏāk* 'that (SG.M)', and
əhnāk 'there'. There are however exceptions in both directions, i.e. cases where
*k is not affricated even though in front-vowel environment and cases which
show affrication of **k* even though not in front-vowel environment, e.g. *bəčān*
[butʃaːn] (also *bəkān* [bukaːn]) 'place',[14] and *kətab* [kɪtɛb] 'he wrote'.[15] Moreover, some lexemes have both forms, with and without affrication of **k*, e.g.
ʔakəl ~ ʔačəl 'food'.

A minimal pair proving the phonemic status of *č* is KhA *bāǧi* 'change (noun)
[money]': *bāči* 'crying'.

3.1.2.6   Reflexes of **m*
OA **m* has generally been preserved but shifted to *b* in some lexemes because of
a second nasal consonant, e.g. *bəkān ~ bəčān* 'place' (however, the form *məkān*
is also used) < OA *makān^{un}*, or *bəsmār* 'nail' < OA *mismār^{un}* (cf. *bismār* in
Kwayriš/Babylon Arabic, Meißner 1903: 114).

3.1.2.7   Reflexes of **ḥ*
OA **ḥ* has generally been preserved but shifted to *h* in the lexeme *əhdaʕaš*
'eleven'.[16]

3.1.2.8   Reflexes of **x*
In KhA, OA **x* is generally realized as a voiceless uvular fricative [χ] in KhA
(compare Ingham 1974: 103, who writes that it is either plain velar or uvular
pharyngealized), e.g. *farax* 'child', *xəmra* 'yeast', and *əxū́* 'his brother'.

---

14   Cf. also Kwayriš/Babylon *mečān* (Meißner 1903:141), but Baghdad *makān ~ mukān* (WB:
      413). An explanation could be that the raising of **a* to [u] has occurred after the affrica-
      tion of **k*.

15   Words derived from the root *k-t-b* often constitute an exception to the historical process
      of fronting and affrication of **k*, cf. *kitab* in Baghdad (WB: 399), *kitab* and *katab* Bahrain
      Arabic (Holes 2001: 451), and *kiteb* in Kwayriš/Babylon Arabic (Meißner 1903: 140).

16   The same phonological process has been documented for the Arabic dialects of Kwayriš/
      Babylon (Meißner 1903: VII: *ihdaʕ(e)š*), Basra (Mahdi 1985: 148: *(i)hdaʕaš*), and Soukhne
      (Syria, Behnstedt 1994: 152: *hdaʕš*). Similar processes occurred in the same word e.g. in the
      dialects of Baghdad (Muslim, Erwin 1963: 261: *daʕaš/ʔidaʕaš*) and Damascus (Berlinches
      2016: 81: *ʔidaʕˤš*).

PHONOLOGY   53

3.1.2.9   Reflexes of *ʔ

OA *ʔ has generally disappeared if not in initial position preceding a vowel and after a pause or in intervocalic position, e.g. *ḥamra* < OA **ḥamrāʔᵘ* 'red (SG.F)'. In intervocalic position, OA *ʔ has shifted to *y*, e.g. *ṣāyər* 'becoming' < OA **ṣāʔirᵘⁿ*.

CA *māʔ* 'water' is an innovation (**y* has shifted to *ʔ* following a long vowel) while KhA *māy* reflects an older form: compare e.g. Geʿez *samāy* (Leslau 1987: 504) and CA *samāʔ*.[17]

In medial pre-vocalic positions, the loss of *ʔ* generally has resulted in the lengthening of the preceding vowel, e.g. *rās* 'head' < OA **raʔsᵘⁿ*. Exceptions are, for example: *səʔal* 'to ask', *taʔmīn* 'security, insurance', Pattern II verbs like *ʔamman—yʔammən* 'to trust', and Pattern V verbs like *tʔaxxar—yətʔaxxar* 'to be late', which, however could simply be loans from CA (compare e.g. the vernacular form *nəšad—yənšəd* for 'to ask'). After a consonant, *ʔ* disappeared completely, e.g. *mara* < (al-)marʔaᵗᵘ 'woman'.

ʔ has an allophone [ʕ] in certain lexemes among some speakers, e.g. *qərʕān* 'Quran', *saʕal* 'to ask',[18] and *səʕāl* 'question'. This phenomenon, however, does not appear to be very common in KhA.

3.1.3   *Assimilations*

In the following the partial and full assimilation processes found in KhA will be described. The forms within square brackets show the exact pronunciation of the assimilated consonants. In the rest of this book, however, these assimilation processes will not be indicated in the transcription so that the underlying root and pattern structures of the KhA words will remain clear to the reader. Assimilation may be partial or complete. In partial assimilation a consonant converges to another consonant in certain regards, usually voice, whereas in full or complete assimilation one consonant becomes identical to another.

3.1.3.1   Regressive

nb > [mb]:   *yənbāg* [jɪmbaːg] 'it (SG.M) is stolen', *nənbīʕ* [nɪmbiːħ] 'we sell'
nl > [lː]:   *ənlaggəḥ* [ɪlːɛgːɪħ] 'we fertilize'

---

17   See also Al-Jallad (2014: 451) on *ʔ-smy* 'the sky' in the Qaryat al-Faw inscription (usually dated between the 1st ct. BCE and 4th ct. CE); and (2014: 456) for general notes on the reconstruction of the Proto-Semitic form for 'sky, heaven'.

18   The use of *saʕal* (with the shift *ʔ* > *ʕ*) is also documented for Šāwi (Procházka 2018c: 283; Bettini 2006: 374) and North-East-Arabian dialects (Ingham 1982b: 252, fn. 36). In KhA, the use of this verb, however, appears to be a loan from CA, cf. the dialectal form *nəšad— yənšəd* 'to ask'.

nr > [rː]:   *ənrūḥ* [ɪrːuːħ] 'we go'

nt > [tː]:   *bənt* [bɪt ~ bɪtː] 'girl', *əntəm* [ɪtːum] 'you (PL.M)'

nṭ > [tˤː]:   *ənṭā-ni* [ɪntˤaːni ~ ɪtˤːaːni] 'he gave me'

The consonant *t* of the verbal inflectional prefixes assimilates completely to a following (palato-)alveolar stop, fricative, or affricate (cf. below on its assimilation as to voice):

tṭ > [tˤː]:   *əttəgg* [ɤtˤːɤgː] 'she hits'

tṯ > [θː]:   *əttāwab* [ɪθːaːwab] 'you (SG.M) yawn'

tḏ > [ðː]:   *ətḏakkrīn* [ɪðːakriːn] 'you (SG.F) remember'

tḏ̣ > [ðˤː]:   *ətḏ̣əbb* [ɪðˤːɪbː] 'you (SG.M) throw', *ətḏ̣əll* [ɪðˤːɤlː] 'she stays/you (SG.M) stay'

ts > [sː]:   *ətsawwi* [ɪsːawːi] 'she makes/you (SG.M) make', *ətsōləf* [ɪsːoːlɪf] 'she tells/you   (M) tell'

tṣ > [sˤː]:   *ətṣīr* [ɪsˤːiːr] 'she becomes/you (SG.M) become'

tš > [ʃː]:   *ətšūf* [ɪʃːuːf] 'she sees/you (SG.M) see'

tz > [zː]:   *ətzawwəǧ* [ɪzːawɪdʒ] 'she marries/you (SG.M) marry'

tǧ > [dʒː]:   *ətǧābəl* [ɪdʒːaːbɪl] 'she is in front of/you (SG.M) are in front of'

tč > [tʃː]:   *ətčəbbīn* [ɪtʃːɪbiːn] 'she pours out/you (SG.F) pour out'

tž > [ʒː]:   not attested in my corpus

The *l* of the definite article *əl-*, the relative pronoun *əlli ~ əl*, the preposition *l-* 'to; for', but also in other words in final position, fully assimilates to the following (palato-)alveolar consonants:

ld > [dː]:   *əl-dīra* [ɪdːiːrɛ] 'the town'

lḏ > [ðː]:   *əl-ḏəkar* [ɪðːɪkar] 'the male'

lḏ̣ > [ðˤː]:   *əl-ḏ̣əhər* [ɤðˤːɤhɤr] 'at noon; the noon'

lt > [tː]:   *əl-tannūr* [ɪtːɛnːuːr] 'the clay oven'

lṯ > [θː]:   *əl-ṯūm* [ɪθːuːm] 'the garlic'

lṭ > [tˤː]:   *əl-ṭīn* [ɤtˤːiːn] 'the clay'

ls > [sː]:   *əl-səčča* [ɪsːɪtʃːɛ] 'the street'

lš > [ʃː]:   *əl-šaṭṭ* [ɪʃːatˤː] 'the river'

lṣ > [sˤː]:   *əl-ṣəbəḥ* [ɤsˤːubuħ] 'the morning'

lz > [zː]:   *əl-zamān* [ɪzːɛmaːn] 'the time'

lẓ > [zˤː]:   *əl-ẓġayyər* [ɤzˤːɣajːɪr] 'the small, young (SG.M)'

lǧ > [dʒː]:   *əl-ǧəwāni* [ɪdʒːuwaːni] 'the bags'

lč > [tʃː]:   *əl-čīma* [ɪtʃːiːmɛ] 'burning firewood in the clay oven'

lž > [ʒː]:   not attested in my corpus

ln > [nː]:   *-əlna* [ɪnːɛ] 'for us, to us', *məṯəl-na* [mɪθɪnːɛ] 'like us', *šəlna* [ʃɪnːɛ] 'we moved', *gəlna* [gɪnːɛ] 'we said', *ahal-na* [ahanːɛ] 'our family'

lr > [rː]:   *məṯəl rōba* [mɪθɪr roːba] 'like yoghurt'

PHONOLOGY   55

3.1.3.2   Progressive

št > [ʃ:]:   *štarētu* [ʃːɛreːtu] 'you (PL.M) bought' (only found in this lexeme; otherwise it is *št*, e.g. *štagēt* [ʃtɛgeːt] 'I missed')

nl > [n:]   *yaṭan-la* [jatˤɑnːɛ] 'they (PL.F) give him'

3.1.3.3   Dissimilation

m may dissimilate to *b* when a second nasal consonant appears in the same lexeme:

m > *b*:   *bəkān ~ bəčān* 'place' (the form *məkān* is also used) < OA *makān^un*, *bəsmār* 'nail' < OA *mismār^un* (cf. 3.1.2.6)

3.1.3.4   Voicing and Devoicing

tg > [dg]:   *ətgūl-la* [ɪdgɪl-lɛ] 'she tells him/you (SG.M) tell him', *ətgūm* [ɪdguːm] 'she gets up, starts to/ you (SG.M) get up, start to'

td > [dː]:   *ətdawwər* [ɪdːawːur] (*ʕala*) 'she looks/you (SG.M) look (for sth.)'

ġt > [xt]:   *təġsəl* [təxsɪl] 'she washes/you (SG.M) wash'

ṣġ > [zˤɣ]:   *ṣġayyər* [zˤɣajːɪr] 'small'

sǧ > [zdʒ]:   *ynəsǧūn* [ɪnɪzdʒuːn] 'they (PL.M) weave'

sg > [zg]:   *ʕasga* [ʕazgɛ] 'palm branch'

šǧ > [ʒg]:   *yfəššgūn* [ɪfɪʒguːn] 'they cut in two, split, halve'

dt > [tː]:   *wālədt-əč* [waːlɪtːɪtʃ] 'your (SG.F) mother'

ʕt > [ħt]:   *məʕtabrīn* [məħtɛbriːn] 'considering (PL)', *ʔəʕtāz* [ʔəħtaːz] 'he needed'

ǧf > [ħf]:   *Ǧaʕfar* [tʃaħfar] 'Ǧaʕfar (name)'

ʕš > [ħʃ]:   *Məšaʕšaʕīn* [muʃaħʃaħiːn] 'Məšaʕšaʕīn (name of a tribal dynasty)'

fḍ > [bðˤ]:   Only attested for the word *ʔəbḍūli* [ʔɪbðˤuːli] 'curious (in a bad way)' (cf. CA *fuḍūli* 'one who busies himself with that which does not concern him', Lane 1863: 2413). This assimilation process has probably occurred in three steps: first, via loss of the vowel in the first open syllable yielding *fḍ*; second, sonorization of *f* > *v* due to its contiguity with the voiced consonant *ḍ*; third, *v* is not part of the KhA consonantal inventory, so it was replaced by *b*.[19]

Desonorization of ʕ is also very common in post- or intervocalic contexts (not only in pausal position), e.g. *ənbīʕ* [ɪmbiːħ] 'we sell', *ətbīʕ sayyārat-ha* [ɪtbiːħ sɛjːaːrathɛ] 'she sells her car', and *šəǧāʕa* [ʃɪdʒaːħa] 'courage'.

---

19   Cf. Mardin *bəzəʕ yəbzaʕ* 'to be afraid' and *bazʕa* 'fear' < √f-z-ʕ, (Vocke and Waldner 1982: 313) and *vazʕit* 'she was afraid' in the dialect of the Çukurova in southern Turkey (Prochazka 2002: 22; these dialects do have a marginal phoneme *v*).

56 CHAPTER 3

Desonorization of *d* was noted only for one speaker [Ḥ1] and only in some words. Where it was found, it was in postvocalic contexts and syllable-final, e.g. *baʕad-ha* [baʕathɛ] 'she has not yet'.

3.1.3.5 Reciprocal Assimilation

When a word ends in *ʕ* and is followed by an object suffix with initial *h*, the sequence *ʕh* becomes *ḥḥ*: first, *ʕ* is devoiced because of the following voiceless consonant *h*; second, *h* assimilates to the pharyngeal *ḥ*.

ʕh > [ħː]:   *yəglaʕ-ha* [jɪglaħːa] 'he plucks her', *ənbīʕ-ha* [ɪnbiːħːa] 'we sell it (SG.F)'

3.1.3.6 Other Assimilation Processes

The affricate *č* [tʃ] may be de-affricated to *š* when immediately preceding a *t*:[20]

čt > [ʃt]:   only found in the lexeme *čtāfāt* [ʃtaːfaːt] 'shoulders' (cf. Ingham 1982a: 163, fn. 5: *štāf* for *čtāf*)

3.1.4 *Consonant Elision*

Generally, *n* and *l* are the consonants most liable to deletion: e.g. *ʔəṭat* < *ʔənṭat* 'she gave', *ʕəd* < *ʕənd-* 'at' and *bət* < *bənt* 'daughter' (cf. 3.7.1). In the 1SG/2SG.M PFV form of the verb *gāl* 'to say', *gələt* 'I/you (SG.M) said', *l* is often deleted when an object suffix is attached to the verb, e.g. **gəl(ə)t-la* > *gət-la* 'I/you (SG.M) said to him'.

3.1.5 *Doubling*

The monosyllabic CV̄C prepositions *mən* 'from, since, of' and *ʕan* 'from, about, of' show gemination of the final consonant when a vowel-initial suffix is added,[21] e.g.:

>   *mən + -i → mənn-i* 'from me'
>   *ʕan + -a → ʕann-a* 'from him'

The 3PL.F IPFV and PFV and (optional) 1SG IPFV verbal suffix *-an* doubles the *-n* when a vowel-initial suffix is added, e.g.:

---

20   Cf. Jastrow (1973: 26) on a comparable process in a south-eastern Anatolian dialect: The affricate *ǧ* is realized as [ʃ] or [ʒ] in constructions: /... vǧCv .../.

21   The doubling of *n* in these two prepositions before vowel-initial suffixes is already attested for CA, cf. Procházka (Procházka 1993: 11, 21).

PHONOLOGY

yšūf-an 'they (PL.F) see' → *yšūf-ann-a* 'they (PL.F) see him'
yxəbz-an 'they (PL.F) bake' → *yxəbz-ann-a* 'they (PL.F) bake it (M)'
xəbz-an 'they (PL.F) baked' → *xəbz-ann-a* 'they (PL.F) baked it (M)'
ʔaḥəṭṭ-an 'I put' → *ʔaḥəṭṭ-ann-a* 'I put it (M)'

The 3SG.F PFV verbal suffix *-at* doubles the *-t* when a vowel-initial suffix is added, which results in a stress shift to the inflection suffix, e.g.:

šāf-at 'she saw' → *šāf-att-a* 'she saw him'
ʔəṭ-at 'she gave' → *ʔəṭ-att-a* 'she gave him'
ḥabbəb-at 'she kissed' → *ḥabbəb-att-a* 'she kissed him'

3.1.6   *Metathesis*
Examples of metathesis in KhA are *ṣəgəd* (but also *ṣədəg*) 'really', cf. CA *ṣidq^{un}* 'truth', and *yawwaz* (< **ǧawwaz*) 'to marry (someone) to (someone else), give in marriage', cf. CA *zawwaǧa*.

3.2   Vowels

3.2.1   *Synchronic Description of the KhA Vowel Inventory*
There are seven phonemic vowels in KhA, with five long vowels and two short vowels.[22]

TABLE 2   Vowel inventory of KhA

	Front	Central	Back
high	*ī*	*ə*	*ū*
mid	*ē*		*ō*
low		*a, ā*	

---

22   Contrast Bahrani and Modarresi Ghavami (2019: 5), who list 11 vowels, adding *i, u, o, e*, and a long back vowel *ā* as separate phonemes (without, however, providing minimal pairs proving their phonemic quality), the first three of which are in the present discussion all subsumed under one archiphoneme *ə* with different allophonic qualities and the last two are treated as marginal phonemes because they appear in loanwords only. In his thesis on KhA phonology, Ingham distinguishes between affix vowel units, *e, i, u, a, aw, ū, ī*, and *ā*, and stem vowel units, *a* and *ə* (1974: 134–144).

58   CHAPTER 3

Marginal Vowel Phonemes

A close-mid front unrounded vowel *e* [e] and a long back vowel *ā* [ɑ:] appear in some Persian loanwords, e.g. *šekel* 'type', *šeker* 'sugar', *āš* 'a thick Iranian soup'.

3.2.1.1   Long Vowels
The following list of minimal pairs shows oppositions between KhA long and short vowels and between long vowels of different quality:

a : *ā*   *bənat* 'she built' vs. *bənāt* 'girls'

ə : *ī*   *dəra* 'he knew' vs. *dīra* 'town'

ə : *ū*   *hədəm* 'piece of clothing, garment' vs. *hədūm* 'clothes, garments'

ā : *ū*   *šāf* 'he saw' vs. *šūf* 'see, look (IMP.SG.M)'

ā : *ī*   *yāb* 'he brought' vs. *yīb* 'bring (IMP.SG.M)'

ā : *ē*   *bāt* 'he spent the night, slept over' vs. *bēt* 'house'

ā : *ō*   *gām* 'he got up' vs. *gōm* 'people, tribe'

ē : *ō*   *ṭēna* 'we gave' vs. *ṭō-na* 'they (PL.M) gave us'

ē : *ī*   *ʕēš* 'bread' vs. *ʕīš* 'live (IMP.SG.M)'; *dēs* '(female) breast' vs. *dīs* 'big serving plate'

ē : *ū*   *frēx* 'child (DIM)' vs. *frūx* 'children'

ī : *ō*   *ʕīd* 'holiday' vs. *ʕōd* 'big, old'

ī : *ū*   *rīḥ* 'wind' vs. *rūḥ* 'spirit'

ō : *ū*   *gōm* 'people, tribe' vs. *gūm* 'get up (IMP.SG.M)'; *bōl* 'urine' vs. *būl* 'urinate (IMP.SG.M)'. This opposition is, however, rather weak, as such varying forms as the following show: *tūlad* ~ *tōlad* 'she gives birth', *gōl* ~ *gūl* 'saying'.

3.2.1.1.1   *ā*
ā is a low central vowel [a:] that can be somewhat backed in the environment of pharyngeals and emphatics (cf. Ingham 1974:152). Examples are *b*[a:]*b* 'door', *r*[a:]*ḥ* 'he went'.

3.2.1.1.2   *ē*
ē is a long mid-front rounded vowel [e:] in non-emphatic contexts following *w*, *r*, *y* or a guttural (*x*, *ġ*, *ḥ*, *ʕ*, *h*): e.g. *ʕ*[e:]*n* 'eye', *h*[e:]*l* 'cardamom', *ġ*[e:]*r* 'other', *w*[e:]*n* 'where', and *y*[e:]*mta* 'when'. In all other non-emphatic contexts, it is a glide from high front [i:] to mid-central [ə] (cf. Fischer 1959:142, fn.1 and the references cited there on the same phenomenon in the dialect of Kwayriš/Babylon), i.e. [i:ə],[23] e.g. *b*[i:ə]*t* 'house', *ʔalf*[i:ə]*n* '2,000', *taʕallm*[i:ə]*na* 'we learned',

---

23   The phonetic contrast between *ē* when realized as [i:ə] and the long vowel *ī* [i:] is perceived as very slight. This is well illustrated by a remark a female informant from Ahvaz

PHONOLOGY   59

lūmīt[iːə]*n* 'two limes', *g*[iːə]*ḏ* 'summer', and *ʕal*[iːə] 'on him'. In emphatic contexts, it is an open-mid front unrounded vowel [ɛː], e.g. *ṭ*[ɛː]*r* 'bird' (cf. Ingham
1974: 152). Some speakers realize *ē* as a high front vowel [iː], e.g. *ʕalī-ha* 'on it'
(cf. Ingham 1976: 68–69, who attributes this feature to the speech of the people living in the area of ʕAmāra and the surrounding marshlands, as well as in
northern and eastern parts of Khuzestan).

3.2.1.1.3   *ī*

ī is a high front vowel [iː]—e.g. *dīra* 'town', *šīl* 'carry (IMP.SG.M)', and *ǧəlīl* 'little,
few'—backed in emphatic contexts (cf. Ingham 1974: 152), e.g. *yṣīr* 'he becomes'.

3.2.1.1.4   *ū*

ū is a high back rounded vowel [uː], e.g. *sūg* 'market', *yāmūsa* 'water buffalo',
and *flūs* 'money'.
   ū is shortened to *ə* in the IPFV forms of the verb *gāl* 'to say' when a pronominal suffix is attached.

3.2.1.1.5   *ō*

ō is a close-mid back rounded vowel [oː] in non-emphatic contexts—e.g. *yōm*
'day'—and an open-mid back rounded vowel [ɔː] in emphatic contexts (cf. Ingham 1974: 152–153), e.g. *ṭōf* 'wall'.
   In some lexemes, there is free variation between *ū* and *ō*, e.g. *yōǧad ~ yūǧad*
'there is', and *yōʕān ~ yūʕān* 'hungry'.

3.2.1.2   Short Vowels

Minimal pairs for the opposition *ə : a* are, for example:

   həyya 'excuse' vs. *hayya* 'snake'
   ḏəll 'stay (IMP.SG.M)' vs. *ḏall* 'he stayed'

3.2.1.2.1   *a*
Non-final

In KhA, the short vowel *a* is realized word-internally as an open-mid front vowel
[ɛ] in non-emphatic and non-guttural contexts, e.g. *d*[ɛ]*mm* 'blood', *kəs*[ɛ]*r-ha*

---

made: She urged me to be careful about using the word *dīs* [diːs] 'big serving plate' because
its sound was almost the same as of the word *dēs* [diːəs] which means '(female) breast' (<
OA *days^un* 'teat'), a word usually avoided in public or in general—even among women: my
informants always just whispered it.

'he broke it (SG.F)', *ḏ*[ɛ]*bb-ha* 'he threw it away', *ys*[ɛ]*mmūn* 'they (PL.M) call', *y*[ɛ]*t* 'she came', *č*[ɛ]*ləb* 'dog', *s*[ɛ]*kk*[ɛ]*r* 'he closed (trans.)'. In the environment of a guttural sound (*x, ġ, ḥ, ʕ, h*), it is realized as backed [a], e.g. *š*[a]*ʕ*[a]*r* 'hair', *ḥ*[a]*ləǧ* 'mouth', *ġ*[a]*n*[a]*m* 'sheep', *m*[a]*r*[a]*g* 'sauce'. In emphatic syllables, it has a backed realization [ɑ], e.g. *š*[ɑ]*ṭṭ* 'river', *ḅ*[ɑ]*ṭən* 'stomach', *ḥəṭ*[ɑ]*b* 'fire-wood', (cf. Ingham 1974: 151).

Final

Word-final *a* tends to be raised (irrespective of its origin as a feminine gender marker, pronominal suffix, or other) to an open-mid front vowel [ɛ]. A few of the many examples in the data are *kəl*[ɛ] 'he ate', *əy*[ɛ] 'he came', *bēt-n*[ɛ] 'our house', *ḏabb-h*[ɛ] 'he threw it (SG.F) away', *b-īd*[ɛ] 'in his hand', *məšā-l*[ɛ] *ġadam* 'he took a step', *naʕy*[ɛ] 'sheep', *ān*[ɛ] 'I'. This phenomenon is known in many other Arabic dialects (Kaye and Daniels 1997: 198).[24]

The raising of final *a* in KhA is not phonemic but can be blocked by a pre-ceding guttural (*x, ġ, ḥ, ʕ, h*), emphatic, or pharyngealized consonant. After a guttural, *r* or *w*, -*a* is mostly realized as [a], e.g. *mənṭaġ*[a] 'area', *sāʕ*[a] 'hour', *əl-əmḥammr*[a] 'Muḥammara', *marr*[a] 'time', *ḥəlw*[a] 'beautiful (F)', *gahw*[a] 'coffee', *ʔəhw*[a] 'he', and *ġəww*[a] 'strength', but especially following *h* raising of final *a* was also noted. Following an emphatic, -*a* is realized as [ɑ], e.g. *maṣ-mūṭ*[ɑ] 'dried fish', *bēḍ*[ɑ] 'white (F)' (cf. Bahrani and Modarresi Ghavami 2019: 7–9; Ingham 1974: 150).

3.2.1.2.2 *ə*

For high (or non-low) short vowels in KhA, the dominant pattern seems to be a single phonemic unit, transcribed here *ə*. The phoneme *ə* has the following allophonic forms: In most non-emphatic and non-guttural contexts, it has an unrounded lax high front allophone [ɪ], e.g. *k*[ɪ]*ll* 'all', *b*[ɪ]*nt* 'girl', *s*[ɪ]*dra* 'lote tree', *nāy*[ɪ]*m* 'sleeping (AP.SG.M)', *y*[ɪ]*gdar* 'he can, is able to', *y*[ɪ]*ft*[ɪ]*k*[ɪ]*r* 'he thinks (intr.)', *ǧ*[ɪ]*ddām* 'in front of' (< *quddām^{un}*). In non-emphatic syllables and in the context of gutturals, it has a mid-central allophone [ə], e.g. *gāʕ*[ə]*d* 'sitting (AP.SG.M)', *ʔ*[ə]*x*[ə]*t* 'sister', *ġ*[ə]*dra* 'power', *ḥ*[ə]*lwa* 'beautiful (F)'. In non-emphatic contexts and when between a labial and a velar or *r*, or when pre-

---

24 Cf. Jastrow on Muslim Baghdadi Arabic and other Iraqi Arabic dialects: "Final -*a* in Muslim Baghdad, irrespective of its origin, is pronounced as a slightly raised and centralized [ä] vowel. In some *gələt* dialects, the raising can reach -*e* (according to the notation of some sources, e.g. Salonen 1980). These pausal allophones tend to be generalized and thus can also occur in context" (2007: 418).

PHONOLOGY   61

ceding *w*, it has a high back rounded allophone [u], e.g. *g*[u]*mət* 'I/you (SG.M)
got up', *m*[u]*dda* 'time', *ḥar*[u]*b* 'war', and *ǧ*[u]*wāni* 'bags' (but *zəl*[ı]*m* 'men', and
nəḥl[ı]*b* 'we milk'). In emphatic non-labial contexts it has a half-close back allophone [ɤ], e.g. *yḥ*[ɤ]*ṭṭ* 'he puts', *ḷ*[ɤ]*tmat* 'she hit herself in grief', or [u] between
a labial and an emphatic, e.g. *yṣ*[u]*ḅḅ* 'he fills', *m*[u]*ṭrat* 'it (SG.F) rained', and
ḅ[u]*ṣal* 'onions'.

Blanc (1964: 36–37) states for Muslim Baghdadi Arabic that syllables in
which "the vowel is flanked by a velar on the one side and a non-back, non-
emphatic, non-labial consonant on the other" appear to preserve the original
vowel. There are some KhA lexemes that appear to follow this rule, e.g. *r*[u]*kba*
'knee' < OA **rukba^tun*. There are, however, also many counterexamples found
in KhA in which the vowel is flanked by a velar on the one side and a non-back,
non-emphatic, non-labial consonant on the other but does not represent the
original vowel, e.g. *yāk*[ı]*l* 'he eats' < OA **yaʔkulu*, and *yāx*[ı]*ḏ* 'he takes' < OA
*yaʔxuḏu.

3.2.1.2.3   Opposition i : u

Generally, it is a common feature of Arabic that the opposition *i : u* is weak,
and already in OA there are very few cases of a full (semantic) contrast (Owens
2006: 51–67; cf. Fischer and Jastrow 1980: 43; 53–54). Fischer and Jastrow attribute the collapse of *i* and *u* as found in many modern dialects of Arabic, as
well as the less common full collapse of all three short vowels, to this fact
(1980: 53). Watson (2007: 21–22) states that the full collapse of the vowels **i*
and **u* into a single short high vowel is characteristic of the Arabic dialects in
north Mesopotamia and Mauritania, and of many Bedouin-type dialects of the
Maghreb; and that in many other dialects the opposition between *i* and *u* has
been greatly reduced (Watson 2007: 22).

In KhA, there are only two cases in which the occurrence of the allophones
i and *u* cannot be traced back to their phonetic environment:

1.   The feminine plural pronominal/object suffixes *-hən* [hin] (3PL.F), and
     -čən [tʃin] (2PL.F) vs. the masculine ones *-həm* [hum] (3PL.M), and *-kəm*
     [kum] (2PL.M). This contrast has most likely been retained to maintain a
     clear contrast between masculine and feminine forms and appears to be
     an old feature going back to the Arabic spoken in pre-diasporic times (cf.
     Owens 2006: 255–256).

     The fact that not all pronominal PL.F forms have [i]—e.g. *-čan* 'you (PL.F)'
     —can be explained as an analogous development to the 3PL.F PFV, IPFV,
     and IMP suffix *-an*—e.g. *rād-an* 'they (PL.F) wanted', *yərd-an* 'they (PL.F)
     want', and *ʔəmšan* 'go (IMP.PL.F)'—and the 2PL.F PFV suffix *-tan*: e.g. *čən-*
     tan 'you (PL.F) were'.

62   CHAPTER 3

2. The opposition *ḥ*[i]*bb* 'kiss (IMP.SG.M)' vs. *ḥ*[u]*bb* 'love (noun)'
    In the first of these two cases, the reason for the retention of the opposi-
    tion *i : u* seems to be related to the marking of a morphological distinction.
    In the second case, the only minimal pair found for this opposition, viz.
    ḥ[i]*bb* 'kiss (IMP.SG.M)' vs. *ḥ*[u]*bb* 'love (noun)', is likely to be explained as
    a consequence of contact influence from MSA or other regional Arabic
    dialects like Iraqi Arabic, or again as a retention of the original forms *ḥibb*
    'kiss (IMP.SG.M)' < *yuḥibbu* 'he loves', and *ḥubb* < *ḥubb^{un}* 'love'. Therefore,
    the *i : u* contrast in this minimal pair does not necessarily imply a phone-
    mic status of these two vowels for the whole vowel system of KhA.

3.2.1.2.4   *Final Vowels* a#, i#, u#

In word-final position, the vowels *a, i, u* are realized as short vowels, also where
they reflect originally long vowels (cf. 3.2.2.1). Their length is preserved wherever suffixes are attached (since they are no longer word-final), e.g. *kəla* 'he ate'
(originally a C_1=ʔ verb reanalyzed as a final weak verb, cf. CA *ramā* 'to throw')
vs. *kəlā-həm* 'he ate them', and *nḥāči* 'we talk (to somebody)' vs. *nḥāčī-č* 'we talk
to you (2SG.F)'.

3.2.2   *Historical Correspondences and Sound Shifts*

3.2.2.1   Long Vowels

As in all modern spoken dialects of Arabic, the OA long vowels *ī, ū,* and *ā* have
(phonetically) lost their long quality in word-final position, e.g. *yəbči* < *yabkī*
'he cries', *kətbu* < *uktubū* 'write (IMP.PL.M)', *məša* < *mašā* 'to go'.

The OA endings *-ā* and *-āʔ* have become *-a* in KhA (as well as in most
other modern spoken Arabic dialects), e.g. *dənya* < *dunyā* 'world', *ġəda ~ ġada*
< *ġadāʔ^{un}* 'lunch', *ḥamra* < *ḥamrāʔ^u* 'red (F)', and *dəwa* < *dawāʔ^{un}* 'medicine'.

The long vowels *ē* and *ō* historically derive from the OA diphthongs *ay* and
aw, e.g. *ṣēd* 'fishing, hunting' < *ṣayd^{un}*; *xēr* 'goods, wealth' < *xayr^{un}*; *yōm* 'day'
< *yawm^{un}*; and *lōn* 'color' < *lawn^{un}*. This process of monophthongization is a
common phenomenon in most modern spoken Arabic dialects (Iványi 2006:
641–642). In my corpus, *ē* was pronounced *ay* in some forms, e.g. *šahrayn* 'two
months', and *ʕayn-i* (~ *ʕēn-i*) 'my eye'.

3.2.2.2   Short Vowels

The two high vowels OA **i* and **u* have merged into one phoneme *ə*, e.g.
qāʕid^{un} > *gāʕəd* 'sitting (AP.SG.M)', and *kull^{un}* > *kəll* 'all, every, each'. As in most
other dialects, *ə* that goes back to OA **i* or **u* is usually elided in unstressed
open syllables, e.g. *gāʕəd + a* > *gāʕda* 'sitting' (AP.SG.F). If the elision results
in an initial CC-cluster, a prothetic vowel *ə* is introduced after a pause and

PHONOLOGY 63

when the preceding word ends in a consonant (cf. 3.7.1), e.g. OA *fulān^{un} >
KhA əflān 'such-and-such, somebody' (cf. Blanc 1964: 35). There are however
exceptions to this rule, e.g. OA *hudūm^{un} > KhA hədūm ~ əhdūm 'clothes, garment'.

With the exception of IPFV Pattern I verbs, in medial syllables ə (< i, u) is
not elided but stressed, e.g. əm'fəlfəl 'one (M) who wants to marry at all costs',
əmfəlfəl + a > əmfəl'fəla 'one (F) who wants to marry at all costs', 'kašməš 'raisins',
but kəš'məš-i (< kišmišī) 'my raisins'.

In IPFV verbs with a vowel-initial inflectional suffix (including the optional
1SG suffix -an used for medial weak and geminated type verbs), the vowel
in the resulting unstressed open syllable is always elided and ə is inserted
after the first root consonant thus breaking up the otherwise resulting three-
consonant cluster. The prefix vowel in the resulting initial open syllable may
also be elided:

> yəktəb + -ūn > *yəktb-ūn > yəkətb-ūn ~ ykətb-ūn 'they (PL.M) write' (cf. OA
> yaktubūn)

Probably in order to preserve a common base for all verbs of this pattern, in
these cases short a is also elided:

> təšrab + -īn > * təšrb-īn > təšərbīn ~ (ə)tšərbīn 'you (SG.F) drink' (cf. OA
> tašrabīn).

OA *a in closed syllables is generally retained, e.g. maglūb < maqlūb^{un} 'turned
over (PP)'.

In open syllables, OA *a is generally raised towards ə in KhA (with different allophones according to their consonantal environment, cf. 3.2.1.2.2 above)
when followed by another a or ā, e.g. səmač < OA *samak^{un} 'fish'; məkān < OA
makān^{un} 'place', and səwāləf < OA sawālif^u 'stories'. This rule also applies to
verbs, e.g. ḍəbaḥ < OA ḍabaḥa 'he killed'. However, many exceptions from this
rule are attested, particularly after gutturals (x, ġ, ḥ, ʕ, ʔ, h) and emphatic consonants, e.g. hawa ~ həwa 'wind', ġada ~ ġada 'lunch', xabar 'news', ġalaṭ 'mistake',
ṣanāyəʕ 'handicrafts', xarāyəb 'destructions'.

KhA a < OA *a has been elided in etymological CaCaCv- sequences in the
second (i.e. unstressed open) syllable, e.g. 'səmča 'a fish' < OA *samaka^{tun},
'məṭrat 'it (SG.F) rained' < OA *maṭarat, but məṭar 'rain' < OA *maṭar^{un}. In
some cases and among some speakers, there is variation regarding the elision or
retention of *a in unstressed open syllables, e.g. ḍəbḥaw ~ ḍəbaḥaw 'they killed,
sacrificed'.

64   CHAPTER 3

If the raised historical *a is in a pre-tonic open syllable, it is often elided, in which case a prothetic vowel is introduced before the resulting initial two-consonant cluster (cf. 3.7.1), e.g. *ərmād* 'ashes' < OA *ramādᵘⁿ. In some lexemes there is variation and both forms are heard, with and without the raising (and elision) of *a, e.g. *əmrākəb ~ marāčəb* 'boats' < OA *marākibᵘ. The forms with original *a* are less common and may be an influence of MSA. If the initial consonant was ʔ, *a is always kept, e.g. *ʔawādəm* 'people, humans' < OA *ʔawādimᵘ (cf. Blanc 1964: 39–40 on this rule in Muslim Baghdadi Arabic).

If the following syllable is -*īC*- or -*ūC*-, OA *a in an unstressed open syllable is generally raised to ə and often consequently elided, in which case, again, a prothetic vowel is introduced before the resulting initial two-consonant cluster (cf. 3.7.1), e.g. *čəbīr ~ əčbīr* < OA *kabīrᵘⁿ 'big, old', and *ğənūb ~ əğnūb* < OA *ğanūbᵘⁿ 'south'. OA *a is, however, usually retained in such structures when the preceding consonant is a guttural, e.g. *xafīf* < OA *xafīfᵘⁿ 'light', *ǧalīl* 'little' (but *ǧəlīl*) < OA *qalīlᵘⁿ, and *ʕarūs* 'bride' < OA *ʕarūsᵘⁿ.[25]

Some speakers do not drop the PFV stem vowel *a* in the syllable preceding a PFV-suffix introduced by -*ē*- (cf. Ingham 1974: 287–288), e.g. *štaǧalēna* 'we worked', and *tamarraḍēt* 'I/you (SG.M) fell sick', although this is contrary to what we would expect because it is in a pre-stressed open syllable.

For the development of historical *a in non-final stressed syllables with gutturals, cf. 3.7.2. Summing up it can be stated that synchronical KhA ə either reflects OA *i, *u, *a, or zero when introduced as an epenthetic vowel (e.g. *galəb* < *qalbᵘⁿ* 'heart').

3.3   Diphthongs

All historical diphthongs have been monophthongized as described in 3.2.2.1.

The monophthongs *ē* and *ō* resulting from this change are sometimes pronounced as diphthongs, e.g. *fawra ~ fōra* 'a boiling', *tawlad ~ tōlad* 'she gives birth', and *ʕayn-i ~ ʕēn-i* 'my eye'.

The KhA shift *ǧ > y has generated new *ay* sequences, e.g. *wayh* < OA *waǧhᵘⁿ 'face', *nayma* < OA *naǧmatᵘⁿ 'star', and *daray* < OA *daraǧᵘⁿ 'ladder, steps'. Wherever a sequence əy resulted (< OA *iǧ), it became *ī*, e.g. *rīl* (< *rəyl*) < OA *riǧlᵘⁿ 'leg, foot'.[26]

---

25   On the raising of *a in CaCīC patterns in OA dialects cf. Shawarbah (2011: 65, fn. 175) and the references mentioned there.

26   Compare Holes (2016: 55) on Bahraini Arabic: "Medially, when in CvCC syllables, the resulting diphthongs became pure long vowels by general rule, e.g. *wēh* 'face' (< *wayh* < *wajh*), *rīl* 'foot, leg' (< *riyl* < *rijl*)".

PHONOLOGY

The 3PL.M PFV verbal suffix -*aw* is an allophonic form of underlying *ō*, which reappears when an object suffix is added, e.g. *šāfaw* 'they (PL.M) saw', but *šāf-ō-ni* 'they (PL.M) saw me' (cf. below, 4.11.15). Similarly, word-final -*ay* usually goes back to *-*ayy(a)* (except for where *y* is the result of the shift *ğ > *y*)—e.g. *ʕal-ay* < *ʕalayya* 'on me'—or to *ayʔ, as in *šay* (also *šī*) < *šayʔun 'thing', and *šway* 'a little bit' < *šuyayʔun 'thing (DIM)'.

3.4 Emphasis

Emphasis is a "phonetic feature characterized by having two points of articulation. The primary point is the dento-alveolar area, and the secondary point engages the upper region of the pharynx" (Al-Ani 2008: 599). For general remarks on the phonetic and acoustic features of emphasis, cf. Card (1983) and Watson (1999).

3.4.1 Emphasis Spread

Emphasis is often analyzed on the basis of the syllable or the word because the phonetic feature of emphasis usually does not concern one emphatic sound, or one segment of a word only but rather extends to adjacent segments. This conditioning of neighboring sounds (both vowels and consonants) or syllables by emphatic consonants is usually called emphasis spread (cf. Al-Ani 2008: 600, who provides a figure illustrating the acoustic effect of emphatics on adjacent long vowels). Emphasis can thus spread from emphatic to non-emphatic consonants in both directions, backwards and forwards, and is also carried by back vowels such as [ɑ] and [u] and their respective long realizations (cf. Mustafawi 2017: 16 on Iraqi Arabic, in which emphasis spread is determined by syllable structure: within a word, it can spread over two open syllables). Vowels affected by emphatic environments are lowered and/or backed, consonants affected by emphatic environments are backed (Mustafawi 2017: 24; cf. also Bakalla 2009: 422).[27] Emphasis spread is usually stopped by front vowels, certain consonants (often alveolars and palato-alveolars, cf. Shawarbah 2011: 57), or certain syllabic structures. In Iraqi Arabic, for example, emphasis spread appears to be blocked within a CvCC type of syllable (cf. Mustafawi 2017: 24 and the reference there).

Ingham uses a word-based analysis of emphasis in his dissertation on KhA phonology, i.e. he considers emphasis in KhA as a feature of certain roots (1974:

---

27 In the following examples, the emphatic quality of vowels affected by emphasis spread will not be indicated separately as this is predictable from the emphatic consonantal context which will be marked with a dot below the consonant.

82). Emphatic roots contain one of the primary emphatic consonants *ṭ*, *ḍ*, or *ṣ* (cf. below), or a certain sequence of consonantal elements associated with emphasis.

Such sequences are mainly combinations of one of the (post)velars (*k*, *g*, *ġ*, *x*),[28] a liquid (*l*, *r*), and/or a bilabial (*b*, *m*, *w*) (cf. Ingham 1974: 118). Examples from KhA for such sequences which cause a word or root to be affected by emphasis are given below. However, in many lexemes that have such consonantal sequences generally associated with emphasis, there is free variation regarding their emphatic or non-emphatic realization. Ingham states that KhA speakers who speak a dialect of the *ʕarab*-type (cf. 2.2.1) sometimes have a non-emphatic realization and *ḥaḍar* speakers an emphatic realization of the same lexeme. He illustrates this with the lexeme *ʔaštaġal* 'to work' (1974: 124–125).

In sum, we find emphaticized words either because of the presence of primary emphatic consonants, or because of certain combinations of consonant types (especially velars, labials, and liquids; cf. Holes 2016: 78–79 on Bahraini Arabic).

3.4.2   *Primary Emphatic Consonants*

The following are minimal pairs (cf. Ingham 1974: 83) for the three primary emphatic consonants found in KhA, *ṭ*, *ḍ*, and *ṣ*,[29] and their plain counterparts:

ṣ : *s*   *ṣabb* 'he poured' vs. *sabb* 'he insulted'
ḍ : *ḏ*   *ḍarr* 'he hurt, damaged' vs. *ḏarr* 'he winnowed'
ṭ : *t*   *ḥaṭṭ* 'he put' vs. *ḥatt* 'it (a leaf) fell', *ṭafal* 'child' vs. *tafal* 'he spat'

Throughout this book, emphasis will only be noted on these three primary emphatic consonants in the transcription.

3.4.3   *Secondary Emphatic Consonants*

In KhA, as in most dialects of Arabic, the secondary or marginal emphatic consonants are *ḷ*, *ḅ*, *ṃ*, *ṛ* (Al-Ani 2008: 600; cf. Holes 2016: 78). For the KhA secondary emphatic consonants, no full minimal pairs with their non-emphatic counterparts were found. The secondary emphatic consonants acquire emphasis in the vicinity of primary emphatic consonants or emphasis-inducing con-

---

28   The phonemes *x* and *q* and the four emphatics, are traditionally called *ḥurūf mustaʕliya*, 'ascending sounds'. These sounds have a backing effect on certain adjacent phonemes and can cause emphatization of certain preceding non-emphatic consonants (Edzard 2009: 2; Blanc 1969: 19).

29   The fourth consonant traditionally listed with the primary emphatic consonants of Arabic, *ḍ*, merges with *ḏ* into *ḏ̣*, as in many other Arabic dialects, cf. 3.1.2.4.

PHONOLOGY

sonantal sequences (see above). In some lexemes, there is no phonetic explanation for the emphasis of these sounds but there seems to be free variation in their emphatic or non-emphatic realization.

Examples for the KhA secondary emphatic consonants *ḷ*, *ḅ*, *ṃ*, and *ṛ* are:

ḷ: *gəḷab* 'he overturned', *gḷōḅ* 'light bulb', *gaḷəḅ* 'heart', *gaḅaḷ* 'before', *gaḷgaḷ* 'he/it (SG.M) shook (intr.)', *xaḷaṭ* 'he mixed', *ġaḷaṭ* 'mistake', *ġaḷa* 'it became expensive', *xaḷag* 'creation', *xaḷāḷ* 'unripe dates', *xāḷa* 'aunt'. *ḷ* also appears in certain forms of the word for God,[30] e.g. *Aḷḷa* 'God', but not where *l* is preceded by *ə* when pronounced [i] or [iː], e.g. *b-əsm-əlla* 'in the name of God'.[31]

ḅ: *ḅāg* 'he stole', *ṃxaḅḅaḷ* 'stupid', *ḅarag* 'electricity'

ṃ: *ʔəṃṃ* 'mother', *xəṃra* 'yeast', *naxṃa* 'mucus'

ṛ: *ṛaxīṣ* 'cheap', *ṛəfas* 'he kicked', *ṛəṃa* 'he shot'

3.5 Syllable Structure

KhA has the following basic syllable types (v = short vowel, v̄ = long vowel):

Cv	*ma.rā.čəb* 'boats', *ḥar.ma* 'woman', *xaš.šə.nat* 'she became angry'
Cv̄	*sā.ʕad* 'he helped', *ma.rā.čəb* 'boat'
CvC	*xaš.šə.nat* 'she became angry', *ta.čab.baš* 'he learned', *ma.rā.čəb* 'boat'
Cv̄C	*bāg* 'he stole', *yīb* 'bring (IMP.SG.M)'
CvCC	*dagg* 'he hit'
Cv̄CC	*dāgg* 'he has hit/is hitting (AP.SG.M)'
CCv̄	*ktā.bi* 'my book'
CCvC	*tšər.ban* 'you (PL.F) drink'
CCv̄C	*trīd* 'you (SG.M) want', *bṭūṭ* 'ducks'
CCvCC	*ftarr* 'he walked around'

All forms with two initial C's, however, usually introduce a prothetic vowel word-initially, or an epenthetic vowel after the first consonant, which of course yields a different syllable structure, e.g. *ʔək.tā.bi* 'my book', *ʔət.rīd ~ tə.rīd* 'you

---

30 An emphatic pronunciation of *l* in this word is already attested for CA (Fischer 1972: 18, Anm. 2).

31 A similar distribution of *ḷ* is also found in other dialects, e.g. in Muslim Baghdadi Arabic (Blanc 1964: 20: "velarization of OA /l/ occurred largely in roots where it was preceded by /x/, /ġ/, or /q/. This /ḷ/ is typical not only of M [Muslim Baghdadi Arabic] but of the *gələt*-dialects as a whole and of Bedouin dialects in other areas as well"); cf. also Fischer and Jastrow (1980: 143).

(SG.M) want', and *ʔəg.ba.lat ~ gəb.lat* (*Sala*) 'she came close, reached' (cf. 3.7.1; cf. Ingham 1973: 536 who additionally gives forms with two initial consonants).

In verbal forms with an initial syllable CvC- or Cv- there is variation in the structure of the prefix sequence. The prefix sequence is either Cv-, e.g. *tə-ṭīḥ* 'she falls/you (SG.M) fall', and *nə-yīb* 'we bring', or əC-, e.g. *ət-ṭīḥ* 'she falls/you (SG.M) fall', and *ən-yīb* 'we bring'. According to Ingham (1976: 74), the prefix sequence Cv- is typical for the nomadic-type dialects of Khuzestan, while (ə)C- is typical of sedentary-type dialects. In my corpus, nomadic forms such as *tərīd* 'she wants/you (SG.M) want', and *təgūl* 'she says/you (SG.M) say', are used by speakers from the cities of Ḥamīdīya, Ahvaz, Tustar, and Hoveyzeh. For the same regions, however, numerous sedentary-type sequences are also attested in my corpus. Thus the strict distinction between nomadic and sedentary-type sequences seems to have been somewhat levelled out. For Pattern I 3SG.F, 3PL.F, and 3PL.M PFV verbs, as well as for some nominal forms ending in *-i* or *-a*, Ingham (1973: 540–541, 543) also states that there is a typical *ḥaḍar* form with an initial sequence CəC- versus an *Sarab* form with an initial sequence CCv-, e.g. *gəlbat* vs. *gləbat* 'she overturned', *xəšba* vs. *xšəba* 'piece of wood', and *šəǧar* vs. *šǧar* 'trees'. In my corpus, only the *ḥaḍar* forms are attested throughout, which implies that the *Sarab*-type syllabic sequences have either never been used or have dropped out of use in the areas and among the families that I investigated.

3.6 Stress

KhA stress rules that are determined by syllabic structure, including regional differences, have been described in detail by Ingham (1974: 62–66)[32] and will therefore only be summarized here and illustrated by examples added from my data.[33]

As Ingham has already stated (1974: 57), one important point in describing KhA stress rules is that stress is not only determined by syllabic structure but also by certain grammatical elements that always attract stress. Such grammatical elements are the interrogative clitics *-man* 'who, whom, which?', and *š-* ...

---

32   One important difference from his analysis and the results of my data analysis is that forms for which Ingham states that stress may be on the penultima or the antepenultima, i.e. final -Cv.Cv(C) patterns (Ingham 1974: 62–65), are now usually stressed on the penultima throughout, e.g. *kə.'ta.la* 'he beat him', and not *'kə.ta.la* 'he beat him'.

33   Nuclear stress will be indicated by a straight apostrophe ' preceding the syllable on which the nuclear stress falls.

PHONOLOGY   69

'what?', as well as the negation particles *lā*, *mā*, and *mū* (Ingham 1974: 58, fn. 1), as described in more detail below.

The general stress rules which are determined by the syllabic structure are summarized in the following (cf. Bahrani and Modarresi Ghavami 2019: 11–12):

(i)   If the last syllable of a word is heavy (-Cv̄ and -CvC) or superheavy (-Cv̄C, -Cv̄CC or -CvCC; cf. Mustafawi 2017: 19 on syllable types in MSA and Arabic dialects), it carries primary stress, e.g. *ḥa.'mām* 'pigeons', *y.'dagg* 'he hits', *y.dǝg.'gūn* 'they (PL.M) hit', and *dǝg.'gó* 'they (PL.M) hit him'.

(ii)   If the last syllable of a word is not heavy, usually the penultimate carries the stress, e.g. *'bēt.na* 'our house', *yǝt.'lō.laḥ* 'it (SG.M) swings', *'xāb.ra* 'call him (IMP.SG.M)', *mǝ.sā.'ʕa.da* 'help, assistance', *'dǝ.wa* 'medicine', *ma.'dǝr.sa* 'school', *yǝf.'tǝ.ḥǝm* 'he understands', *'šǝr.ka* (also *ša.'rī.ka*) 'company', and *'gā.lat* 'she said'. This includes verbs with object suffixes which form one phonological word, e.g. *gā.'lat.li* 'she said to me'.

(iii) In Dual forms, stress usually falls on the syllable preceding the Dual suffix, e.g. *'bē.tēn* 'two houses' (also in Iraqi, Erwin 1963: 42–43).

Some grammatical elements attract stress, resulting in stress positions that do not correspond to the above outlined rules. These grammatical elements are mainly negation particles, such as *mā* and *lā*, and interrogative pronouns such as *š- ...?* 'what?'. To put the main stress on the first element in negative structures is a feature not only shared with other North East Arabian dialects (cf. Erwin 1963: 43 on Muslim Baghdadi Arabic) but also with some Persian and Turkish varieties: compare, e.g. *'ne-midunam* (Tehrani Persian) and KhA *má-adri* ['ma:.dri ~ 'ma.ʔad.ri], both meaning 'I don't know' (Ingham 2005: 178–179). Considering the distribution of this feature, Ingham's arguing that this is a *Sprachbund* phenomenon[34] appears very likely.

Examples from my KhA data for interrogative pronouns attracting stress on the first syllable are: *'šǝ-trīd?* 'What do you (SG.M) want?', *'šǝ-aʕrǝf?* 'What do I know?', *'š-ǝnsawwi?* 'What do (can) we do?', *'yāhu rāḥ?* 'Who (SG.M) went?', and *'wēn rāḥ?* 'Where did he go (to)?'.

3.7   Phonotactics

3.7.1   *Consonant Clusters and Anaptyxis*
Generally, there are never more than two consonants in one cluster.
    On the epenthetic vowel in verbal prefixes, cf. 3.5 above.

---

34   This describes the situation when a region develops a new common characteristic as a result of its long history of contact due to trade, war, etc. (Winford, 2003: 70–74).

70   CHAPTER 3

i.   Initial

In syllables beginning with two consonants, usually a prothetic vowel is introduced before the first consonant, e.g. *əbṭūṭ* 'ducks', and *əbyūt* 'houses'.

It also happens that speakers introduce a prothetic vowel even after a word
ending in a vowel and before an initial structure CvC-, e.g. *lamma əkəbar* 'when
he grew up'. The introduction of a prothetic vowel before an imperative of the
structure CəCC-v (i.e. IMP.SG.F, IMP.PL.F, and IMP.PL.M; or IMP.SG.M with a
vowel initial object suffix)—e.g. *əkətbi* 'write (IMP.SG.F)'—has been described
by Ingham as a rural feature (1973: 542). In my corpus, it is attested for speakers
from Ahvaz.

ii.   Medial

Medial two-consonant clusters are found, for example, in PFV verbs with vowel
initial inflectional suffixes where a short vowel has been elided, e.g. *ḏəbḥaw*
'they killed, sacrificed'.

In IPFV verbs with a vowel-initial inflectional suffix, the vowel in the resulting unstressed open syllable is elided and *ə* is inserted after the first root consonant, thus breaking up the otherwise resulting tri-consonant cluster. The
prefix vowel in the resulting initial open syllable may also be elided (cf. 3.2.2.2
above):

> *yəktəb-* + *-ūn* > **yəktb-ūn* > *yəkətb-ūn* ~ *ykətb-ūn* 'they (PL.M) write'
> *təšrab-* + *-īn* > ** təšrb-īn* > *təšərbīn* ~ *(ə)tšərbīn* 'you (SG.F) drink'

The form *ma-'dər-sa* 'school' has probably developed from *'madrasa* via deletion of **a* in the second (unstressed open) syllable followed by insertion of
ə to avoid the otherwise resulting tri-consonant cluster. Finally, since there
is no heavy syllable, stress shifted to the penultimate: *'madrasa* > **'madrsa* >
*'madərsa > *ma-'dər-sa*.

In a tri-consonant cluster of the form $C_1C_1C_2$, i.e. in which the first two
are the same (geminated), one of the geminated consonants is elided, e.g.
ynaḏḏf-a [inɑðˤfɛ] 'he cleans it (M)'. Though the gemination is not articulated,
this consonant reduction will not be reflected in the transcription in order
to make the meaning and grammatical information of a verb clearer to the
reader.

Geminated SG.M PFV verbs optionally insert an anaptyctic long vowel *-ā-*
before consonant-initial suffixes to avoid an otherwise resulting three-consonant cluster (cf. Ingham 1974: 251; and Holes 2016: 71 on the same phenomenon

PHONOLOGY   71

in sedentary-type Bahraini Arabic), e.g. *ḥaṭṭ-ā-ha* ~ *ḥaṭṭ-ha* [ḥatˤha] 'he put it (SG.F) down'. However, the fact that an anaptyctic *-ā-* also appears in some medial weak 3SG.M PFV verbs—e.g. *gāl-ā-lha* ~ *gāl-əlha* 'he told her'—suggests that the insertion of *-ā-* before object suffixes is not purely motivated by a cluster-reduction rule. This phenomenon may have developed in analogy to final weak 3SG.M PFV verbs, which show vowel lengthening before a pronominal suffix, e.g. *ləgā-həm* 'he found them' (cf. Holes 2016: 71, fn. 32 and 79 on the fact that in some urban sedentary dialects of Bahrain *ā*-insertion after 3SG.M PFV verbs is also not limited to geminated verbs).

The preposition *ʕənd-* 'at' is often reduced to *ʕəd-* via deletion of *n* before any pronominal suffix. A similar deletion is noted for the noun *bənt* 'daughter', which is often reduced to [bɪt], both in genitive constructions and before pronominal suffixes, e.g. *bətt-man?* [bɪtmɛn] 'Whose daughter?', *bətt-ak* [bɪtɛk] 'your (SG.M) daughter' (cf. Holes 2016: 73 on the same developments in sedentary-type Bahraini Arabic).

iii.   Final

Final consonant clusters in pausal position (-CC#), or when followed by a consonant-initial word (-CC C), are not allowed except when the two consonants are identical. When they are not identical, an epenthetic vowel, mostly *ə* but in some cases *a* (usually after a guttural), is introduced between the two final consonants, e.g. *gələt* 'I/you (SG.M) said' < *qult(-u)*, *ḥarab* 'war' < *ḥarb^{un}*, *məṭəl* 'like' < *miṭl^{un}*, *baḡal* 'mule' < *baḡl^{un}*, and *šahar* 'month' < *šahr^{un}*. However, this epenthetic vowel is not needed wherever a vowel-initial suffix is added, e.g. *məṭl-a* 'like him', and *ḥarb-i* 'my war'.

3.7.2   g(a)hawa-*Syndrome*

The so-called *g(a)hawa*-syndrome is a feature typical of Eastern Bedouin-type dialects (Rosenhouse 2006: 262; Johnstone 1967: 6–7; cf. De Jong 2007: 151 and the references there; Holes 2016: 78; 2018b: 137). The *g(a)hawa*-syndrome denotes the resyllabification of non-final syllables of the type C_1aC_2 to C_1C_2a when C_2 is a guttural (*ḡ, x, ʕ, ḥ,* or *h*). This phonological process has occurred in two steps (cf. De Jong 2007: 151–152): first, a vowel is introduced after C_2— e.g. *gahwa* 'coffee' becomes *gahawa*—and, second, (though not in all dialects that have the *g(a)hawa*-syndrome) stress shifts to the second vowel and the first vowel is deleted, e.g. *gahawa* 'coffee' becomes *ghawa*.

Examples from KhA are *ənʕaraf* 'we know' < *naʕrifu*, *yʕaraf* 'he knows' < *yaʕrifu*, *yḡazəl* (also *yəḡzəl*) 'he spins' < *yaḡzilu*, *ʔahalīya* 'relatives, family' (cf. WB: 19: *ʔahlīya*), and *naʕaya* 'ewe' < *naʕḡa^{tun}*.

In some originally *hamza*-initial forms the glottal stop together with the vowel from the first syllable might be dropped resulting in the guttural as the initial consonant (cf. De Jong 2007: 152). Examples from KhA are: *ḥamar ~ ʔaḥamar* 'red' (the latter form representing the intermediate stage < *ʔaḥmarᵘ*), *xaḍar ~ ʔaxaḍar* 'green' (< *ʔaxḍarᵘ*), and *ḥal-i* (but also *ʔahal-i*) 'my family' (< *ʔahl-i*). Compare also KhA *xaras* 'dumb' (< **ʔaxaras < ʔaxras*, cf. CA *ʔaxrasᵘ*, Lane 1863: 722), which has dropped the initial syllable, and KhA *ʔaṭraš* 'deaf' (cf. CA *ʔaṭrašᵘ*, Lane 1863: 1841), which has kept it because C$_2$ is not a guttural. As the examples show, both forms are attested for KhA: those in which the first syllable was dropped altogether, and the intermediate form in which the first syllable is still there but a vowel is already inserted after the guttural.

The *g(a)hawa*-syndrome has ceased to be an active phonological process in KhA and has survived only in a few common words, especially colors (cf. the examples above; cf. Holes 2016: 130; and 2007: 612 on same situation in Bahraini and Kuwaiti Arabic) and certain verbs. In fact, in most KhA words of the structure as described above, the resyllabicated form is no longer in use, e.g. KhA *gahwa* (and not *ghawa*) 'coffee', *maḥlūl* (and not *mḥalūl*) 'open (PP)', and *ṣaxla* (and not *ṣxala*) 'a goat (kid)'. Ingham (1973: 543–544) still lists some of these words such as *ghawa* 'coffee' and *ṣxala* 'a goat (kid)' for *ʕarab*-type dialects.

Johnstone (1967: 7) already described in the 1960s that the productivity of this feature has strongly receded in the Gulf Arabic dialects due to the spread of literacy and the influence of modern media and that it was rarely found anymore in the Kuwaiti Arabic of his time.

CHAPTER 4

Morphology

This chapter discusses the morphology of pronouns, adverbs, prepositions, conjunctions, particles, quantifiers, nouns, numerals, and verbs.

4.1 Pronouns

The morphological patterns of KhA independent and suffixed pronouns and the retention in KhA PL.F forms of the 2nd as well as the 3rd persons are more characteristic of Bedouin than sedentary dialects (cf. Procházka 2014: 129; cf. Vicente 2008: 584 on the Bedouin-type paradigms for personal pronouns) and of *gələt* rather than *qəltu* dialects, which, e.g. have 1SG *ana*, 1PL *nəḥna*, and 2PL.M *əntəm* (Palva 2009: 27–28).

4.1.1 *Independent Personal Pronouns*
As shown in Table 3, KhA has ten independent pronouns:

TABLE 3   Independent personal pronouns

	SG	PL
1	*ʔāna* [ʔaːne]	*ʔəḥna, ḥənna*
2M	*ʔənta*	*ʔəntəm* [ʔətːum] (north)
		ʔəntam (Tustar)
		ʔəntu (south)
2F	*ʔənti*	*ʔəntan*
3M	*həwa ~ ʔəhwa ~ ʔəhəwa*	*ʔəhma ~ ʔəhəma ~ həmma*
3F	*hīya ~ ʔəhya ~ ʔəhəya*	*ʔəhna ~ hənna*

Gender Distinction

As in most other dialects of Arabic (Procházka 2014: 135), the feminine plural forms[1] in KhA distinguish themselves from their masculine counterparts

---

1 Preservation of gender distinction in the 2nd person as well in the 3rd person plural in pro-

---

© BETTINA LEITNER, 2022 | DOI:10.1163/9789004510241_005

74   CHAPTER 4

via the contrast (feminine) *n* versus (masculine) *m*. Moreover, the vowel *ə* in
the 3rd person feminine plural pronouns all have an allophone [i] contrasting
with the allophone [u] characteristic of the masculine 3rd person pronouns.
This characteristic allophonic pattern used to distinguish gender is also found
in many other dialects and is usually explained as a retention of the original
Semitic pattern (Procházka 2014: 135; cf. Fischer and Jastrow 1980: 79).

Only the 2PL.F pronoun *ʔəntan* and the respective suffix form -*čan* have a
vowel *a*, not *ə* [i] (cf. Ingham 2007: 574). This same vowel pattern is found
among other Arabic dialects, among them those of Khorasan and the Lower
Gulf, and some dialects of the Najd (Procházka 2014: 137–141).

3rd Person

As shown in Table 3, the 3rd person plural pronouns generally have a disyl-
labic form and are frequently heard with an initial vowel, e.g. *ʔəhwa* (3SG.M),
ʔəhma (3PL.M) (cf. Mahdi 1985: 152 on these forms in Basra). Ingham describes
these forms as typical of the Šaṭṭ al-ʕArab and southern KhA dialects as well
as of dialects of the Banū Lām north and east of ʕAmāra (Ingham 1976: 70,
fn. 29; 2007: 574 gives only the forms with initial vowel). The same feature is
also found in the dialects of Khorasan, Jabal Fayfāʔ (Hijaz, Saudi Arabia), and
im-Maṭṭah (Oman) (Procházka 2014: 136). In my corpus, the *ʔəC*-initial forms
are used by speakers from Fəllāḥīya (especially [A10]), Xafağīya, Hoveyzeh, and
Muḥammara, and thus, at least synchronically, cannot be exclusively attributed
to southern dialects. Similarly, the *CəC*-initial forms are used by speakers from
Ahvaz, Fəllāḥīya, Muḥammara, Xafağīya, and Abadan and therefore cannot be
attributed to northern dialects only. The *ʔəC*-initial form has very likely developed via morphological alignment with the vowel-initial forms of the 1st PL and
2nd person SG and PL. A development similar to the KhA example is found in
the Arabic dialects of Siirt and Sason: the forms of the 3rd person pronouns
have, as a result of intraparadigmatic convergence aligning with the forms
of the 2nd person, lost their initial *h* (Procházka 2018: 273). Procházka (2014:
134 and 2018: 273) describes a parallel development in the Arabic dialects of
W-Syria, Cilicia, and Central Asia, where, the 2nd person forms adopted the
initial *h*- of the 3rd person, yielding, for example, *hinti(n)* for 2SG.F.

---

nouns and verbs is generally a feature found mainly in Eastern Bedouin-type dialects of Arabic (Palva 2006: 606). The Bahraini dialects have lost this feature in the course of time along
with some other changes (Holes 2018b: 134; Ingham 1982a: 38–39), probably due to various
factors such as dialect contact, or social and demographic changes (especially urbanization).

MORPHOLOGY

2nd Person

The most common form of the 2PL.M is *?əntəm*, which appears 22 times in my corpus. The form *?əntu*, which has lost the final *-m* as the result of morphological alignment with the respective inflectional suffix of the perfect (Procházka 2014: 131), occurs only once in my corpus (speaker [M1]) but has been confirmed from other speakers from Muḥammara and Abadan. The form *?əntam* is restricted to the area of Tustar (Pers. Šuštar). In the dialect of Tustar, also the 2nd and 3rd PL.M verbal suffixes end on *-tam* and *-am*, respectively, e.g. *šəftam* 'you (PL.M) saw' and *?əyam* 'they (PL.M) came' (cf. 4.11.1.1). The suffix of the 2nd and 3rd PL.M PFV verbs *-tam* and *-am* as well as the 2nd and 3rd PL.M pronouns *?əntam* and *hamma* and their respective suffix forms *-kam* and *-ham* are typical of Šammari dialects.[2]

The 2PL.F form *?əntan* has developed by analogy with the respective inflectional suffix of the perfect, e.g. *čəntan* 'you (PL.F) were' (cf. Procházka 2014: 132).

1st Person

The form *ḥənna* for the 1PL was only recorded among the semi-nomadic speakers at the outskirts of Ahvaz. This form of the 1PL pronoun is also documented for ʕAnazi and Šammari-type dialects in Syria and Iraq (cf. Behnstedt 1997: 511 and 1035 on Syria; and Ingham 1982a: 139 on a Šammari dialect spoken around Karbala: "*ḥinna ṭalāṭīn* ... 'We were thirty men ...'"; cf. also Rosenhouse 1984: Table 5.1). Johnstone (1967: 14) also gives this form ([*i*]*ḥinna*) for Qatari Arabic and he adds that "in the Syrian Desert the Syro-Mesopotamian dialects have *iḥna* and tge others mostly *ḥinna*. The Šammari dialect of ʕAnaiza also has *ḥinna*".

Functions

Independent pronouns in KhA can function as overt subjects. Often they are used for the expression of emphasis (cf. Vicente 2008: 585).

i. Verbless clauses

As subjects, the pronouns often, but not necessarily, appear in verbless clauses.

---

2 Cf. Procházka (2014: 132), who discusses possible origins of 2nd and 3rd M.PL pronominal and verbal forms ending in *-am*; Ingham (1976: 69, fn. 23) mentions that this form occurs in the ʕAmāra area and in the speech of the Kawāwila, a gypsy tribe living in Ahvaz

76

CHAPTER 4

(1) [A10]
ʔəhwa bəlʕān.
3SG.M rich
'He is rich.'

ii. Disambiguation

Independent pronouns can be used for disambiguation in utterances such as the following (2). If there was no independent pronoun in example (2), it would not be clear to which person the active participle *sāknīn* 'living (AP.PL.M)' refers without context.

(2) [A1]
mən zamān əsnīn ʔəhna sāknīn   əb-hāy l-manāṭəġ.
from time   years 1PL   live.AP.PL.M in-DEM DEF-regions
'For many years (now) we have been living in this region.'

iii. Emphasis

When used for the expression of emphasis, the independent pronoun usually appears after the element it emphasizes, both in subject and non-subject position.

(3) [A6]
ġanam-na ʔəhna, əl-ʕarab   ʔəhna
sheep-1PL 1PL   DEF-Arabs 1PL
'our sheep, of us, us Arabs'

(4) [A10]
mā bī-ya, mā ʔagdar   ʔāna.
NEG in-1SG NEG be_able_to.IPFV.1SG 1SG
'I'm not able to, I can't.'

iv. Contrast

Independent pronouns are also used to contrast different individuals, as in example (5): the independent pronoun following the first noun, *əbū-y* 'my father', can also be interpreted as a means of emphasizing that his father, and no one else, had been the one who had planted the palms.

MORPHOLOGY 77

(5) [A9]
əbū-y   həwwa əl   zraʕ   hāḏ ən-naxal, w-āna
father-1SG 3SG.M REL plant.PFV.3SG.M DEM DEF-palms and-1SG
mən baʕad-a   ham taʕalləmət.
from after-3SG.M also learn.PFV.1SG
'My father was the one who planted these palms, and I learned (this job)
from him.'

v.   Topicalization

Independent pronouns may also introduce verbal clauses.

(6) [Ḥ1, describing how she and her relatives would go to Basra to sell home-
     made yoghurt]
ʔəḥna nəgḍi   w   nəštəri   w   hāy ...
1PL   finish_work.IPFV.1PL and buy.IPFV.1PL and DEM
'(As for us,) we finish our work and we shop and so (on) ...'

In object position, independent pronouns usually appear as suffixed enclitics
(cf. 4.1.2), with the exception of topicalized objects, as in (7):

(7) [A10]
ʔəhya māxəḏ-ha   ʔəbn əl-malək.
3SG.F take.AP.SG.M-OBL.3SG.F son DEF-king
'The king's son took her (as his wife).'

4.1.2 Suffixed Personal Pronouns
The pronominal suffixes can be added to nouns, prepositions, and verbs. The
morphological forms of the suffixes presented in Table 4 and Table 5 differ only
in the 1SG (*-i* or *-y* after nouns and prepositions vs. *-ni* after verbs).

The 3SG.M pronominal suffix *-a* is typical of some Bedouin-type dialects,
both Eastern and Western (cf. Vicente 2008: 586), and is very common in
the whole Mesopotamian and Gulf area (cf., for example, Holes 2016b: 83 on
Bahraini Arabic; Seeger 2013: 313 on Khorasan and Qashqadarya Arabic; and
Ingham 1982a: 66). Only in rare cases is a final *h* heard, e.g. after the object
marker *yyā* used for double (pronominalized) object constructions (cf. 4.1.5).
This can be interpreted as a trace of an older form of the 3rd person SG.M
pronominal suffix, which still had an element *h*. Ingham (2007: 574) gives *-a(h)*
as the KhA 3rd person SG.M pronominal suffix. When a 3SG.M suffix is added to
a word ending in a vowel, this vowel is lengthened and stressed, e.g.

(1) [T2]
ġassalnā́.
wash.PFV.1PL.OBL.3SG.M
'We washed it.'

TABLE 4 Pronouns suffixed to nouns and
prepositions

	After consonants	After vowels
1 SG	*-i*	*-y, -ya*
2 SGM	*-ak*	*-k*
2 SGF	*-əč*	*-č*
3 SGM	*-a*	*-´*
3 SGF	*-ha*	*-ha*
1 PL	*-na*	*-na*
2 PLM	*-kəm*	*-kəm*
2 PLF	*-čan*	*-čan*
3 PLM	*-həm*	*-həm*
3 PLF	*-hən*	*-hən*

TABLE 5 Pronouns suffixed to verbs

šāf- 'he saw'	After consonants	After vowels
1 SG	*-ni*	*-ni*
2 SGM	*-ak*	*-k*
2 SGF	*-əč*	*-č*
3 SGM	*-a*	*-´*
3 SGF	*-ha*	*-ha*
1 PL	*-na*	*-na*
2 PLM	*-kəm*	*-kəm*
2 PLF	*-čan*	*-čan*
3 PLM	*-həm*	*-həm*
3 PLF	*-hən*	*-hən*

MORPHOLOGY   79

When attached to nouns (including the genitive exponent *māl*, see 4.6), the pronominal suffixes are used to express possession (2). Cf. 4.6.1 on an alternative construction for the expression of possession.

(2) [Ḥ1]
     dəkkān-ha
     shop-3SG.F
     'her shop'

When added to finite verbs or active participles (with verbal force), pronominal suffixes are used to express direct objects (3) and attached to pronouns they express prepositional objects. Cf. 4.11.15 on the morphological processes that occur when pronouns are suffixed to verbs.

(3) [Ḥ1]
     ḥaṭṭēnā-ha
     put.PFV.1PL-OBL.3SG.F
     'we put it'

(4) [A4, telling the woman we were interviewing that I already knew how a *fānūs* 'oil lamp' looked like]
     ʕārəft-a,   *šāyft-a*   *həyya,*
     know.AP.SG.F-OBL.3SG.M   see.AP.SG.F-OBL.3SG.M   3SG.F
     ʕārəft-a,   *ʕārəft-a.*
     know.AP.SG.F-OBL.3SG.M   know.AP.SG.F-OBL.3SG.M
     'She knows it, she's seen it, she knows it.'

Pronouns attached to the preposition *l-* express indirect objects when following a verb (cf. Table 6) or possession when standing alone (cf. 4.1.3.2, Table 7, and 4.11.14.2).

4.1.2.1   Short Forms
There are enclitic short forms of the independent pronouns that occur in certain contexts, but always in combination with another element. These elements are mainly:

i.   *mā-*, yielding the negative pronouns (cf. 4.1.4)
ii.   the adverb *baʕad-*, yielding the adverbial expression 'still' (cf. 4.3.1.24), or, with a negation, 'not yet' (cf. 4.3.1.25)
iii. the adverb *gadd-mā-*, meaning '(it is) so ... (that)' (cf. 4.3.2.15)
iv.   the interrogative *yā* 'which?', yielding the interrogative *yā-hu* 'who? (SG.M)' (SG.F: *yā-hi*) (cf. 4.1.11.4)

CHAPTER 4

TABLE 6   Indirect object suffixes complementing to a verb

	After consonants	After vowels
1 SG	*-li*	*-li*
2 SGM	*-lak*	*-lak*
2 SGF	*-ləč*	*-ləč*
3 SGM	*-la*	*-la*
3 SGF	*-əlha*	*-lha*
1 PL	*-əlna*	*-lna*
2 PLM	*-əlkəm*	*-lkəm*
2 PLF	*-əlhən*	*-lhən*
3 PLM	*-əlhəm*	*-lhəm*
3 PLF	*-əlčan*	*-lčan*

TABLE 7   Pseudoverb *ʔəl-* plus pronoun for possession

1 SG	*ʔəli*
2 SGM	*ʔəlak*
2 SGF	*ʔələč*
3 SGM	*ʔəla*
3 SGF	*ʔəlha*
1 PL	*ʔəlna*
2 PLM	*ʔəlkəm*
2 PLF	*ʔəlhən*
3 PLM	*ʔəlhəm*
3 PLF	*ʔəlčan*

Distinct short forms of the independent pronouns exist only for the 3rd person SG.M, *-hu ~ -haw*, and SG.F, *-hi ~ -hay*. For all other forms either the full independent pronoun is used, e.g. *m-əḥna* 'we are not' (cf. negative pronouns, 4.1.4), or the pronominal suffix form e.g. *mā-hən* 'they (F) are not', *yā-həm* 'who (PL.M)?', and *baʕad-na* 'we are still'.

MORPHOLOGY 81

(5) [A4]
mən awwal-mā tṣīr ətsammūn-ha ṭəlyān
from first-REL become.IPFV.3SG.F call.IPFV.2PL.M-OBL.3SG.F lambs
w tʕadda-l-ha farəd ṭəlṭ təšhər
and pass.PFV.3SG.M-for-3SG.F INDEF three months
š-ətsammūn-a? baʕad-hu ṭəlyān?
what-call.IPFV.2PL.M-OBL.3SG.M still-3SG.M lambs
'When they [i.e. the lambs] have just been born you call them ṭəlyān
(lambs). But after some three months, what do you call them? Are they
still (called) ṭəlyān?'

4.1.3 *Indirect Object Suffixes*
Pronominalized indirect objects of verbs are expressed by a combination of the
preposition *l-* 'to, for' plus a pronominal suffix, e.g. *-l-i* 'to me', attached to the
verb.

Combined with a consonant-initial pronoun and when preceded by a consonant, the base form is *əl-* (1). Similarly, Muslim Baghdadi Arabic has the two
base forms *l-* and *il-* in the same distribution (Erwin 1963: 142–143; cf. Procházka
1993: 155).

(1) [Ḥa1]
ʔasōləf-əl-həm.
tell.IPFV.1SG-to-3PL.M
'I tell them.'

All forms of the pronominalized indirect objects are given in Table 6 above (p.
80).

4.1.3.1 *gāl* 'to Say, Tell' + Indirect Object Suffixes
When indirect object suffixes are attached to a form of the verb *gāl* 'to say, tell'
that has a long vowel in its base (*ā* in the PFV, *ū* in the IPFV)—e.g. *gālat* 'she
said, told', *ygūl* 'he says, tells', and *gūli* 'tell (IMP.SG.F)'—the long vowel is usually shortened (*ā* to *a*; *ū* is shortened and lowered to *ə*) and the *l* of the root
doubled when intervocalic (cf. Blanc 1964: 106 on this feature in Muslim Baghdadi Arabic)

> *gāl* + *li* → *gal-li* 'he told me'
> *ygūl* + *la* → *ygəl-la* 'he tells him'
> *ʔagūl* + *ləč* → *ʔagəl-ləč* 'I tell you (SG.F)'
> *gūl* + *li* → *gəl-li* 'tell (IMP.SG.M) me!'
> *gūlan* + *li* → *gəllan-li* [gəl:al:i] 'tell (IMP.PL.F) me!'

82   CHAPTER 4

Especially the forms ending in a vowel, but also others, show variation regarding the shortening of the long vowel and the doubling of *l*, e.g.:

> *gālat + li → gallat-li ~ gālat-li* 'she told me'
> *gālaw + li → gallō-li ~ gālō-li* 'they (PL.M) told me'
> *ygūlūn + la → ygə(l)lū-la ~ ygūlū-la* 'they (PL.M) tell him'
> *gūlu + li → gəl(l)ū-li ~ gūlū-li* 'tell (IMP.PL.M) me!'
> *gələt + əlhəm → gəlt-əlhəm ~ gallēt-əlhəm* 'I told them (PL.M)'
> *gəlna + əlhəm → gəlnā-lhəm ~ gallēnā-lhəm* 'we told them (PL.M)'

This is a very widespread phenomenon attested for many dialects (cf. Erwin 1963 on Muslim Baghdadi Arabic; Cowell 1964 on Syrian Arabic; or Holes 2016 on Bahraini Arabic).

Finally, a long vowel *-ā* can be inserted between the 3SG.M PFV verb *gāl* 'he said' and an indirect object suffix.

(2)   [A14], Elicited
      gālā-l-ha[3]
      tell.PFV.3SG.M-to-3SG.F
      'he told her'

4.1.3.2   Pseudoverb *ʔəl-* Plus Pronominal Suffix for Possession
As also listed in 4.11.14 on the so-called 'pseudoverbs', the preposition *ʔəl-* plus a pronominal suffix is used to express possession and the meanings 'to, for' (all forms are given in Table 7). In this case the combination *ʔəl-* + pronoun is not enclitic but a separate prosodic unit. Muslim Baghdadi Arabic similarly attaches pronominal suffixes to a base *il-* when it is not enclitic but a separate prosodic unit (Blanc 1964: 120, who transcribed the base as *el-*; cf. Procházka 1993: 151)

4.1.4   *Negative Pronouns*
The so-called negative pronouns (cf. Vicente 2008: 586) are used for the negation of nominal clauses with non-past and non-future reference. Negative pronouns consist of the NEG particle *mā* + a shortened and partly phonologically adapted form of the independent pronoun, which is also used with the adverb *baʕad* 'still' (cf. 4.3.1.24). *mā* is shortened to *m-* before full-form vowel-initial

---

3   Alternatively, *gāl-əl-ha*, without the insertion of *ā*, is also heard.

MORPHOLOGY

83

TABLE 8   Negative pronouns

	SG	PL
1	*mā-ni* 'I am not ~ am I not'	*m-əḥna*
2M	*m-ənta*	*m-əntəm*
2F	*m-ənti*	*m-əntan*
3M	*mā-hu ~ mā-haw*	*mā-həm*
3F	*mā-hi ~ mā-hay*	*mā-hən*

pronouns such as 2SG.F *ʔənti*. The negative pronouns of the 3rd person have two variant forms each, ending either in a vowel (*mā-hu, mā-hi*) or in a diphthong (*mā-haw, mā-hay*). The latter forms, i.e. those ending in a diphthong, are also documented for Basra Arabic (Mahdi 1985: 239).

Examples

(1) [Ḥa1, answering the question *čam yōm yəṭawwəl tannūr?* 'How long does (the construction of) a clay oven take?']
maṯal āna w   nəḏərt-i ʔāna, lō nāḏra   maṯal asawwi
like   1SG and vow-1SG 1SG   if vow.AP.SG.F like   do.IPFV.1SG
*yōmēn,   lō maṯal hēč **mā-ni**   nāḏra   ʔasawwi   ṯələṯ*
two_days if like   DP NEG-1SG vow.AP.SG.F do.IPFV.1SG three
tayyām ha-š-šəkəl.
days   DEM-DEF-kind
'It depends on me and my vow: if I have vowed, I do (it) like in two days; if I, for example, have not vowed, it takes me three days—like that.'

(2) [T2]
*āna baʕad-ni bnayya **mā-ni**   čəbīra.*
1SG still-1SG girl   NEG-1SG big.SG.F
'I am still a girl; I am not a grown-up (yet).'

(3) [Ḥ1]
*la,   **mā-hu**   blēt,   xəšab.*
NEG NEG-3SG.M metal_plate wood
'No, it is not (made of) metal (plates), (it is made of) wood.'

84

CHAPTER 4

(4) [A12]
mā-hən   *bṭūṭ-na,*   *ḏann əbṭūṭ-na.*
NEG-3PL.F ducks-1PL DEM ducks-1PL
'(These) aren't our ducks; those are our ducks.'

(5) [A6]
daḡīḡa   *mawḡūdāt,*   *ʕad-na zḡār*   *baʕad-hən* **mā-hən**
young_ewe exist.AP.PL.F at-1PL young.PL still-3PL.F NEG-3PL.F
mwalldāt.
give_birth.AP.PL.F
'We have young ewes;[4] we have young ones, they have not yet given birth.'

In some instances, we find the full pronoun attached to the NEG particle *mā*,
e.g.

(6) Ahvaz, unidentified person
mā-hīya   *īrānīya.*
NEG-3SG.F Iranian.SG.F
'She is not Iranian.'

4.1.5   *Double (Pronominalized) Object Constructions and the Object Marker -əyyā-*

For KhA verbs that usually govern two objects, e.g. *ʔanṭa* 'to give (sth. to sb.)'
and *rāwa* 'to show (sth. to sb.)', the object marker *-əyyā-* can be used.[5] In the
following discussion we will distinguish between the types of the two objects:
they can be either a direct and an indirect object, or two direct objects.

i.   Direct and Indirect Object

If both objects are pronominalized, the pronominal suffix that refers to the
indirect object is suffixed directly to the verb and the pronominal suffix that
refers to the direct object follows, suffixed to the object marker *-əyyā-*. This construction is used only with direct objects that refer to 3rd persons, e.g.:

---

4   Definition for *daḡīḡa* provided by informants: *naʕaya ṣaḡīra, hāya llaḏi baʕad-hi mā-hi wālda*
"a young ewe, one that has not yet given birth" and is about 9 to 10 months old. Once it has
given birth, it is called *naʕaya*. On this word in CA cf. Wahrmund (1877: 673) s.v. *daqīqa*: "a
sheep"; and Lane (1863: 896) s.v. *daqīqa* "small cattle; i.e. sheep or goats; opposed to *ḡalīla*
which signifies camels".

5   For similar constructions cf. Blanc (1964: 67) on Muslim Baghdadi Arabic, and Holes (2016:
65) on Bahraini Arabic. In the latter, however, the direct object is usually suffixed to the verb
and the indirect object to the object marker *-iyya-*.

MORPHOLOGY

waddēnā-lha-ǝyyā-ha 'we sent it (SG.F) to her (SG.F)'
yībī-li-yyá! 'bring (IMP.SG.F) it (SG.M) to me!'

Such constructions are a single prosodic unit and carry the main stress on the *ā* of the object marker *-ǝyyā-*.

Alternatively, the direct object can be suffixed directly to the verb and the indirect object pronoun follows, attached to the preposition *(ʔǝ)l-* 'to, for'. The object pronoun can be combined either with the non-enclitic or the enclitic form of the preposition *(ʔǝ)l-*, in the former case yielding a separate prosodic unit. When the direct object does not refer to a 3rd person, or when the indirect object is to be translated as 'for …', constructions with the preposition *(ʔǝ)l-* 'to, for' are always preferred over the one with *-ǝyyā-*, e.g.:

waddēt-ak ʔǝla 'I sent you (SG.M) to him'
ǧīb-hā ʔǝli! 'bring it to me!'
ʔāxǝd-ha' ʔǝlna 'I take her for us'

Combined with the enclitic form of the preposition *(ʔǝ)l-*, it forms one single prosodic unit together with the verb, e.g.:

waddētī-hā-li 'you (F) sent it (F) to me'
ḥaṭṭēnā-hā-lhǝm 'we served it (F) [the food] to them'

ii. Two Direct Objects

If two direct objects are added to a verb, the first is usually directly suffixed to the verb and the second combined with the object marker *-ǝyyā-*, e.g.:

ṭī-ni-yyá! 'give (IMP, SG) it (M) to me!'
ʔaṭī-k-ǝyyā-ha 'I give it (F) to you (M.SG)'
ʔarāwī-č-ǝyyá 'I'll show it (M) to you (F.SG)'.

Further examples from the corpus are:

(1) [A3]
   kān   *ʕad-ha ha-š-šǝkǝr   al-aṣfar,   hǝwa hāḏa, mǝn*
   be.PFV.3SG.M at-3SG.F DEM-DEF-sugar DEF-yellow 3SG.M DEM when
   tǝrḥīn   adallī-č-ǝyyá.
   go.IPFV.2SG.F show.IPFV.1SG-OBL.2SG.F-OBJ.SG.M
   'She had this yellow sugar, that's it; when you go, I will show it to you!'

(2) [A19]
ḏīča, ḏāk əl-mənyal ġēr ᴾšekelᴾ, hassa
DEM DEM DEF-sickle other shape   now
arāwī-č-əyyá   *hnāka.*
show.IPFV.1SG-OBL.2SG.F-OBJ.SG.M there
'That one, that sickle has another shape; I'll show it to you now.'

(3) [F1]
əl-ġaṣər,   hāḏa həwa, əlli ḏāk əl-yōm
DEF-castle DEM 3SG.M REL DEM DEF-day
rāwēt-əč-əyyá,   *gət-l-əč*   *mhaddam.*
show.PFV.1SG-OBL.2SG.F-OBJ.SG.M tell.PFV.1SG-to-2SG.F destroyed
'The castle, the one which I showed to you that day, I told you (that it was)
destroyed.'

4.1.6 *Demonstrative Pronouns*

This chapter is divided into sections on proximal and distal demonstratives
following a short introduction with general remarks on both types. In both
sections, all forms are first given in a table and then discussed individually
regarding their frequency and main syntactical properties (including illustra-
tive examples for different types of usage and position).

The existence of PL.F forms is, again, more characteristic of Bedouin than of
sedentary dialects (cf. Fischer 1959; Behnstedt 1993; Rosenhouse 1984). The PL.F
forms *haḍann* (proximal) and *ḏākann* (distal) developed as a combination of
the SG.M demonstratives *hāḏ(a)* (proximal)/*ḏāk* (distal) and the 3PL.F inflectional suffix *-an* (cf. Fischer 1959: 114 on the etymology of this and similar forms
and their occurrences in other dialects of Arabic).

All demonstrative pronouns can be used either as attributive adjectives (i.e.
as appositions to a definite noun) or as (self-standing) pronouns. In principle,
there are three possible positions for demonstratives (though not all positions
are attested for all forms in my corpus): (i) preceding the noun or predicate, as
in (3) or (5) below, (ii) following the noun or predicate, as in (4) or (6) below,
or (iii) both preceding and following the noun or predicate. The last option is
usually used only with SG demonstratives (cf. Fischer 1959: 97–98 on the combination of demonstratives).

There are variants with final -*a* for all (proximal and distal) demonstratives
except for the PL.F forms (cf. Fischer 1959: 91, fn. 5, who discusses the etymology
of forms with final -*a* and their function as intensifying demonstratives). Similarly, there are variants with final -*i* for the PL proximal demonstratives (PL.F
haḍann, ḍann, and PL.M *haḍōl*) and the SG.F distal demonstrative (*ḏīč*).

MORPHOLOGY

TABLE 9   Proximal demonstratives

'this, these'	SG	PL
M	*hāḏ, hāḏa*	*haḏōl, haḏōla, haḏōli, ḏōl, ḏōla*
F	*hāḏi, hāy, hāya*	*haḏann, haḏanni, ḏann, ḏanni*

The (plural) proximal demonstratives forms with *ha-* are more frequently used than their counterparts without *ha-*. By contrast, the distal demonstratives with *ha-* (cf. Table 10 below) appear less frequently than their counterparts without *ha-*.

4.1.6.1   Proximal
The proximal demonstratives of KhA are similar to the forms used in Muslim Baghdadi Arabic (Erwin 1963: 290; cf. Blanc 1964: 139), Basra Arabic (Mahdi 1985: 155), and al-Shirqat Arabic (Salonen 1980: 67–71). For Muslim Baghdadi Arabic, however, there are no documented PL.F forms (Erwin 1963: 290). But because of the recently increasing influence of rural speakers on the Muslim dialect of Baghdad, the PL.F forms do appear to be gaining ground. Al-Shirqat Arabic (Salonen 1980: 67) has SG proximal forms without the initial *ha-* (viz. *ḏe, ḏi*), which are unknown to KhA.

4.1.6.1.1   *SG.M*
The SG.M proximal demonstrative *hāḏa* occurs 299 times in my corpus, while *hāḏ* occurs 144 times. Generally, *hāḏ* is more often used attributively, as in (1), than pronominally, as in (2).

As examples (1) and (2) suggest, *hāḏ* usually comes before its head.

(1)   [Ḥa1]
    hāḏ əl-wakət əl   marr   ʕalē-na
    DEM DEF-time REL pass.PFV.3SG.M on-1PL
    'the time that has passed [lit. "on us"]'

(2)   [A9]
    hāḏ yḏ̣əll   ḏəxər.
    DEM remain.IPFV.3SG.M storage
    'This remains (in) storage.'

88   CHAPTER 4

hāda[6] is also used both as an attribute, as in (3) and (4), and as a pronoun, as in (5) and (6). *hāda* can be used preceding a definite noun, as in (3), or following a definite noun, as in (4).

(3) [A4]
     yəmma, ***hāda*** *l-mašḥūf əb-šənhi   msawwīn-a,*
     mother DEM DEF-boat with-what make.AP.PL.M-OBL.3SG.M
     əb-xəšab   w   blēt?
     with-wood and metal_plate
     'My dear, this *mašḥūf* [a kind of a boat[7]], with what did they make it? With wood and metal (plates)?'

(4) [A10]
     əl-walad ***hāda*** *rabbṓ.*
     DEF-boy DEM raise.PFV.3PL.M.OBL.3SG.M
     'They raised this boy.'

(5) [Ḥa1]
     *ʕūd hāy   ḥamāma yōm əl-xēr   ʔəlli fāt   w   **hāda***
     DP DEM pigeon   day DEF-good REL pass.PFV.3SG.M and DEM
     həlāl.
     crescent
     'I think this is a pigeon—the good day that has passed—and this (one is) a crescent.'

(6) [A4]
     *čānūn   **hāda**, hā?*
     coalpan DEM   DP
     'This is (called) a *čānūn*, right?'

hāda can also be used referring to PL.F or SG.F, as in (7)–(9):

(7) [A1]
     hāda *d-dəkrāyāt*
     DEM DEF-memories
     'these memories' [*dəkrāyāt* 'memories' as a non-human plural is grammatically PL.F in KhA]

---

6 See Fischer (1959: 71) on the development of *hāda* < OA *dā* (+ *hā*).
7 Cf. Edzard (1967: 311), who describes *mašḥūf* as a "Schnabelboot".

MORPHOLOGY 89

(8) [A4]
hāḏa šənhi?
DEM what.SG.F
'What is this (SG.F)?'

(9) [M1]
hāḏa čəlmat əl-fārsi, əs-sərka
DEM word.CS DEF-Persian DEF-vinegear
'This is a Persian word (SG.F), sərka ("vinegear").'

4.1.6.1.2 *SG.F*
It appears that *hāy* has largely replaced the SG.F DEM *hāḏi*: *hāy* occurs 351 times[8] in my corpus, *hāḏi* occurs only 19 times (cf. Fischer 1959: 53 on the same development in Damascus Arabic). *hāya*, occurs 4 times in the corpus and is usually used as a pronoun.

hāy, also found in most other Mesopotamian dialects, mostly refers to a SG.F subject, as in (10), and probably derives from the DEM proclitic *ha-* + feminine ending (see Stokes 2018: 130, fn. 3 and the reference mentioned there; and Fischer 1959: 52–55).

(10) [Ḥa1]
hāy xōš mara.
DEM good woman
'This is a good woman.'

It can, however, also refer to a SG.M noun (11) a. and b., a COLL noun (12), or a PL.F noun (13).

(11) [Ḥ1]
a. **hāy** šəʕāʕ.
DEM nose_ring
'This is a nose ring (SG.M).'

b. **hāy** l-əglād
DEM DEF-necklace
'this necklace (SG.M)'

---

8 The high number is of course also due to the fact that *hāy* is also used with PL nouns and for vague reference, see below.

90   CHAPTER 4

(12) [A19]
   *əḥna **hāy** əl-ʕarab   **hāy***
   1PL   DEM DEF-Arabs DEM
   'we Arabs (COLL)'

(13) [A9]
   *dbāb   **hāy** əl-plāstəkīyāt*
   barrels DEM DEF-plastic.PL.F
   'these plastic barrels (PL.F)'

The last example shows an unusual syntagm: INDEF noun_DEM_DEF-ADJ.
   Though their position before the noun/predicate prevails, *hāy* and *hāḏi* can
also follow its head:

(14) [M4]
   *əstəfādat-na **hāy***
   benefit-1PL   DEM
   '(this) our benefit'

Both *hāy* and *hāḏi* can be used as a self-standing pronoun (15), as well as attributively (16):

(15) [A1]
   ***ha**-l-ġanam   əl   ʕad-ak **hāy** ʔəl-i, mā-hu   ʔəl-ak!*
   DEM-DEF-sheep REL at-2SG.M DEM to-1SG NEG-3SG.M to-2SG.M
   'These sheep that you have, they belong to me, not to you!'

(16) [A9]
   hāy** əl-karab   **hāḏa
   DEM DEF-nodules DEM
   'these nodules here'

hāy for Vague Reference

hāy is often used for vague reference, as in *w hāy* 'and so on' (cf. Holes 2016:
86 on the same function of the Bahraini Bedouin-type F proximal demonstra-
tive *ḏi*), *lō hāy* 'or the like, or so' (17), and *hāy hīya* 'that's it, that's all'. Similarly,
in colloquial Persian *o-īnhā* can have the meaning 'and so on, and things like
that'.

MORPHOLOGY   91

(17) [Ḥa1]
 čūla   ham hassət ha-l-wakət   maṭal,   yrūḥ
 stove also EXIST DEM-DEF-time for_example go.IPFV.3SG.M
 *maṭal,   msāfarǧi lō **hāy** ham nyīb-l-a ...*
 for_example traveler   or DEM also bring.IPFV.1PL-to-3SG.M
 'A little stove (*čūla*) ... it also exists ... nowadays, like (if) one goes, for
 example, travelling or so, we also bring it ...'

(18) [Ḥ1]
 *ṭalʕēna   ʕawēšat-na⁹   w   **hāy**.*
 take_out.PFV.1PL   bread.DIM-1PL and DEM
 'We took our bread [out of the bread box[10]] and so on.'

4.1.6.1.3   *PL.M*

The PL.M demonstrative *haḏōl* occurs 10 times in my corpus and its variant
haḏōli 8 times. *ḏōla* occurs twice. The forms *haḏōla* and *ḏōl* do not occur in
my corpus but their use was confirmed by consultants.

   All forms were consistently used in the corpus with PL.M reference and both
as attributes and as self-standing pronouns. The PL.M demonstratives mostly
occur before the definite noun when used attributively, and before the predicate when used pronominally.

(19) [A3]
 ***haḏōl** əl   ʕad-həm ḥaywān*
 DEM   REL at-3PL.M cattle
 'these, who have cattle'

(20) [M1]
 ***haḏōli** frūx   ʔəxū-y*
 DEM   children brother-1SG
 'These are my brother's children.'

(21) [A12]
 *ʔahal-i   **ḏōla**!*
 family-1SG DEM
 'These are my family!'

---

9   Diminutive of *ʕēš* 'bread': cf. 4.9.4.
10   Called *ǧəḏər ʕēš*.

4.1.6.1.4   *PL.F*

The PL.F demonstrative *haḏann* occurs 14 times in my corpus, its variant *haḏanni* 34 times. *ḏann* occurs twice. The form *ḏanni* does not occur in my corpus but its use was confirmed by consultants.

All forms were consistently used in the corpus with PL.F reference and both as attributes and as self-standing pronouns. *haḏann* and *haḏanni* were more often used as pronouns than as attributes. The PL.F demonstratives mostly occur before the definite noun when used attributively and preceding the predicate when used pronominally.

(22) [Ḥ1]

    haḏan *nǝnzaḥ*   **ḏann** *ǝl-ḥǝlwāt,*   *yaʕni*
    DEM   take_off.IPFV.1PL DEM DEF-beautiful.PL.F DP
    nḏamm-hǝn.
    store.IPFV.1PL-OBL.3PL.F
    'We took these off, these beautiful (clothes); I mean we put them away/ stored them.'

(23) [Ḥa1, talking about her tattoos]

    ča *ǝš-ḥalā-hǝn*   **haḏanni** *yaʔ*[11]*!*
    DP what-beauty-3PL.F DEM   DP
    '(Don't you) see, how beautiful these are [lit. "how their beauty is"]!'

4.1.6.1.5   *ha-*

In addition to the forms in Table 9, an invariable proclitic form *ha-* can be prefixed to a definite noun of any gender and number:[12]

(24) a. *ha-l-ḥǝdūd*

       DEM-DEF-frontiers
       'these frontiers'

---

11   The particle *yaʔ* in this context expresses approximately 'What do you think?! Of course, they were simply stunning!'.

12   For examples on the use of *ha-* with M, F, and PL nouns in various Arabic dialects cf. Fischer (1959: 42–43). On the development of this invariable form *ha-* not from the DEM *hāḏa* but from first an interjection/presentative and (demonstrative) sentence introducer and then into a DEM cf. Rosenhouse (1984: 250) and Fischer (1959: 47). As in some other dialects of Arabic (Rosenhouse 1984: 250; Fischer 1959: 50), this sentence-introductory/vocative function of *ha-* is still in use in KhA; see §4.8.4 and the examples given there, which illustrate the functions of *ha- ~ hā-* ranging between presentative and DEM.

MORPHOLOGY   93

b. *ha-s-saʕfa*   *hāy*
   DEM-DEF-palm_frond DEM
   'this palm frond (here)'

c. *ha-l-ḥāla*   *hāy*
   DEM-DEF-condition DEM
   'this condition'

d. *ha-š-šəkəl*   *hāḏ*
   DEM-DEF-shape DEM
   'like this'

The proclitic demonstrative *ha-* occurs 72 times in my corpus. As shown in the last three examples, the DEM *ha-* is often combined with another DEM following the noun (cf. Fischer 1959: 46; 97–98; Rosenhouse 1984: 251–252, who suggests that this pattern might be typical of Bedouin-type dialects).

ha- is also used for various adverbial and other fixed expressions (cf. Holes 2016: 88 on similar expressions in Bahraini Arabic), e.g. *ha-n-namūna ~ ha-š-šəkəl* 'like that, that way', *ha-l-gadd(āt)* 'this much' (cf. 4.3.2.14), *ha-l-kəṭər* 'this much', *ha-n-nōb(a)* 'then', *hassa* (< *ha-s-sāʕa* 'this hour'; cf. Fischer 1959: 149; and 4.3.1.1) 'now', and *ha-l-ḥadd* 'this … (big, long, etc.)' as in the following example:

(25) [A10]
     ygūl   *əya*,   *ləgā-l-a*   *šāyəb*,
     say.IPFV.3SG.M come.PFV.3SG.M find.PFV.3SG.M-for-3SG.M old_man
     ha-l-ḥadd   *laḥīt-a.*
     DEM-DEF-point beard-3SG.M
     'Then he came and found an old man, with a beard that long.'

(26) [A9]
     hāy əl-faḥla   *tṣīr*   *čəbīra w   hāy*
     DEM DEF-male_palm become.IPFV.3SG.F big.F   and DEM
     ən-naxla   *la,   zəġīra, ēh, zəġīra, tağrīban*
     DEF-palm_tree NEG small.F yes small.F ca.
     ha-l-gaddāt-ha   *tṣīr.*
     DEM-DEF-amounts-3SG.F become.IPFV.3SG.F
     'This male palm grows big, but this palm not, small, yes small, it's going to be about that big.'

94   CHAPTER 4

4.1.6.1.6   hēč *'Such; This; like That'*
As a demonstrative pronoun (cf. 4.3.2.1 on *hēč* as a demonstrative adverb), *hēč*
modifies nouns and is very similar in its functions to German 'so'. It usually
immediately precedes the noun it modifies. That to which the noun is compared to can precede the phrase containing *hēč*.

(27) [Ḥ1]
    zamān gabəl yadda,[13]   *lā*   *lbāsāt,* *lā*   *ša(y)* **hēč** *hədəm.*
    time   past grandmother NEG trousers NEG thing DEM garment
    'In former times, there were no trousers, there was no such garment.'

Further specification of a noun modified by *hēč*, frequently follows the NP.

(28) [AB1]
    hēč *ləbəs-həm.*
    DEM clothes-3PL.M
    'Their clothes (look) like that [lit. "such are their clothes"].'

(29) [A3]
    bə-ǧənūb aktar šī   **hēč** *akəl yḥəbbūn,*   *təmən w*   *ḥalīb*
    in-south most thing DEM food love.IPFV.3PL.M rice   and milk
    w   *rōba.*
    and yoghurt
    'In the south they mainly like (to eat) this food: rice, milk, and yoghurt.'

(30) [A10]
    əḥčāyat əš-šēna   *təgləb-ha*   *zēna, yaʕni* **hēč**
    talk.CS DEF-bad.F turn_into.IPFV.3SG.F-OBL.3SG.F good.F DP   DEM
    mara   *ḏarba zēna.*
    woman clever.F good.F
    'She turns bad speech into good, she (indeed) was such a clever and good
    woman.'

It is also used in the following fixed expression, very frequently used by speaker
[A19]:

---

13   Yassin (1977: 297) describes "the use of a senior kin-term to address the junior" in Kuwaiti
    Arabic as "a function of familiarity and endearment on the basis of generational asymme-
    try"; this description fits the frequent use of senior kin-terms to address juniors in KhA,
    too.

MORPHOLOGY 95

(31) [A19]
 *əb-**hēč** ṭarīǧa*
 in-DEM way
 'like this, this way, in such a way'

hēč also occurs substantivized, as in the following examples:

(32) [M4]
 *wāyəd aḥsan mən **hēč** yṣīr.*
 a_lot better than DEM become.IPFV.3SG.M
 'It becomes much better than this.'

(33) [X1]
 mā yənwəčəl,   *əy walla,* *hassa **hēč**.*
 NEG be_eaten.IPFV.3SG.M yes by_God now DEM
 '(The food nowadays) can't be eaten, by God; now it's like that [that bad]'

As the following example shows, a phrase with nominalized *hēč* can even be made definite by prefixing the definite article to the demonstrative *hēč*. In general, such constructions are very unusual for Arabic.

(34) [Ḥa1], [A18]
 [Ḥa1]: *zamān gabəl, yadda,* *hēč šəfət,* *hēč*
    time past grandmother DEM see.PFV.1SG DEM
    šəfət ...
    see.PFV.1SG
 [A18]: *šənhu?* *ēh, l-hēč* *šəfət* *w l-hēč*
    what.3SG.M yes DEF-DEM see.PFV.1SG and DEF-DEM
    šəfət *w-əḥna nrīd-hən.*
    see.PFV.1SG and-1PL want.IPFV.1PL-OBL.3PL.F
    'In former times, I have seen this and that ...—A: What (exactly have you seen)? Exactly this "I've seen this and that" is what we want (to hear).'

4.1.6.2 Distal

All distal forms have an element *-k-* or its affricated counterpart *-č-* (if after the long front vowel *ī*), in most forms in word-final position.[14] The KhA distal

---

14 Cf. Fischer (1959: 82) on the etymology of suffix *-k* for distal demonstratives; and Müller-

96   CHAPTER 4

TABLE 10   Distal demonstratives

'that, those'	SG	PL
M	*haḏāk, ḏāk, ḏāka*	*haḏōlāk, ḏōlāk, ḏōlāka, ḏōlāki, ḏakōl, ḏakōli*
F	*haḏīč, ḏīč, ḏīči, ḏīča*	*ḏākan, ḏakan, haḏannīč, ḏannīč, ḏannīča,* *ḏannīči, ḏīčan*

demonstratives are similar to the forms used in Muslim Baghdadi Arabic (cf. Blanc 1964: 139), Basra Arabic (Mahdi 1985: 155), and al-Shirqat Arabic (Salonen 1980: 67–71). For Muslim Baghdadi Arabic, however, there are no PL.F forms documented (Erwin1963: 290).

4.1.6.2.1   SG.M

The SG.M distal demonstrative *haḏāk* occurs twice in my corpus, *ḏāk* occurs 58 times and *ḏāka* 7 times. The high number of occurrences of *ḏāk* is due to its frequent use in story-introductory phrases like *ḏāk əl-yōm* 'that day', and *ḏāk əl-wakət* 'that time'.

All forms were consistently used with SG.M reference in the corpus and both as attributes and as self-standing pronouns. The form *ḏāka* is mainly used pronominally, as in (36). In the corpus, the SG.M distal demonstratives mostly occur preceding the definite noun when used attributively and preceding the predicate when used pronominally.

(35) [Ḥa1]
    zamān ḏāk əl-wakət ən-nəswān   maṯal   yṭəḥnan.
    time   DEM DEF-time DEF-women for_example mill.IPFV.3PL.F
    'During that time, the women were for example milling.'

(36) [M1]
    w   ḏāka rayyāl-na   hāy baṭn-a
    and DEM husband-1PL DEM belly-3SG.M
    šaggō-ha.
    rupture.PFV.3PL.M-OBL.3SG.F
    'And that one, my [lit. "our"] husband—his belly was ruptured.'

Kessler (2003: 641) on the distal demonstrative pronouns *h'z'k* and *h'zyk* in pre-Classical Mandaic.

MORPHOLOGY

4.1.6.2.2 *SG.F*

The SG.F distal demonstrative *ḏīč* occurs 36 times in my corpus and *ḏīča* thrice. The form *haḏīč* does not occur in my corpus but its use was confirmed by consultants. *ḏīči* appears only twice, in a recording of a speaker from Fəllāḥīya (living in Kuwait). All forms were used both as attributes and as self-standing pronouns. The form *ḏīča* was mainly used pronominally.

(37) [A10]
    xayāl   **ḏīč**   *əl-bənt*   *əl-ḥəlwa*   *ydəgg*   *b-əl,*
    reflection DEM DEF-girl DEF-beautiful.F hit.IPFV.3SG.M in-DEF
    b-əl-māy.
    in-DEF-water
    'That pretty girl('s face) was mirrored in the, in the water.'

(38) [A19]
    hāḏi *hna* *ʕand-na* *həndəba,* **ḏīča.**
    DEM here at-1PL   endive   DEM
    'This, here we have endive, this one.'

4.1.6.2.3 *PL.M*

The PL.M distal demonstrative *ḏōlāk* occurs once in my corpus: (39). The forms *haḏōlāk, ḏōlāki, ḏōlāka, ḏakōl,* and *ḏakōli* do not occur in my corpus but their use was confirmed by consultants. All forms can be used both as attributes and as self-standing pronouns.

(39) [Ḥa1]
    xō, **ḏōlāka** *laḥagaw*   *w-əḥna* *mā* *laḥagna*
    DP DEM   live_to_see.PFV.3PL.M and-1PL NEG live_to_see.PFV.1PL
    əl-ʔawwalīyīn.
    DEF-old_days
    'Well, those (still) lived to see (that); (but) we did not live to see (the days of) the past.'

4.1.6.2.4 *PL.F*

The PL.F distal demonstrative *ḏannīč* occurs thrice in my corpus, *ḏākan* occurs 4 times. The forms *ḏannīča, ḏannīči* and *haḏannīč* do not occur in my corpus, but their use was confirmed by consultants.

All forms can be used both as attributes, see for example (40), and as self-standing pronouns, see for example (41). In all four instances of *ḏākan*— all from the same speaker, [A19]—the word stress was on the final syllable (*ḏa'kan*).

(40) [Ḥa1]

> *əb-zamān ham əl-ġadīmīyāt,*   *dannīč ən-nəswān ...*
> in-time   DP   DEF-ancestors.PL.F DEM   DEF-women
> 'In the time of the (women) ancestors, those women ...'

(41) [A1]

> *lākən mən kəbbarna*   *dannīč rāḥat*   *w yārēt hāḏ*
> but   when grow_up.PFV.1PL DEM   go.PFV.3SG.F and if_only DEM
> *əl-ʔayyām tərǧaʕ.*
> DEF-days   come_back.IPFV.3SG.F
> 'But when we grew up, these (memories) passed and if only these days
> came back.'

(42) [A19]

> *hāḏ əl-makānīs šūfi*   *ʔaku əzġār, ʔaku ḏāk əl ——*
> DEM DEF-brooms see.IMP.SG.F EXIST small.PL EXIST DEM REL
> *ḏākan, əl lēǧād, ḏākan mū haḏann, məṭəl ḏāka šūfi*
> DEM   REL over_there DEM   NEG DEM   like   DEM see.IMP.SG.F
> *ḏākan, ḏākan.*
> DEM   DEM
> 'These brooms, see, there are small ones, there are those that—those,
> which are over there, those, not these, like that one, see, those, those.'

4.1.7 Indefinite Pronouns

We will regard as indefinite pronouns those "whose main function is to express indefinite reference" (Haspelmath 1997: 11). But, in contrast to Haspelmath (1997: 12), we will also include the generic pronoun *bnādəm* 'one' (German 'man') in this discussion.

KhA shares most indefinite pronouns with the neighboring dialects of Iraq, as indicated below. However, the KhA indefinite pronoun *hīč* + NEG 'nothing, not anything'[15] and the generic pronoun *bnādəm* are not documented for Iraqi Arabic.

4.1.7.1 əbnādəm 'One' (German 'Man')

This generic indefinite pronoun derives from the expression *ʔibn ādam* 'son of Adam'.

---

15   *hīč* in Iraqi usually means 'like this, so', cf. KhA *hēč* 4.3.2.1; but according to my informants from Baghdad, today it may also be heard in one-word sentences with the meaning 'nothing' and is perceived as a southern rural influence.

MORPHOLOGY 99

(1) [A14], Elicited
əbnādəm kūn mā yčaddəb.
one must NEG lie.IPFV.3SG.M
'One must not lie.'

4.1.7.2 *flān* 'Somebody'

(2) [Ḥ1; explaining what they used to do in the past when someone got married]
bāčər, mū maṭal ʕərs əflān?
tomorrow NEG like wedding someone
'For example, (if) tomorrow there is a wedding of someone [lit. "tomorrow, isn't there like a wedding of someone?"].'

4.1.7.3 *wāḥəd* (M), *waḥda* (F) 'Someone, Anyone, One'; with NEG 'No One, Nobody'

This indefinite may optionally be used with the indefinite *kəll* 'all', yielding *kəll wāḥəd* 'everyone', or with the indefinite article *farəd* (< OA *fardᵘⁿ* 'single, individual', cf. Lane 1863: 2363 on CA "*fard* 'single; sole; only; one, and no more; ... a single, or and individual, person or thing'"), yielding *farəd wāḥəd* 'someone'. Cf. Salonen (1980: 77) on the use of this widespread indefinite pronoun in the dialect of al-Shirqat, Erwin (1963: 297) on Muslim Baghdadi Arabic, Mahdi (1985: 164) on Basra Arabic, and Meißner (1903: XVII) on the Arabic of Kwayriš/Babylon.

(3) [Ḥa1]
ʔəla wāḥəd ysawwī-l-a māy həwa
if someone make.IPFV.3SG.M-for-3SG.M water air
yǧəsm-a wīya yār-a, wīya xú.
share.IPFV.3SG.M-OBL.3SG.M with neighbor-3SG.M with brother.3SG.M
'If someone made himself *māy həwa* [lit. "air water", a very simple dish of red sauce without meat], he shared it with his neighbor, with his brother.'

(4) [A2], Elicited
ʔaku wāḥəd mən ʕad-kəm yəgdar
EXIST someone of at-2PL.M be_able_to.IPFV.3SG.M
ysāʕəd-ni?
help.IPFV.3SG.M-OBL.1SG
'Can anyone of you help me?'

(5) [A10]
ḥāṭṭ-l-a *wāḥəd* *ham yxədm-a.*
put.AP.SG.M-for-3SG.M someone also serve.IPFV.3SG.M-OBL.3SG.M
'He also had given him someone to serve him.'

(6) [A7]
wāḥəd *mā* *yʕarəf* *əṯ-ṯāni.*
someone NEG recognize.IPFV.3SG.M DEF-other
'One does not recognize the other.'

(7) [Ḥ1; telling us how they used to play and bathe in the river]
waḥda ġəslat *waḥda.*
one.F wash.PFV.3SG.F one.F
'One washed the other.'

(8) [A1]
lā *wāḥəd kān* *ytarǧəm-na.*
NEG one be.PFV.3SG.M translate.IPFV.3SG.M-OBL.1PL
'No one was translating for us.'

4.1.7.4 *Ɂaḥḥad* 'Somebody, Someone'; with NEG 'Nobody, No One, Not ... Anyone'

The use of this indefinite pronoun is widespread: it is found, for example, in the Arabic dialects of Basra (Mahdi 1985: 162), Muslim Baghdad (Erwin 1963: 296), al-Shirqat (Salonen 1980: 76), and Kwayriš/Babylon (Meißner 1903: XVII).

(9) [M1]
gaʕadət *tānēt* *Ɂaḥḥad* *ʕēn-i* *wāyəd əl*
sit.PFV.1SG wait.PFV.1SG someone dear-1SG a_lot REL
əyī-l-i.
come.IPFV.3SG.M-to-1SG
'I was waiting a long time [lit. "I sat and waited"] for someone to come for me.'

(10) [A10]
lamma əltəftat *mā šāfat* *Ɂaḥḥad Ḥamda.*
when turn_around.PFV.3SG.F NEG see.PFV.3SG.F someone Ḥamda
'As she turned around, Ḥamda didn't see anyone.'

MORPHOLOGY

101

4.1.7.5   *maḥḥad* 'Nobody, No One'

The indefinite pronoun *maḥḥad* is a compound of the negation particle *mā* and the indefinite pronoun *ʔaḥḥad* 'one'. The non-compound form is also attested, especially when in non-subject position, as example (10) above shows. Both forms are also used in, for example, the Arabic dialects of Basra (Mahdi 1985: 162–163), Muslim Baghdad (Erwin 1963: 296), and al-Shirqat (Salonen 1980: 76–77).

(11) [A10]
> **maḥḥad** mā   yədri   b-əl-āxar.
> nobody   NEG know.IPFV.3SG.M with-DEF-other
> 'No one recognized the other.'

4.1.7.6   *šay ~ šī* 'Something'; with NEG 'Nothing, Not Anything'

For this indefinite pronoun in Basra cf. Mahdi (1985: 163); in Muslim Baghdadi Arabic cf. Erwin (1963: 296); in al-Shirqat cf. Salonen (1980: 78); in Kwayriš/ Babylon cf. Meißner (1903: XVII). It may be used with the indefinite *kəll* 'all', yielding *kəllšī ~ kəllšay* 'everything' (cf. below 4.1.7.7), and the indefinite article *farəd*, yielding *farəd šī* 'something'.

(12) [A10]
> **šī**   xafīf, b-əl   — mət̲əl yḥabbūn   rōba   w   ʕēš.
> something light in-DEF   like   love.IPFV.3PL.M yoghurt and bread
> '(They eat) something light [for breakfast], with—for example, they like yoghurt and bread.'

(13) [A14], Elicited
> ʔaku **šī**   mət̲əl ər-rōba   yāklūn-ha
> EXIST something like   DEF-yoghurt eat.IPFV.3PL.M-OBL.3SG.F
> b-ər-rəyūg.
> with-DEF-breakfast
> 'There is something like yoghurt, that they eat for breakfast.'

šay ~ šī can be the head of a relative clause, as in:

(14) [A1]
> **šay**   əlli ʕad-na hənāka ...
> thing REL at-1PL there
> 'Something that we have there, (is) ...'

102   CHAPTER 4

(15) [A14], Elicited
    mā   sawwēt   šī ~ šay.
    NEG do.PFV.1SG thing
    'I haven't done anything.'

šī may also be combined with the indefinite article *farəd*, in some cases even
in a negated clause:

(16) [M1]
    lā   dəktūr w   lā   farəd šī.
    NEG doctor and NEG INDEF thing
    'There are no doctors nor anything.'

4.1.7.7   *kəllšay ~ kəllšī* 'Everything'; with NEG 'Not ... Anything, Nothing'
Cf. Salonen (1980: 78) on this indefinite pronoun in al-Shirqat, Erwin (1963:
296–297) on Muslim Baghdadi Arabic, and Mahdi (1985: 164) on Basra Arabic.

(17) [A10, explaining why the pigeon in her story could talk]
    gabəl   kəllšī   yaḥči.
    in_former_times everything speak.IPFV.3SG.M
    'In former times everything could talk.'

(18) [A10]
    šadd   ʕala l-faras   w   məša,   ygūl
    grasp.PFV.3SG.M on   DEF-horse and walk.PFV.3SG.M say.IPFV.3SG.M
    rāḥ   ḥammal   kəllšay   alli ahəwa ḷḷa
    go.PFV.3SG.M carry.PFV.3SG.M everything REL 3SG.M God
    xālġ-a,   ʕala l-faras,   mən daryāt axyūṭ, mən
    create.AP.SG.M-OBL.3SG.M on   DEF-horse from spools threads from
    kəllšay.
    everything
    'He took the horse and left; he took everything he found [lit. "that God has
    created"], on the horse, spools, everything.'

As in the following example, *kəllšī* 'everything' also commonly precedes a
negated verbal phrase to emphasize the negation of the verb (cf. Bar-Moshe
2019: 217 on an example of the same construction in Jewish Baghdadi; and
Erwin 1963: 297 on Muslim Baghdadi Arabic).

MORPHOLOGY 103

(19) [Ḥ1]
əl-ʕarūs **kəllši** *mā nsawwī-l-hən.*
DEF-bride everything NEG do.IPFV.1PL-to-3PL.F
'The bride(s), we didn't do anything with them [no henna, etc.] ~ we did nothing with them.'

4.1.7.8 *kəllman* 'Each (One), Everyone'
Cf. Salonen (1980: 75) on *kull man ~ kull min* 'everybody who' in al-Shirqat Arabic, Erwin (1963: 297) on *kull-man* 'everyone, each' in Muslim Baghdadi Arabic, and Holes (2016: 97) on *kilmin* 'everyone (who)' in the sedentary-type dialects of Bahrain.

(20) [M1]
kəllman *xaḏa* *flūs-a* *w-rāḥ.*
everyone take.PFV.3SG.M money-3SG.M and-go.PFV.3SG.M
'Each one took his money and left.'

(21) [A14], Elicited
kəllman *yədfaʕ* *əḥsāb-a.*
everyone pay.IPFV.3SG.M bill-3SG.M
'Everyone pays his (own) bill.'

4.1.7.9 *hīč* 'Nothing, Not Anything'
The indefinite *hīč* 'nothing' is borrowed from Persian *hīč* which has the same meaning.
hīč either occurs either in combination with a negated phrase, as in (22), or as a one-word-sentence, as in (23). The same construction is, for example, known for the Arabic dialect of the Çukurova in southern Turkey, where it was probably borrowed from Tur. *hiç* which has the same meaning (cf. WAD IV: map 469b).

(22) [A14], Elicited
hīč *mā šəfət.*
nothing NEG see.PFV.1SG
'I haven't seen anything.'

(23) [A14], Elicited
š-sawwēt? — **hīč.**
what-do.PFV.2SG.M nothing
'What have you done?—Nothing.'

104 CHAPTER 4

4.1.8 *Partitives*

4.1.8.1 *šī* 'Some'

KhA *šī* < OA *šayʔ^{un}* '(some)thing' functions as an existential partitive with the meaning '(there is) one (, who/that); (there are) some (, who/that)'. *šī* is similarly used as an existential marker with the meaning 'there is' in the Bedouin-type Šāwi dialects of the Harran-Urfa region in Turkey, as well as in Arabic dialects of South Arabia, the Gulf, Oman, and Yemen (Procházka 2018c: 279, fn. 59; Johnstone 1967: 170). The negated form of the existential marker *šī*, as found in the aforementioned dialects, is *māməš* (< *mā min šayʔ* 'there is nothing'), which is widespread in South Iraqi and the Gulf dialects (Procházka 2018c: 279). *māməš* is also used as a negative existential marker in KhA (cf. *māməš* in 4.8.1.6), as well as its variant *māmən* (cf. 4.8.1.7), in which the last element of the original phrase *mā min šayʔ* was deleted (Procházka 2018c: 279).

(1) [Ḥ1]
šī   mən-həm šī   mgaffla w   šī   baʕad-hi,   əd-dəkākīn
some of-3PL.M some closed.F and some not_yet-3SG.F DEF-shops
əs-sūg.
DEF-market
'Some [stores] are (already) locked and some not yet, the shops of the market.'

(2) [A6]
əl-hən   asmāʔ, šī   ʔəsəm-ha   barša, w   šī   ʔəsəm-ha
to-3PL.F names some name-3SG.F *barša* and some name-3SG.F
ġarra, w   šī   ʔəsəm-ha   ʕašma, w   šī   ʔəsəm-ha   dərʕa
ġarra and some name-3SG.F *ʕašma* and some name-3SG.F *dərʕa*
— əl-asmāʔ   čəṯīr.
    DEF-names many
'They have [many different] names: there are some who are called *barša*; there are some who are called *ġarra*; there are some who are called *ʕašma*; there are some who are called *dərʕa*—there are a lot of names.'

(3) [X1]
šī   bī-na   ṭābəg əṣ-ṣəbəḥ.
some among-1PL *ṭābəg* DEF-morning
'Among us are some who (eat) *ṭābəg* [typical dish of fish baked inside a bread] in the morning.'

MORPHOLOGY   105

4.1.8.2   *bī*-PRO 'There Are Some (among Them) That/Who, Some of Them'
bī-PRO 'there are some (among them) that/who, some of them' appears to be
elliptic for *ʔaku bī*-PRO 'there are (some) among (them)'.

(4)   [A6]
      bī-ha   *mā   twallad.*
      among-3SG.F NEG give_birth.IPFV.3SG.F
      'There are some that don't give birth.'

(5)   [A6]
      bī-ha   *yaʕni ydawwər*   *ʕala l-lōn*   *əl-aswad.*
      among-3SG.F DP   look_for.IPFV.3SG.M for   DEF-color DEF-black
      'There are some (people) who look for a black color [regarding sheep
      wool].'

(6)   [A19]
      bī-həm   *ydəggūn-a*   *'fence', bī-həm*
      among-3PL.M hit.IPFV.3PL.M-OBL.3SG.M fence   among-3PL.M
      ydəggūn-a   ᴾ*sīm xārdār*ᴾ.16
      hit.IPFV.3PL.M-OBL.3SG.M barbed_wire_fence
      'There are some (who) put up a fence, there are some (who) put up a
      barbed-wire fence.'

4.1.8.3   *wāḥəd mən*, F *waḥda mən* 'One of'

(7)   [M1]
      wāḥəd mən xəwān ...
      one   of   brothers
      'One of (the) brothers ...'

(8)   [Ḥ2]
      waḥda mn-ən-nəswān bāyra,   bāyra.17
      one   of-DEF-women unloved.F unloved.F
      'One of the [sultan's seven] wives was unloved, unloved.'

---

16   < Pers. *sīm-e xār-dār* 'barbed-wire fence'.
17   Cf. WB (47): "*bāyir* 'waste, uncultivated, unused, unwanted'" and "*bāyra* 'an old maid; a
      woman whose husband has married a second wife'".

106   CHAPTER 4

4.1.9 *Relative Pronoun* ʔəlli, ʔəl

Among some educated speakers *ʔalladi* might be heard, but this form appears to be a loan from MSA. The dialectal (and most common) forms of the relative pronoun are *ʔəlli* and *ʔəl*. The origin of the latter, i.e. the relative pronoun *ʔəl*, most likely goes back to the definite article (see Stokes 2018: 145 and the references given there). Stokes (2018: 143) convincingly traces the origin of *ʔəlli* back to a form **ʔallay*, which itself is a combination of the definite article *al* and the demonstrative **ʔulay*, which according to Rabin has already been used as a relative in Proto-Arabic.[18]

Similar forms are found in Iraqi Arabi dialects, cf. *elladi, elli*, and *el* in Kwayriš/Babylon Arabic (Meißner 1903: XVI), *ʔälli/ʔelli/ʔilli* and *ʔäl/ʔel* in al-Shirqat (Salonen 1980: 73–75), *ʔilli/lli* in Basra Arabic (Mahdi 1985: 256–257), *l* and *illi* in Baghdad Arabic (Blanc 1964: 120), and *illi* in the Arabic dialects of Bahrain and Kuwait (see Stokes 2018: 128–129 and the references given there).

The final *-l* in the form *ʔəl* usually assimilates to a following alveolar or palato-alveolar consonant, i.e. *t, ṯ, ṭ, d, ḏ, ḍ, s, ṣ, š, z, ẓ, ǧ, ž, č, l, n, r* (cf. 3.1.3 and 4.9.6.1 on the same assimilation process regarding the definite article).

(1) [A18]
    hāy   əl-bənt   ət   təḥāčī-č   mā-hīya   īrānīya.
    DEM DEF-girl REL talk_to.IPFV.3SG.F-OBL.2SG.F NEG-3SG.F Iranian.F
    'This girl, who is talking with you, she is not Iranian.'

The form *ʔəl* (plus assimilated variants) appears 99 times in my corpus. *ʔəlli* appears about half as often, 46 times, and was mostly used by speaker [A1], who uses a somewhat more educated register.

4.1.9.1 Relative Clause with a Definite Head Noun

The most common form of syndetic relative clauses in KhA is that with a definite head noun preceding the relative pronoun. However, relative clauses with indefinite heads are also frequent in KhA (cf. below).

---

18   Cf. also Huehnergard and Pat-El (2018) for a discussion on the origin of the Semitic relative marker.

MORPHOLOGY 107

(2) [A1]
w-ġəsəm mən əš-šaʕb   əl-ʕarab   əl-ʔaḥwāzi   ʔəlli ʕāyšīn
and-part of   DEF-people DEF-Arab DEF-Ahvazi REL live.AP.PL.M
b-əl-əḤwēza ...
in-DEF-Hoveyzeh
'A group of the Arab people of Ahvaz, who live in Hoveyzeh ...'

4.1.9.2   Relative Clause with an Indefinite Head Noun
As already said above, relative constructions in which the relative pronoun
follows an indefinite noun are quite frequent in KhA—elsewhere this phenomenon is rare (for an overview see Brustad 2000: 91–99). Its frequent use
in KhA might be a consequence of the dialect's peripheral status and the lack
of influence from MSA.

(3) [A10]
šay   əlli fakkr-a,   mū əhya
thing REL think.PFV.3SG.M-OBL.3SG.M NEG 3SG.F
təfakkr-a.
think.IPFV.3SG.F-OBL.3SG.M
'What [lit. "thing, which"] he thought wasn't what she thought.'

(4) [A1]
l-maḥal   sənt   əlli əd-dənya   mā təmṭar.
DEF-*maḥal* year.CS REL DEF-world NEG rain.IPFV.3SG.F
'*maḥal* (is) a year in which it doesn't rain.'

(5) [A12]
ʕand-i bənt   ʕamm əlli məṭəl mā šāfat   əl-ʕēn.
at-1SG daughter uncle REL like   NEG see.PFV.3SG.F DEF-eye
'I marry [lit. "I have"] my cousin [lit. "paternal uncle's daughter"] who is
stunningly beautiful [lit. "as the eye hasn't seen before"].'

(6) [A10]
yāhu   əl   əmḥāčī-k?
who.SG.M REL talk_to.AP.SG.M-OBL.2SG.M
'Who is (the person) that has talked to you?'

In the following example, the indefinite pronoun *kəllšay* 'everything' (cf. 4.1.7.7)
is the head of the relative clause:

108   CHAPTER 4

(7)   [A10]
      šadd   *ʕala l-faras*   *w*   *məša,*   *ygūl*
      grasp.PFV.3SG.M on   DEF-horse and walk.PFV.3SG.M say.IPFV.3SG.M
      rāḥ   *ḥammal*   *kəllšay*   *alli* *əhəwa ḷḷa*
      go.PFV.3SG.M carry.PFV.3SG.M everything REL 3SG.M God
      xālǧ-a,   *ʕala l-faras,*   *mən daryāt əxyūṭ,*   *mən*
      create.AP.SG.M-OBL.3SG.M on   DEF-horse from spools threads from
      kəllšay.
      everything
      'He took the horse and left; he took everything he found [lit. "that God has
      created"], on the horse, spools, everything.'

4.1.9.3   Non-attributive Relative Clauses
These are relative clauses without a referent or head noun. In my corpus, such
relative clauses are introduced by *əl*.

(8)   [A6]
      əl   *mā* *tawlad*   *əl-hassa*   *ngəl-ha*
      REL NEG give_birth.IPFV.3SG.F until-now call.IPFV.1PL-OBL.3SG.F
      daǧīǧa.
      young_ewe
      'The one that has not yet given birth, we call it *daǧīǧa*.'

(9)   [A4]
      əl   *aktar yḥəbbūn-ha*   *ən-nās*   *b-rās-ak*
      REL most love.IPFV.3PL.M-OBL.3SG.F DEF-people in-head-2M.SG
      ətfakkər,   *yāhi?*
      think.IPFV.2SG.M which.SG.F
      'The one [city] that the people like most, in your opinion, (what do) you
      think, which one (is it)?'

4.1.10   *Reflexive Pronoun* rūḥ-*PRO '... Self' PL* rwāḥ-*PRO '... Selves'*
As in many other dialects, the reflexive pronoun is expressed via the substantive *rūḥ* lit. 'soul', PL *rwāḥ*, to which an enclitic pronoun is attached.

(1)   [A14], elicited
      ʔašūf   *rūḥ-i*   *b-əl-məšūfa.*
      see.IPFV.1SG self-1SG in-DEF-mirror
      'I see myself in the mirror.'

MORPHOLOGY

(2) [A14], elicited
ʔənšūf **rwāḥ-na** *b-əl-məšūfa.*
see.IPFV.1PL selves-1PL in-DEF-mirror
'We see ourselves in the mirror.'

(3) [A14], Elicited
təḥči *wīya rūḥ-ha.*
speak.IPFV.3SG.F with self-3SG.F
'She talks to herself.'

4.1.11 *Interrogative Pronouns*
Though KhA shares similar forms of interrogative pronouns expressing 'what?'
and 'which?' with the neighboring dialects of Iraq, its forms for 'who?' are different.

4.1.11.1 *š- ~ ʔəš-* 'What?'
The Arabic dialects of al-Shirqat, Hilla (Salonen 1980: 72–73), Basra (Mahdi 1985: 158), Kwayriš/Babylon (Meißner 1903: XV–XVI), and Muslim Baghdadi Arabic (Erwin 1963: 293) all use the same or similar forms of this interrogative. The forms used in Khorasan (*ēš*) and Central Asian Arabic (*ēš, eyš, īš, iš šay, iš-, yēš*) differ from those of KhA mostly in the vowels (Seeger 2013: 314). The form closest to KhA is *iš-*, which is documented for Afghanistan (Seeger 2013: 314).

The interrogative *š- ~ ʔəš-* 'what?' is mainly used in object function, i.e. to ask for the argument of a verb.

(1) [A4]
š-ətsawwūn *bī-ha?*
what-do.IPFV.2PL.M with-3SG.F
'What do you do with it?'

It may however also be used with the genitive exponent *māl* (cf. 4.6 below), with the existence particle *ʔaku*, or with a noun.

(2) [A18]
š-əsm *əl-ləʕēbi?*
what-name DEF-game
'What's the name of the game?'

In combination with a noun, *š-* can also have an exclamatory sense, similar to the English 'how ...!' (cf. Holes 2016: 93 on Bahraini Arabic).

110   CHAPTER 4

(3)   [Ḥa1, talking about her tattoos]
      ča   aš-ḥalā-hən   haḏanni yaʔ[19]!
      DP   what-beauty-3PL.F DEM   DP
      '(Don't you) see, how beautiful these are [lit. "how their beauty is"]!'

The combination of the interrogative pronoun ʔaš- 'what?' with the relative particle mā yields the subordinating conjunction ʔaš-mā 'whatever' (cf. 4.7.2.35).

4.1.11.2   šənhu, F šənhi (mən) 'What? What Kind of?'
The same forms—i.e. a base šən- with the suffixed short forms of the personal
pronouns—are found in al-Shirqat Arabic (Salonen 1980: 71), and Bedouin-type
Bahraini Arabic (Holes 2016: 93). Basra (Mahdi 1985: 157) and Muslim Baghdadi
Arabic (Erwin 1963: 293) use a similar form, šinu 'what?'.
    šənhu is mainly used in one-word questions and with nouns. In some cases
it may also be used in verbal sentences, for which, however, š- is normally preferred.

(4)   [A19]
      šənhu?
      what.SG.M
      'What [here: "what else can I do?"]?'

(5)   [A17]
      šənhu   hāḏ?
      what.SG.M DEM
      'What is this?'

(6)   [A4]
      nəfs əs-saʕfa   lō l-xūṣa   lō šənhi?
      self DEF-palm_frond.SGT or DEF-palm_leaves or what.SG.F
      'The palm frond itself or the (palm) leaves or what?'

(7)   [A18]
      ʔanti ḏāk əl-wakət **šənhi**   čānat   məhənt-əč?
      2SG.F DEM DEF-time what.SG.F be.PFV.3SG.F profession-2SG.F
      'What was your profession during that time?'

─────────

19   The particle yaʔ in this context expresses approximately 'What do you think?! Of course,
      they were simply stunning!'.

MORPHOLOGY 111

In combination with the preposition *mən* 'from, of', it usually means 'what kind of?'

(8)   [A4]
      šənhi   ***mən*** *səmač*   *əhnā aktar hənā yənṣād,*
      what.SG.F of   fish.COLL here most here be_fished.IPFV.3SG.M
      yā   *nōʕ?*
      which type
      'What kind of fish is mainly caught here, what type?'

With verbs in the past, *šənhu / šənhi* is often preferred over *š-*.

(9)   [A4]
      wāld-əč,   ***šənhi***   *čān*   *ydāwəm?*
      father-2SG.F what.SG.F be.PFV.3SG.M work.IPFV.3SG.M
      'Your father, what work did he do?'

šənhu is frequently used in the phrase *mā ʔadri šənhu* or *māʔadri šənhi* 'I don't know what', which in rapid speech is often condensed to *mā-šənhu* and *mā-šənhi*, respectively.

(10) [Ḥaı, answering the question what they gave women, who have just given birth, to eat]
      həwa hāda əl-ḥarūrāt   *maṯal fəlfəl,*   ***mā-šənhi.***
      3SG.M DEM DEF-warm_things like   pepper NEG-what.SG.F
      'This is it [what she said before], like warm things: pepper (and) whatnot [lit. "I don't know"].'

In some cases, the base *šən-* is also combined with the full form of the personal pronoun *həwa* or *hīya*, as in the next example:

(11) [A10]
      šənhəwa   *trīd ...?*
      what.SG.M want.IPFV.2SG.M
      'What is it that you want?'

4.1.11.3   *yā* + SG Noun 'Which?'
The attributively used interrogative pronoun *yā* is invariable. In al-Shirqat Arabic, the form *hayy* (invariable) 'which? what?' (Salonen 1980: 71) is found; for Basra Arabic both forms, *ayy* and *yā*, are attested (Mahdi 1985: 160–161).

112   CHAPTER 4

(12) [A4]
ʔənti yā   bəlda ʔəl-əč   wāyəd ʕazīza?
2SG.F which city   to-2SG.F a_lot   dear.F
'Which city (of Khuzestan) do you like a lot [he means "most"]?'

(13) [A4]
yā   ṣaff təġra   dərəs? yā   glāṣ tədrəs?
which class study.IPFV.2SG.M lesson which class study.IPFV.2SG.M
'In which grade are you? In which grade do you study?'

4.1.11.4   M *yāhu ~ yāhaw,* F *yāhi,* PL.M *yāhəm,* PL.F *yāhən* 'Who? Which?'
KhA has no separate lexemes for 'who?' and 'which?' in subject position: both
are expressed by *yā-* followed by the shortened forms of the 3rd person pronouns.

The interrogative base that expresses 'who?' is used with the enclitic short
forms of the personal pronouns in several other dialects of the region, too, but
with a different base (*min*) than that of KhA (*yā*). The Arabic dialect of Basra
(Mahdi 1985: 157) and Muslim Baghdadi Arabic (Erwin 1963: 292) have *minu*;
al-Shirqat Arabic (Salonen 1980: 71–72) uses *minhu/min/mīn*. The dialects of
Kwayriš/Babylon (Meißner 1903: XV), Hilla and Nasiriya (cf. Salonen 1980: 72),
and those of Bahrain (Holes 2016: 93) all use a base *min-* before attaching the
enclitic pronouns.

Basra (Mahdi 1985: 160–161) as well as Muslim Baghdadi Arabic (Erwin 1963:
295) also have *yāhu* for 'which?'. Al-Shirqat Arabic, however, uses the suffixed short forms of the personal pronouns attached to a base *ʔay-* (Salonen
1980: 71). Kwayriš Arabic knows both base forms, *ay-* and *yā-* (Meißner 1903:
XVI).

KhA *yāhu* 'who? which?' can be used in one-word questions, as the head of
a relative clause, or as the subject of verbal as well as of nominal sentences.
The enclitic pronoun usually agrees in gender and number with the item asked
about.

(14) [A12]
yāhu?   — *Fēḍal.*
who.SG.M   Fayḍal
'Who?—Fayḍal.'

MORPHOLOGY 113

(15) [A4]
əl aktar yḥəbbūn-ha   *ən-nās*   *b-rās-ak*
REL most love.IPFV.3PL.M-OBL.3SG.F DEF-people in-head-2M.SG
ətfakkər,   *yāhi?*
think.IPFV.2SG.M which.SG.F
'The one [city] that the people like most [of all cities in Khuzestan], in your opinion, (what do) you think, which one (is it)?'

(16) [A10]
yāhu   *əl*   *əmḥāči-k?*
who.SG.M REL talk_to.AP.SG.M-OBL.2SG.M
'Who is (the person) that has talked to you?'

(17) [A14], Elicited
yāhi   *mən əs-səyāyīr?*
which.SG.F of DEF-cars
'Which one of the cars?'

4.1.11.5   *-man* 'Who? Whom? Whose? (Which?)'
The enclitic interrogative *-man* may be attached to verbs, prepositions, nouns, the genitive exponent *māl*, and the pseudoverb *ʔəl-* 'belong to' (cf. 4.11.14.2). Hence, it is obligatory in all non-subject positions.

Cf. Mahdi (1985: 157–158) on this enclitic interrogative in Basra Arabic, Erwin (1963: 292) on Muslim Baghdadi Arabic, and Meißner (1903: XV) on Kwayriš/ Babylon Arabic.

(18) [A14], Elicited
*šəftī-**man**?*
see.PFV.2SG.F-who
'Whom did you (SG.F) see?'

(19) [A14], Elicited
*hāy sayyārat-**man**?*
DEM car.CS-who
'Whose car is this?'

(20) [A15]
ča l-baṭṭa   *mālat-**man**?*
DP DEF-duck GL.SG.F-who
'Say, whose duck is that?'

114   CHAPTER 4

(21) [A14], Elicited
     *mā ʔadri   ʔəl-**man** hāy   əs-sayyāra.*
     NEG know.IPFV.1SG to-who   DEM DEF-car
     'I don't know to whom this car belongs.'

(22) [A14], Elicited
     *xaḏēt-**man**?*
     take.PFV.2SG.M-who
     'Whom did you marry?'

Note also the use of -*man* in the following question:

(23) [A2]
     *əlḥadd-**man**?*
     until-which
     'Until where [lit. "to which frontier/limit"]?'

4.2   Quantifiers

Contrary to what is often stated in traditional grammars, quantifiers represent
a separate category and are not related to indefinite pronouns (Haspelmath
1997: 11–12), though formally some quantifiers are similar to some indefinite
pronouns—compare, for example the quantifier *kəll* 'every' and the indefinite
pronoun *kəll šī* 'everything'.

4.2.1   čam + SG 'Some, Several'

(1) [A12]
     *baʕad **čam** səna*
     after   some year
     'after some years'

(2) [A19]
     *ʔagaṣṣī-l-əč   **čam** waḥda ...*
     cut.IPFV.1SG-for-2SG.F some one.F
     'I (will) cut you some [viz., *məkānīs* 'brooms', SG *məknāsa*] ...'

MORPHOLOGY   115

4.2.2   šwayy ~ šwayyūn *Some, a Little*

(3)   [F1]
      šwayy   maləḥ
      some   salt
      'some salt'

(4)   [A16]
      šwayyūn maləḥa   ham əṭḥaṭṭūn   əntəm?
      a_little   salt.SGT also   put.IPFV.2PL.M 2PL.M
      'Do you also add a little bit of salt [to your coffee]?'

4.2.3   kəll-*PRO* *'All'*

kəll- + a suffixed pronoun usually follows a definite subject. Cf. Erwin (1963: 358)
on this construction in Muslim Baghdadi Arabic.

(5)   [M1]
      əẓḏād-i   kəll-həm   ʕarab.
      ancestors-1SG all-3PL.M Arabs
      'My ancestors are all Arabs.'

(6)   [A9]
      māy   kārūn marraḍ   hāḏ ən-naxīl   kəll-a.
      water Karun sicken.PFV.3SG.M DEM DEF-palms all-3SG.M
      'The water from the Karun river makes all these palms ill.'

4.2.4   kəll + *Noun 'Every, Each; All, the Whole'*

Before an indefinite SG noun, *kəll* means 'every, each' (cf. Erwin 1963: 358 on this
construction in Muslim Baghdadi Arabic):

(7)   [A9]
      kəll   səna
      every year
      'every year'

Before a definite SG or PL noun, it means 'all, the whole' (cf. Erwin 1963: 358 on
Muslim Baghdadi Arabic):

116 CHAPTER 4

(8) [A12]
kəll əxwān-a
all   brothers-3SG.M
'all his brothers'

4.2.5 *čəṯīr* (*mən*) '*Many* (*of*)'

(9) [A14], Elicited
čəṯīr   mən-həm   ydāwmūn   b-šarəkat   ən-nafəṭ.
many   of-3PL.M   work.IPFV.3PL.M   in-company.CS   DEF-oil
'Many of them work in the oil company.'

4.3   Adverbs

Adverbs are a separate lexical category or word class on their own. Since they often do not—and in the case of KhA never—have clear morphological markers of category membership, they are usually defined by their syntactic function as adverbials, i.e. as verbal or sentential modifiers. Like prepositions, they are uninflected; unlike prepositions, they have a phrasal status (Maienborn and Schäfer 2019: 479–480).

A number of KhA adverbs are shared with CA and many other modern dialects of Arabic: e.g. *əl-lēla* 'tonight'; *əl-yōm* 'today'; *əl-ʕaṣər* 'in the late afternoon'; and *fōg* 'above, up'. Some KhA adverbs are also heard in all Iraqi dialects, such as *hassa* 'now'[20] and *farəd marra* (cf. Erwin 1963: 357 on Muslim Baghdadi Arabic). Two typical south-Mesopotamian *gələt*-features, outside Khuzestan only documented for Basra, are *ǧədd* 'straight ahead' (Mahdi 1985: 181;cf. WAD IV: map 455a) and *harfi* 'early' (Mahdi 1985: 183;cf. WAD IV: map 463).[21] Some KhA adverbs are typical of many Iraqi and Gulf (and sometimes also Central Asian) Arabic dialects, e.g. *kalləš* 'very, totally';[22] *ḥadər* 'below,

---

20   Outside Mesopotamia, cognate forms of *hassa* are also used in e.g. Sudan, Chad, Nigeria, Uganda, Kenya, Afghanistan, and Uzbekistan (WAD IV: map 461a).

21   Cf. Holes (2016: 13)on this lexeme in Bahraini Arabic, where it has the meaning 'fresh, young (meat); early (crop)', and the related Akkadian lexeme *xurpū* 'early crop'; in Iraqi *harfi* means 'newborn, young' (WB: 479). In South Arabian, the root *ḫ-r-f* means 'autumn crop', 'year', 'lamb', see Beeston (1982:62), and http://sabaweb.uni-jena.de/Sabaweb/Suche/Suche.

22   Cf. WB (410) on Iraqi; Holes (2016: 101) on Bahraini; Holes (2007: 614) on Kuwaiti; and Holes (2008: 484) on Omani Arabic. In addition to Gulf and Iraqi Arabic, it is also used in Saudi Arabia/Naǧd (see WAD IV: map: 468a for an overview of its occurrences).

MORPHOLOGY

down'[23] (cf. 4.4.21 on the homophone preposition *ḥadər*); *ha-l-gadd* 'this much, this ...';[24] *baʕad* (optionally plus pronominal suffixes) 'still';[25] *tawwa* or *taw(w)-*PRO 'just now, a moment ago'.[26] Yet other KhA adverbs can be considered typical of (Eastern) Bedouin-type dialects or are at least shared with some other Bedouin-type dialects (also outside the Mesopotamian and Gulf area), e.g. *lēǧād* (and its cognate forms) '(over) there'[27] and its counterpart *lēyāy* (and its cognate forms) '(over) here', which appears to be less common (Qasim Hassan, pers. comm. 2020, however, confirmed its use for southern Iraq); *wāyəd* 'very, much, a lot';[28] *əl-ʕām* 'last year';[29] *bsaʕ* 'immediately, straightaway';[30] and *ḥēl* 'fast, in a loud voice; very'.[31] Finally, the use of some adverbs seem to be virtually limited to KhA or not documented (in the same use and meaning) for other dialects: *ʕalēman?* 'on what? for what? why?', *halbat* 'maybe, per-

---

23   Cf. Procházka (1993: 226–227 and the references cited there) on Central Arabia, Uzbekistan, and the Gulf littoral; Holes (2001: 104; 2016: 101) on the Gulf littoral; and Brockett (apud Klingler 2017: 122) on Oman/Khabura. Cf. WAD IV: map 457 for an overview of its occurrences, which in addition to the just-mentioned places include Basra, Jordan/Salṭ, and Saudi Arabia/Naǧd.

24   Cf. Bar-Moshe (2019: 31, fn. 5 and the references cited there) on the Jewish Baghdadi and the Muslim dialects of Mosul; and Holes (2016: 88) on Bahraini Arabic.

25   Cf. Rosenhouse (1984b: 51) on Bedouin dialects in N-Israel; Holes (2016: 100; and 2001: 46) on Bahraini Arabic, Johnstone (1967: 68) on Gulf Arabic; Erwin (1963: 311) on Muslim Baghdadi Arabic.

26   Cf. WB (61) on Iraqi, Qafisheh (1996: 128) and Holes (2016: 100) on Gulf Arabic.However, this adverb also exists in other Bedouin-type and urban dialects in the Maghreb, e.g. Tunis Arabic (Rosenhouse 1984b: 51 and the references mentioned there on *touwa* or *tau* expressing 'now').

27   Cf. Rosenhouse (1984b: 50, 112) on various Bedouin-type dialects; and Fischer and Jastrow (1980: 151), who called it a typical rural *gələt* feature; cf. Fischer (1959: 130–131) and Procházka (1993: 115) on cognate forms of both *lēǧād* and *lēyāy* in various eastern and western dialects of Arabic.

28   Cf. Jastrow (2007: 423) on S-Iraq; Holes (2007: 614) on Kuwait; Holes (2008: 484) on Oman and (2016: 101) on Bahrain; cf. WAD IV: map 467, which also mentions its occurrence in (eastern) Yemen, provides a general overview of its distribution, and states that this lexeme mainly occurs among Bedouin-type dialects. Cf. Lane (1863: 2925) on the related CA adjective *wāǧid* 'rich; possessing competence, or sufficiency; in no need; without wants, ...'.

29   Cf. Holes (2016: 311) on Bahraini Arabic; Rosenhouse (1984b: 112) on Bedouin dialects in N-Israel; and WB (330) on Iraqi Arabic. Yousuf AlBader, pers. comm. 2020, confirmed its use in Kuwaiti Arabic. Cf. WAD IV: map 465a for a general overview of its distribution.

30   Cf. Rosenhouse (1984b: 51, 112) on Bedouin-type dialects in N-Israel.

31   Cf. Rosenhouse (1984b: 51 and the references mentioned there) on Negev Arabic. Yousuf AlBader, pers. comm. 2020, confirmed its use in Kuwaiti Arabic.Cf. WAD IV: map 468b for a general overview of its distribution.

118 CHAPTER 4

haps, probably';[32] *nōba* 'once';[33] and the adverbial expressions *mənnā w ǧādi* 'soon' and *mən-*PRO *w hēč* 'shortly, very soon', which are to the best of my knowledge not documented for other dialects. Further, many spoken dialects of Arabic have no adverb that expresses 'again',[34] but rather express repeated actions with certain verbs:[35] thus, the KhA adverb *ərdūd* 'again', which not documented for the neighboring dialects of Iraq,[36] can be considered a rare feature.

Because adverbs are usually classified according to their lexical semantics (cf. Maienborn and Schäfer 2019: 481), the following sections are arranged in the three semantic categories: "adverbs of time", "adverbs of manner", and "adverbs of location". Within each category, demonstrative adverbs will generally be listed first.

This list of adverbs should represent all frequent-used items with examples of their usages, but does not claim to be complete.

4.3.1 *Adverbs of Time*
4.3.1.1 *hassa* 'Now'
The adverb *hassa* developed from a compound of the proclitic demonstrative *ha-* and the noun *s-sāʕa* 'hour, moment, instant' yielding *ha-s-sāʕa* 'this moment' (cf. Fischer 1959: 149; Lane 1863: 1467–1468 on CA *sāʕa* 'hour, a little while'; *fī sāʕatin* 'in a short time, in a moment'; and even *as-sāʕata* 'just now'; cf. 4.1.6.1.5 above).

(1) [A19]
   hassa *hāy* *əl-ʔaraḍ* — *xō* *gəlt-l-əč* *tawwa* — *hāy*
   now DEM DEF-land DP say.PFV.1SG-to-2SG.F just DEM
   əl-ʔaraḍ *həna* *kāḍḍīn-ha* *ʔāǧār.*
   DEF-land here take.AP.PL.M-OBL.3SG.F rent
   'Now this field—well, I have just told you—this field here, we rent it.'

---

32   In addition to KhA, this item is also documented for some dialects of Palestine, and Egypt, (WAD IV: map 470c).

33   (WB: 473) does not document this adverbial use of *nōba* for Iraqi Arabic but only its use as a noun meaning 'turn; time, instance' as also used in KhA. Qasim Ḥassan, pers. comm. 2020, however did confirm that in S-Iraqi *nōba* was used as a temporal adverb meaning 'once'. In Omani it has the meaning 'sometimes, also' (Holes 2008: 484) and in Bahraini it means 'time, occasion' (Holes 2001: 533).

34   I thank Prof. Stephan Procházka for drawing my attention to this point.

35   Bahraini Arabic, for example, uses the verb *radd*, cognate with the KhA adverb *ərdūd* 'again', to express a repeated action (Holes 2016: 316).

36   However, Qasim Hassan, pers. comm. 2020, states that it is also used in southern Iraq.

MORPHOLOGY 119

4.3.1.2 *əl-yōm* 'Today'

(2) [A14]
əl-yōm šəft Māǧəd b-əṣ-ṣədfa.
DEF-day see.PFV.1SG Majed with-DEF-chance
'Today I saw Majed accidentally.'

4.3.1.3 *ʔaməs* 'Yesterday'
Cf. CA *ʔams* 'yesterday, the day before the present day by one night; what is before that, a short time before' (Lane 1863: 99). Reflexes of *al-bāriḥa* are, in contrast to many other dialects of the Syro-Mesopotamian region (cf. WAD IV: map 459), not used to denote the (whole) preceding day, but only the last evening or night (cf. 4.3.1.6), a use which is already attested for CA (Lane 1863: 182–183).

(3) [A14], Elicited
ʔaməs rəḥna l-əs-sūg.
yesterday go.PFV.1PL to-DEF-market
'Yesterday we went to the market.'

4.3.1.4 *ʔawwal ʔaməs* 'the Day before Yesterday'
Cf. CA *ʔawwalu min ʔamsi* 'the day before yesterday'(Lane 1863: 99).

(4) [A14], Elicited
ʔawwal ʔaməs əyō-na xəṭṭār.
before yesterday come.PFV.3PL.M-OBL.1PL guests
'The day before yesterday we had guests.'

4.3.1.5 *əl-lēla* 'Tonight'

(5) [Ḥ1]
gālaw əl-lēla ʕarəs.
say.PFV.3PL.M DEF-night wedding
'They said (that) tonight there is a wedding.'

4.3.1.6 *əlbārḥa* 'Last Night'

(6) [A14], Elicited
əlbārḥa šəfna məsalsal b-ət-tələbzōn.
last_night see.PFV.1PL soap_opera in-DEF-television
'Last evening we were watching a soap opera on TV.'

120 CHAPTER 4

4.3.1.7 *bāčər* 'Tomorrow'

KhA *bāčər* is related to CA *bukra* 'the early morning' (Lane 1863: 241). This adverb (or a cognate form) is widespread, used from Libya, Egypt, and all countries (though not all dialects) of the Mashreq, and further documented for Nigeria, Chad, Sudan, South-Sudan, and Uganda (WAD IV: map 460).

(7) [Ḥ1]
bāčər,   *mū*   *maṭal*   *ʕərs*   *əflān?*
tomorrow NEG like   wedding someone
'For example, (if) tomorrow there is a wedding of someone [lit. "tomorrow, isn't there like a wedding of someone?"].'

4.3.1.8   *ʕəgəb bāčər* 'the Day after Tomorrow'

(8) [A14], Elicited
ʕəgəb bāčər   *ənrūḥ*   *əl-Kərbala.*
after tomorrow go.IPFV.1PL to-Kerbala
'The day after tomorrow we go to Kerbala.'

4.3.1.9   *hāy əs-səna, ha-s-səna, əs-səna* 'This Year'

(9) [A14], Elicited
ha-s-səna   *rāḥ ənšīl*   *ṣōb*   *əlḤamīdīya.*
DEM-DEF-year FUT move.IPFV.1PL towards Ḥamīdīya
'This year we will move to Ḥamīdīya.'

4.3.1.10   *əl-ʕām* 'Last Year'

(10) [A6]
əl-ʕadad   *māl-ha*   *ḥadd əl-ʕām*   *čānat*   *xaməs*
DEF-number GL.SG.M-3SG.F until DEF-year be.PFV.3SG.F five
mīya.
hundred
'Its [i.e. the sheep's] number was 500 until last year.'

4.3.1.11   *sənt əl-yāya, sənt əl-əxra, ʕām əl-yāy* 'Next Year'

(11) [A9]
sənt   *əl-yāya,*   *ənnaḍḍəf*   *hāḏ əl-karab.*
year.CS DEF-come.AP.SG.F clean.IPFV.1PL DEM DEF-nodules
'Next year, we clean these nodules [of the palm tree].'

MORPHOLOGY 121

4.3.1.12   *əṣ-ṣabəḥ* 'in the Morning'

(12) [A14], Elicited
    əṣ-ṣabəḥ   *nətrayyəg*   *ʕēš*   *w*   *ḥalīb.*
    DEF-morning eat_breakfast.IPFV.1PL bread and milk
    'In the morning we have bread and milk for breakfast.'

4.3.1.13   *ġəbša ~ ġabša* 'in the Early Morning, at Dawn'

(13) [Ḥ1]
    nəmši   *ġabša.*
    go.IPFV.1PL dawn
    'We go in the early morning.'

4.3.1.14   *əḍ-ḍaḥa* 'in the Late Morning'

(14) [A14], Elicited
    balkat əḍ-ḍaḥa   *təyī-l-na.*
    maybe DEF-late_morning come.IPFV.2SG.M-to-1PL
    'Maybe you (can) come (to visit) us in the late morning.'

4.3.1.15   *əḍ-ḍəhər* 'at Noon'

(15) [A14], Elicited
    ʔaxalləṣ   *mən əš-šaġəl*   *əḍ-ḍəhər.*
    finish.IPFV.1SG from DEF-work DEF-noon
    'I finish work at noon.'

4.3.1.16   *əl-ʕaṣər* 'in the Late Afternoon'

(16) [A14], Elicited
    šəft-a   *l-ʕaṣər.*
    see.PFV.1.SG-OBL.3SG.M DEF-late_afternoon
    'I saw him in the late afternoon.'

4.3.1.17   *b-əl-lēl* 'in the Evening, at Night'

(17) [A14], Elicited
    b-əl-lēl   *ašūf-ak.*
    in-DEF-night see.IPFV.1SG-OBL.2SG.M
    'I see you in the evening.'

4.3.1.18　*farəd wakət* 'Once, One Day'

(18) [M4]
    čān   farəd wakət baraka b-əš-šaṭṭ.
    be.PFV.3SG.M INDEF time   blessing in-DEF-river
    'Once there was blessing in the river.'

4.3.1.19　*farəd marra, farəd nōba* 'Once, One Time, Sometime'

(19) [A14], Elicited
    əlḥadd hassa farəd marra ṭalaʕt   mən īrān.
    until   now   INDEF time   go_out.PFV.1SG from Iran
    'Until now I have only once gone outside Iran.'

4.3.1.20　*mədda, farəd mədda* 'Some Time, a Certain Time'

(20) [A12]
    ḍallēna   mədda   b-əŠǧənnība.
    stay.PFV.1PL time_span in-Šǧənnība
    'We stayed for some time in *Šǧənnība*.'

(21) [A19]
    rəǧaʕət   l-əl-əkwēt   ḍallēt   ham farəd mədda,
    return.PFV.1SG to-DEF-Kuwait stay.PFV.1SG DP   INDEF time_span
    ən-nōb   baʕad, əyēt   baʕad   mā rəḥat.
    DEF-time then   come.PFV.1SG anymore NEG go.PFV.1SG
    'I came back to Kuwait, stayed (there) for some time, then came back and
    I didn't go (abroad) anymore.'

4.3.1.21　*ḏāk al-wakət* 'Then, during That Time'

(22) [Ḥa1]
    ʔasōləf   al-mā   ǧara   ʕala-y ḏāk al-wakət.
    tell.IPFV.1SG DEF-REL happen.PFV.3SG.M on-1SG DEM DEF-time
    'I tell what happened to me during that time.'

MORPHOLOGY 123

4.3.1.22 *ʔawwal ~ zamān əl-awwal* 'in the Old Days, in the Past, Formerly'

(23) [M1]
 ʔawwal čānat ə d-dənya ḥalu xāḷa, mū mətəl hassa.
 formerly be.PFV.3SG.F DEF-world beautiful aunt NEG like now
 'In the past everything was fine, not like today.'

4.3.1.23 *harfi* 'Early'

(24) [A1]
 *rəḥna **harfi** l-əl-mədərsa.*
 go.PFV.1PL early to-DEF-school
 'We went to school early.'

4.3.1.24 *baʕad* (+PRO) 'Still'

(25) [Ḥa1]
 *mən **baʕad** rayl-i ʕadal, mən zamān ḏāk əl-wakət, **baʕad***
 when still husband-1SG alive when time DEM DEF-time still
 əzləmt-i ʕadal.
 husband.CS-1SG alive
 'When my husband was still alive—at that time, when my man was still
 alive.'

With covert subjects, *baʕad* is always used with a shortened and partly phonologically adapted form of the independent pronoun (cf. 4.1.2.1).

(26) [A14], Elicited
 ***baʕad-hi** əttānī-k.*
 still-3SG.F wait.IPFV.3SG.F-OBL.2SG.M
 'She is still waiting for you.'

4.3.1.25 *baʕad* with NEG 'Not Yet'
baʕad with NEG is usually used with a shortened, enclitic form of the independent pronoun (cf. 4.1.2.1).

124　　　　　　　　　　　　　　　　　　　　　　　　　　　　CHAPTER 4

(27) [A6]
baʕad-hi *mā-hi*　　*wālda.*
still-3SG.F NEG-3SG.F give_birth.AP.SG.F
'She has not yet given birth.'

4.3.1.26　*baʕad* + NEG 'Not Anymore, No Longer'
Followed by a negated verb, but without a shortened, enclitic form of the independent pronoun, *baʕad* has the meaning 'not anymore, no longer':

(28) [M4]
bass *mən* *ṣār*　　　　*al-ḥarəb, ḍall*　　　　　*baʕad*
but　when　become.PFV.3SG.M　DEF-war remain.PFV.3SG.M anymore
mā *yədxəl*　　　　*ḥaməl* *b-əl-əmḥammra.*
NEG enter.IPFV.3SG.M charges in-DEF-Muḥammara
'But when the war began, charges were no longer shipped to Muḥammara.'

4.3.1.27　*ərdūd* 'Again'

(29) [A15]
ḥəblat　　　　　　　　　　*ərdūd?*
become_pregnant.PFV.3SG.F again
'Did she get pregnant again?'

4.3.1.28　*ǧərīb* 'Soon'

(30) [A6]
ǧərīb *təyīb*　　　　　　*tawlad.*
soon give_birth.IPFV.3SG.F give_birth.IPFV.3SG.F
'Soon she [i.e. the ewe] will give birth.'

4.3.1.29　*mənnā w ǧādi* 'Soon'

(31) [A12]
mənnā　　*w* *ǧādi*　　　*ywəldan.*
from_here and go.AP.SG.M give_birth.IPFV.3PL.F
'They [i.e. the ewes] will soon give birth.'

MORPHOLOGY   125

4.3.1.30   *mən*-PRO *w hēč* 'Shortly, Very Soon'

(32) [A6]
    mən-ha   **w**   **hēč**   *əl-ha*   *l-əl-əwlād.*
    from-3SG.F and DEM to-3SG.F to-DEF-children
    'She [i.e. the ewe] will give birth to the lambs soon.'

4.3.1.31   *bsaʕ* 'Immediately, Straightaway'
bsaʕ etymologically is a contraction of *bi-sāʕatin* or *bi-sāʕatihi* (cf. Lane 1863:
1468 on CA *fī sāʕatin* 'in a short time, in a moment', and *min sāʕatihi* 'at the
moment thereof, instantly').

(33) [X1]
    sawwēt-a   *ʕēš*   *ṭabəg* *ʕalamūd-mā* *yəgʕad*
    make.PFV.1SG-OBL.3SG.M bread *ṭābəg* for-REL   get_up.IPFV.3SG.M
    əz-zəlma w-yṣalli   *w*   *hāy, əbsaʕ*   *gəmət.*
    DEF-man and-pray.IPFV.3SG.M and DEM immediately get_up.PFV.1SG
    'I made him *ṭābəg* [typical dish of fish baked inside a bread], so (that it is
    ready) when my husband [lit. "the man"] gets up and prays and so forth:
    I got up immediately (to make him breakfast).'

(34) [A18] and [X1]
    d-dōša,   *əšgadd*   *yṭawwəl?*   — **bsaʕ.**
    DEF-fishing_net how_much last.IPFV.3SG.M   immediately
    'The *dōša* [a type of fishing net], how long does it take (to make one)?—
    (It is ready) immediately.'

4.3.1.32   *tawwa* 'Just, Just Now, a Moment Ago'

(35) [A14], Elicited
    tawwa   *yat.*
    just_now come.PFV.3SG.F
    'She has just come.'

4.3.1.33   *taww-* + PRO 'Just, Just Now, a Moment Ago'

(36) [A19]
    taww-na   *bazarēna.*
    just_now-1PL seed.PFV.1PL
    'We have just seeded (it).'

126　　　　　　　　　　　　　　　　　　　　　　　　　　　　　CHAPTER 4

4.3.1.34　*tāli* 'Then, Next'

This temporal adverb (< AP of OA *talā* 'to follow'; cf. MSA *bi-t-tāli* 'then') is often combined with the adverb *ən-nōb*, which also means 'then'.

(37) [A4]

    xō, ən-nōb,　sōlfi-l-na,　　　　　tāli　ṣār　　　　　　　　　zēn?

    DP DEF-time tell.IMP.SG.F-to-1PL then become.PFV.3SG.M good

    'Well; and then, tell us, did he then recover?'

4.3.1.35　*ən-nōb ~ ən-nōba* 'Then'

(38) [A1]

    w-ən-nōb　　　mən　baʕəd-mā yəbas,

    and-DEF-time when after-REL dry.PFV.3SG.M

    ygəṣṣūn-a　　　　　　　　w-ən-nōba　　ynaḍḍfūn-a

    cut.IPFV.3PL.M-OBL.3SG.M and-DEF-time clean.IPFV.3PL.M-OBL.3SG.M

    mən　əl-warag　w-ən-nōb　　yfəššgūn-a.

    from DEF-leaves and-DEF-time cut_in_halves.IPFV.3PL.M-OBL.3SG.M

    'And then, when it has dried, they cut it, and then remove the leaves, and then they cut it in two (halves).'

4.3.1.36　*nōba* 'Once'

(39) [A10]

    nōba, nōbtēn, ṭalāṯ ...

    once twice three

    'Once, twice, three times [she told the people that story] ...'

4.3.1.37　*nōbtēn* 'Twice'

(40) [A4] and [A12]

    čam　　　marra tnəšrīn　　　　　b-əl-yōm?　— nōbtēn, nōbtēn.

    how_many time　graze.IPFV.2SG.F in-DEF-day　twice　twice

    'How many times do you take (the sheep) to graze each day?—Twice, twice.'

MORPHOLOGY

4.3.1.38   *wāyəd* 'Often, a Lot, a Long Time'

(41) [M1]
*gaʕadət   tānēt   ʔaḥḥad   ʕēn-i   **wāyəd** əl*
sit.PFV.1SG wait.PFV.1SG someone dear-1SG a_lot   REL
əyī-l-i.
come.IPFV.3SG.M-to-1SG
'I was waiting a long time [lit. "I sat and waited"] for someone to come for me.'

(42) [A14], Elicited
wāyəd *ənrūḥ   ʕala š-šaṭṭ.*
often   go.IPFV.1PL on DEF-river
'We often go to (sit by) the river.'

4.3.1.39   *yōmīya* 'Daily, Every Day'

(43) [A10]
*ham əl-bəšət   yəntagg   rīḥa w **yōmīya** səbəḥ.*
also DEF-cloak be_hit.IPFV.3SG.M odor and daily   bath
'Also, the *bəšət* [a summer cloak] was perfumed and every day [the man was given] a bath.'

4.3.1.40   *marrāt, nōbāt* 'Sometimes'

(44) [F1]
*ʔabū-y   **marrāt**   ygūl   gabəl   čəntu*
father-1SG sometimes say.IPFV.3SG.M formerly be.PFV.2PL.M
tāklūn   māy həwa.
eat.IPFV.2PL.M water air
'My father sometimes says (that) you used to eat *māy həwa* [lit. "air water", a very simple dish of red sauce without meat].'

4.3.1.41   *dāyman* 'Always'

(45) [Ḥ1]
*waḷḷa   **dāyman** hēč   mā nəlbas.*
by_God always   like_this NEG dress.IPFV.1PL
'We really don't always dress like this.'

128 CHAPTER 4

4.3.1.42   *kəll wakət* 'All the Time, Always'

(46) [A19]
   kəll wakət hənā ʕala š-šəǧəl.
   all time here on DEF-work
   '(We are) always here at work.'

4.3.1.43   *yalla* 'Finally'[37]

(47) [A10]
   b-ət-tālta   dagg   ʕalī-ha   əl-bāb,
   with-DEF-third.F knock.PFV.3SG.M on-3SG.F DEF-door
   əftəhmat,   ət-tālta   **yalla** əftəhmat.
   understand.PFV.3SG.F DEF-third.F finally understand.PFV.3SG.F
   'The third time he knocked on her door [in the middle of the night], she
   understood, the third time she finally understood.'

(48) [A6]
   sāʕa b-əs-sabʕa   w   nəṣṣ ḥna b-ət-tamānīya **yalla**
   hour with-DEF-seven and half 1PL with-DEF-eight finally
   nəgʕad   mən ən-nōm.
   get_up.IPFV.1PL from DEF-sleep
   '(It is) half past seven (or) eight (when) we finally get up from sleep.'

4.3.2   *Adverbs of Manner*

The three manner adverbs *wāyəd* (4.3.2.16), *ḥēl* (4.3.2.17), and *kəlləš* (4.3.2.18), all
of which can be used as intensifiers with the meaning 'very', do not only modify verbal and sentential referents in line with the definition of adverbs given
above, but may also modify adjectives and even other adverbs, as in (35) below.
Like English adverbs such as *extremely* or *very*, these KhA adverbs therefore
represent an adverbial subclass (cf. Maienborn and Schäfer 2019: 480).

4.3.2.1   *hēč ~ hēči* 'Like This, This Way'

The KhA demonstrative adverb *hēč ~ hēči* is distinguished from the Muslim
Baghdadi Arabic form, *hīč ~ hīči* (Erwin 1963: 360–361; also used in many other

---

37   Cf. Ingham (1994: 127) on a similar meaning of this adverb in Najdi Arabic: "*yalla* Qualificatory 'just, barely' … in this use, it precedes a verb"; and Procházka (2012: 392–393)
on Moroccan Arabic: "*yallah* [transcription adapted] serves as a temporal adverb" and
denotes "only such brief intervals of time as 'this moment', 'just', 'immediately', 'as soon as'".

MORPHOLOGY   129

dialects of Iraq: cf. WAD IV: map 466), only by the quality of the long middle
vowel. *hēč ~ hēči* as well as *hīč ~ hīči* derive from the demonstrative **haykā* (Fischer 1959: 140; cf. WAD IV: map 466 on occurrences of this and cognate forms
in other dialects of Arabic; and Behnstedt 1993: 88–89).

hēč has also been considered an "adverb of manner" (cf. Owens 1993: 199,
who describes the Nigerian equivalent to KhA *hēč* as "deictic and manner morpheme"). Here, I will follow scholars such as Fischer (1959: 140) and Fischer and
Jastrow (1980: 151) in describing it as a demonstrative adverb.

Some scholars include the adverbs 'there' and 'here' among the "demonstrative adverbs" (for example, Fischer and Jastrow 1980: 151). In this study, however,
I classify them as "adverbs of location".

Functions

i.   Concrete Reference

When referring to a concrete element of an utterance, the adverb *hēč* most
often modifies a verb that describes a physical action or mental process such as
'thinking'. When modifying a verb that describes a physical action, the phrase
in which it is used is frequently accompanied by a gesture made by the speaker.
This was for example the case in (1), in which the speaker explained and
demonstrated to me how she used to swim in the river when she was a child.
As the examples below illustrate, *hēč* can precede or follow the verb it modifies.

(1)   [F1]
      *ʔarīd   afūy   **hēč**   afūy,   ʕal-īday-ya*
      want.IPFV.1SG swim.IPFV.1SG like_this swim.IPFV.1SG on-hands-1SG
      ***hēč**   afūy,   ʔarīd   afūy   ʕal-ṣaḥan*
      like_this swim.IPFV.1SG want.IPFV.1SG swim.IPFV.1SG on-side
      *gəfā-y[38] **hēč**   w-aġrəf   b-īday-ya   afūy,*
      back-1SG like_this and-paddle.IPFV.1SG on-hands-1SG swim.IPFV.1SG
      *ʔarīd   afūy   maṭal **hēč**   wādəm wīya əl-xōra*
      want.IPFV.1SG swim.IPFV.1SG like   like_this people with DEF-vortex
      mālt   əl-māy,   wāyəd aʕarəf   afūy.
      GL.SG.F DEF-water a_lot   know.IPFV.1SG swim.IPFV.1SG

---

38   Cf. CA *qafā* 'back'; the use of this lexeme is also attested for some Arabic dialects in Yemen,
      the Negev, Ghaza, and Lebanon/Baskinta (WAD I: 157).

130   CHAPTER 4

'(Whenever) I want to swim, like this I swim, with [lit. "on"] my arms I swim like this; I swim on the side of my back, and paddle like this with my arms, I swim like this; people make a vortex [i.e. they swam in circles to create a vortex in the water]. I can swim very well.'

(2)   [M4]
ʔaktar əl-marāčəb əl   tšūf-hən   *nāymāt   lō*
most   DEF-boats   REL   see.IPFV.2SG.M-OBL.3PL.F   sleep.AP.PL.F   or
ʕāyfīn-hən   *hēči.*
leave.AP.PL.M-OBL.3PL.F   like_this
'Most of the boats you see are asleep [i.e. not working], or they have left them like this.'

(3)   [M4]
mā   təgdər   *ətfakkər*   *hēči!*
NEG   be_able_to.IPFV.2SG.M   think.IPFV.2SG.M   like_this
'You can't think like that!'

In the next example, *hēči* is used similarly to the German 'so (etwa) ...' or the English 'about ..., ... or so'.

(4)   [A4] and [M1]
ʕəmr-əč?   — hēči,   sabʕīn   xamsīn sittīn ysawwi
age-2SG.F   like_this seventy fifty   sixty make.IPFV.3SG.M
ha-š-šəkəl.
DEM-DEF-type
'How old are you?—About 70, 50, 60, about this age.'

ii.   Discourse Particle

Cf. below, 4.8.5.7.

4.3.2.2   *bass* 'Only'
bass derives from Pers. *bas* 'many, more; very much; enough, sufficient; often; yes, certainly' (cf. Steingass 2001: 185).

(5)   [M3]
bass *ʔanta   mən   əl-ʕāyla   tdāwəm*   *b-əs-sūg?*
only   2SG.M   from   DEF-family   work.IPFV.2SG.M   at-DEF-market
'Of the family, only you work at the market?'

MORPHOLOGY   131

4.3.2.3   *b-waḥad-* + PRO 'Alone, On Somebody's Own'

(6) [M4]
     əb-waḥd-a
     with-alone-3SG.M
     'he alone, on his own'

(7) [A10]
     mən   ʕāf-ha   *w-məša*   *hīya*
     when leave.PFV.3SG.M-OBL.3SG.F and-go.PFV.3SG.M 3SG.F
     ḍallat   ***əb-waḥad-ha***.
     remain.PFV.3SG.F with-alone-3SG.F
     'When he had left her and had gone, she remained on her own/alone.'

4.3.2.4   *b-rūḥ-*PRO 'by … Self, Independently, Alone'

(8) [F1, jokingly asking me why I had not invited her when we cooked fish]
     mā   ʕazamtī-ni,   *xallēti*   *l-ḥaǧǧīya*
     NEG invite.PFV.2SG.F-OBL.1SG leave.PFV.2SG.F DEF-Ḥaǧǧīya
     tākəl   ***əb-rūḥ-ha***   *səmčāt, əš-māl-əč?*
     eat.IPFV.3SG.F with-self-3SG.F fishes   what-GL.SG.M-2SG.F
     'You did not invite me (and) let the Ḥaǧǧīya eat fish alone: What is wrong
     with you?'

4.3.2.5   *ham ~ hamma* 'Also, Too'
This adverb is originally Persian and used in many Mesopotamian but also Gulf
Arabic dialects (cf. Holes 2016: 36 on Bahraini; 2007: 614 on Kuwaiti; WB: 483
on Iraqi).
    Wherever *ham ~ hamma* refers to a verb, it is usually stressed.

(9) [A12]
     b-əš-šəta   ***ham*** *ənšīl.*
     in-DEF-winter also move.IPFV.1PL
     'We also move (to another place) in winter.'

In statements in which it refers to a noun, it usually comes after this noun and
does not attract stress (but rather the preceding noun is stressed).

132   CHAPTER 4

(10) [Ḥa1]

 ... əb-zamān-na la, baʕad məntəkrāt[39] **ham** ġalīlāt.
 in-time-1PL NEG still cars also few.PL.F
 '... in our times no, there were also less cars.'

In question it usually appears in initial position.

(11) [A4]

 ham ʕad-əč ʕamām b-əl-ʕərāg?
 also at-2SG.F relatives in-DEF-Iraq
 'Do you also have relatives in Iraq?'

ham ... ham ... means '(both) ... as well as ...'.

(12) [A6]

 taʕab **ham** b-əš-šəta w **ham** b-əl-gēḏ.
 exhaustion also in-DEF-winter and also in-DEF-summer
 'It [working as a shepherd] is exhausting in winter as well as in summer.'

4.3.2.6 *balkat* 'Maybe, Perhaps, Probably'

KhA *balkat* is most likely of Turkish origin (cf. Aksoy 1963: 620 on *belke, belkit, belkim, belkime,* and *belliki* 'maybe' in Eastern Turkish dialects; and Reinkowski 1998: 242 on Turkish loanwords in Baghdad-Arabic). Also, Holes (2016: 291, fn. 107) states that (sedentary-type) Bahraini and Iraqi Arabic *balki* and *balkat* were "probably borrowed from Turkish, though the ultimate origin is Persian" (Steingass 2001: 198 translates Persian *bal-ki* as 'but, however, perhaps; nay, no; still more; moreover; besides; rather, on the contrary').Malaika (1963: 35) also derives Baghdadi Arabic *belki* 'rather, maybe' from Turkish, as does Seeger (2009: 28) for Ramallah Arabic *balki, balkīš, balkin* 'maybe; possibly; probably'.[40]

---

39 *məntəkār ~ mətəkār* 'car' PL *məntəkrāt* < Engl. *motorcar*.

40 Cognate forms of this adverb are further found in, e.g. Negev Arabic (Shawarbah 2011: 377: *balki(n)* 'perhaps'). Cf. also Holes (2016: 291) on its occurrence in sedentary-type Bahraini and Iraqi Arabic. According to Yousuf AlBader, pers. comm. 2020, it is not used in present-day Kuwaiti Arabic; cf. WAD IV: map 470b for an overview of the occurrences of this adverb in a great number of Arabic dialects.

MORPHOLOGY 133

(13) [A16] and [X3] [Nādya (N) is telling Maryam's aunt (M) how they use to prepare coffee in Ahvaz]

N: *šwayyūn mələh ygūl* *ʕan* *əl-ḥalāl*
a_little salt say.IPFV.3SG.M from DEF-allowed
w-əl-ḥarām *əhnā lēǧād* *ysawwūn.*
and-DEF-forbidden 1PL over_there make.IPFV.3PL.M

M: **balkat** *ysawwūn-ha* *wāyəd ḥəlwa*
probably make.IPFV.3PL.M-OBL.3SG.F very good.F

N: '(With) a little salt—they say it is for the best [lit. 'for the allowed and the forbidden']—we over there [she means in Ahvaz, since we were in Xafaǧīya during the recording] prepare (the coffee).'
M: 'They probably make it very good.'

4.3.2.7 *məmkən ~ yəmkən* 'Maybe, Perhaps, Probably'
Both forms are used in the majority of all Arabic dialects (cf. WAD IV: map 470a).

(14) [M4]
hāḏ *əš-šaṭṭ* *ənta* *tšūf* *čān* *əb-zamān-a*
DEM DEF-river 2SG.M see.IPFV.2SG.M be.PFV.3SG.M at-time-3SG.M
čān *yəḥkəm,* *hassa* **məmkən** *āna mā* *čənət,*
be.PFV.3SG.M reign.IPFV.3SG.M now maybe 1SG NEG be.PFV.1SG
ʔabbahāt-na čānaw *ysōlfūn.*
fathers-1PL be.PFV.3PL.M tell.IPFV.3PL.M
'This river, you see, was in his time very strong [lit. "ruling"]; (that) maybe (was when) I was not (born yet)—our fathers used to tell (this).'

(15) [A9, talking about how air pollution affected the palms]
hassa tənzəl — *ətḍəbb* *al-ʕəṭəǧ*[41]
now go_down.IPFV.3SG.F throw.IPFV.3SG.F DEF-corymb
b-əl-gāʕ, *ytēḥ* *kəll-a* *trāb,* **yəmkən** *ytēḥ*
at-DEF-ground fall.IPFV.3SG.M all-3SG.M dust maybe fall.IPFV.3SG.M
kəll-a *trāb.*
all-3SG.M dust
'Now it [the palm tree] takes down—it throws the corymb [cluster of dates] to the ground, it all falls down like dust, it might all fall down like dust.'

---

41 Cf. CA √ʕdq: Lane (1863: 1988) *ʕidq* 'a raceme of a palm-tree, or of dates'.

134 CHAPTER 4

4.3.2.8 *halbat* 'Maybe, Perhaps, Probably'

The source of KhA *halbat* is probably Persian *al-batte* 'certainly, necessarily, in every manner, altogether' (Steingass 2001: 92: s.v. *al-batta*), or (Ottoman) Turkish: cf. *helbet* 'surely, definitely, doubtlessly' in Eastern Turkish dialects (Aksoy 1974: 2330) and Ottoman *elbet ~ elbette* 'certainly, decidedly, surely; in the end' (Devellioğlu 2006: 214). Comparing the meanings of Persian *al-batte* and Turkish *helbet, elbet ~ elbette* with the meanings of KhA *halbat*, we can see that a semantic attenuation from 'certainly' to 'maybe, perhaps, probably' must have occurred (cf. WAD IV: map 470c on the same semantic development in two other dialects, in which this form occurs: Egyptian and Palestinian).

(16) [M4]

nəyīb *ğahāl-na* *w* *nəgſad* *əhnā,* **halbat**
bring.IPFV.1PL children-1PL and sit.IPFV.1PL here maybe
ənkaḍḍ-əl-na *səmča.*
catch.IPFV.1PL-for-1PL fish.SGT
'We take our kids and sit here, and maybe we catch one fish.'

4.3.2.9 *xāf* 'Maybe'

This adverb is etymologically a grammaticalization of the 1SG IPFV form *ʔaxāf* 'I fear' (i.e. 'I fear, that' > 'maybe (it happens, that)', cf. WAD IV: map 470c). It is also used in some dialects of Oman and Yemen. In some other regions, e.g. Salṭ in Jordan, the Negev (Shawarbah 2011: 39), and Sinai, a similar form, viz. *xāfaḷḷa*, with a similar meaning is documented (WAD IV: map 470c).

(17) [A16]

xāf *əl-banāt* *yərdan* *nsāſəd-hən* *xāḷa?*
maybe DEF-girls want.IPFV.3PL.F help.IPFV.1PL-OBL.3PL.F aunt
'Maybe the girls [preparing lunch] want us to help them, aunt?'

(18) [Ḥa1]

xāf *ənḍəll* *əb-ġēr* *zād* *mā* *ſad-na* *ṭḥīn,*
maybe remain.IPFV.1PL with-other_than food NEG at-1PL flour
w-ənḍamm-a.
and-store.IPFV.1PL-OBL.3SG.M
'Maybe we are left without food, without flour, and so we store it [the flour].'

MORPHOLOGY

4.3.2.10   *bəhdāy* 'Slowly, Quietly, with a Low Voice, Calmly'

(19) [A15], Elicited
bəhdāy, lā   ṭṭagṭag!   *ʔəḥči   bəhdāy!*
quietly   NEG make_noise.IPFV.2SG.M speak.IMP.SG.M quietly
'Be quiet, don't make such noise! Talk quietly!'

(20) [A15], Elicited
ʔəmši   bəhdāy!
walk.IMP.SG.F quietly
'Walk slowly!'

4.3.2.11   *šwayy ~ šwayyūn* 'a Little (Bit)'

(21) [AB1]
ləǧat-na   əšwayy təxtələf   wīya əl-əʕrāg.
language-1PL a_little differ.IPFV.3SG.F with DEF-Iraq
'Our language differs a little bit from (that spoken in) Iraq.'

4.3.2.12   *šwayy əšwayy* 'Little by Little, Slowly'

(22) [A3]
šwayy əšwayy yəstəwi.
little   little   be_cooked.IPFV.3SG.M
'Little by little it cooks.'

4.3.2.13   *ḥatta* '(Not) Even'

(23) [A19]
tara ḥatta xārəǧ   ham hēč.
DP   even abroad also like_this
'They even (have) this abroad.'

Within a negated clause, its meaning is 'not even'.

(24) [F1]
hassa saṭla   rōba   mā ywaččəl   ḥatta nafar, mā
now   bucket yoghurt NEG feed.IPFV.3SG.M even person NEG
ywaččəl.
feed.IPFV.3SG.M
'Nowadays one bucket of yoghurt does not feed even one person.'

136 CHAPTER 4

4.3.2.14 *ha-l-gadd ~ ha-l-gaddāt* 'This Much, This …'
When a pronoun is suffixed to the adverb *ha-l-gadd*, it can have the form
ha-l-gaddāt-, i.e. with the external PL.F morpheme added. The same form is
also known for Arabic dialects in Iraq (cf. Bar-Moshe 2019: 31, fn. 5 and the references cited there on the Jewish dialect of Baghdad and the Muslim dialects
of Mosul; and Erwin 1963: 360 on Muslim Baghdadi Arabic).

(25) [A9]
    kəll   səna tgəṣṣ   **ha-l-gadd**   *mən ən-naxla.*
    every year cut.IPFV.2SG.M DEM-DEF-amount from DEF-palm_tree
    'Each year you cut this much of the palm-tree.'

(26) [A9]
    tağrīban   **ha-l-gaddāt-ha**   *tṣīr.*
    approximately DEM-DEF-amounts-3SG.F become.IPFV.3SG.F
    'It's going to be about this big [the palm-tree].'

4.3.2.15 *gadd-mā* + PRO '(It Is) so/This … (That)'
The adverbial expression *gadd-mā-* '(it is) so/this … (that)' is combined with
the short forms of the independent pronouns as described in 4.1.2.1 Holes (2001:
415–416; 2016: 399)mentions for Bahraini Arabic an expression quite similar to
this KhA adverbial expression: *min gadd mā* 'it is so … that', and he also gives
examples like *min gadd mā hu ʕēb* 'it is so shameful, that …'.

(27) [AB1]
    maḥammra **gadd-mā-hi**   *ḥəlwa*   *čānat …*
    Muḥammara so_much-REL-3SG.F beautiful.F be.PFV.3SG.F
    'Muḥammara was this beautiful …'

4.3.2.16 *wāyəd* 'Very, Much, a Lot'

(28) [A10]
    ʔəhəya **wāyəd** *ətrīd*   *əl-ḥamām.*
    3SG.F much want.IPFV.3SG.F DEF-pigeons
    'She loves pigeons very much.'

(29) [Ḥa1]
    wāyəd *taʕabna.*
    very   tire.PFV.1PL
    'We worked very hard [lit. "we got very tired"].'

MORPHOLOGY   137

(30) [A14], Elicited
    *ʕand-a   flūs   **wāyəd** ~ **wāyəd** *ʕand-a   flūs.*
    at-3SG.M money a_lot   a_lot   at-3SG.M money
    'He has a lot of money.'

4.3.2.17   *ḥēl* 'Fast, in a Loud Voice; Very'

(31) [A14], Elicited
    *lā   təmši   **ḥēl!***
    NEG   go.IPFV.2SG.M fast
    'Don't go so fast [with the car]!'

(32) [A10]
    *həlwa   **ḥēl.***
    beautiful.F very
    '(She is) very beautiful.'

(33) [T2]
    *ʔəḥči   **ḥēl   ḥaǧǧīya!***
    speak.IMP.SG.F loudly Ḥaǧǧīya
    'Speak up, Ḥaǧǧīya!'

4.3.2.18   *kalləš* 'Very, Totally'
Cf. Erwin (1963: 359) on *kulliš* 'very' in Muslim Baghdadi Arabic.

(34) [M1]
    *byūt-na   ḍallan   ṭāḥan   **kalləš.***
    houses-1PL remain.PFV.3PL.F fall_down.PFV.3PL.F totally
    'Our houses remained (empty, i.e. people had left them): they were totally
    destroyed.'

As the next example shows, KhA *kalləš* may also be used to further modify
another adverb:

(35) [A14], Elicited
    *yəḥči   **kalləš ḥēl.***
    speak.IPFV.3SG.M very   loudly/fast
    'He talks very loudly/fast.'

138   CHAPTER 4

4.3.2.19   *zēn* 'Well'

(36) [A14], Elicited
     əsmaʕ-ni   **zēn!**
     listen.IMP.SG.M-OBL.1SG well
     'Listen to me well!'

4.3.2.20   *xōš* 'Well'
The KhA adverb *xōš* (cf. 4.8.5.9 on the homophone KhA DP *xōš*) derives from
the Persian element *xoš* basically meaning 'good, well' (cf. Steingass 2001: 487
on the whole range of its meanings), which is used as a prefixed (lexicalized)
element preceding some nouns and verbs to coin compound adjectives, nouns,
and verbs (Majidi 1990: 411, 413): e.g. Pers. *xoš-andām* 'handsome' (< *andām*
'shape; body'), and *xoš-nevīs* 'calligrapher' (< present stem *nevīs-* 'to write'). It is
also used in Iraqi Arabic (cf., for example, Erwin 1963: 352 on Muslim Baghdadi
Arabic). In KhA the use of this element has been
    further developed so that it may also be used as an adverb meaning 'well',
as in (37) (Erwin 1963: 352 describes *xōš* only as a 'noun modifier' in Muslim
Baghdadi Arabic).
    In KhA, as in Iraqi Arabic, *xōš* is also used as an attributive adjective; in such
cases it precedes nouns, without agreeing in gender or number with them: e.g.
xōš walad 'a good boy', *xōš əbnayya* 'a good girl' (cf. Leitner 2020a: 126).

(37) [A18]
     hīya **xōš** *təsʔal.*
     3SG.F well ask.IPFV.3SG.F
     'She asks good questions [lit. "she asks well"].'

4.3.2.21   *farəd marra* 'Totally, Completely'

(38) [M4]
     əl-əmḥammra   *mayyta baʕad,* **farəd   marra.**
     DEF-Muḥammara dead.F DP   INDEF time
     'Muḥammara is completely dead (now).'

4.3.2.22   *farəd nōb* 'Totally, Completely'

(39) [M1]
     baʕad ʕəyūn-i   xānan   *bī-ya.   rāḥan*   **farəd   nōb.**
     then   eyes-1SG betray.PFV.3PL.F with-1SG go.PFV.3PL.F INDEF time

MORPHOLOGY 139

'Then I became blind [lit. "my eyes betrayed me"]. They [his eyes] left (me) completely.'

4.3.2.23   *ṣədfa ~ b-əṣ-ṣədfa* 'Accidentally, Coincidentally'

(40) [A14], Elicited
əl-yōm   šəft   Māğəd b-əṣ-ṣədfa.
DEF-day see.PFV.1SG Majed with-DEF-chance
'Today I saw Majed accidentally.'

4.3.2.24   *səwa ~ səwīya* 'Together'

(41) [M1]
mā   gaʕdaw   səwa.
NEG sit.PFV.3PL.M together
'They didn't stay [lit. "sit"] together.'

4.3.2.25   *nəwīya* 'Together'

(42) [A2]
gāʕdīn   nəwīya.
sit.AP.PL.M together
'We sit together.'

4.3.2.26   *ʔaṣlan* + NEG 'Not at All'

(43) [A4]
lā, hīya mā tʕaraf   ʕağam, ʔaṣlan ʕağam hīya mā
NEG 3SG.F NEG know.IPFV.3SG.F Persian at_all   Persian 3SG.F NEG
tʕaraf.
know.IPFV.3SG.F
'No, she does not know Persian; she does not know Persian at all.'

4.3.3   *Adverbs of Location*
4.3.3.1   *lēyāy* '(Over) Here'
lēyāy '(over) here' developed analogously with *lēğād(i)* '(over) there' via the active participle of the verb *ʔəya* 'to come': *yāy* 'coming (AP)', forming the counterpart of *ğādi* 'going (away) (AP)'. It is remarkable that in KhA *yāy* can be used not only to express direction, but also as a local adverb.

140   CHAPTER 4

(1) [M1]
     gət-l-a   *hā* **lēyāy**   ^P*yād*   *gerefti*^P   *fārsi*
     say.PFV.1SG-to-3SG.M   DP over_here memory take.PFV.2SG Persian
     ʕarabi?
     Arabic
     'I said to him, "Tell me, have you learned Persian (or) Arabic here?"'

(2) [Ḥ1]
     əlḥadd əlli **lēyāy**
     until   REL over_here
     'until here'

(3) [A12]
     taʕāl   **lēyāy!**
     come.IMP.SG.M over_here
     'Come (over) here!'

4.3.3.2   *lēġād ~ lēġādi ~ ġād ~ ġādi* '(Over) There'
The adverb *lēġād ~ lēġādi ~ ġād ~ ġādi* 'there' developed from the active participle *ġādi*, as used in (1), which goes back to the OA verb *ġadā* 'leave, go (forth)'
(cf. WAD IV, comments on map 450b), which is not attested as a finite verb in
KhA.

(1) [X1]
     zād mā-hu   *ḥəlu, hāy* **ġādi,**   *gabəl*   *aḥsan.*
     food NEG-3SG.M good DEM go.AP.SG.M formerly better
     'There is no good food; that has gone; in former times (it was) better.'

As is common in most other eastern dialects of Arabic that make use of this
adverb (cf. Fischer 1959: 131), the most common form is the one without the
final -*i*, as in the following examples:

(2) [A16] [Nādya is telling Maryam's aunt how they use to prepare coffee in
     Ahvaz]
     šwayyūn mələḥ ygūl   *ʕan əl-ḥalāl*   *w-əl-ḥarām*
     a_little salt   say.IPFV.3SG.M from DEF-allowed and-DEF-forbidden
     əḥnā **lēġād**   *ysawwūn.*
     1PL   over_there make.IPFV.3PL.M
     '(With) a little salt—they say it is for the cattle and the women—we over
     there [in Ahvaz: during the recording we were in Xafaǧīya] prepare (the
     coffee).'

MORPHOLOGY 141

(3) [A19]
šūfi   dīča lēǵād,   dāka!
see.IMP.SG.F DEM overthere DEM
'See, that one over there, that one!'

(4) [A15], Elicited
rūḥ   lēǵād!
go.IMP.SG.M over_there
'Go (over) there!'

Many dialects have three levels of local distance, 'here—there—over there', and forms of *ǵādi* often indicate the third level ('over there') and by that a greater distance than implied by forms of *hnāk* 'there' (cf. WAD IV, comments on maps 450a–450b; Watson 2006: 23). Behnstedt (1993: 88), likewise states that in most dialects which use *ǵād(i)* it denotes a great distance ('over there').

KhA *ǵād* is also used metaphorically to indicate distance in time, as in the next example. In this case, *ǵād* cannot be replaced by *ʔəhnāk*.

(5) [AB1]
nākəl-ha   baʕad b-əl-īd   mū   b-əl-xāšəg
eat.IPFV.1PL-OBL.3SG.F DP   with-DEF-hand NEG with-DEF-spoon
čān   ǵād.
be.PFV.3SG.M there
'We used to eat it [the fish] with the hand, not with the spoon, back then.'

The next example shows that KhA *lēǵād* does not necessarily indicate greater distance than *ʔəhnāk*, being used here with reference to something pointed at by the speaker—i.e. something at a visible distance. In this case, *lēǵād* may be replaced by *ʔəhnāk*.

(6) [A19]
dāk al lēǵād,   dāk əl   mənnāka mən wara
DEM REL over_there DEM REL over_there from behind
ən-naxla.
DEF-palm_tree
'That one which is there, that which is there, behind the palm-tree.'

We can therefore assume that KhA no longer strictly follows the threefold spacial remoteness-system still used by many other dialects. Synchronically, KhA *yāy* and *ǵād* appear to present in most cases a second set of distal and proximal

142   CHAPTER 4

local (and directional) adverbs used interchangeably with *ʔəhnā* and *ʔəhnāk*, and their frequency of use varies according to speaker provenance.

Ingham (1976: 67, fn. 16) states that *yāy* and *ġād* can have the meanings 'this way' and 'that way' in all *ġələt*-dialects and describes their use with the meanings 'here' and 'there' (with local, rather than directional significance) as limited to the ʕAmāra regions (1976: 67, fn. 16). However, the examples found in my corpus prove that the use of *ġād* and *yāy* (and their cognate forms) with the meanings 'here' and 'there' (i.e. as local adverbs) is also attested for present-day Ahvaz, Fəllāḥīya, and Muḥammara. The forms with the prefixed preposition *lē*- 'to' (*lē-yāy* and *lē-ġād*) are not mentioned by Ingham.

According to Fischer and Jastrow, the use of the AP *ġādi* as an adverb with the meaning 'there' is typical of the rural *ġələt* dialects (1980: 151; cf. Meißner 1903: 136).[42] Muslim Baghdadi Arabic instead uses *hnāk ~ hnāka* for 'there' (Fischer and Jastrow 1980: 151), but has *ġād* for 'yonder, over there' (WB: 332). While Fischer and Jastrow do not mention whether they consider its counterpart *ǧāy* (KhA *yāy*) 'here'—which appears to be less commonly used in general—also a typical rural *ġələt* feature, they mention *hnā* and *hēn* as typical rural *ġələt* forms for 'here' (Fischer and Jastrow 1980: 151; cf. Palva 2009: 28).

4.3.3.3   *ʔəhnā ~ hnā ~ həna ~ hān* 'Here'

Especially in the south of Khuzestan, the forms *ʔəhnā* and *ʔəhnāk* (cf. 4.3.3.4) are preferred over *yāy* and *ġād* (or one of their allomorphs). In Muslim Baghdadi Arabic mainly *hnā ~ hnāna* are used for 'here' (Blanc 1964: 139) and in the Gulf dialects mainly *hnī ~ ihna* (Johnstone 1967: 17, 68; Holes 2006: 248; Fischer 1959: 117).

Both KhA *ʔəhnā* 'here' and *ʔəhnāk* 'there' carry the main stress on the last syllable (cf. Fischer 1959: 115, who supposes that also in the original forms the stress was already on the final syllable).

(7)   [A12]
ḥōš-na   hāḏa ʔəhnā māl   əl-ōlād   əb-Xazāmi.
house-1PL DEM here   GL.SG.M DEF-children in-Xazāmi
'Our house here belongs to the children in Xazāmi [neighborhood in Kūt ʕAbd-Allah, Ahvaz].'

The alternative form *həna* (as well as *hənāk ~ hənāka*, cf. below) has been—with very few exceptions—recorded only for speakers from Fəllāḥīya, Muḥammara, and Abadan.

---

42   On cognate forms of these two adverbs in other dialects of Arabic cf. WAD IV (map 450 on *ġād* and map 449 on *yāy* in the Maghreb and Mashreq); Fischer (1959: 130–131); and

MORPHOLOGY

(8) [A19]
hāy al-ʔaraḍ həna kāḍḍīn-ha   ʔāǧār.
DEM DEF-land here take.AP.PL.M-OBL.3SG.F rent
'This field here, we rent it.'

The form *hān* 'here' appears only once in my corpus (9) (cf. Fischer 1959: 123, who derives *hān* from *hāhunā* and gives references for the occurrence of *hān* and cognate forms in many Bedouin-type and rural dialects, "Fellaḥen-mundarten", of Syria, Palestine, and Yemen). Ingham's statement, that "the use of the form /hāna/ is characteristic of *bādiya* speech in Khuzistan, contrasting with *hnā*, the form of the Riverine Arabs" (Ingham 1982a: 170) was confirmed by my consultants, who added that *hān* was used mainly in the northern parts of Khuzestan in places like Tustar and Sūs. Interestingly, in my corpus *hān* is only used by one speaker from Fəllāḥīya (now he lives in Ahvaz), where a *ḥaḍar* dialect is spoken (cf. Ingham 2007: 572).

(9) [A19, explaining why he has put a barbed-wire fence around his field]
ᴾ*sīm xārdār*ᴾ   — *mkarram s-sāməʕ*   — *ʕala   l-xanzīr*
barbed_wire_fence   respected DEF-listener   so_that DEF-pig
lā   ʔəyi   lō ḥaywān lā   ʔəyi   mən hān.
NEG come.IPFV.3SG.M or animal NEG come.IPFV.3SG.M from here
'(We put up a) barbed-wire fence—excuse the expression—so that pigs won't come (and eat the crop) or (so that) the animals won't come from here.'

4.3.3.4   *ʔəhnāk(a) ~ hnāk ~ hənāk(a)* 'There'
Of the variant forms *ʔəhnāk(a) ~ hnāk ~ hənāk(a)* all meaning 'there', the most common is *ʔəhnāk*. There is a similar variation in the pronunciation of this form in al-Shirqat "*hnāk ~ henāk ~ hunāk*" (Salonen 1980: 98).

(10) [A1]
yamm   Mūsīyān əhnāk ʔaktar nās   ʕad-həm ǧannāma.
next_to Musian there most   people at-3PL.M shepherds
'There, near Musian [city in Ilam Province of Iran], most people are shep-herds.'

hənāk ~ hənāka (as well as *hənā*, cf. above) have been—with very few excep-tions—recorded only for speakers from Fəllāḥīya, Muḥammara, and Abadan.

Procházka (1993: 115); cf. Behnstedt (1993: 88) on *ǧād(i)* in eastern dialects of Syria, e.g. Palmyra, Soukhne, and Dēr iz-Zōr.

144 CHAPTER 4

(11) [A19]
mū āna čənt əb-xārəǧ hənāka?
NEG 1SG be.PFV.1SG in-abroad there
'Haven't I been abroad there?'

4.3.3.5   *mənnā* 'from Here, Over Here, Here'
The adverbs *mənnā* 'from here, over here' (12) and *mənnāk ~ mənnāka* 'from there, over there' (13) derive from a combination of the preposition *mən* plus the adverb *hnā*, or *hnāk(a)* via loss of *h* (cf. Fischer 1959: 117–116 on this adverb and references to its occurrence in other dialects of Arabic).

(12) [M1]
*w-əftarrēna   **mənnā**   w   **mənnā**.*
and-go_around.PFV.1PL from_here and from_here
'And we went around from here and from here.'

4.3.3.6   *mənnāk ~ mənnāka* 'From There, Over There, There'

(13) [Ḥ1]
*əl-bəšət,   hassa, yō lō štarētú   **mənnāk***
DEF-cloak now   or or buy.PFV.2.MPL.OBL.3SG.M from_there
mxayyaṭ   w   ǧəbtú   mən əl-Mašhad.
tailor.PP.SG.M and bring.PFV.2.MPL.OBL.3SG.M from DEF-Mashhad
'The *bəšət* [a summer cloak], now, if (for example) you bought it from there tailored and you brought it from Mashhad ...'

(14) [A19]
*ḏāk əl lēǧād,   ḏāk əl **mənnāka** mən wara*
DEM REL over_there DEM REL over_there from behind
ən-naxla.
DEF-palm_tree
'That one which is there, that which is there, behind the palm tree.'

4.3.3.7   *ha-ṣ-ṣōb* 'Over Here, This Way'

(15) [A14], Elicited
*wēn   rāyəḥ?   taʕāl   **ha-ṣ-ṣōb!***
where go.AP.SG.M come.IMP.SG.M DEM-DEF-direction
'Where are you going? Come over here!'

MORPHOLOGY

145

4.3.3.8   *ḏāk əṣ-ṣōb* 'Over There, That Way'

(16) [A14], Elicited
   rūḥ   *ḏāk əṣ-ṣōb!*
   go.IMP.SG.M DEM DEF-direction
   'Go that way!'

4.3.3.9   *ʕa-l-ʕasma* '(to the) Left'
For the etymology of *ʕasma* cf. CA *ʕasima* 'it (a man's hand and his foot) was, or became, distorted' (Lane 1863: 2047). Cognate forms are documented for Arabic dialects spoken on the Arabian Peninsula and Gulf Arabic dialects in the meaning 'lefthanded' (WAD I: 221, map 78). Similar semantic developments from 'crooked', 'lame', or 'flaccid' to 'left' are also documented for other dialects of Arabic—e.g. some Algerian and Yemeni Arabic dialects (cf. WAD IV: map 454).

(17) [A14], Elicited
   b-əč-čarra[43]   *tləff*   *ʕa-l-ʕasma.*
   at-DEF-crossroad turn.IPFV.2SG.M to-DEF-left
   'At the crossroad, turn left.'

4.3.3.10   *ʕal-yamna* '(to the) Right'
Reflexes of this lexeme are found in the majority of all dialects of Arabic and go back to the OA adjectives *yamīn^{un}* and *ʔayman^u*, both meaning 'right' (Lane 1863: 3064, cf. WAD IV: map 453). KhA *yamna* goes back to the feminine form of the adjective, *yumnā*. Similarly, in many other Mesopotamian dialects— such as those of Basra, Baghdad, al-Shirqat, Urfa, and Kwayriš/Babylon—and in parts of Morocco, Algeria, and Palestine reflexes of *yimna* are used (cf. WAD IV: map 453).

(18) [A14], Elicited
   b-əč-čarra   *tləff*   *ʕa-l-yamna.*
   at-DEF-crossroad turn.IPFV.2SG.M to-DEF-right
   'At the crossroad, turn right.'

4.3.3.11   *ǧədd* 'Straight Ahead'
On its etymology, cf. CA *ǧudda* and *ǧādda* 'a beaten way marked with lines [...] or a road, or way (leading to water)' (Lane 1863: 387; cf. WAD IV: map 455).

---

43   < Pers. *čahār-rāh* 'crossroad'.

146 CHAPTER 4

(19) [A14], Elicited
trūḥ *ǧədd!*
go.IPFV.2SG.M straight
'Go straight!'

4.3.3.12 *ǧəddām* 'in Front'

(20) [A14], Elicited
əl-akbar *yrūḥ* *ǧəddām.*
DEF-oldest go.IPFV.3SG.M in_front
'The oldest one goes in front.'

4.3.3.13 *fōg* 'Above, up, on Top'

(21) [X1]
ḥaṭṭēt *əs-səmča* *fōg.*
put.PFV.1SG DEF-fish.SGT on_top
'I put the fish on top/above.'

(22) [M4]
əl-māy *yəṣʕad* *fōg.*
DEF-water ascend.IPFV.3SG.M up
'The water comes up.'

4.3.3.14 *ḥadər* 'Below, Down'

(23) [A11]
ča xaḏā-hən *nəzlaw* *ḥadər l-əš-šaṭṭ.*
DP take.PFV.3SG.M-OBL.3PL.F descend.PFV.3PL.M down to-DEF-river
'He took them [the water buffaloes] down to the river.'

(24) [A14], Elicited
ʔəhma sāknīn *ḥadər.*
3PL.M live.AP.PL.M below
'They live below.'

4.3.3.15 *dāxəl* 'Inside'

In most parts of Iraq, *ǧawwa* is used instead of *dāxəl* to express 'inside' (WAD IV: map 452). However, Basra and Muslim Baghdadi Arabic, also know reflexes of *dāxəl* for 'inside' (besides *ǧawwa* 'inside') as used in KhA. *dāxəl* is also used in Kuwaiti and Baḥraini Arabic (WAD IV: map 452).

MORPHOLOGY   147

(25) [A14], Elicited
ydəššūn   ***dāxəl.***
enter.IPFV.3PL.M inside
'They go inside (e.g. the house).'

4.3.3.16   *barra* 'Outside, Abroad'
This adverb is widespread and used in many dialects in the Mashreq as well
as in the Maghreb (cf. WAD IV: map 451) and already attested for CA: "*xaraǧtu
barr-an* 'I went forth outside the [house or] town, or into the desert'" (Lane
1863: 176).

(26) [F1]
ṭəlʕī   ***barra***
go_out.IMP.SG.F outside
'Go outside!'

(27) [A9]
əs-saʕamrān,   ... *məṣādara yṣadrūn-a*   ***barra* ...**
DEF-Saʕamrān   export   export.IPFV.3PL.M-OBL.3SG.M abroad
ēh, yəmši   ***barra.***
yes go.IPFV.3SG.M abroad
'The Saʕamrān [name of a kind of date], ... they export it abroad; yes, it
goes abroad.'

4.3.3.17   *wara* 'Behind, Back'

(28) [A14]
ʔəšmər   *əč-čǝffīya,*   *dəbb-ha*   ***wara!***
throw.IMP.SG.M DEF-Keffiyeh throw.IMP.SG.M-OBL.3SG.F back
'Throw the [your] Keffiyeh, throw it back!'

4.3.4   *Interrogative Adverbs*
4.3.4.1   *yēmta ~ ḷyēmta* 'When?'
Similar forms of this interrogative adverb are found in various Iraqi Arabic
dialects: in Kwayriš/Babylon (Meißner 1903: 148: *yemta*, besides *ešwak(i)t*),
(Muslim) Baghdad (Blanc 1964: 138: *yamta/yemta*, but *šwaket* is preferred), Ana
(ʕĀna) and Mosul (Blanc 1964: 138: *wēmta* and *ēmati*, respectively). Elsewhere,
we find cognate forms, e.g., in Uzbekistan Arabic (Fischer 1961: 260: *īmta*). These
forms are derived from a combination of the two interrogative adverbs *ayy*
'which?' and *matā* 'when' (cf. Procházka 2018c: 277 and Fischer 1961: 260).

148 CHAPTER 4

The combination of the interrogative adverb *yēmta* 'when?' with the relative particle *mā* yields the subordinating conjunction *yēmta-mā* 'whenever' (cf. 4.7.2.40).

(1) [A19]
yēmta *nkarrb-a?*
when plow.IPFV.1PL-OBL.3SG.M
'When do we plow it?'

(2) [A14]
ḷyēmta *yərǧaʕ?*
when come_back.IPFV.3SG.M
'When does he come back?'

(3) [A14]
əlḥadd **yēmta** *təbǧa?*
until when stay.IPFV.2SG.M
'Until when do you stay?'

4.3.4.2 *lēš* 'Why?'[44]

(4) [M1]
lēš *təḥči* *ʕayam?*
why speak.IPFV.2SG.M Persian
'Why do you speak Persian?'

4.3.4.3 *əl-man* 'Why?, What for?'

(5) [A19]
hāḏa karrbṓ *ʔōmāda*[45] — **əl-man?** *šān*
DEM plow.PFV.3PL.M.OBL.3SG.M preparation for-what because_of
əl-ḥanṭa *w* *əš-šaʕīr.*
DEF-wheat and DEF-barley
'This, they plowed it in preparation—What for? For [growing] wheat and the barley.'

---

44 Cf. 4.7.2.33 on the temporal conjunction *lēš-mā* 'when'.
45 < Pers. *āmāde kardan* 'to prepare'.

MORPHOLOGY   149

4.3.4.4 *ʕalēman?* 'on What? for What? Why?'

This interrogative adverb is a combination of the preposition *ʕala* 'on' and the interrogative enclitic *-man* 'what, who?', between which the consonant *y* was introduced: *ʕalayman > ʕalēman*. To the best of my knowledge, this adverb is not documented for other dialects. (However, Qasim Hassan, pers. comm. 2020, confirmed its use in S-Iraqi).

(6)   [A9]
    w   yṭəbxūn-a   hāḏ ət-ṭabəx w
    and cook.IPFV.3PL.M-OBL.3SG.M DEM DEF-dish and
    yrəššūn-a   ʕalēman? ʕala t-tamər.
    sprinkle.IPFV.3PL.M-OBL.3SG.M on_what on DEF-dates
    'And they cook this thing and on what do they (then) sprinkle it? On the dates.'

(7)   [Ḥ2]
    ʔāna ʕalēman āna hāy bət-i   ʔadbaḥ-ha,   ʔāna
    1SG why 1SG DEM daughter-1SG kill.IPFV.1SG-OBL.3SG.F 1SG
    hāy bət-i,   ʔarīd   ʔawaddī-ha
    DEM daughter-1SG want.IPFV.1SG send.IPFV.1SG-OBL.3SG.F
    l-əl-marābi.
    to-DEF-orphanage
    'Why should I kill my daughter? This is my daughter; I want to take her to the orphanage [instead of killing her].'

4.3.4.5 *šlōn* 'How?'

(8)   [A4, asking the farmer what dairy goods he produces]
    ***šlōn** təstəfādūn   man ʕad-a?*
    how use.IPFV.2PL.M from at-3SG.M
    'How do you make use of it [the milk]?'

4.3.4.6 *wēn* 'Where?'

(9)   [A10]
    ***wēn** təlgīn-a?*
    where find.IPFV.2SG.F-OBL.3SG.M
    'Where do you find him?'

150   CHAPTER 4

4.3.4.7   *wēn* 'Where to?'

(10) [A14]
    wēn   *tərḥīn?*
    where go.IPFV.2SG.F
    'Where are you going to?'

4.3.4.8   *bēš* 'How Much?'
bēš usually refers to a price or time.

(11) [A14]
    bēš   *əs-sāʕa*   ~ *əs-sāʕa*   **bēš?**
    how_much DEF-hour   DEF-hour how_much
    'What's the time?'

(12) [A14]
    bēš   *əṭ-ṭamāṭa?*
    how_much DEF-tomato
    'How much are the tomatoes?'

(13) [M1]
    hassa əṭḥīn, xamsīn kīlu **bēš**   *yṣīṛ?*
    now   flour fifty   kilo how_much become.IPFV.3SG.M
    'Nowadays flour, how much are 50 kilos?'

4.3.4.9   *šgadd* 'How Many; How Much?', with *ʕəmr*-PRO 'How Old?'

(14) [A4]
    əšgadd   *mən naxīl-kəm*   *hēč b-əl-mīya*   *təmarraḍ*
    how_many of   palms-2PL.M DP in-DEF-hundred fall_sick.PFV.3SG.M
    mən ət-təlwīṯ?
    of   DEF-pollution
    'How many per cent of your palms like that fell sick because of the pollution?'

(15) [A14]
    šgadd   *ʕand-ak əflūs?*
    how_much at-2SG.M money
    'How much money do you have?'

MORPHOLOGY   151

(16) [A18]
    šgadd   *ʕəmr-ak?*
    how_much age-2SG.M
    'How old are you?'

4.3.4.10 *čam ~ kam* 'How Many?', with *ʕəmr*-PRO 'How Old?'

(17) [A17]
    čam   *əṣbūra kaḍḍēt?*
    how_many Ṣabūra catch.PFV.2SG.M
    'How many Ṣabūra [name of a kind of fish] did you catch?'

(18) [A4]
    čam   *marra tnəšrīn*   *b-əl-yōm?*
    how_many time   graze.IPFV.2SG.F in-DEF-day
    'How many times do you take (the sheep) to graze each day?'

(19) [A4]
    kam   *ʕəmr-əč?*
    how_much age-2SG.F
    'How old are you (SG.F)?'

4.3.4.11 *bī-ma, bēš* 'with What?'

(20) [A4]
    bī-ma   *ysəffūn-ha?*
    with-what braid.IPFV.3PL.M-OBL.3SG.F
    'With what do they braid it?'

(21) [A4]
    bēš   *ətgəṣṣūn-a?*
    with_what cut.IPFV.2PL.M-OBL.3SG.M
    'With what do you cut/fleece it [the sheep wool]?'

4.3.4.12 *mnēn ~ mən wēn* 'from Where?'
mnēn has an anaptyctic vowel in initial position or between *m* and *n* (*əmnēn* or
mənēn) unless it follows a word that ends in a vowel.

(22) [A4]
wālədt-ak   əmnēn?
mother-2SG.M from_where
'Where is your mother from?'

(23) [X3]
mnēn   əl-ġandi   yā-ni   ča?
from_where DEF-diabetes come.PFV.3SG.M-OBL.1SG DP
'From where did I get my diabetes do you think? [Of course from the bad food we eat nowadays.]'

4.4   Prepositions

The following is an extensive, but not complete, list of the most frequently used KhA prepositions with examples of their usages. The selection of the KhA prepositions included in the following list is based upon the rough definition of the nature of prepositions provided by Stephan Procházka: "Prepositions may be defined as function words indicating the relation of a noun or pronoun to other words in the clause." (Procházka 2008: 699). Nevertheless, defining prepositions, and especially deciding on whether or not a noun has already become a full preposition, is extremely difficult.

The relation indicated by a preposition is very often temporal or local. In many cases, however, this relation is not temporal or local but has developed other functions by metaphorical usage. To such extended usages of prepositions belongs, e.g. the expression of an instrument or an item's price via the preposition *b-* (cf. Procházka 2008: 701).

In the following, the KhA prepositions are first listed with their translations[46] or explanations of their functions, and references to examples of their usage follow. Whenever attested, examples of prepositions that are combined with pronominal suffixes will also be given.

The combination of prepositions in general, and the combination of prepositions with the preposition /min/ 'from' especially, are very common and already attested for CA (cf. Procházka 1993: 37, 68, 184). In KhA as well as in other dialects (cf. Procházka 1993: 68), *mən* usually does not add anything semantically when combined with other prepositions. The preposition that

---

46   I have tried to provide the basic or most frequent English equivalents for the prepositions. However, because many prepositions have adopted diverse metaphoric functions, the translated meanings listed are not meant to be complete.

can be combined with a certain other preposition will be given in parentheses before the main preposition, e.g. (*mən*) *baʕad* 'after'. Morphological variants of a preposition are given after the symbol ~.

Compound prepositions consist of a preposition and another word (cf. Prochâzka 2008: 700). These are not listed separately because they are usually perceived as one element by the speakers. In some cases this leads to a contraction, as in *mən šān* > *mšān* 'because of'.

Some prepositions are further used to connect verbs with their indirect objects specifying the semantic range of the verb in question (cf. Prochâzka 2008: 701), e.g. *ṭāḥ b-* 'to take (sth.)', and *ǧāwab ʕan* 'to answer (sb.)'.

Before listing the KhA prepositions, I will discuss some general differences between KhA and other Arabic dialects, especially Iraqi Arabic, and point out some remarkable features of KhA regarding its prepositions. While many prepositions are used by the majority of Arabic dialects, e.g. *fōg* 'above, over, on' (4.4.20), and *bēn* 'between' (4.4.11), some KhA prepositions can be considered typical of the Mesopotamian dialect group and are thus shared with Iraqi Arabic, e.g. *yamm* 'next to' (4.4.25), *ʕalamūd* 'because of, for' (4.4.28), and the genitive exponent *māl* (4.6). Among the differences between KhA and Iraqi Arabic is the preposition *ǧawwa* 'inside, under', which is used in Iraqi (Erwin 1963: 301) but not in KhA, which instead uses *ḥadər* 'under'. The latter is also documented for some Arabic dialects in Central Arabia, the Gulf littoral, and Uzbekistan (cf. Prochâzka 1993: 226–227 and the references cited there; Holes 2001: 104–105).

Among the remarkable features of KhA are the occasional use of *b-* with a goal, the very frequent combinations of two or more prepositions, as in (64) below, and the temporal use of the originally local prepositions *ǧəddām* 'in front of, before (temporal)' (4.4.5) and *wara* 'behind, after (temporal)' (4.4.7). The temporal use of *ǧəddām* can be considered a peripheral phenomenon because—to my knowledge—it is elsewhere only found in Chad and some west-Algerian Bedouin dialects (Prochâzka 1995a: 421). Temporal use of *wara* appears to be a bit more widespread because it is also known in Nigerian Arabic (Owens 1993: 224), many Maghribi dialects, and, in the east, though less frequently, in several Gulf Arabic and *gələt* dialects (Prochâzka 1995a: 421, fn. 23).

154 CHAPTER 4

4.4.1 b- 'in; at (*Temporal and Local*); to [*Goal*]; with (*Instrumental*); [*Price*]'

KhA uses only reflexes of OA *bi-* 'in; with' but none of OA *fī* 'in'.[47] Its form varies according to its linguistic environment. In most cases it is *b-*, especially when a vowel follows (e.g. of the definite article *əl-*), as in (1)–(4). When a Cv- structure follows and the word preceding the preposition ends in a vowel, it is frequently *b-*, as in (5) and (6), but also *əb-*, as in (8). When a Cv- structure follows and the preceding word ends in a consonant, its form is usually *əb-*, as in (7), or *bə-*, as in (9).

(1) [A6]
     b-əl-bēt
     in-DEF-house
     'in the house'

(2) [A16]
     b-əl-lēl
     at-DEF-night
     'at night'

(3) [A1]
     tšūf   *əl-mədīr*   *b-əl-bāb.*
     see.IPFV.2SG.M DEF-headmaster at-DEF-door
     'You see the headmaster at the door.'

(4) [A6]
     ngəṣṣ-ha   *b-əz-zwaw.*
     cut.IPFV.1PL-OBL.3SG.F with-DEF-shears
     'We fleece it [the sheep] with shears.'

The preposition *b-* is also used to indicate a price:

(5) [A14]
     kēlo ṭamāṭa b-xamsīn.
     kilo tomato with-fifty
     'A kilo of tomatoes costs 50.'

---

47   Cf. Procházka (Procházka 2008: 702; 1995a: 418) on the fact that all Iraqi dialects south of
     Mosul, and many Arabian Bedouin dialects, have reflexes only of OA *bi-* and none of OA
     fī.

MORPHOLOGY

(6) [A14]
štarēna   *bēt-na*   *b-xaməsmīyat məlyōn.*
buy.PFV.1PL house-1PL with-500.CS   million
'We bought our house for 500 million.'

(7) [A10]
yəhaləs   *əb-laḥīt-a*   *w   yxayyṭ*
pluck.IPFV.3SG.M with-beard-3SG.M and sew.IPFV.3SG.M
əb-mazwīt-a.
with-cloak-3SG.M
'He pulls out (hair) from his beard and sews (from it) a *mazwīya* [a winter cloak].'

(8) [A10]
nəgrat-ha   *əb-ʕēn-ha.*
peck.PFV.3SG.F-3SG.F in-eye-3SG.F
'It [the pigeon] pecked her in her eye.'

(9) [Ḥ2]
dəbaḥna   *dəyāya*   *w*   *ḥattēna*   *damm-ha*   *bə-šiša.*
kill.PFV.1PL chicken.SGT and put.PFV.1PL blood-3SG.F in-bottle
'We killed a chicken and poured her blood into a bottle.'

(10) [A9]
yxallūn   *l-saḥan*   *bə-waṣṭ-a.*
leave.IPFV.3PL.M DEF-plate in-middle-3SG.M
'They leave the plate at its center [of the tablecloth on the floor].'

Twice in my corpus, the preposition *b-* is used with a goal: see the next two examples. This is uncommon for Arabic in general and could be an influence from the use of the Persian preposition *be* 'in; to; for' (in Persian, this preposition is however also often omitted in rapid speech).

(11) [M3]
rəḥna   *b-əd-dəyar.*
go.PFV.1PL to-DEF-villages
'We went to the villages.'

156   CHAPTER 4

(12) [M4]
    yaʕni hassa mən   ətrūḥ   b-əl-bandar ətbawwəʕ
    DP   now   when go.IPFV.2SG.M to-DEF-port see.IPFV.2SG.M
    əl-markab.
    DEF-ship
    'So, when you go to the port now, you see the ship.'

4.4.2   mən ~ mn- *'from (Temp. and Local); Since, for; of (Partitive and Material); Than'*

The preposition *mən* has a reduced form *mn-* which may be used before a vowel (mostly in contexts where *mən* precedes the definite article *əl*). *mn-* has an initial anaptyctic vowel, yielding *əmn-*, as in (15), unless it follows a word that ends in a vowel, as in (14).

(13) [Ḥ1]
    ǧəbtū́   mən əl-Mašhad.
    bring.PFV.2.MPL.OBL.3SG.M from DEF-Mashhad
    'You brought it from Mashhad.'

(14) [M3]
    ʔāna mn-əl-əmḥammra.
    1SG   from-DEF-Muḥammara
    'I am from Muḥammara.'

(15) [A19]
    əmn-əṣ-ṣəbəḥ   əlḥadd əl-ʕaṣər
    from-DEF-morning until   DEF-late_afternoon
    'from the morning until the late afternoon'

(16) [A19]
    hāḏa ham mən ṣəǧər   yəštəǧəl   čān.
    DEM also from childhood work.IPFV.3SG.M be.PFV.3SG.M
    'This one [pointing at his son] has also been working since (his) childhood.'

(17) [A12]
    hassa mā nʕarəf   nǧazəl   gəmna,   mən zamān
    now   NEG know.IPFV.1PL spin.IPFV.1PL begin.PFV.1PL from time
    mā   nǧazəl.
    NEG spin.IPFV.1PL

MORPHOLOGY 157

'Now, we don't know how to spin anymore; for a long time (now) we haven't spun.'

(18) [F1]
waḥda mən əl-banāt
one.F of DEF-girls
'one of the girls'

(19) [A19]
... ʔaḥsan mən dəhən əl-ḥaywān.
better than lard DEF-animal
'[Dates are] ... better than animal lard.'

4.4.3 ḥadd ~ əlḥadd 'until, up to (Temporal and Local)'

(20) [A9]
əṭḍəll ḥadd bərəǧ sātt.
stay.IPFV.3SG.F until month sixth
'She stays until the sixth month [of the Iranian/Solar Hijri calendar].'

(21) [A9]
ənnaḍḍəf hāḏ əl-karab nṭēḥ-ha,
clean.IPFV.1PL DEM DEF-nodules take_down.IPFV.1PL-OBL.3SG.F
ənxallī ḥadd as-saʕaf əl-xaḍar.
leave.IPFV.1PL.OBL.3SG.M until DEF-palm_fronds DEF-green
'We clean these nodules; we take them down; we leave it until the green palm fronds.'

4.4.4 gabəl ~ ġabəl 'before, ... Ago'
The epenthetic vowel *ə* between the last two consonants in the preposition *gabəl ~ ġabəl* 'before, ... ago' can be elided in before a following vowel.

(22) [F1]
gabəl ar-rəyūg
before DEF-breakfast
'before breakfast'

(23) [A6]
ġabəl sanawāt
before years
'years ago'

158 CHAPTER 4

(24) [M3]
ġabl   əl-ḥarəb
before DEF-war
'before the war'

4.4.5   ǧəddām *'in Front of, before (Temporal)'*

(25) [A14]
əs-sayyāra ǧəddām   əl-bēt.
DEF-car   in_front_of DEF-house
'The car is in front of the house.'

The temporal use of the originally local preposition *ǧəddām* expressing anteriority is not very widespread, though also known for Chad and some west-Algerian Bedouin dialects (cf. Procházka 1993: 192–193; 1995a: 420–421). For the *gələt* dialects of al-Shirqat and Kwayriš/Babylon, only a local meaning of *ǧəddām* is documented (Salonen 1980: 92; Meißner 1903: XXXII).

(26) [A19]
čān   ḥayāt-na ʔaḥsan ǧəddām əl-ḥarəb.
be.PFV.3SG.M life-1PL better before   DEF-war
'We had a better life before the war.'

4.4.6   əgbāl *'in Front of, Opposite from/of'*
Cf. Erwin (1963: 304) on this preposition in Muslim Baghdadi Arabic.

(27) [A14]
ʔəgʕəd   əgbāl-i!   xall asōləf-l-ak!
sit.IMP.SG.M in_front_of-1SG let   tell.IPFV.1SG-to-2SG.M
'Sit down in front of me! Let me tell you stories!'

(28) [A14]
əs-sayyāra əgbāl   əl-bəstān.
DEF-car   in_front_of DEF-garden
'The car is in front of the garden.'

(29) [A14]
əl-əmḥammra   ətṣīr   əgbāl   ʕAbbādān.
DEF-Muḥammara become.IPFV.3SG.F in_front_of Abadan
'Muḥammara is situated in front of Abadan.'

MORPHOLOGY

4.4.7 (mən) wara *'behind, after (Temporal)'*
wara is mainly used to express that something is behind something else in a
local sense (cf. Procházka 1993: 202).

(30) [A14]
    əl-bəstān   wara   l-bēt.
    DEF-garden behind DEF-house
    'The garden is behind the house.'

However, as (31) shows, it can also be used in a temporal sense expressing pos-
teriority (cf. Procházka 1993: 203). Temporal use of the originally local preposition *wara* is also known in, e.g. Nigerian Arabic (Owens 1993: 224) and many
Maghribi dialects, but also in the east in several Gulf Arabic and *gələt* dialects
(Procházka 1995a: 421, fn. 23). In this sense, KhA *wara* is interchangeable with
the KhA preposition *baʕad.*

(31) [X2]
    mən wara l-karāb
    from after DEF-plowing
    'after plowing'

4.4.8 (mən) baʕad *'after'*

(32) [A3]
    mən baʕad fatra
    from after while
    'after a while'

4.4.9 l- *'to, until (Local and Temporal), for,* [POSS]'
Before Cv-structures the form of this preposition is usually *ʔəl-*, as in (34); before
a vowel, it is *l-*, as in (33), (37), and (38). Before two consonants the form is always *l-*; but an epenthetic vowel is introduced before the two initial consonants
yielding *l-əCC*, e.g. *l-əbyūt-na* 'to our houses'. With the preposition *l-*, the same
morpho-phonological rules apply as for the definite article, cf. 4.9.6.1, also regarding the possible assimilation to a following alveolar or palato-alveolar consonant. However, as (34) shows, exceptions to this assimilation rule do occur.

(33) [H1]
    waṣalna   l-ahal-na.
    arrive.PFV.1PL to-family-1PL
    'We came to our family.'

160 CHAPTER 4

(34) [Ḥ1]
tətlaʕ al-dəkkān-ha.
go_out.IPFV.3SG.F to-shop-3SG.F
'She goes to her shop.'

(35) [A4]
l-əs-sāʕa bēš?
to-DEF-hour how_much
'Until when?'

(36) [A6]
əl mā tawlad al-hassa ngəl-ha
REL NEG give_birth.IPFV.3SG.F until-now call.IPFV.1PL-OBL.3SG.F
daǧīǧa.
young_ewe
'The one [sheep] that has not yet given birth, we call (it) *daǧīǧa.*'

(37) [Ḥa1, talking about her work as a midwife]
mən ʕašyāt l-əṣ-ṣəbaḥ
from evenings until-DEF-morning
'from night till morning'

(38) [Ḥ1]
ham l-ahl al-bēt.
also for-family DEF-house
'[We brought lunch] also for the family of the house.'

For its function to express possession in combination with suffixed object pronouns, cf. 4.1.3.2 and 4.11.14.2. The preposition *l-* is not used to mark a definite
object as in Cypriot Arabic (cf. Procházka 1993: 161) or Muslim Baghdadi Arabic
(Erwin 1963: 332).

Goals are most commonly expressed by using the preposition *l-*, as in (33)
above. However, especially in questions, the preposition *l-* can be omitted, as
the next three examples illustrate (Procházka 1993: 157 states that this is a common feature found in many Arabic dialects):

(39) [A14]
wēn rəḥət?
where go.PFV.2SG.M
'Where did you go to?'

MORPHOLOGY 161

(40) [A12]

gabəl   rāḥaw   wəyyā-na Karbəla.
formerly go.PFV.3PL.M with-1PL Karbala
'In the past they went with us to Karbala.'

(41) [M3]

kəll   bəčān   məšēna.
every place go.PFV.1PL
'We went to all places.'

4.4.10   lē ~ lī *'until, to'*

Apart from the local adverbs *lēyāy* 'here' and *lēġād* 'there' (cf. 4.3.3), the preposition *lē* is only used in some fixed expressions, like:

(42) [Ḥ2]

təyūn   lē-na.
come.IPFV.2PL.M to-1PL
'You come to us.'

(43) [A1]

lī-hassa   mā   taġaddēt.
until-now NEG eat_lunch.PFV.1SG
'Until now I haven't eaten (any) lunch.'

4.4.11   bēn *'between'*

(44) [A14]

wāyəd aḥəbb   əl-bəstān   əl bēn   ḥōš-na   w
a_lot love.IPFV.1SG DEF-garden REL between house-1PL and
ḥōš-kəm.
house-2PL.M
'I really like the garden between our and your house.'

(45) [A14]

hāḏ əl-ḥači yəbġa   bēn-i   w bēn-ak.
DEM DEF-talk remain.IPFV.3SG.M between-1SG and between-2SG.M
'This talk remains between you and me/among us.'

162   CHAPTER 4

4.4.12   bēnāt + *PL PRO 'between, among'*
The form *bēnāt* (cf. Procházka 1993: 97; and 1995a: 422–423 for etymological
remarks on this form which also exists in other Semitic languages) is used only
with plural pronominal suffixes and with plural nouns. The same meaning can
often be expressed by a repetition of *bēn* + PRO. Compare the next example
and example (45) above, both of which may be translated as 'This talk remains
among us.'

(46) [A14]
    hāḏ   əl-ḥači   yḏ̣əll   bēnāt-na.
    DEM DEF-talk remain.IPFV.3SG.M between-1PL
    'This talk remains among us.'

(47) [A14]
    bēnāt-na   ʔaku   masāfa   čbīra.
    between-1PL EXIST distance big.F
    'There is a big distance between us.'

(48) [A14]
    bēnāt-na   ʔaku   zaʕal.
    between-1PL EXIST fight
    'There is a (little) fight between us.'

4.4.13   ṭūl *'during (the whole)'*

(49) [A10]
    ʔāna hāy ṭūl   əs-sənīn   ansa   mən ayi
    1SG   DEM during DEF-years forget.IPFV.1SG when come.IPFV.1SG
    ʔagəl-l-əč.
    tell.IPFV.1SG-to-2SG.F
    'During (all) these years, when(ever) I came (home), I (always) forgot to
    tell you.'

(50) [A15]
    ʔāna ṭūl   əl-yōm   mašḡūla bī-ha.
    1SG   during DEF-day busy.F   with-3SG.F
    'During the whole day I am busy with her [she means her daughter].'

4.4.14   barra *'outside'*
This preposition is homophone with the adverb *barra* (cf. 4.3.3.16).

MORPHOLOGY 163

(51) [A14]
 əl-ʔawlād   **barra**   *l-bēt.*
 DEF-children   outside   DEF-house
 'The children are outside the house.'

4.4.15   (mən) ʕand ~ ʕad ~ ʕənd ~ ʕəd 'at; [POSS]'

ʕand (and its variant forms) is used for the expression of proximity (cf. Proch+ázka 1993: 80) and possession (cf. 4.11.14.3).

 The pronunciation of the vowel in the preposition *ʕand* can vary between *a* and *ə* (cf. Procházka 1993: 76–78 for a discussion of the form of the CA preposition *ʕinda* 'at' in modern spoken dialects of Arabic). Procházka states that, apart from the bigger cities in Syria, parts of Anatolia, northern Yemen, and Oman, in which *ʕand* is the common form, the majority of the other Eastern dialects use *ʕind* (1993: 77). Damascus Arabic, like KhA, also seems to know both variants (cf. Procházka 1993: 77, fn. 65).

 The preposition *ʕand ~ ʕəd* regularly shows elision of *n*, yielding *ʕad* or *ʕəd*, before consonant-initial suffixes as. Before vowel-initial suffixes both forms with and without elision of *n* are heard.

(52) [Ḥ1]
 təthanna   **ʕad** *ahal-ha.*
 apply_henna.IPFV.3SG.F   at   family-3SG.F
 'She applies the henna at her family's place.'

KhA *ʕand* is frequently introduced between the preposition *mən* and a pronominal suffix, but without adding any semantic information or changing the meaning of *mən*:

(53) [Ḥ1, describing the way they used to fix and embellish their scarfs with
   jewels and stones]
 wə-nḥəṭṭ   *waḥda šaḏra,*   *ḥaḏər*   *mən* *ʕad-ha.*
 and-put.IPFV.1PL   one.F   golden_bead   beneath   of   at-3SG.F
 'And we put one golden bead beneath it.'

4.4.16   dāxəl 'inside'

(54) [A14]
 dāxəl   *əl-bēt*
 inside   DEF-house
 'inside the house'

164 CHAPTER 4

4.4.17 *dāyər dawār, dōr mā dawār, dār mā dawār '(All) around'*

(55) [A14]
dāyər   dawār   Vəyanna kəll-a   šə̆ğar.
turn.AP.SG.M going_around Vienna   all-3SG.M trees
'All around Vienna are a lot of trees [lit. "it is all trees"].'

dāyər is frequently used in the phrase *mən dāyər səna əd-dāyər səna* 'from year to year, from one year to the next, all around the year'.

4.4.18 (b-)wasaṭ ~ wəṣṭat *'in the Middle of'*
The KhA preposition *wasaṭ* 'in the middle of' is usually combined with the preposition *b-* 'with'. This combination is known for many other dialects of Arabic, among them that of Kwayriš/Babylon (Meißner 1903: XXXIII; cf. Procházka 1993: 205, 207).

(56) [M1]
əb-wasaṭ   əd-dīra
in-middle DEF-town
'in the middle of the town'

As the next example shows, the preposition *wasaṭ* can be combined with pronominal suffixes. When the suffix is vowel-initial, the second vowel *a* of the preposition is elided, yielding a base *wasṭ-*:

(57) [A9]
xallī́   b-əs-səfra,   maṯal ġəda,
leave.IMP.SG.OBL.3SG.M at-DEF-table_cloth like   lunch
yxallūn   l-saḥan   bə-wasṭ-a.
leave.IPFV.3PL.M DEF-plate in-middle-3SG.M
'You leave them [the dates] on the table cloth, like (at) lunch, they put a plate in its center.'

The variant form of this preposition, *wəṣṭat*, occurs twice in my corpus (both in the same sentence), once in combination with the preposition *b-* and once without it. In Muslim Baghdadi Arabic the first form, *wasaṭ*, can also be used without the preposition *b-* (Malaika 1963: 32; cf. Procházka 1993: 205–206).

MORPHOLOGY   165

(58) [AB1]
əb-waṣṭat ət-təmən ənḥašši   əs-saməč w   ənḥaṭṭ-a
in-middle DEF-rice fill.IPFV.1PL DEF-fish and put.IPFV.1PL-OBL.3SG.M
waṣṭat   ət-təmən.
middle DEF-rice
'(We put the fish) in the middle of the rice; we fill the fish and we put it in
the middle of the rice.'

4.4.19 əbbaṭən 'in the Middle of, inside'

(59) [Ḥ1]
əbbaṭn   əl-hōr
in_the_middle_of DEF-marsh
'in the middle of the marshes'

(60) [X3]
darīša, ngaʕʕəd   bī-ha   l-əmmaʕīn mətəl hāy
window put_down.IPFV.1PL in-3SG.F DEF-vessels like   DEM
əṭ-ṭāṣa,   mətəl hāy l-əmmāʕīn ngaʕʕəd   əbbaṭən-ha.
DEF-bowl like   DEM DEF-vessels put_down.IPFV.1PL inside-3SG.F
'(The) window, we put the vessels in it; for example, this bowl, or these
vessels, we put (them) inside it.'

4.4.20 fōg 'above, over, on'

(61) [A19]
ʔāna fōg   əs-sabʕīn.
1SG   above DEF-seventy
'I am above seventy.'

(62) [X1]
ḥaṭṭēt   əs-saməča   fōg,   fōg   əč-čīma
put.PFV.1SG DEF-fish.SGT on_top above DEF-embers
əd-dāwīya.
DEF-burn.AP.SG.F
'I put the fish on top, on the burning embers.'

(63) [X3]
w-yḥaṭṭ   fōg-a   šakar.
and-put.IPFV.3SG.M on-3SG.M sugar
'And he puts sugar on it.'

166   CHAPTER 4

4.4.21   (mən) ḥadər 'under, beneath'

ḥadər 'under' is etymologically related to the CA verbal noun ḥadr connected
with the CA verb ḥadara—yaḥduru 'let, put down' (Procházka 1993: 227).

This preposition is also used in some dialects of Central Arabia and the Gulf,
and in the Arabic dialect of Uzbekistan (cf. Procházka 1993: 226–227 and the references cited there; Holes 2001: 104–105 on Bahraini Arabic, in which it is used
either as an adverb meaning 'below, underneath', or as an adjective meaning
'low-lying'). Most Iraqi dialects use the preposition ǧawwa for 'under' (Erwin
1963: 301).

In the next example the combination of ḥadər with mən is not optional,
because mən ḥadər īd ... 'under the hand (of) ...' is a fixed idiomatic expression.

(64) [Ḥa1]
      tačabbašət   mən ḥadər īd-ha.
      learn.PFV.1SG from under hand-3SG.F
      'I have learnt (it) from her [lit. "under her hand"].'

(65) [X1, describing a recipe for a traditional fish dish called ṭābəg, for which
      the fish is baked inside bread]
      ən-nōb   ḥaṭṭētī-l-əč   ḥadər-ha.
      DEF-time put.PFV.2SG.F-for-2SG.F under-3SG.F
      'Then you put it [the bread] under it [the fish].'

As the next example shows, direct suffixation of a pronoun to the preposition
ḥadər can be avoided by adding two more prepositions, mən and ʕand, the latter of which more commonly precedes pronominal suffixes (cf. Syrian Arabic
mən taḥt and fōʔ mən, Cowell 1964: 486).

(66) [Ḥ1, describing the way they used to fix and embellish their scarfs with
      jewels and stones]
      wə-nḥaṭṭ   waḥda šaḏra,   ḥadər mən ʕad-ha.
      and-put.PFV.1PL one.F golden_bead beneath of   at-3SG.F
      'And we put one golden bead beneath it.'

4.4.22   ṣōb 'towards, in Direction of, in the Vicinity of'

(67) [M1]
      rəḥna   hēč,   ṣōb   əl-Gəṣba.
      go.PFV.1PL like_this towards al-Guṣba
      'We went like that, towards al-Guṣba [Pers. Arvandkenar; port city south
      of Abadan].'

MORPHOLOGY   167

(68) [A18], Elicited
ʔəḥna sāknīn,   ṣōb   əl-əḤwēza.
1PL   live.AP.PL.M close_to DEF-Hoveyzeh
'We live close to Hoveyzeh.'

(69) [M1]
dīrat-həm   ṣōb   ʕAbbādān.
town-3PL.M   close_to Abadan
'Their town is close to Abadan ~ in the direction of Abadan.'

4.4.23 ʕan 'from, of, about (a Topic)'
Both *ʕala* and *ʕan* are used in a revelative function—i.e. for stating the topic
one wants to talk about (cf. Procházka 1993: 74–75).

(70) [F1]
sōlfi   ʕan   gabəl!
tell.IMP.SG.F about past
'Tell us about the past!'

(71) [A14]
dāyman yəḥči   ʕan   nafṣ-a.
always talk.IPFV.3SG.M about self-3SG.M
'He always talks about himself.'

Its local use with the meaning 'from, of' is restricted to idiomatic expressions
like *baʕad ʕan* 'go away, leave'. Procházka (1995a: 418) states that most "dialects
which use both *min* and *ʕan*, use *min* in an ablative sense while *ʕan* is used to
mark a topic".

(72) [A10]
hīya baʕdat   ʕan   ən-nazīl.
3SG.F go_away.PFV.3SG.F from DEF-camp
'She went away from the camp.'

4.4.24 ʕala ~ ʕa 'on, about (a Topic), against, at'

(73) [A14]
ʕala l-mēz
on   DEF-table
'on the table'

168 CHAPTER 4

In only a few cases (of these, *ʕa* always precedes the definite article *l*), KhA *ʕala* is shortened to *ʕa-*, as in (74):

(74) [A3]
al-māy   māl-a   ḥaṭṭaw   ʕa-l-gās.
DEF-water GL.SG.M-3SG.M put.PFV.3PL.M on-DEF-gas
'Its water, they put (it) on the gas (oven).'

(75) [A18]
sōlfī-l-na   ʕala   z-zarāʕa!
tell.IMP.SG.F-to-1PL about DEF-agriculture
'Tell us about (the) agriculture!'

(76) [A14]
ad-daray   mantačča   ʕala   ṭ-ṭōf.
DEF-ladder lean.AP.SG.F against DEF-wall
'The ladder leans against the wall.'

(77) [A14]
kall-ham   ʕala-yya.
all-3PL.M against-1SG
'They are all against me.'

(78) [A19]
kall wakat hanā ʕala š-šaǧal.
all time here at   DEF-work
'(We are) always here at work.'

The next example shows the use of this preposition in the phrase *ʕala gūlt al-*
... 'as the ... say':

(79) [A19]
w   ʕand-ač ḥalba,   hāy al-marra,   ʕala gūlt
and at-2SG.F fenugreek DEM DEF-bitter.F as   saying.CS
al-ʕaǧam   ygalū-l-a   hīya ygalū-l-a
DEF-Persians say.IPFV.3PL.M-to-3SG.M 3SG.F say.IPFV.3PL.M-to-3SG.M
ᴾšembelīleᴾ
fenugreek
'[And then], there is fenugreek, this bitter one; (or,) as the Persians call it *šenbelīle*'

MORPHOLOGY   169

Combined with the suffixed interrogative -man 'what', it has a base form ʕalē-
(cf. 4.3.4.4).

4.4.25 yamm 'next to, near'

(80) [A10]
yamm _ḏāk əl-bēt_
next_to DEM DEF-house
'next to that house'

(81) [A1]
gaʕad   **yamm-a**
sit.PFV.3SG.M next_to-3SG.M
'He sat next to him.'

(82) [A1]
yamm _Mūsīyān əhnāk ʔakt_ar nās   ʕad-həm ġannāma._
next_to Musian there most people at-3PL.M shepherds
'There, near Musian [city in Ilam Province of Iran], most people are shepherds.'

4.4.26 ʕala šān ~ ʕašān ~ šān 'because of, for'

(83) [A19]
yxallūn-a   — _šənhu?_ **ʕašān** _əl-akəl_   **šān**
leave.IPFV.3PL.M-OBL.3SG.M   what.SG.M for DEF-food for
b-əš-šəta.
in-DEF-winter
'They leave it [the stored dates]—What (for)? For the food, for (in) winter.'

4.4.27 mən šān ~ mšān 'because of, for'

(84) [AB1]
... _baʕad hāy əl-ḥāməḏ nāxəḏ_   **əmšān** _əl-ḥašu._
then   DEM DEF-lemon take.IPFV.1PL for   DEF-filling
'... then we take this lemon for the filling [of the fish].'

4.4.28 ʕalamūd 'because of, for, for the Sake of'
The preposition ʕalamūd might be cognate with the preposition _mayd_ used in
southern Arabia with the same meaning (cf. Procházka 1993: 231–232). It is also

used in Baghdadi Arabic (cf. Blanc 1964: 154). On the conjunction *ʕalamūd-mā* 'because when, so (that) when' cf. 4.7.2.7.

(85) [A14]
    yēt   *ʕalamūd-ak.*
    come.PFV.1SG because_of-2SG.M
    'I came for you.'

4.4.29   (mən) *ġēr 'Other (Than), Nothing but, apart from, besides, except for, without'*

(86) [Ḥ2]
    mā   *yat-ak*   *ġēr*   *bət-ak.*
    NEG come.PFV.3SG.F-OBL.2SG.M other_than daughter-2SG.M
    'Nobody (else) but your daughter came to you.'

(87) [Ḥ1]
    mən ġēr   *əl-ʕaṣar,*   *nṭīḥ*[48]   *yaʕni nōbtēn,*
    from other_than DEF-late_afternoon go_down.IPFV.1PL DP   twice
    ēh, nōbtēn nṭayyəḥ.
    yes twice   take_down.IPFV.1PL
    'Apart from the late afternoon [when they always bring the buffaloes down to the river], we take (them) twice (down to the river).'

(88) [A14]
    ʔəyaw   *kəll-həm*   *mən ġēr-ak.*
    come.PFV.3PL.M all-3PL.M from except_for-2SG.M
    'All came but you.'

4.4.30   *ġēr ~ b-ġēr 'without'*

(89) [Ḥa1]
    əyēt   *əb-ġēr*   *ʕabāya.*
    come.PFV.1SG with-other_than abaya
    'I came without an abaya.'

---

48   Probably a *lapsus linguae* as the expected form for 'we take down', which also appears at the end of the sentence, would be *nṭayyəḥ*; *nṭīḥ* usually means 'we fall' in KhA.

MORPHOLOGY 171

(90) [Ḥa1]

xāf   ənḍəll   əb-ǧēr   zād.
maybe remain.IPFV.1PL with-other_than food
'Maybe we are left without food (one day).'

4.4.31 blāya 'without'

In Baghdad the form for 'without' is *blayya* (cf. Procházka 1993: 112).

(91) [A10]

ča   ʔanti mā yṣīr   ətḍallīn   əblāya šəǧəl!
DP 2SG.F NEG become.IPFV.3SG.M remain.IPFV.2SG.F without work
'Hey you, you can't just stay here without work(ing)!'

4.4.32 bədūn 'without'

(92) [X2]

ḍall   bədūn   ᴾkart   melliᴾ.
remain.PFV.3SG.M without ID_card national
'He remained without an identity card.'

4.4.33 məṭəl ~ maṭal 'like'

(93) [A14]

məṭəl əl-yāhəl
like   DEF-child
'like a child'

(94) [Ḥ1]

kəll   wakət, maṭal ʕīd,   maṭal farah,   maṭal ʕəd-na
every time   like   holiday like celebration like   at-1PL
ʕərəs.
wedding
'(We) always (wear these kind of clothes); like (for the) *ʕīd*, for a celebration, like (when) we have a wedding.'

When the noun following this preposition is indefinite and begins with an alveolar or palato-alveolar consonant, the final *l* often assimilates to this first consonant, as in the next example: *məṭəl rōba* [mɪθɪr roːba] 'like yoghurt':

172   CHAPTER 4

(95) [Ḥ1]
   ġədā-na   māxdīn-a   wəyyā-na, məṭəl rōba.
   lunch-1PL take.AP.PL.M-OBL.3SG.M with-1PL   like   yoghurt
   'Our lunch we brought with us, like yoghurt.'

məṭəl can also be used with pronominal suffixes:

(96) [A1]
   *ʔəhwa **məṭl**-ak.*
   3SG.M like-2SG.M
   'He is like you.'

(97) [A10]
   *tara ysawwī-č   **məṭəl**-na.*
   DP   make.IPFV.3SG.M-OBL.2SG.F like-1PL
   'Because (otherwise), it [i.e. the vulture] will do to you as he did to us.'

4.4.34   gadd ~ əbgadd *'at the Age/Size of ...'*

(98) [A1]
   *čənt   əzġīr, **gadd**   Māhər.*
   be.PFV.1SG young at_the_age_of Maher
   'I was young, at the age of Maher.'

(*əb*)*gadd* can also be used with pronominal suffixes:

(99) [Ḥa1, telling what they used to play when they were girls]
   *ham aku   banāt **əbgadd**-i*
   also EXIST girls   at_the_age_of-1SG
   'There were also some girls of my age.'

4.4.35   wīya ~ wayya ~ wəya *'(Together) with, at the Time of [Synchronously]'*

The origin of the preposition *wīya* is a contraction of OA **wa-ʔiyyā-* (cf. Procházka 1993: 24, 197–198). In KhA, the form *wīya* is more common than its alternative forms *wayya*, as in (101) and (103) and *wəya*, as in (102). According to some consultants from Baghdad, Muslim Baghdadi Arabic also has an alternative pronunciation of this preposition with only one *y*. Ingham (1973: 550; cf. Procházka 1993: 198) gives only the form with one *y*, *wəya*, for KhA. In Tikrīt the first vowel is *a* (cf. Procházka 1993: 199–200 and the references cited there).

MORPHOLOGY   173

(100)   [Ḥa1]
        Ɂəla wāḥəd   ysawwī-l-a   māy   həwa
        if   someone make.IPFV.3SG.M-for-3SG.M water air
        yǧəsm-a   wīya yār-a,   wīya
        share.IPFV.3SG.M-OBL.3SG.M with neighbour-3SG.M with
        xǘ.
        brother.3SG.M
        'When someone made *māy həwa* [lit. "air water", a very simple dish
        of red sauce without meat] he shared it with his neighbor, with his
        brother.'

(101)   [A6, telling us how many sheep he owns]
        hassa bī-ha   Ɂarbaʕ mīya,   Ɂarbaʕ mīya   w   xamsīn
        now   EXIST-3SG.F four   hundred four   hundred and fifty
        taġrīb, ǧēr   əṣ-ṣəxūl   hassa xō, mā nəḥsəb-hən
        ca.   without DEF-goats now   DP NEG count.IPFV.1PL-OBL.3PL.F
        wayya əl-ġanam.
        with   DEF-sheep
        'Now there are 400 [sheep], about 450, (but) without (counting) the
        goats; well, we don't count them with the sheep.'

(102)   [A4]
        wāyəd ʕad-na wəyā-č   səwāləf.
        many at-1PL with-2SG.F stories
        'We have many things to talk about with you.'

The next example shows that this preposition can also be used to express temporal coincidence.

(103)   [Ḥ1]
        nōṣal   yaʕni l-əd-dīra,   əd-dīra
        arrive.IPFV.1PL DP   to-DEF-village DEF-village
        nōṣal-ha,   wayya la- əl-adān.
        arrive.IPFV.1PL-OBL.3SG.F with   DEF DEF-prayer_call
        'We came to the village, we came to the village, at the time of [lit. 'with']
        the, the prayer call.'

174   CHAPTER 4

4.5   Paradigms of Prepositions with Pronominal Suffixes[49]

In the following, full paradigms will be provided for those prepositions that can combine with pronominal suffixes and that show morphological changes when the suffixes are attached.

i.   *ʕand ~ ʕad ~ ʕənd ~ ʕəd* 'at; [POSS]'

The preposition *ʕand ~ ʕənd* usually elides *n* before consonant-initial suffixes, yielding a base *ʕad ~ ʕəd* (cf. Procházka 1993: 79–80 on this same process in Muslim Baghdadi Arabic and other Mesopotamian and Gulf Arabic dialects). *n* may also be elided before vowel-initial suffixes, but this elision is not as regular as before consonant-initial suffixes (cf. Procházka 1993: 80, fn. 78, on a comparable observation for Muslim Baghdadi Arabic).

1 SG	*ʕand-i ~ ʕad-i*
2 SGM	*ʕand-ak ~ ʕad-ak*
2 SGF	*ʕand-əč ~ ʕad-əč*
3 SGM	*ʕand-a ~ ʕad-a*
3 SGF	*ʕad-ha*
1 PL	*ʕad-na*
2 PLM	*ʕad-kəm*
2 PLF	*ʕad-čan*
3 PLM	*ʕad-həm*
3 PLF	*ʕad-hən*

ii.   Prepositions Ending in *-a*: *ʕala* 'on', *wīya* '(Together) with', *wara* 'behind'

The preposition *ʕala* generally has the form *ʕalay-* before suffixes (cf. Procházka 1993: 59, 63), which in KhA yields the base *ʕalē-* via monophthongization of *ay* > *ē*. Only with the 1 SG pronominal suffix is the diphthong word-final and retained, yielding *ʕalay* or *ʕalayya*. *wara* goes back to OA **warāʔa* via loss of the final syllable. As stated above, the origin of the preposition *wīya* is a contraction of OA **wa-ʔiyyā-* (cf. Procházka 1993: 24, 197–198). Since both KhA *wara*

---

49   For the full paradigm of the preposition *l-* 'to, for, until' with pronominal suffixes cf. Table 6 and Table 7.

MORPHOLOGY   175

and *wīya*, unlike *ʕala*, do not go back to a (medial) form with a final diphthong
before suffixes, their final vowels are simply lengthened before a suffix.

1 SG	*ʕalay* ~ *ʕalayya*	*wəyyā-y*	*warā-y*
2 SGM	*ʕalē-k*	*wəyyā-k*	*warā-k*
2 SGF	*ʕalē-č*	*wəyyā-č*	*warā-č*
3 SGM	*ʕalé* [ʕaliːə] ~ *ʕalī-h*	*wəyyá*	*wará*
3 SGF	*ʕalē-ha*	*wəyyā-ha*	*warā-ha*
1 PL	*ʕalē-na*	*wəyyā-na*	*warā-na*
2 PLM	*ʕalē-kəm*	*wəyyā-kəm*	*warā-kəm*
2 PLF	*ʕalē-čan*	*wəyyā-čan*	*warā-čan*
3 PLM	*ʕalē-həm*	*wəyyā-həm*	*warā-həm*
3 PLF	*ʕalē-hən*	*wəyyā-hən*	*warā-hən*

iii.   Prepositions Ending in *-n*: *ʕan* 'from, of, about (a Topic)', *mən* 'from, of,
       Than (Comparative)'

ʕan 'from, of, about (a topic)' and *mən* 'from, of, than (comparative)' show gemination of the final *-n* before vowel-initial suffixes, yielding homophonic forms
for when these prepositions are combined with the suffixes of the 3SG.M and
the 1PL (cf. 3.1.5; and Procházka 1993: 73, 180). However, as stated above, the
preposition *ʕand* is frequently introduced between the preposition *mən* and
the pronominal suffix, as in (53). With this intermediate preposition there is a
clear difference between 3SG.M (*mən ʕand-a*) and 1PL (*mən ʕad-na*).

1 SG	*ʕann-i*	*mənn-i*
2 SGM	*ʕann-ak*	*mənn-ak*
2 SGF	*ʕann-əč*	*mənn-əč*
3 SGM	*ʕann-a*	*mənn-a*
3 SGF	*ʕan-ha*	*mən-ha*
1 PL	*ʕann-a*	*mənn-a*
2 PLM	*ʕan-kəm*	*mən-kəm*
2 PLF	*ʕan-čan*	*mən-čan*
3 PLM	*ʕan-həm*	*mən-həm*
3 PLF	*ʕan-hən*	*mən-hən*

176   CHAPTER 4

iv.   *b-* 'with; in'

The preposition *b-* has a base *bī-* before suffixes, which is also common in many other dialects of Arabic (cf. Procházka 1993:102). Procházka (1993:102) explains the development of the long *ī* in *bī-* as an analogy with the preposition *fī* 'in' or a merger with *fī* in dialects where *fī* has become obsolete, as is the case in KhA. The form with the 3SG.M suffix, which is only marked by a stress on the final long vowel, *bí* [biːə], has developed from *bī-* + **-h*.

1 SG	*bī-ya*
2 SGM	*bī-k*
2 SGF	*bī-č*
3 SGM	*bí*
3 SGF	*bī-ha*
1 PL	*bī-na*
2 PLM	*bī-kəm*
2 PLF	*bī-čan*
3 PLM	*bī-həm*
3 PLF	*bī-hən*

4.6   *māl* Constructions and the Analytic Genitive

The noun *māl* originally meant 'property'. As a noun, it occurs as the head of NPs, which usually express relations of various kinds (cf. 4.6.2).

It has been further grammaticalized and developed into a linker for nominal attribution—i.e. for the construction of the analytic genitive (cf. 4.6.1).[50] In this function it is usually labeled in Arabic dialectology as a "genitive exponent" or "genitive marker" (cf. Eksell 2006; cf. Bettega 2019: 228, fn. 4 and the references mentioned there on the different labels used for such markers).

māl syntactically functions like a preposition expressing the periphrastic genitive (such as English *of*, French *de*, etc.). However, unlike real prepositions, KhA *māl* is not invariable but can be inflected for gender and number according to the grammatical gender and number of its head noun. All forms of *māl* can be combined with a pronominal suffix.

---

50   Parallel developments are not restricted to Arabic dialects but found in many Semitic languages; for an overview see Rubin (2005: 51–57).

MORPHOLOGY

TABLE 11   Total numbers of occurrences of *māl* without a pronominal suffix

	SG		PL	
M	*māl*	90	*mālīn*	5
F	*mālat ~ mālt*	53	*mālāt*	3

TABLE 12   Total numbers of occurrences of *māl* with a pronominal suffix

	SG		PL	
M	*māl*	49	*mālīn*	0
F	*mālat ~ mālt*	16	*mālāt*	2

Its forms and numbers of occurrence in my corpus are presented in Tables 11 and 12 above.

Once in my corpus *māl(at)* is used in a diminutive form, *maylat*, by speaker [Ḥ1] from Hoveyzeh (cf. example (8) below). Other consultants of Ahvaz confirmed the use of the diminutive form *əmwēlt-i* [ʁmːeːlti] for 'mine'.

Outside Khuzestan, *māl* is also used in many other dialects, though mostly not inflected for number, and only rarely for gender, especially those of the Mesopotamian and Gulf dialect area. Among these are Kwayriš/Babylon Arabic (Meißner 1903:XXVI, who also mentions a F form *mālat* and a PL.F form *mālāt*, but not the PL.M form *mālīn*) and most other dialects in Iraq (Blanc 1964: 156; Palva 2006: 607); Bahraini Arabic (Holes 2016: 223–227, besides *ḥagg*); Omani Arabic (Bettega 2019: 229–230, besides *ḥaqq*, which is used in Dhofar); and Kuwaiti Arabic (Holes 2007: 614; Brustad 2000: 72–73 and the references mentioned there, who writes that *ḥagg* is also used, albeit only as an indirect object marker that has the same meaning as /li-/ 'to, for'). Central Asian Arabic dialects do not make use of a genitive exponent at all (cf. Blanc 1964: 156), but rather express nominal attribution via the so-called "dialectal tanwīn" (cf. Holes 2018a: 132, fn. 41).

In the following I outline the most important semantic and syntactic aspects of the two main ways in which the element *māl* is used, which are for the analytic genitive and in independent *māl*-phrases. The semantic categories presented are not a complete account of all possible functions (e.g. there probably

178   CHAPTER 4

exist also analytic genitive constructions used for quantification). These sections simply provide a general view of the various functions of *māl* based on my corpus and some elicited data.

4.6.1   *Analytic Genitive*

The analytic genitive is a syntagm used as an alternative to synthetic nominal attribution (unless the second element is an adjective; cf. 4.9.3 on synthetic nominal attribution and the use of the nouns *ʔəmm* 'mother' and *ʔəbu* 'father' to express possession or to specify a noun's qualities). The two default types of this syntagm are: NOUN + MĀL + NOUN and NOUN + MĀL-PRONOMINAL SUFFIX. There are also examples in which the element after *māl* is an adverb, as in (10).

4.6.1.1   Semantic Aspects

The analytic genitive is used to express possession and affiliation in the widest sense: it marks relations in time, space, and society (particularly origin). It is generally limited to alienable, non-intimate relations and preferred over synthetic nominal attribution for pragmatic reasons like the wish to express textual prominence or focus (Brustad 2000: 76; cf. Bettega 2019: 239), or for formal reasons, when the head noun is a loanword or ends in a vowel (cf. below).

The analytic genitive is usually not used for inalienable relations such as body parts, thoughts, or personal relations such as kinship, friendship, or neighborhood (cf. Eksell 2006: 83; and Melcer 1995: 61–67 for a range of semantic fields in Jewish Baghdadi in which pronominal suffix constructions are usually preferred over *māl*-constructions to express possession).

The main functions of KhA *māl*-phrases are summarized in the following:

i.   Possession

In addition to pronominal suffixation (cf. 4.1.2), *māl*-constructions are frequently used to express possession. In this function, they often have pronominal suffixes, as in the next example, where we have both ways of expressing possession next to each other, with the same noun and uttered by the same speaker: *hawīt-i* (pronominal suffixation) and *hawīya mālt-i* (analytic genitive), both meaning 'my identity card'.

MORPHOLOGY   179

(1) [A19]
     as-saǧal **māl-i**   ṯamānīya w   xamsīn, šlōn angūl   hawīya
     DEF-ID GL.SG.M-1SG eight   and fifty   how say.IPFV.1PL ID
     mālt-i,   hawīt-i   ṯamānīya w   xamsīn bass āna fōg
     GL.SG.F-1SG ID.CS-1SG eight   and fifty   but 1SG above
     as-sabʕīn.
     DEF-seventy
     'My identity card (says that I am) 58; as we call (it)[51] my identity card, my
     identity card (says) 58, but (actually) I am above 70.'

In some cases, as in the next example, we find both methods combined. This
doubled expression of possession—especially with a postposed independent
personal pronoun—is used for emphasis.

(2) [M1]
     mū   ʕala ġaṣd-i   **mālt-i**   ʔāna.
     NEG about intention-1SG GL.SG.F-1SG 1SG
     '(This is) not *my* intention/what I mean.'

The use of a *māl*-construction is often preferred over a synthetic genitive construction when the head noun ends in a vowel (cf. Bettega 2019: 240).

(3) [A12, explaining a type of singing/lamenting expressed by the verb
     naʕa—yənʕi]
     al-ġana   **māl-a**   ḥazīn.
     DEF-singing GL.SG.M-3SG.M sad
     'Its (way of) singing is sad.'

ii. Origin

As the next example shows, the head noun can also be substituted with a
demonstrative pronoun (cf. Melcer 1995: 72 on Jewish Baghdadi).

(4) [A6]
     ʕad-na ʔaḥna hāy **mālt**   Īza.
     at-1PL 1PL   DEM GL.SG.F Izeh

---

51 He is apparently aware of the fact that the term *saǧal* for 'identity card' is only used among
    KhA speakers and therefore repeats the phrase with the term *hawīya*, which is commonly
    used in the Arab states.

180   CHAPTER 4

'We have these (sheep) from Izeh [city in Khuzestan, about 180 km east of Ahvaz].'

(5)   [A19]
      Ɂəhna Ɂaṣlīyat-na   māku?[52]   *haḏōl Ɂarab yaɁni kəll Ɂarab*
      1PL   origin.CS-1PL NEG.EXIST DEM   Arabs DP   all   Arabs
      Xūzestān aṣlīyat-ha   māl   əl-yaman, kəll-ha mālt
      Khuzestan origin.CS-3SG.F GL.SG.M DEF-Yemen all-3SG.F GL.SG.F
      əl-yaman   hənāka.
      DEF-Yemen there
      'Our origin—right?—These Arabs, or rather all Arabs of Khuzestan, their origins go back to Yemen, they are all from Yemen, (from) there.'

māl is also usually preferred over the synthetic annexation structures where the head noun is a loanword (cf. Melcer 1995: 74 on Jewish Baghdadi; Brustad 2000: 74; Eksell Harning 1980: 36).

(6)   [Ḥa1]
      əl-bēhdāš[53]   *māl   əs-salaf*
      DEF-health_care_center GL.SG.M DEF-district
      'the health center of the [she means: "my"] district'

iii.   Material

The element *māl* is also used to denote the material of which an item is made:

(7)   [Ḥ1]
      Ɂəxwāṣ mālat fəḍḍa
      rings   GL.SG.F silver
      'rings (made) of silver'

(8)   [Ḥ1]
      əšwēlat-ha   maylat   balbūl
      shawl.DIM-3SG.F GL.SG.F.DIM balbūl
      'her thin shawl [lit. "made of (the material) *balbūl*"[54]]'

---

52   *māku* lit. 'there is not' is often used in rhetorical questions to put the focus on the topic of the sentence, in this case the tribe's origin.

53   < Pers. *behdāšt* 'hygiene, healthcare' (Junker and Alawi 2002: 108).

54   Cf. Steingass (2001: 197) on the Pers. term *bulbul čašm* 'a sort of silk'.

MORPHOLOGY 181

iv.   Type

The element *māl* is also used to specify a noun's qualities or its type (cf. also
example (16) below, and 4.9.3 on a similar use of the nouns *ʔəmm* 'mother' and
ʔəbu 'father'). This function is of course closely linked to its use to describe an
item's material. Such *māl*-constructions often correspond to a compound noun
in English or German.

(9)   [A3]
      naštəri   čərʕān   mālāt   əl-əʕyūl,   mālāt   əl-həwāyəš.
      buy.IPFV.1PL cow_legs GL.PL.F DEF-calves GL.PL.F DEF-cows
      'We buy legs (and feet) of calves, of cows.'

v.   Relation in Time and Space

māl can also function as a linker between a noun and an expression of time or
space.

(10) [A2]
      hāḏ   əz-zād   māl   ʔaməs   fāčč.
      DEM DEF-food GL.SG.M yesterday gone_bad
      'This food from yesterday has gone bad.'

(11) [A3]
      w   əl   sāknīn   b-əl-maġrəb māl   əl-aḥwāz
      and REL live.AP.PL.M in-DEF-west GL.SG.M DEF-Ahvaz
      'And those who live to the west of Ahvaz ...'

vi.   Purpose

The element *māl* is also used for expressing a noun's purpose. In this function
it is often translated as 'for ...' or corresponds to a compound noun in English
or German.

(12) [A3]
      xəmra mālt   əl-ǧəbən
      rennet GL.SG.F DEF-cheese
      'rennet for cheese ~ cheese rennet'

182 CHAPTER 4

(13) [X3]
d-dalla **mālt** *əd-dəhən*
DEF-jug GL.SG.F DEF-lard
'the jug for the lard'

vii. Quantity

māl can also express quantity. This use of *māl* also appears in other dialects of
Arabic (cf. Woidich 2006: 228 on Cairo Arabic, in which the genitive exponent
bitāʕ can be combined with numerals: "*bitāʕ xamsīn kīlu* 'ca. 50 kg' ").

(14) [X3]
fəṣṣ **māl** *dəhən*
handful GL.SG.M lard
'a handful of lard'

4.6.1.2   Syntactic Aspects
Determination

Three of the possible four definiteness combinations of two nouns circumpos-
ing *māl* are attested for KhA: INDEF *māl* INDEF, INDEF *māl* DEF, and DEF *māl*
DEF. We lack evidence only for DEF *māl* INDEF.

i. INDEF *māl* INDEF (cf. Holes 2016b: 223 on such phrases in Bahraini Arabic; Blanc 1964: 156 on examples from Baghdad Arabic):

(15) [A10]
farəd *ġaṣar* **māl** *malək*
INDEF castle GL.SG.M king
'a castle of a king'

(16) [A10]
... *gəšəf*[55] *daḥrūya w* *gəšəf hāḏa w* *gəšər* **māl** *raggi*
shell   egg   and shell DEM and rind GL.SG.M watermelon
'... an eggshell and a shell of this, and a watermelon rind'

---

55   Probably the speaker wanted to say *gəšər* 'shell'.

MORPHOLOGY 183

ii. INDEF *māl* DEF

(17) [A3]
nəštəri   čərʕān   mālāt   əl-əʕyūl,   mālāt   əl-həwāyəš.
buy.IPFV.1PL cow_legs GL.PL.F DEF-calves GL.PL.F DEF-cows
'We buy legs (and feet) of calves, of cows.'

(18) [A10]
rəmmanāt   əṯnēn māl   əd-dahab
pomegranates two   GL.SG.M DEF-gold
'two pomegranates of gold ~ two golden pomegranates'

The following example, already cited above, shows that a pronominal suffix can be either attached to the head (*aṣlīyat-na* 'our origin') or to the element *māl* (*aṣəl māl-na* 'our origin'), and that *māl*-constructions can appear both in subject/object as well as in predicate position. This example further proves that there are *māl*-phrases in KhA in which the head (*aṣəl* 'origin') is indefinite but the whole expression is semantically definite. Such constructions are also known for other dialects of Arabic.[56]

(19) [A19]
Ɂəḥna   Ɂaṣlīyat-na   māl   Šādəgān. Ɂaṣəl   aṣəl   māl-na
1PL   origin.CS-1PL GL.SG.M Shadegan origin origin GL.SG.M-1PL
Bani Tamīm, Ɂaṣəl   māl-na   māl   əl-yaman   mū   māl
Banū Tamīm origin GL.SG.M-1PL GL.SG.M DEF-Yemen NEG GL.SG.M
əhnāk.
there
'We are originally from Shadegan. Our ultimate origin is the [tribe] Banū Tamīm. Our origins go back to Yemen, not there [i.e. Khuzestan].'

iii. DEF *māl* DEF

(20) [Ḥ1]
əṣ-ṣīnīya mālt   ət-təmmən
DEF-tray GL.SG.F DEF-rice
'the rice-tray'

---

56   Cf. Holes (2016: 224, fn. 27) on Bahraini Arabic; Bettega (2019: 240, fn. 22) on Omani Arabic; Blanc (1964: 125–126) on Christian Baghdadi Arabic; and Procházka (2018a: 253–254) on Mosul Arabic.

184 CHAPTER 4

Elliptic Constructions

There are several examples, in which the head is not explicitly named and can be considered elliptic or implicit. Bettega (2019: 235) describes similar cases for Omani Arabic and calls the head of such constructions "implicit PD [Possessed, i.e. the first or head noun]". As Bettega writes, a head can be omitted "when the speaker reckons that no ambiguity could possibly arise from this omission".

In the next example, the head, 'clothes', is elliptic; but from the verb and the context it is obvious that the speaker is referring to clothes.

(21) [Ḥ1, describing how the women reserved their beautiful dresses for weddings, and on a regular day dressed casually]
ləbasna   mālat   əl-ġaraḍ.
dress.PFV.1PL GL.SG.F DEF-work
'We dressed [in casual clothes] for work.'

The next example shows especially well that the boundaries between analytic genitive constructions with an elliptic head and independent *māl*-phrases are very weak. In this example, *māl* almost appears to be used like a substantivized possessive pronoun (cf. German 'eures').

(22) [A4]
mā-dri[57]   bí   ṯ̬ələǧ ʕamma mālat-kəm?
NEG-know.IPFV.1SG in.3SG.M ice aunt GL.SG.F-2PL.M
'I don't know, is there ice in yours [referring to the blue bottle called *kolma* used for iced water or buttermilk]?'

In the next example, the head, the sheep's types, is omitted.

(23) [A8; asking me to make sure I knew the terms she was using]
tʕarfin   māl   ġanam?
know.IPFV.2SG.F GL.SG.M sheep
'Do you know (the names) of the sheep?'

4.6.2 *Independent* māl-*Phrases*
Apart from the analytic genitive, *māl* is also used as the head of independent noun phrases. Independent *māl*-phrases usually stand in predicative position

---

57   < *mā ʔadri* 'I don't know'.

MORPHOLOGY   185

and often introduce verbless copula complements, but they can also appear in subject or object position. From its use in independent *māl*-phrases, especially in examples such as (25), we can see a diachronically earlier stage when it was still used as a noun expressing 'possession'. The basic syntagm for independent *māl*-phrases is: MĀL—NOUN / PRO / ADVERB / INTERROGATIVE.

4.6.2.1   Semantic Aspects

The semantic functions of independent *māl* NPs do not fundamentally differ from those described above for analytic genitive constructions with *māl*.

i.   Possession and Belonging

Because independent *māl* NPs are usually used predicatively they more often denote belonging than possession.

For ascertaining the ownership of an object (in both questions and statements), *māl*-constructions have to be used (cf. Bettega 2019: 240, fn. 23). In Kuwait, which also has *māl* for the analytic genitive, such phrases can only be expressed with *ḥagg* (Brustad 2000: 73, 78, e.g. *ḏahab ummha ḥagg Nūra* 'Her mother's gold is for/belongs to Nura', but *šaʕar māl sibiʕ* 'hair of a lion').

(24) [A14], Elicited
    hāḏa māl-əč?   — *lā mū māl-i,   māl   əxt-i.*
    DEM GL.SG.M-2SG.F   NEG NEG GL.SG.M-1SG GL.SG.M sister-1SG
    'Is this yours?—No, it's not mine, it belongs to my sister.'

(25) [A12]
    ḥōš-na   hāḏa ʔəhnā māl   əl-ōlād   əb-Xazāmi.
    house-1PL DEM here GL.SG.M DEF-children in-Xazāmi
    'Our house here belongs to the children in Xazāmi [neighborhood in Kūt ʕAbd-Allah, Ahvaz].'

(26) [M1]
    mū   ʔəḥna mālīn   ən-naxal.
    NEG 1PL   GL.PL.M DEF-palm_trees
    'We do not have palm trees [lit. "we are not the possessors of the palm trees"].'

186   CHAPTER 4

ii.   Origin

(27) [M3]
      *ʔāna **mālat** ʕAbbādān.*
      1SG   GL.SG.F Abadan
      'I am from Abadan.'

(28) [M1]
      *əğdād   əğdād-i   **māl**   hənā.*
      grandfathers grandfathers-1SG GL.SG.M here
      'My ancestors are from here [Muḥammara].'

iii.   Material

(29) [H1]
      *hāy l-əglād   əlli lēyāy   ham **māl**   ḏahab.*
      DEM DEF-necklace REL over_here also GL.SG.M gold
      'This necklace here is also made of gold.'

iv.   Idiomatic Use

Finally, *māl*, is also typically used in questions such as (30), when a person asks
after another's condition or health. In such phrases, *māl* is never inflected.

    Woidich (2006: 363) writes that in such Cairo Arabic constructions as *mālik
taʕbāna?* 'What is (wrong) with you? Are you tired?', *māl* can still be recognized
as **mā li* + interrogative clause (cf. Reichmuth 1983: 118 on the use of *māl-* plus
PRO in eastern Sudan, which could also reflect etymological *mā l-*). The possibility of course exists, that such KhA constructions also reflect etymological *mā
+ l-*, which has subsequently become intransparent so that it could be further
combined with the interrogative *š-* 'what?':

(30) [A12]
      *š-**māl**-čan?*
      what-GL.SG.M-2PL.F
      'What is wrong with you? What troubles you?'

v.   Quantity

As was noted above, *māl* is also used to express quantity, or, as in the next example, an approximate quantity like 'a little bit of …, some':

MORPHOLOGY 187

(31) [X3, talking with Umm Amǧad about types of sugar and the fact that nowadays you can no longer find 'yellow sugar' and the quality of sugar has become very bad]

hassa lā,   hāḏ   baʕad,   hassa ham yšəbšūn-əl-na
now   NEG DEM anymore now   also   mix.IPFV.3PL.M-for-1PL
ʕalé   māl   ət-təryāg,   mā   ʔadri
on.3SG.M GL.SG.M DEF-opium NEG know.IPFV.1SG
š-yšəbšūn   wəyyá.
what-mix.IPFV.3PL.M with.3SG.M
'Now (we) don't (have it) [the yellow sugar] anymore: nowadays they also mix some opium into it—I don't know what they mix it with.'

4.6.2.2   Syntactic Aspects

As already stated, the syntagm for independent *māl*-phrases is: MĀL—NOUN / PRO / ADVERB / INTERROGATIVE. This means that the nature of the modifying element following *māl* is not limited to nouns and pronominal suffixes, but can also be an adverb or even an interrogative:

(32) [A15]
ča   l-baṭṭa   mālat-man?
DP DEF-duck GL.SG.F-who
'Say, whose duck is that?'

(33) [A4]
əṭ-ṭōg   māl   šənhi?
DEF-necklace GL.SG.M what.SG.F
'What is the *ṭōg*[58] made of?'

The next example shows that an independent *māl*-phrase does not necessarily need a head to which to refer (cf. also example (31) above) and can thus stand in subject position. Such examples are often hard to distinguish from elliptic constructions as described above.

(34) [A12]
mālat   əl-awwalīya kəll-a   məšat.
GL.SG.F DEF-past   all-3SG.M go.PFV.3SG.F
'All (things) of the past are gone.'

---

58   Kind of jewelry: a golden or silver ring used as a necklace.

188   CHAPTER 4

Determination

In independent *māl*-phrases, in which the modifying element is a noun, the noun can be either definite or indefinite.

MĀL INDEF

(35) [A14; Joking tone among friends, the second person is obviously not some-
      body who would go on the Hajj]
      *lēš   mā   trūḥ   l-əl-ḥaǧǧ?   — baḷḷa ʔāna **māl**   ḥaǧǧ?*
      why NEG go.IPFV.2SG.M to-DEF-Hajj   DP   1SG GL.SG.M Hajj
      'Why don't you go on the Hajj? Do I look like I go on the Hajj? [lit. "By God,
      am I of the Hajj?"]'

MĀL DEF

Cf. (25) above.

4.6.3   *Conclusion and Notes on Agreement*
The nominal linker *māl* might be in the process of losing its ability to inflect (cf. Bettega and Leitner 2019: 18, fn. 14; Bettega 2019: 233; Rubin 2005: 54). The analysis of my corpus shows that the SG.M form *māl* can also be used with a SG.F head (cf. (5) *ʔaṣlīya* 'origin'), or even a PL.M head (cf. (28) *əǧdād əǧdād* 'ancestors').

The speaker in example (5) uses two different forms of *māl*, first the 3SG.M form (*māl*) and then the SG.F form (*mālt*), even though both instances refer to a SG.F head. The first is *ʔaṣlīya* 'origin', and the second the COLL *ʕarab* 'Arabs' (cf. 4.9.2.1 on the fact that verbs, pronouns, and adjectives referring to collectives are usually SG.F when the collective is perceived as one entity).

Of those forms without pronominal suffixes, all five occurrences of the PL.M form *mālīn* are in independent *māl*-constructions, all three instances of the PL.F form *mālāt* are in analytic genitive constructions, and the SG.F form *mālat* ~ *mālt* is used more often in analytic genitive (38/53 occurrences) than in independent *māl*-constructions (15/53 occurrences). The SG.M form *māl* occurs in total 90 times without pronominal suffixes: 63 times in analytic genitive con-
structions, and 27 times in independent *māl*-constructions. Out of the 63 times used in analytic genitive constructions, 49 times it refers to SG.M and 14 times to PL.M, SG.F, or PL.F. Out of the 27 times used in independent *māl*-constructions, it refers 21 times to SG.M and 6 times to PL.M, SG.F, or PL.F. Though the size of my sample might not permit a general statement, the result of this analy-

MORPHOLOGY 189

sis suggests an important tendency: in both analytic genitive and independent *māl*-constructions *māl* is not inflected in 22.22% of all instances (i.e. it does refer to a PL.M, SG.F, or PL.F head but its form is still SG.M).

There is a slight tendency of inflected forms to appear in analytic genitive rather than in independent *māl*-constructions. This can probably be explained by the fact that in analytic genitive constructions the head (and its grammatical gender and number) is usually more transparent than it is in independent *māl*-constructions. Another motivation behind the inflection is probably a semantic one and connected to how far grammaticalized the element *māl* is in certain uses: where it is used to describe a material or origin, as in (29) above, for directions, as in (11) above, or as in the last two examples above, *māl* usually does not inflect and comes closest to real prepositions.

4.7 Conjunctions

Conjunctions are "a closed class of uninflected words which serve the joining of words, phrases, clauses, or sentences and simultaneously express a specific semantic relationship between the conjoined elements" (Waltisberg 2006: 467).

Morphologically, we can distinguish between simple and compound conjunctions. Whereas simple conjunctions consist of only one lexical morpheme, such as *bass* 'but', compound conjunctions are usually combinations of prepositions and the relative particle *mā*,[59] such as *gabəl-mā* 'before', of interrogatives and the particle *mā*, such as *yēmta-mā* 'whenever', or of two simple conjunctions, like *ḥatta lō* 'even if'.

Syntactically, there are two main groups of conjunctions: coordinating and subordinating conjunctions. As their names indicate, coordinating conjunctions such as *w-* 'and', and *lō* in the meaning 'or', coordinate syntactically equivalent items if they belong to the same sort (words, phrases, clauses, or sentences), whereas subordinate conjunctions, such as *lō* in the meaning 'if', introduce syntactically subordinate clauses. We should bear in mind that, as the example of *lō* shows, the same conjunction can however be used for different semantic and syntactic functions.

---

59 Called *mā al-maṣdariyya* in Arabic grammar (cf. Badawi, Carter, and Gully 2016: 578–602), which is used for the construction of many MSA conjunctions, e.g. *bayna-mā* 'while, during', *ʕinda-mā* 'when', *miṭla-mā* 'as, like', etc. (cf. Badawi, Carter, and Gully 2016: 587–599).

190   CHAPTER 4

This chapter is divided along the two main syntactic categories of 'coordinating' and 'subordinating' conjunctions. Subordinating conjunctional clauses can be subdivided according to their semantic nature: temporal, causal, final, conditional, adversative, and concessive. As will become clear from the examples below, KhA conjunctional clauses can either precede or follow the matrix clause.

KhA exhibits several conjunctions only rarely attested in other dialects of Arabic, among them: *ʔamman* 'but', *lēš-mā* 'when', *ǧəddām-mā ~ ǧəddām-lā* 'before', *mənāla-mā* 'until', *čē* 'because', *ʕala* 'if', and *māku* in the sense of 'otherwise'.

For each conjunction at least one example will be provided to illustrate its use.

4.7.1   *Coordinating Conjunctions*

4.7.1.1   *w- ~ wa* 'and'

This conjunction can be considered pan-Semitic and is used as the main coordinating conjunction in all varieties of Arabic. Its main function is additive or sequential (cf. Holes 2016b: 369). It has two main allomorphs: *w-* before a vowel, and *wa*, which is mainly used before a consonant or before a pause.

(1)   [A3]
       nətrəb-əl-na   rās   bəṣal, w-ənḥəṭṭ   fəlfəl.
       cut.IPFV.1PL-for-1PL head   onion and-put.IPFV.1PL pepper
       'We cut an onion and we put pepper (in it).'

4.7.1.2   *lō* 'or',[60] *lō ... lō ...* 'Either ... or ...'

KhA *lō* is used as a coordinating conjunction 'or' (i.e. to join two equal alternatives) and as a conditional conjunction 'if'. While it shares the latter function with its CA cognate *law* and most other dialects which have it, its use as a coordinating conjunction is more restricted. Outside Khuzestan, *lō* is used in the above two functions in all dialects of Baghdad (Blanc 1964: 156; Erwin 1963: 307), the dialect of Kwayriš/Babylon (Meißner 1903: XXXV), and in the sedentary-type Baḥārna dialects of Bahrain (the Bedouin-type ʕArab dialects of Bahrain—like most other Gulf Arabic dialects—use *lō* merely as a conditional particle, Holes 2016: 17, 371; 2018b: 122–123). Basra appears to use *walla* or *ʔaww* instead (Mahdi 1985: 186–187; Qasim Hassan, pers. comm. 2020, however, states that *lō* is also used as a coordinating conjunction in southern Iraq).

---

60   Cf. 4.7.2.24 on the homophone subordinate conjunction used for conditional relations.

MORPHOLOGY   191

Because its Akkadian cognate *lū* has these same two functions (among others), Holes argues that the existence of *lō* as a coordinating conjunction might go back to an ancient Akkadian substrate influence (2016: 17). Accordingly, the use of *lō* as a coordinating conjunction in KhA probably also goes back to an Akkadian substrate as its geographical distribution suggests.

(2)   [A6]
      nawāḥi həndəyyān mā həndəyyān[61], *əl-yarāḥi,*   *ʕad-həm əstəfāda*
      regions Hendijan REL Hendijan   DEF-Jarahi at-3PL.M use
      mən ʕad-ha məzāwi,   *lō bšūta ...*
      of   at-3SG.F winter_cloaks or summer_cloaks
      '(In) the surroundings of Hendijan, Hendijan and its surroundings, (and in) Jarahi, they make of it [i.e. of black sheep wool] winter cloaks or summer cloaks.'

The double conjunction *lō ... lō ...* is used to express double choice 'either ... or ...', as in the following example:

(3)   [Ḥ1]
      lō nṣəbġ-a   *azrag, lō nṣəbġ-a*
      or color.IPFV.1PL-OBL.3SG.M blue   or color.IPFV.1PL-OBL.3SG.M
      šwayy məṯəl ygəlū-l-a   *təryāgi.*
      a_little like   say.IPFV.3PL.M-to-3SG.M opium_colored
      'We either color it blue, or we color it like what they call *təryāgi*.'[62]

4.7.1.3   *yō* 'or', *yō ... yō ...* 'Either ... or ...'
yō is also used to join two equal alternatives. The form *yō* might be a contamination of *lō* and *yā*, the latter of which is ultimately Persian (Steingass 2001: 1523 *yā* 'or', *yā ... yā ...* 'either ... or ...'), but also found in modern Turkish (*veya* 'or', Parker 2008: 484) and Ottoman Turkish (*yā ... yā ...* 'either ... or ...', Zenker 1866: 945). From these languages its use as a coordinating conjunction equivalent to English 'or' (or, when doubled, 'either ... or ...') spread to various Arabic dialects in, e.g. Anatolia (Vocke and Waldner 1982: 466), Syria (Cowell 1964: 395), Israel (cf. Rosenhouse 1984: 113, who describes *yā* 'or' as a sedentary feature in the otherwise Bedouin-type dialects of northern Israel; Shawarbah 2011: 277 on Negev Arabic), and Khorasan (Seeger 2013: 318, 320, sentence 8: "*yā yimūtan yā mā*

---

61   Cf. 4.8.2.2 on this construction.
62   < Pers. *teryāk* 'opium', i.e. a brown color like that of opium.

yimūtan 'entweder sie sterben, oder sie sterben nicht' [either they die or they don't die]"). Outside Khuzestan, the form *yō* is also documented for Uzbekistan Arabic (Fischer 1961: 235, fn. 2: "*jō* 'oder' < pers. *jā*").

(4) [A18, asking the elderly woman who was sharing with us her memories of the past with what they used to mill their wheat]

əl-yāwan   yō əl-hāwan?
DEF-mortar or DEF-mortar
'The *yāwan* [i.e. a wooden mortar] or the *hāwan* [i.e. a mortar made of stone]?'[63]

The double conjunction *yō ... yō ...* is used to express double choice 'either ... or ...', as in the following example:

(5) [Ḥ1]

əhdūm, maṭal ča yō xaḍar yō ʔaḥmar.
clothes like   DP or green or red
'(The) clothes, you see, (they used to be) like either green or red.'

4.7.1.4   *lā ... wa-lā ...* 'Neither ... nor'

lā ... wa-lā ... is an adversative double conjunction expressing 'neither ... nor' and is also used in other dialects like Muslim Baghdadi Arabic (Erwin 1963: 306).

(6) [A1]

*lā   ʕad-həm tannūr **wa-lā**   ʕad-həm ší.*
NEG at-3PL.M oven   and-NEG at-3PL.M thing
'They had neither an oven nor anything.'

4.7.1.5   *bass* 'but'[64]

The conjunction *bass* used to express an adversative relationship is an ancient loan from Persian. It appears 152 times in my corpus. This conjunction is used in

---

63   Ḥassūnizadeh 2015:891–892: "*yāwan*, PL *yəwāwən, yāwnāt*: 'خشبة محفورة يوضع الأرز الغير' ؛ 'مقشّر في داخلها ويضرَب عليه بالميجنة حتى تنفَصَل القشور عن اللّب'"؛ cf. Persian *hāwan* 'mortar' (Steingass 2001: 1487), but also *ǧāwan* is documented for Persian (Dehkhoda online: https://vajje.com/en, s.v., جاون ؛ «ه»؛ ابدال «ه» جاون: لغتی است در هاون. (يادداشت بخط مولف). جوفن. جوغن «ج» به «به». Cf. Edzard (1967: 309), who states that among the *Məʕdān* Arabs *ǧāwan* was a mortar used for rice and made of palm wood, but that the word's origin was unclear.

64   Cf. 4.7.2.9 on the homophone subordinate conjunction used for temporal relations.

MORPHOLOGY

many Eastern dialects of Arabic, among them Muslim Baghdadi Arabic (Erwin 1963: 306), Basra Arabic (Mahdi 1985: 186), al-Shirqat Arabic (Salonen 1980: 110), Bahraini Arabic (Holes 2016: 372, but only as a less common alternative to *lākin*), the Bedouin dialects of northern Israel (Rosenhouse 1984: 114, who describes *bas*, as a sedentary feature) and the Negev (Shawarbah 2011: 278), Syrian Arabic (Cowell 1964: 397–398), and Egyptian Arabic (Woidich 2006: 158).

(7) [A19]
 *hawīt-i tamānīya w xamsīn **bass** āna fōg as-sabʕīn.*
 ID.CS-1SG eight and fifty but 1SG above DEF-seventy
 'My identity card (says I am) 58 (years old), but (actually) I am above 70.'

4.7.1.6 *lākən ~ wa-lākən* 'but'
The conjunction *lākən ~ wa-lākən* is only rarely used in KhA (20 times in my corpus, 17 times by speaker [A1] who has a high command of literary Arabic) and can be considered a loan from MSA.

(8) [M3]
 b-əl-əmḥammra   xō tədrūn   bī-ha yaʕni ʔašġāl
 in-DEF-Muḥammara DP know.IPFV.2PL.M in-3SG.F DP jobs
 wāyda b-əl-əmḥammra, lākən mū l-ahal-ha.
 many.F in-DEF-Muḥammara but NEG DEF-people-3SG.F
 'In Muḥammara—well, you know of course, there are many jobs in Muḥammara, but not for its people [he means that all jobs are reserved for Persians and foreigners].'

4.7.1.7 *ʔamman* 'but, However'
While the form *ʔamma* for 'but' is known for other dialects of Arabic, among them al-Shirqat-Arabic (Salonen 1980: 110), the Bedouin dialects of northern Israel (Rosenhouse 1984: 114) and the Negev (Shawarbah 2011: 278), and Syrian Arabic (Cowell 1964: 396–397), the KhA form *ʔamman* (ending in *-n*) is only rarely attested elsewhere and appears to be a KhA innovation.

We do, however, find *ʔaman*—besides *ʔama*— in some Arabic-speaking villages in Cilicia (Procházka 2002: 164). The source of the KhA form *ʔamman* is unclear; but it might be a construction analogous to forms such as *lamman* 'when'.[65]

---

65 I am grateful to Prof. Stephan Procházka (pers. comm., April 2020), who brought its use in Cilicia to my attention.

194   CHAPTER 4

ʔamman occurs in my corpus only 6 times and only among speakers from Fəllāḥīya, Muḥammara, and Abadan.

(9)   [AB1]
      āna dərasət   ***amman ...*** *māku*   *wāyəd šəġəl.*
      1SG study.PFV.1SG but   NEG.EXIST many job
      'I have studied (to be a teacher) but ... there are not many jobs (in Iran).'

4.7.2   *Subordinating Conjunctions*

Particularly in colloquial Arabic, certain clauses may as well be subordinated asyndetically, i.e. without a conjunction between the two elements (Bloch 1965; and Cowell 1964: 398–400 on Syrian Arabic; Woidich 2006: 379–380 on Cairene Arabic; Procházka 2018b on northern Iraq).

All conjunctions that are homonymous with an interrogative, like *yāhu* 'who?; whoever', or compounds of an interrogative + *mā* will be listed at the end of this chapter.

4.7.2.1   *w-* 'while' (Circumstantial Clauses)

w- is also used for the expression of circumstantial clauses, most often corresponding to English 'while' (cf. Holes 2016: 433 on Bahraini Arabic):

(1)   [A14], Elicited
      Māġəd gāʕəd yəgra   *dərəs əb-dār-a*   *w-əḥna*
      Majed CONT read.IPFV.3SG.M lesson in-room-3SG.M and-1PL
      gāʕdīn   *b-əl-bəstān.*
      sit.AP.PL.M in-DEF-garden
      'Majed is studying in his room, while we are sitting in the garden.'

4.7.2.2   *ʔəlli* 'That'

The conjunction *ʔəlli* 'that' is not used very often, but rather replaced by an asyndetic construction. My corpus has no example of the use of this conjunction.

(2)   [A2], Elicited
      ətgūl   *əlli l-yōm*   *mā rāḥ ətrūḥ*   *l-əš-šəġəl.*
      say.IPFV.3SG.F that DEF-day NEG FUT go.IPFV.3SG.F to-DEF-work
      'She says that today she won't go to work.'

4.7.2.3   *ḥatta* 'so (That), in Order to'

This conjunction is used for final clauses and also found in, for example, Muslim Baghdadi Arabic (Erwin 1963: 306), Basra Arabic (Mahdi 1985: 186), and

MORPHOLOGY   195

al-Shirqat Arabic (Salonen 1980:108). In KhA, the verb in the subordinate clause
introduced by this conjunction is always IPFV.

(3) [A14], Elicited
     taʕāl   *ṣōb-i*   ***ḥatta***   *asōlaf-l-ak*   *əš*
     come.IMP.SG.M towards-1SG so_that tell.IPFV.1SG-to-2SG.M what
     ṣār   *bī-ya.*
     happen.PFV.3SG.M with-1SG
     'Come over here (to me) so I can tell you what happened to me.'

4.7.2.4   *ḥatta lō* 'Even If'
This conjunction is also used in, for example, Basra (Mahdi 1985: 255). In KhA,
the verb in the subordinate clause introduced by this conjunction is always
IPFV.

(4) [AB1]
     lō aḷḷa yənṭī-ni   *farəd farax* ***ḥatta lō***
     if God give.IPFV.3SG.M-OBL.1SG INDEF child even if
     yṣīr   *nəsar.*
     become.IPFV.3SG.M vulture
     'If God (just) gave me one child!—Even if it turned out to be a vulture.'

4.7.2.5   *məṭəl-mā* 'like, as'
This conjunction is also used in, for example, Baghdad (WB: 433; Erwin 1963:
308), Basra (Mahdi 1985: 192), al-Shirqat (Salonen 1980: 108), Bahrain (Holes
2001: 491–492), and the Bedouin dialects of northern Israel (Rosenhouse 1984:
114). In KhA, the verb in the subordinate clause introduced by this conjunction
is usually PFV.

(5) [A14], Elicited
     ʔəḥna mā nʕīš   ***məṭəl-mā** ʕāšaw*   *ahal-na.*
     1PL   NEG live.IPFV.1PL like-REL   live.PFV.3PL.M family-1PL
     'We don't live as our ancestors used to live.'

(6) [A1], Elicited
     ***məṭəl-mā** gālaw*   *ahal-na   gabəl,   əl   mā*
     like-REL   say.PFV.3PL.M family-1PL formerly REL NEG
     yənṭi   *zəbīl-a,*   *maḥḥad yʕabbī-l-a.*
     give.IPFV.3SG.M basket-3SG.M nobody fill.IPFV.3SG.M-for-3SG.M
     'As our ancestors used to say, the one who does not give/offer a basket,
     won't have it filled (by) anyone.'

(7) [A3], Elicited

*kūn asawwi   **maṭəl-mā** gālat   əmm-i.*
must do.IPFV.1SG like-REL say.PFV.3SG.F mother-1SG
'I have to do as my mother said.'

4.7.2.6   *mən* 'When'

This conjunction is also used in (Muslim) Baghdad (Erwin 1963: 307), Basra (Mahdi 1985: 189), al-Shirqat (Salonen 1980: 105–106), and Bahrain (Holes 2016: 422–423, 425–426). Like *lamman-mā*, KhA *mən* is used to describe completed past-time events (in this case the verb in the conjunctional clause is PFV).

(8) [M4]

*bass **mən** ṣār   əl-ḥarəb, ḍall   baʕad*
but when become.PFV.3SG.M DEF-war remain.PFV.3SG.M anymore
mā yədxəl   ḥaməl b-əl-əmḥammra.
NEG enter.IPFV.3SG.M charges in-DEF-Muḥammara
'But when the war began, charges were no longer shipped to Muḥam-mara.'

(9) [Ḥ1]

*hāḏa **mən** əyēna   l-əl-ʕarəs.*
DEM when come.PFV.1PL to-DEF-wedding
'This (we wore) when we went [lit. "came"] to a wedding.'

The conjunction *mən* can, however, also be used to describe events that are timeless or refer to the present, similar to *yēmta-mā* (in this case the verb in the conjunctional clause is IPFV).

(10) [A15]

*šwayya **mən** ʔayūʕ,   ən-nōba rūḥ-i   təlʕab*
a_little when get_hungry.IPFV.1SG DEF-time soul-1SG play.IPFV.3SG.F
w-rās-i   yōyaʕ-ni.
and-head-1SG hurt.IPFV.3SG.M-OBL.1SG
'Sometimes [lit. "a little"], when I get hungry, then I feel dizzy [lit. "my soul wiggles"[66]] and my head hurts.'

---

66   Cf. Iraqi Arabic *liʕab, yilʕab*, which also can mean 'to be loose, have play in it, wiggle, move, stir' (WB: 422, where we also find the example *lamma ʔaftarr, nafsi dgūm tilʕab* 'When I spin around, I begin to get nauseated').

MORPHOLOGY   197

4.7.2.7   *Salamūd-mā* 'because When, so (That) When'
This conjunction appears only twice in my corpus, both times uttered by the
same speaker, an elderly woman from Xafağīya:

(11) [X1]
    sawwēt-a   *Sēš*   *ṭabəg*   **Salamūd-mā***
    make.PFV.1SG-OBL.3SG.M bread ṭābəg so_that-REL
    yəgSad   *əz-zəlma w-yṣalli*   *w*   *hāy,*
    get_up.IPFV.3SG.M DEF-man and-pray.IPFV.3SG.M and DEM
    əbsaS   *gəmət.*
    immediately get_up.PFV.1SG
    'I made him *ṭābəg*-bread;[67] so that (it was ready) when my husband got
    up and prayed and so on, I quickly got up (and made him breakfast).'

(12) [X1]
    ḥaṭṭēt   *əs-səmča*   *fōg,*   *fōg*   *əč-čīma*
    put.PFV.1SG DEF-fish.SGT on_top above DEF-embers
    əd-dāwīya   *təstəwi*   *əs-səmča;*   **Salamūd-mā***
    DEF-burn.AP.SG.F be_cooked.IPFV.3SG.F DEF-fish.SGT so_that-REL
    ʔaḥaṭṭ   *əl-Sayīn,*   *ḥaṭṭēt-a*   *hēč ...*
    put.IPFV.1SG DEF-dough put.PFV.1SG-OBL.3SG.M DEM
    'I turn it, put the fish on top, on top of the burning embers, and the fish
    bakes; so when I put the dough, I put it like that [describing then how she
    prepares the dough].'

4.7.2.8   *b-əl-yōm* 'When, as; While, during'
Cognate forms of *b-əl-yōm*—which diachronically is a grammaticalization of
yōm 'day', i.e. 'the day when'—are used in many other dialects with this or a
similar meaning, among them Basra Arabic (Mahdi 1985: 189), and Bahraini
Arabic (Holes 2016: 114, with the meaning '(at the time) when'). In KhA, it is
usually used with past-time reference and therefore with a verb in the PFV.

(13) [A14], Elicited
    b-əl-yōm   *čənna*   *gāSdīn*   *səwīya,*   *əbū-y*   *čān*
    at-DEF-day be.PFV.1PL sit.AP.PL.M together father-1SG be.PFV.3SG.M
    ySammər   *əb-sayyārt-a.*
    repair.IPFV.3SG.M with-car.CS-3SG.M
    'While we were sitting together, my father was repairing his car.'

---

67   Traditional dish in which a fish rolled in bread is baked in a clay oven.

198   CHAPTER 4

4.7.2.9   *bass* 'as Soon as'

bass is also used to express a temporal relationship. In this function it is also used, e.g., in Bahraini Arabic (Holes 2016: 430) and the Bedouin dialects of northern Israel (Rosenhouse 1984: 114). In KhA, the verb in the subordinate clause introduced by this conjunction is always IPFV.

(14) [A10]

bass   *əyi*   *əbū-k*   *yəmma,* **bass**
as_soon_as   come.IPFV.3SG.M father-2SG.M mother as_soon_as
əyi   *əbū-k,*   *ʔāna ʔayōz-ak*
come.IPFV.3SG.M father-2SG.M 1SG   marry.IPFV.1SG-OBL.2SG.M
mara, ʔaḥsan bətt əmn-əl-ʕašīra.
woman best   girl of-DEF-tribe
'As soon as your father comes back [from the Hajj], my beloved (son), as soon as your father is back, I will marry you to the best girl of the tribe.'

4.7.2.10   *ʔawwal-mā* 'First When; at First; as Soon as'

This temporal conjunction is also used in, for example, al-Shirqat (Salonen 1980: 108), Kwayriš/Babylon (Meißner 1903: XXXVI), and Bahrain (Holes 2001: 25–26). In KhA, the verb in the subordinate clause introduced by this conjunction is always IPFV.

(15) [A6]

ʔawwal-mā *tṣīr*   *ətsammūn-ha*   *ṭəlyān.*
first-REL   become.IPFV.3SG.F call.IPFV.2PL.M-OBL.3SG.F lambs
'When they [i.e. the lambs] have just been born you call them *ṭəlyān* (lambs).'

4.7.2.11   *lamman-mā ~ lamma ~ lamman* 'When'

This conjunction, already found in CA (cf., e.g. Quran 28:14: *wa-lammā balaǧa ʔašuddahu* ... 'And when he attained his full strength/maturity ...'), is also used in, for example, the Arabic dialects of Basra (Mahdi 1985: 190), al-Shirqat (Salonen 1980: 105), Kwayriš/Babylon (Meißner 1903: XXXVI), Kuwait (Johnstone1967: 150), Bahrain (Holes 2016: 421, 424; Johnstone1967: 159), the United Arab Emirates (Johnstone 1967: 172), and the (Bedouin) dialects of northern Israel (Rosenhouse 1984: 114) and the Negev (Shawarbah 2011: 278). In KhA, the verb following this conjunction is usually PFV.

MORPHOLOGY 199

(16) [M1]

lamman-mā ʔəya   dawwar   ʕalē-na mā
when-REL   come.PFV.3SG.M search.PFV.3SG.M for-1PL NEG
ṭāḥ   bī-na.
find.PFV.3SG.M with-1PL
'When he came (back), he looked for us (but) didn't find us.'

4.7.2.12   *mā-ṭūl-*PRO 'as Long as'
This conjunction is also used in Basra (Mahdi 1985: 190, who however translates it as 'since'; but from the example he gives, it could also mean 'as long as')
and Kwayriš/Babylon (cf. Meißner 1903: XXXVI). In Bahrain we instead find the
invariable phrase *mā dām* (Holes 2016: 114, 431–432). In KhA, the verb in the
subordinate clause introduced by this conjunction is always IPFV. The 1SG PRO
is *-ni*—i.e. the form used for pronouns attached to verbs (cf. 4.1.2, Table 5).

(17) [A14], Elicited

mā-ṭūl-a   yədrəs,   yʕīš   wəyyā-na
REL-as_long_as-3SG.M study.IPFV.3SG.M live.IPFV.3SG.M with-1PL
b-əl-bēt.
in-DEF-house
'As long as he studies, he will live with us in the house.'

(18) [A14], Elicited

mā-ṭūl-ni   ʔaštəġəl   əb-hāy əš-šarīka,   ʕəd-na mā
REL-as_long_as-1SG work.IPFV.1SG in-DEM DEF-company   at-1PL REL
yəkfī-na   l-əl-ačəl.
suffice.IPFV.3SG.M-OBL.1PL for-DEF-food
'As long as I work in this company, we will have enough to eat.'

4.7.2.13   *ʕəgəb-mā* 'after'
This temporal conjunction is also used in, for example, Basra (Mahdi 1985: 192),
Kwayriš/Babylon (Meißner 1903: XXXVI), Bahrain (Holes 2016: 427), and the
Bedouin dialects of northern Israel (Rosenhouse 1984: 114). In KhA, the verb
in the subordinate clause introduced by this conjunction is always PFV.

(19) [A14], Elicited

ʕəgəb-mā kəbar   ṭahharṓ.
after-REL grow_up.PFV.3SG.M circumcise.PFV.3PL.M.OBL.3SG.M
'After he had grown up, they circumcised him.'

200   CHAPTER 4

(20) [A14]
    ʕəgəb-mā ḍaraṭ   ṣamm   ʕazz-a.
    after-REL fart.PFV.3SG.M close.PFV.3SG.M ass-3SG.M
    'After he farted, he closed his ass.' [Said about a person who tries to make
    up for a bad thing s/he has done]

4.7.2.14   *baʕəd-mā* 'after'

This temporal conjunction is also used in many other dialects, among them
Muslim Baghdadi Arabic (Erwin 1963: 308), and the dialects of Basra (Mahdi
1985: 192), Kwayriš/Babylon (Meißner 1903: XXXVI), Bahrain (Holes 2016: 427),
and the Bedouin dialects of northern Israel (Rosenhouse 1984: 114). In KhA, the
verb in the subordinate clause introduced by this conjunction is always PFV.

(21) [A1]
      w-ən-nōb   mən baʕəd-mā yəbas,
      and-DEF-time when after-REL dry.PFV.3SG.M
      ygəṣṣūn-a   w-ən-nōba   ynaḍḍfūn-a
      cut.IPFV.3PL.M-OBL.3SG.M and-DEF-time clean.IPFV.3PL.M-OBL.3SG.M
      mən əl-warag   w-ən-nōb   yfəššgūn-a.
      from DEF-leaves and-DEF-time cut_in_halves.IPFV.3PL.M-OBL.3SG.M
      'And then, when it has dried, they cut it and then remove the leaves and
      then they cut it in two (halves).'

4.7.2.15   *ǧəddām-mā ~ ǧəddām-lā* 'before'

This temporal conjunction is also used, for example, in Kwayriš/Babylon Arabic
(Meißner 1903: XXXVI). In KhA, the verb in the subordinate clause introduced
by this conjunction can be PFV or IPFV. The temporal use of *ǧəddām*, originally
a local preposition expressing anteriority, is not very widespread (cf. 4.4.5).

(22) [A2]
    ǧəddām-mā ʔarūḥ   l-əš-šəǧəl   anaḍḍəf   əl-bēt
    before-REL go.IPFV.1SG to-DEF-work clean.IPFV.1SG DEF-house
    w-ən-nōba   ʔamši.
    and-DEF-time go.IPFV.1SG
    'Before I go to work, I clean up the house and then I leave.'

4.7.2.16   *gabəl-mā ~ gabəl-lā* 'before'

We also find this conjunction in Basra (Mahdi 1985: 192), al-Shirqat (Salonen
1980: 105), (Muslim) Baghdad (Erwin 1963: 308), Kuwait (Johnstone 1967: 150),
Qatar (Johnstone 1967: 167), the United Arab Emirates (Johnstone 1967: 172),

MORPHOLOGY   201

and among the Bedouin dialects of northern Israel (Rosenhouse 1984: 114). In
KhA, the verb in the conjunctional phrase containing the temporal conjunction
gabəl-mā is usually IPFV, even when referring to the past, as in the following
example (cf. Holes 2016: 426 on the same rule with the same conjunction in
Bahraini Arabic):

(23) [F1]
    *yaʕni mā   ḥabbēti   l-ḥaǧǧi   **gabəl-mā***
    DP   NEG love.PFV.2SG.F DEF-Ḥaǧǧi before-REL
    tatzawwaǧīn-a.
    marry.IPFV.2SG.F-OBL.3SG.M
    'So you did not love grandpa [lit. "the Ḥaǧǧi; pilgrim"] before you married
    him?'

4.7.2.17   *mənāla-mā* 'until'

mənāla-mā is used as a temporal conjunction equivalent to English 'until'.
The use of this conjunction is, to the best of my knowledge, not attested for
any other dialect of Arabic (Qasim Hassan, pers. comm. 2020, states that this
conjunction is also used in southern Iraq but in a slightly different form:
mənālam-mā). Its origin appears obscure, but it might be related to CA *manāl*
'obtainment' + (KhA) 3SG.M PRO -*a* yielding '(it is) his obtainment (that) …'.

The verb in the subordinate clause introduced by this conjunction can be
PFV or IPFV.

(24) [A3]
    *… **mənāla-mā** ykəḍḍ   rūḥ-a,   šwayyūn*
    until-REL   grasp.IPFV.3SG.M self-3SG.M a_litte
    yəǧməd,   w-yṣīr   maḥrūg əs-səbʕa.
    congeal.IPFV.3SG.M and-become.IPFV.3SG.M Maḥrūg əs-Səbʕa
    '(You keep stirring it) … until it has become solid; (when) it has congealed
    a little, (then) it becomes Maḥrūg əs-Səbʕa [bread soup, a traditional
    dish].'

(25) [A14], Elicited
    ***mənāla-mā** āna ʔaṭbəx   w-axalləṣ,   ənta   balla*
    until-REL   1SG cook.IPFV.1SG and-finish.IPFV.1SG 2SG.M DP
    šūf   dars-ak.
    see.IMP.SG.M lesson-2SG.M
    'Until I finish cooking, you do your studies.'

202 CHAPTER 4

4.7.2.18 *xāṭər ~ əl-xāṭər* 'so That, in Order to'

This conjunction is used to express final relations. The verb in the subordinate clause introduced by this conjunction is always IPFV.

(26) [M4]

ʔakbar markab, ġarragṓ   *b-əl-ḥarəb īrān*
biggest ship   drown.PFV.3PL.M.OBL.3SG.M in-DEF-war Iran
ġarrag-a,   *b-əd-ᴾdahaneᴾ — **xāṭər** šənhi?*
drown.PFV.3SG.M-OBL.3SG.M at-the-mouth   so_that what.SG.F
***xāṭər** əl-ʕərāǧīya lā ygədrūn*   *yʕabrūn*
so_that DEF-Iraqis NEG be_able.IPFV.3PL.M cross.IPFV.3PL.M
ha-ṣ-ṣafḥa.
DEM-DEF-side
'The biggest ship, they sunk it in the war, Iran sunk it, at the mouth (of the river)—What for? So that the Iraqis could not cross from this side.'

xāṭər in combination with the verbal negator *lā* expresses 'lest, so that ... (would) not'. The verb in the subordinate clause is then always IPFV.

(27) [A3, describing the recipe for stuffed chicken]

šədd   *ərlī-ha,*   ***xāṭər** lā təḥtəll*
close.IMP.SG.M legs.CS-3SG.F so_that NEG open.IPFV.3SG.F
b-əl-marag   *w-yəṭlaʕ*   *əl-ḥašu*   *māl-ha.*
in-DEF-sauce and-come_out.IPFV.3SG.M DEF-filling GL.SG.M-3SG.F
'Close its [the chicken's] legs, so that it doesn't open in the sauce and its filling comes out.'

4.7.2.19 *čē* 'because, since'

This conjunction is used to express causal relations. The origin of the form *čē* has hitherto not been discussed, but it might be connected to a colloquial Persian form *čē* used in the same meaning (which is, to the best of my knowledge, only attested for historical varieties of Persian).[68] It could also be a shortened

---

68   I am grateful to Chams Bernard, who drew my attention to the fact that already 11th century Judaeo-Persian has used an element *čē* (*čy*) with the meaning 'because, for, since' (Paul 2013: 171; cf. MacKenzie 1968: 262, line M8, *et passim*); it appears that most published Early Jewish Persian (used until the early 13th century) documents, which "reflect some old forms of New Persian (NP), and display a transitional stage between Middle Persian (MP)

MORPHOLOGY   203

form of the conjunction *čēf* 'because, as', as used in, for example, Muslim Baghdad Arabic (see Erwin 1963: 307).[69] Outside Khuzestan, its use is also documented for Kwayriš/Babylon Arabic (Meißner 1903: 140: "*ka, ča, čē(i)* 'da; wie; weil [since, because]'", and XXXVI: "*čē(i)mā* 'a) als ob [as if]; b) da, weil [since, because]'"). It is also used in certain dialects spoken in Southern Iran (e.g. on the island of Shif, Bushehr),[70] where it alternates with the form *čēf* which strongly supports the theory that KhA *čē* is also derived from *čēf*.

In KhA, the verb in the subordinate clause introduced by this conjunction can be PFV or IPFV.

(28) [A17]

   əl-kūlər   *mā   mṭaffin-a?*   *lā*
   DEF-air_conditioner NEG turn_off.AP.PL.M-OBL.3SG.M   NEG
   sāmḥīn,   *čē*   *ysaǧǧəl*   *w   mā*
   excuse.AP.PL.M because record.IPFV.3SG.M and NEG
   yəṭlaʕ   *tamām, sāmḥīn*   *xāḷa.*
   turn_out.IPFV.3SG.M fine   excuse.AP.PL.M aunt
   '(Shouldn't) we turn off the air conditioner? Sorry, (it is) because we record [lit. "it records"] and it [i.e. the recording] doesn't turn out well (otherwise); we are sorry.'

(29) [Ḥa1]

   w   rādaw   *w   ṭō-ni*   *kərət*[71] *bass āna*
   and want.PFV.3PL.M and give.PFV.3PL.M-OBL.1SG license but 1SG
   čē   *mā   ʕad-i   s-səǧən*[72]   *xāḷa awwal-mā fāl,*
   because NEG at-1SG DEF-citizenship aunt first-REL   beginning[73]
   ərəfaḍət   *hāy əs-sālfa.*
   hinder.PFV.1SG DEM DEF-story

---

and NP", probably originated in the southwestern Iranian provinces of Fārs and Khuzestan (Gindin 2009: 133–136). Thus, *čē* has been, or is likely to have been, used in other historical as well as currently-spoken dialects of Persian, too.

69   Cf. (Ingham 2006: 30) on Afghanistan Arabic *kē/ki* 'why', which he also derives from *kēf*.

70   Data from the FWF-funded research project "Arabic in Southern Iran" (https://south -iranian-arabic.uni-graz.at/de/), in which the author was employed from 2020–2021.

71   < Pers. *kārt* 'license; (playing, debit, identification ...) card'.

72   Probably < *səǧəl* 'register, record', cf. WB (213).

73   The use of *fāl* in this phrase does not appear to be connected to CA *faʔl* 'omen' as can be seen from the translation. Cf. Hassan (2019: 211) on the use of the phrase *ʔawwal fāl* 'first of all; first; basically; above all' in Southern Iraq and the Middle Euphrates area.

204   CHAPTER 4

'And they wanted to give me a license [i.e. the official certification for being a midwife]. But since I did not have a citizenship at that time, I hindered this story.'

4.7.2.20   *ləʔan(na)* ~ *laʔan(na)* ~ *lan* 'because'

The conjunction *ləʔan(na)* (occurs thrice in my corpus) ~ *laʔan(na)* (occurs twice) ~ *lan* (occurs 4 times) occurs only rarely in my corpus and, except once, is only used only by speakers [A1] and [A6], who have a good command of Standard Arabic. This conjunction can therefore be considered a loan from the literary language. The verb in the subordinate clause introduced by this conjunction can be PFV or IPFV.

(30) [A6]

*ḏkūra mā   nxalli   bī-ha ...   **ləʔanna** ḏ-ḏakar   əstəfāda*
males   NEG leave.IPFV.1PL with-3SG.F because   DEF-male use
mā   bi.́
NEG with.3SG.M

'We don't keep the rams [lit. "leave them with it", i.e. the ewes] ... because there is no use for the ram [except for fertilization].'

4.7.2.21   *ḥadd-mā* 'as Long as, until'

ḥadd-mā is used as a temporal conjunction equivalent to English 'as long as, until'. The verb in the subordinate clause introduced by this conjunction can be PFV or IPFV.

(31) [M3]

***ḥadd-mā** nās   mawǧūd,   əḥna mawǧūdīn,   **ḥadd-mā** nās*
until-REL people existing.SG.M 1PL   existing.PL.M until-REL people
təštəri,   mawǧūdīn.
buy.IPFV.3SG.F existing.PL.M

'As long as people are here, we stay here [at the market, selling things]; as long as people are buying (things), we stay here.'

4.7.2.22   *ʕašān* 'so That, in Order to'

The use of this conjunction, which also expresses final relations like *xāṭər*, is, according to my consultants, limited to Fellāḥīya. The verb in the subordinate clause introduced by this conjunction is always IPFV.

MORPHOLOGY 205

(32) [A1]

> *taʕāl*   *ṣōb-i*   **ʕašān**   *nataʕallam.*
> come.IMP.SG.M towards-1SG so_that study.IPFV.1PL
> 'Come to me so we can study (together).'

4.7.2.23 *ʕan-lā* 'in Order Not to, Lest'

This conjunction is used to express final relations. It is also attested for other dialects, for example the Arabic dialects of Bahrain (Holes 2001: 365). In KhA, the verb in the subordinate clause introduced by this conjunction is always IPFV:

(33) [X3]

> *nsawwi*   *d-dalla mālt*   *əd-dəhən* — *hā*   *ʕalū-ha*   —
> make.IPFV.1PL DEF-jug GL.SG.F DEF-lard   DEM height-3SG.F
> *w*   *tḥəṭṭ*   *asfal-ha*   *tamər ʕan-lā*
> and put.IPFV.2SG.M beneath-3SG.F dates from-NEG
> *yxīs*   *əd-dəhən yəxrab.*
> turn_rancid.IPFV.3SG.M DEF-lard go_bad.IPFV.3SG.M
> 'We make the jug for the lard—(it was) that big—and you put on its bottom dates, so the lard doesn't turn rancid.'

4.7.2.24 *lō* 'If'

The conjunction *lō* (or its cognate forms *law* and *lū*) is used for conditional clauses in the majority of all—Eastern as well as Western—dialects of Arabic.

In KhA, *lō* is used both for real conditions (with an IPFV verb in the protasis) as well as for hypothetical conditions (with a PFV verb in the protasis):

(34) [Ḥ2]

> *w*   *lō tərdīn*   *əs-səwāləf ġadīmīya, farəd yōm*
> and if want.IPFV.2SG.F DEF-stories old.SG.F   INDEF day
> *ʔayīban*   *əmm-i*   *w-axallī-č*
> bring.IPFV.1SG mother-1SG and-leave.IPFV.1SG-OBL.2SG.F
> *ətsaġġlīn*   *mən ʕad-ha.*
> record.IPFV.2SG.F from at-3SG.F
> 'And if you want the old stories, one day I (will) bring my mother and I will let you record her.'

206   CHAPTER 4

(35) [A14], Elicited
    lō čān   *ʕand-i flūs,*   *ča*[74] *štarēt*   *sayyāra.*
    if   be.PFV.3SG.M   at-1SG money   DP   buy.PFV.1SG car
    'If I had money, I would buy a car.'

4.7.2.25   *ʔəla, ʔəḏa* 'When, If'

These two conjunctions are used to express a conditional relation. Whereas *ʔəḏa* is used in a great number of Arabic dialects and directly reflects OA *ʔiḏā* 'if', the form *ʔəla* is a dialectal innovation (although probably also quite old, cf. Johnstone 1967: 16, fn. 6) that emerged via an unusual sound change (cf. Bravmann 1934: 338–340). The use of *ʔəla* is, however, by far not limited to KhA, but also documented for many dialects spoken in the Maghreb (cf. Caubet 2007: 286 on the realis in Moroccan Arabic) as well as on the Arabian Peninsula (cf. Johnstone 1967: 16, fn. 6, and 69).

In KhA, *ʔəḏa* and *ʔəla* are used in a mere temporal sense (usually with a PFV verb) and for real conditions (with an IPFV or PFV verb in the protasis):

(36) [A3]
    əl-səmač əla   *yəbas,*   *yṭīḥūn*   *bí*
    DEF-fish   when   dry.PFV.3SG.M   take.IPFV.3PL.M   with.3SG.M
    ygəššrūn-a.
    skin.IPFV.3PL.M-OBL.3SG.M
    'When the fish is dry, they take it and skin it.'

(37) [A6]
    ʔəla ṣārat   *bēḏa*   *way-ha*   *ʔaswad,*
    if   become.PFV.3SG.F   white.F face-3SG.F black
    əngəl-ha   *barša.*
    call.IPFV.1PL-OBL.3SG.F   barša
    'If she [i.e. the ewe] is white (and) her face black, we call her *barša.*'

(38) [A4]
    ʔəḏa naṯya, tsammūn-ha   *barša w*   *ʔəḏa ḏəkar, abraš.*
    if   female call.IPFV.2PL.M-OBL.3SG.F barša and if   male   abraš
    'If (she is) [i.e. the sheep] female, you call it *barša* and if it is male, *abraš.*'

---

74   Like the KhA discourse particle *ča* (cf. 4.8.5.4) in this example, the discourse particle *ṛā-* in Tunisia, Libya, and Morocco also appears in the introduction of the apodosis of conditional clauses (Procházka and Dallaji 2019: 60–63).

MORPHOLOGY 207

4.7.2.26 *ʕala* 'If'

This conjunction is also used to express a conditional relation. Etymologically, this form either goes back to *ʔəla* via pharyngealization of *ʔ* (cf. 3.1.2.9 for other examples from KhA that have this phonological process), or it is a cognate of the preposition *ʕala*: compare *ʕalwān* used in Urfa (Turkey) for the introduction of irreal optative clauses, e.g. *ʕalwān inte šāyif hāda* 'if you had seen this!' (Procházka 2003: 84), and *ʕalawwa* in Soukhne, e.g. *ʕalawwa cīt* "If you had come!" (Behnstedt 1994: 324; and more examples on 191). Cf. also 4.7.2.27 below for the conjunction *ʕala-mā* 'until, while, when' used in KhA and Basra Arabic.

(39) [Ḥ2]

> *hāy al-bant bant-i tayībūn-ha,*
> DEM DEF-girl daughter-1SG bring.IPFV.2PL.M-OBL.3SG.F
> *tayībūn-ha ʕala talʕat bant-i,*
> bring.IPFV.2PL.M-OBL.3SG.F if turn_out.PFV.3SG.F daughter-1SG
> *kūn āna ʔadbaḥ-ha.*
> must 1SG kill.IPFV.1SG-OBL.3SG.F
> 'This girl, my daughter, bring her, bring her. If she turns out to be my daughter, I must kill her.'

4.7.2.27 *ʕala-mā* 'until, While, When'

ʕala mā 'until; while' is also used in Basra (Mahdi 1985: 192).

(40) [A3]

> *ʕala-mā tastawi našlaʕ-a.*
> when-REL be_done.IPFV.3SG.F take_out.IPFV.1PL-OBL.3SG.M
> 'When it [the bread] is done, we take it out [of the oven].'

(41) [A12]

> *lēš-mā tgūlīn, ʕala-mā yāb-əl-ha*
> when-REL say.IPFV.2SG.F when-REL bring.PFV.3SG.M-to-3SG.F
> *lə-blāla*[75] *yāb-əl-ha l-məxbāza,*
> DEF-reed_mats bring.PFV.3SG.M-to-3SG.F DEF-məxbāza
> *dannag al-walad b-ət-tannūr, ṭāḥ*
> lean.PFV.3SG.M DEF-boy in-DEF-oven fall.PFV.3SG.M
> *w-əštəwa.*
> and-be_grilled.PFV.3SG.M

---

75 *balla* PL *blāla* 'palm mat'.

208   CHAPTER 4

'And then, when he had brought her [his mother] the palm mats, and had brought her the *maxbāza* [utensil made of straw and white cloth used to spread the dough for sticking it onto the wall of the clay oven], the boy leaned into the oven, fell (into it), and was grilled.'

4.7.2.28   *w-* 'Although, But (Still)'

As in some other dialects of Arabic (e.g. Holes 2016: 369 on Bahraini Arabic), KhA *w-* can also have an adversative function, similar to English 'but' and 'although', as in the following example:

(42)   [A14], Elicited
       həwwa marīḏ̣ kəll-a   w-hāy   w-rāḥ   l-əš-šəġəl.
       3SG.M sick   all-3SG.M and-DEM but-go.PFV.3SG.M to-DEF-work
       'He was totally sick, but he went to work.'

4.7.2.29   *māku* 'Otherwise'

māku, lit. 'there is not', is also used as a concessive conjunction equivalent to English 'otherwise'.

(43)   [A14], Elicited
       hassa lāzəm anām,   māku   bāčər   rāḥ atʕab
       now   must sleep.IPFV.1SG NEG.EXIST tomorrow FUT tire.IPFV.1SG
       b-əš-šəġəl.
       at-DEF-work
       'I have to (go to) sleep now, otherwise I will be very tired at work tomorrow.'

4.7.2.30   *yāhu* 'Whoever'

Cf. 4.1.11.4 on the homophone interrogative pronoun *yāhu* 'who? which?'

(44)   [X3]
       yāhu   əl   yōʕān w   yrūḥ
       whoever REL hungry and go.IPFV.3SG.M
       yəšlaʕ-l-a   fəṣṣ   māl   dəhən,
       take_out.IPFV.3SG.M-for-3SG.M handful GL.SG.M lard
       w-yḥəṭṭ-a   b-ʕēš-a,   w-yḥəṭṭ
       and-put.IPFV.3SG.M-OBL.3SG.M in-bread-3SG.M and-put.IPFV.3SG.M
       fõg-a   šakar wa laff-a   w
       on-3SG.M sugar and fold.PFV.3SG.M-OBL.3SG.M and
       kəlá́.
       eat.PFV.3SG.M.OBL.3SG.M

MORPHOLOGY   209

'Whoever is hungry goes and takes out a handful of lard, and puts it on his bread, and puts sugar on it, and folds it and eats it.'

4.7.2.31   *kəll-mā* 'Whenever, Each Time (That)'

This temporal conjunction is also used with the same meaning in Basra (Mahdi 1985: 194), al-Shirqat (Salonen 1980: 105), and Kwayriš/Babylon (Meißner 1903: XXXVI). In KhA, the verb in the subordinate clause introduced by this conjunction is usually IPFV.

(45) [A10, telling a fairy-tale]
    kəll-mā   *təmšī-l-ak*   *ġadama*[76]
    every_time-REL walk.IPFV.2SG.M-for-2SG.M step
    təksar-l-ak   *rəmmāna*   *w*
    break.IPFV.2SG.M-for-2SG.M pomegranate and
    ḏabb-ha   *b-əš-šaṭṭ.*
    throw.IMP.SG.M-OBL.3SG.F in-DEF-river
    'Whenever you take a step, you break a pomegranate and throw it into the river.'

4.7.2.32   *čann-PRO* 'as If'

Cognate forms of the conjunction *čann-PRO* 'as if' used for hypothetical comparisons are found in various other dialects of Arabic, for example, in Basra (Mahdi 1985:70; cf. WB: 87–88), Kwayriš/Babylon (Meißner 1903: XXXVI), and the Gulf (Johnstone 1967: 69: *činn* 'as if'). *čann-PRO* appears only once in my corpus.

(46) [A14], Elicited
    təḥči   **čann-ha**   *šēxa.*
    speak.IPFV.3SG.F as_if-3SG.F old_woman
    'She speaks as if she were an old woman.'

4.7.2.33   *lēš-mā* 'When'

In my corpus, this temporal conjunction is only used by the semi-nomadic speakers [A12] and therefore might be an *ʕarab* feature. However, the same conjunction is also attested in a similar meaning for Jewish Baghdadi (cf. Bar-Moshe 2019: 192, who translates the phrase *lēš-ma ʕāyan* as 'Then he saw ...').

---

76   < Pers. *ġadam* (*bar-dāštan*) 'to (take a) step'.

210 CHAPTER 4

The semantic development of this conjunction from the interrogative *lēš* 'why?' is not clear, and there seem to exist only few parallels in other dialects of Arabic: the dialect of Siirt in Anatolia, for example, has *ašam lē* in the meaning 'as, when' < *ašám ~ ayšám* 'how?' + *lē*, which equals KhA *mā* (Vocke and Waldner 1982: 26).[77]

The KhA (fixed) phrase *lēš-mā tgūlīn*, as in (41), which contains the conjunction *lēš-mā* and literally means 'when you (SG.F) say', is often used by women to introduce a new event in stories.

(47) [A12]
lēš-mā   *radd*   *l-ahal-a,*   *ləga*
when-REL come_back.PFV.3SG.M to-people-3SG.M find.PFV.3SG.M
hal-a   *ṭaggat-həm*   *gōm.*
people-3SG.M hit.PFV.3SG.F-OBL.3PL.M tribe
'When he came back to his people, he found them attacked by a tribe/an enemy.'

4.7.2.34   *šlōn-mā* 'as, However, in Whatever Way'
This conjunction is also used in, e.g. Muslim Baghdadi Arabic (Erwin 1963: 309), Basra Arabic (Mahdi 1985: 194), and Urfa Arabic (Stephan Próchazka, pers. comm. 2020).

(48) [A4, telling me not to be shy about the picture we were taking with the shepherd]
ham məṯəl əbū-k   *kān,*   *əṯḥaṭṭīn-a*
DP   like   father-2SG.M be.PFV.3SG.M put.IPFV.2SG.F-OBL.3SG.M
īd-əč   *ʕala ktāf-a*   *māku*   *məškəla, Bettina,*
hand-2SG.F on   shoulder-3SG.M NEG.EXIST problem Bettina
māku   *məškəla, ətkəḍḍīn-a*   *mən čtāf-a,*
NEG.EXIST problem grasp.IPFV.2SG.F-OBL.3SG.M from shoulder-3SG.M
šlōn-mā trīdīn.
how-REL want.IPFV.2SG.F
'It's as if he was your father: put your hand on his shoulder [for the picture-taking]—that's no problem, Bettina, no problem—put your hand on his shoulder [lit. "take him from his shoulder"], as you like.'

---

77   I have to thank Prof. Stephan Procházka for drawing my attention to this fact.

MORPHOLOGY   211

4.7.2.35 *ʔəš-mā* 'Whatever'

This conjunction is also used in, e.g. Muslim Baghdadi Arabic (Erwin 1963: 309) and Basra Arabic (Mahdi 1985: 193). The verb in the subordinate clause introduced by this conjunction is always IPFV.

(49) [A10]

hāḏa l-farax **əš-mā** *yəlʕab,* *yəǧləb.*
DEM DEF-child what-REL play.IPFV.3SG.M win.IPFV.3SG.M
'This kid: whatever he plays, he wins.'

4.7.2.36 *wēn-mā* 'Wherever'

This conjunction is also used in Basra (Mahdi 1985: 193), Muslim Baghdadi Arabic (Erwin 1963: 309), and the Bedouin dialects of northern Israel (Rosenhouse 1984: 114). The verb in the subordinate clause introduced by this conjunction can be PFV or IPFV.

(50) [A14], Elicited

wēn-mā *čān,* *aṭīr*
where-REL be.PFV.3SG.M fly.IPFV.1SG
w-ayīb-a-l-ak.
and-bring.IPFV.1SG-OBL.3SG.M-to-2SG.M
'Wherever it is [i.e. the thing you want], I will fly (there) and bring it to you.'

(51) [A12]

b-əš-šəta *ham ənšīl.* *baʕad b-əš-šəta* **wēn-mā**
in-DEF-winter also move.IPFV.1PL DP in-DEF-winter where-REL
dagal yṣīr ...
grass become.IPFV.3SG.M
'In winter we also move ... in winter, wherever grass grows (we go there) ...'

(52) [A14], Elicited

wēn-mā *čānat* *əǧ-ǧamba ətrūḥ* *əṭṭīr*
where-REL be.PFV.3SG.F DEF-jacket go.IPFV.2SG.M fly.IPFV.2SG.M
wə-təyīb-ha, *tara əl-lēla* *dašša māku* *lō*
and-bring.IPFV.2SG.M-OBL.3SG.F DP DEF-night entry NEG.EXIST if
mā tyīb-ha.
NEG bring.IPFV.2SG.M-OBL.3SG.F

'Wherever the [your lost] jacket is, fly (there) and bring it (back): otherwise you can't come home tonight [lit. "there is no entry"], if you don't bring it (back).'

4.7.2.37 *škaṭər-mā* 'However Much, No Matter How Much'

This conjunction is also used in, e.g. Basra Arabic (Mahdi 1985: 256). In KhA, it is used exactly in the same way as *šgadd-mā*.

(53) [A2], Elicited
Pəkli *škaṭər-mā* *tərdīn!*
eat.IMP.SG.F how_much-REL want.IPFV.2SG.F
'Eat as much as you want!'

4.7.2.38 *šgadd-mā* 'However Much, No Matter How Much, as Much as'

This conjunction is also used in, e.g. Muslim Baghdadi Arabic (Erwin 1963: 309) and Basra Arabic (Mahdi 1985: 194).

(54) [A2], Elicited
Pəsəʔli *šgadd-mā* *tərdīn!*
ask.IMP.SG.F how_much-REL want.IPFV.2SG.F
'Ask as much as you want!'

4.7.2.39 *šwakət-mā* 'Whenever'

This conjunction is also used in, e.g. Muslim Baghdadi Arabic (Erwin 1963: 309), and Basra Arabic (Mahdi 1985: 193–194). In KhA, the verb in the subordinate clause introduced by this conjunction is usually IPFV.

(55) [A14], Elicited
šwakət-mā tərdīn, *taʕay* *ṣōb-i!*
when-REL want.IPFV.2SG.F come.IMP.SG.F towards-1SG
'Whenever you want, come to me!'

4.7.2.40 *yēmta-mā ~ əlyēmta-mā* 'Whenever'

This conjunction is also used in, e.g. Basra (Mahdi 1985: 194). In KhA, the verb in the conjunctional phrase containing the temporal conjunction *yēmta-mā* is always IPFV and refers to possible future actions.

MORPHOLOGY

213

(56) [A19]
yēmta-mā tərdūn   āna əb-xədmat-kəm,
when-REL want.IPFV.2PL.M 1SG at-service.CS-2PL.M
ʔāxəd-kəm.
take.IPFV.1SG-OBL.2PL.M
'Whenever you want, I am at your service (to) take you [to interview a shaykh].'

(57) [A2], [voice message sent to me]
əlyēmta-mā ṭḥəbbīn   āna mawǧūd w-əb-xadəmt-əč.
when-REL   want.IPFV.2SG.F 1SG present and-at-service.CS-2SG.F
'Whenever you want, I am there (for you) to help you.'

4.8   Particles

Particles are small invariable words that have a grammatical or discursive function. In traditional grammar descriptions, the discussion of particles mostly includes prepositions, interrogatives and conjunctions (e.g. Meißner 1903: XXXI–XXXIII; Shawarbah 2011: 259–286; Erwin 1963: 299–312; and Holes 2016: 103–116). For the sake of a better overview, prepositions and conjunctions are treated separately and not within this chapter. Also, the numerous compound prepositions and conjunctions do not really fit the definition of particles as "small invariable words".

4.8.1   *Existence and Non-existence*
In this section, the expressions of existence are followed by the expressions used for non-existence. Whereas some expressions of existence have a negative counterpart, e.g. *ʔaku* 'there is' vs. *māku* 'there is not', others do not have a negative (or positive) counterpart, e.g. *māmən* 'there is not', and *hassət* 'there is'.

4.8.1.1   *ʔaku* 'There Is/Are'
Apart from Khuzestan, *ʔaku* 'there is' (and its negative *māku* 'there is not'; cf. below) is also used throughout Iraq (Blanc 1964: 146–147), and in some (northern) Gulf Arabic dialects of Kuwait and Bahrain (mostly sedentary-type villages; cf. Holes 2018b: 120). In the Anatolian village of Āzəx (turk. Idil) in the Turkish province of Mardin (Jastrow 1981: 164, fn. 1), *māku* is also used for 'there is not', but its positive counterpart is *kīkū* 'there is' (a contraction of the present tense prefix *kū* and the verb *ykūn* 'he is').

214   CHAPTER 4

There is still no consensus about the origin of the existential particles *ʔaku* 'there is' and its negative *māku* 'there is not'. Müller-Kessler traces *ʔaku* back to the Aramaic particle of existence *ʼyt* 'there is' (and *lyt* 'there is not'), which in central and southeastern Babylonian Aramaic dialects such as Mandaic was augmented by the deictic element *k'* (2003: 642, 643, 645). In Neo-Mandaic this augmented particle of existence has survived as *ekko ~ ekka* 'there is' and *lekko ~ lekka* 'there is not' (Müller-Kessler 2003: 642–643). Holes relates its origin to the Akkadian verb and noun *makū* 'want, lack, need; to be absent, missing', with *aku* being a later (Arabic internal) reanalysis of *māku/makū* as *mā* (NEG particle) + *aku* (2018b: 120–121; 2016: 17). Diem suggests an Arabic-internal development, interpreting *ʔaku* as combination of the deictic element *k* with the 3SG.M pronoun (cf. Müller-Kessler 2003: 644). Jastrow also gives an Arabic internal interpretation, tracing *māku* back to **mā yakūn* 'there is not', with *aku* being a back formation from *māku*, which has been reanalyzed as **mā + aku* (2018: 90). Examples for the use of *ʔaku* from my data are:

(1) [A3]
w-**aku**   ḥawār, ygūlū-l-a   ḥawār māl   ḥəssu.
and-EXIST spices say.IPFV.3PL.M-to-3SG.M spices GL.SG.M ḥəssu
'And there are spices; they call them spices for *ḥəssu*.'

(2) [Ḥa1]
ham **aku**   banāt əbgadd-i.
also EXIST girls at_the_age_of-1SG
'There are also girls in my age.'

4.8.1.2   *hast ~ hassət* 'There Is'

hast ~ hassət 'there is' is of Persian origin and elsewhere also found in Kuwait, Lower Iraq, and Bahrain (Holes 2018b: 122). Ingham notes that *hassət* is typical for the south, while *ʔaku* was used elsewhere in Khuzestan (Ingham 1976: 71). My data that this geographical alignment is not maintained in contemporary KhA. In my corpus, *hassət* is used by speakers from northern cities such as Ahvaz or Ḥamīdīya, whilst speakers from the southern cities of Abadan and Muḥammara also use *ʔaku*. In general, *hassət ~ hast* (8 times) occurs less frequently than *ʔaku* (30 times) in my corpus.

(3) [A6]
ēh, ḏəkar w   naṭya **hassət**.
yes male and female EXIST
'Yes, there are male and female [sheep].'

MORPHOLOGY   215

4.8.1.3 *bī* 'There Is'

The use of *bī* (< *b-* + 3SG.M PRO) for the expression of existence is also known for several other dialects (e.g. the Bedouin dialects of the Syrian Desert, cf. Procházka 1993: 109, 125).

(4) [A2, Abu Khazʕal was talking about the buffaloes' eating habits when Muḥammad jokingly asks:]

ham marrāt   ***bī***   *taḥtūma?*
also sometimes EXIST midnight_snack
'Do they [the buffaloes] also have [lit. "is there also"] midnight snacks at times?'

4.8.1.4 *māku* 'There Is Not'

The most common negative existential marker in KhA is *māku*, occurring 63 times in my corpus.

(5) [F1]

ʔāna gabəl   *əntəm mā baʕad-kəm,* ***māku***   *lā*
1SG in_former_times 2PL.M NEG still-2PL.M NEG.EXIST NEG
sayyāra, ***māku,***   *ʔabadan, sayyāra māmən,*   ***māku***   *sayāyīr.*
car   NEG.EXIST at_all   car   NEG.EXIST NEG.EXIST cars
'Me, in the past, when you were not (born) yet, there were no cars, there were none, no way, there were no cars, there were no cars.'

(6) [F1]

ēh gabəl…   *al-ʕarīs*   *yḥannūn-a,*
yes in_former_times DEF-groom apply_henna.IPFV.3PL.M-OBL.3SG.M
al-ʕarīs   *yḥannūn-a,*   *hassa la*   *baʕad*
DEF-groom apply_henna.IPFV.3PL.M-OBL.3SG.M now   NEG anymore
ḥənna ***māku.***
henna NEG.EXIST
'Yes, in the past, they apply henna on the groom, they put henna on the groom; now not, now there is no henna anymore.'

4.8.1.5 *mā bī* 'There Is Not'

(7) [F1]

mā bī   *ṭamāṭa.*
NEG EXIST tomato
'There were no tomatoes (in the past).'

216   CHAPTER 4

4.8.1.6   *māməš* 'There Is Not'
The form *māməš* does not occur in my corpus, but its use was confirmed by
consultants, who also provided example (8). According to my consultants, this
form is rather typical of the speech of the *ḥaḍar*, e.g. the people of Fəllāḥīya.
māməš is also used in Lower Iraq (cf. Blanc 1964: 146) and in Bahraini Arabic
(Holes 2018b: 121).

(8)   [A14, imagined scenario: when a person A calls every day asking regard-
       ing a person B's health, and then one day, there is no call and B calls A
       him/herself, s/he would say:]
       hā? əl-yōm   māməš?
       DP   DEF-day NEG.EXIST
       'So what? Today there is no (call)?'

4.8.1.7   *māmən* 'There Is Not'
māmən 'there is not' < *mā min šay?* 'there is nothing' developed via deletion of
the last element of this phrase (Procházka 2018c: 279). *māmən* is also used in
the Šāwi-dialects of the Harran-Urfa region in Turkey (Procházka 2018c: 279)
and in Bahraini Arabic (Holes 2016: 104–105). This form occurs only five times
in my corpus.

(9)   [Ḥ1, describing how in former times it was not necessary to have an invi-
       tation in order to go to a wedding]
       māku   maṯal hēč ənaʕzəm,   māku   ʕazīma,   la,
       NEG.EXIST like   DEM invite.IPFV.1PL NEG.EXIST invitation NEG
       māmən   ʕazīma.
       NEG.EXIST invitation
       'There was no, like this, invitations [lit. "we invite"], there was no invita-
       tion, no, there was no invitation.'

(10)   [X3, explaining that they used to prepare chicken and not lamb for dinner
       when guests came, because they had no lambs]
       māmən   ṭəli.
       NEG.EXIST lamb
       'There were no lambs.'

4.8.1.8   *mā čān* 'There Was No(t)'
With reference to the past, non-existence is also expressed by a negated form
of the verb *čān* 'to be', e.g.:

MORPHOLOGY   217

(11) [AB1]
      *tɔlɔfɔzyōn **mā** **čān**.*
      television NEG be.PFV.3SG.M
      'There was no television.'

4.8.2 *Negation*
The main negation particles used in KhA, are *mū*, *mā*, and *lā*. These negation
particles always bear the main stress (cf. 3.6; Ingham 1974: 22). On the negative personal pronouns cf. 4.1.4. A prohibitive particle *lāykūn*, as documented
for KhA by Ingham (1974: 22, 32: "*lāykūn yɔktɔb* 'I hope he does not write'"),
does not occur in my corpus. According to my consultants, it is rarely used
at all, and if so, then in the meaning of 'maybe', as in the following example:

(12) [A3]
      lāykūn *mɔša*   *wɔyyā-hɔm.*
      maybe go.PFV.3SG.M with-3PL.M
      'Maybe he went with them.'

4.8.2.1   *mū* 'Not, Don't'
This negation particle is mostly used to negate nouns but may also be used to
negate verbs:

(1) [M4]
     mū *bass āna ʔasōlɔf.*
     NEG only 1SG talk.IPFV.1SG
     'It is not only me complaining [lit. "talking"].'

(2) [Ḥ1]
     ʔēh, bɔšɔt   *xafīf yaʕni,* **mū** *mɔtīn.*
     yes summer_cloak thin DP   NEG thick
     'Yes, the *bɔšɔt* [a summer cloak] is thin, not thick.'

(3) [A10]
     mū *rɔdɔt*   *mara?*
     NEG want.PFV.2SG.M wife
     'Didn't you want (to have) a wife?'

In addition, *mū* is often used for rhetorical questions:

218 CHAPTER 4

(4) [A19]

mū āna čənt əb-xārəǧ hənāka?
NEG 1SG be.PFV.1SG in-abroad there
'Haven't I been abroad there?'

4.8.2.2 *mā* 'Not, Don't'

The negation particle *mā* is the most frequently used particle in KhA for the negation of verbs (IPFV as well as PFV), participles, and pseudoverbs (cf. Ingham 1974: 33).

(5) [A19]

əyēt basad mā rəḥət.
come.PFV.1SG anymore NEG go.PFV.1SG
'I came back [to Ahvaz] and then I didn't go (abroad) anymore.'

(6) [A19]

mā sand-i farəd šəġla ġēr bəkān.
NEG at-1SG INDEF job other place
'I don't have any job anywhere else.'

(7) [A10]

mā bī-ya, mā ʔagdar āna.
NEG in-1SG NEG be_able.IPFV.1SG 1SG
'I'm not able (to do this job), I can't.'

(8) [X1]

mā yənwəčəl,
NEG be_eaten.IPFV.3SG.M
'(This food) can't be eaten.'

(9) [A12]

mā tšərbūn čāy?
NEG drink.IPFV.2SG.M tea
'Don't you (want to) drink tea?'

Once in my corpus *mā* was used at the end of an utterance for emphasis, as in the English 'right?' or 'isn't it?':

MORPHOLOGY   219

(10) [A4, who addresses the following question to the woman because her son
     just said the number of the class he was entering in Persian, *šišom* 'sixth
     (grade)', and not in Arabic]
     ətˤallmīn-a   *ˤağam, mā?*
     teach.IPFV.2SG.F-OBL.3SG.M Persian NEG
     'You teach him [your son] Persian, right/don't you?'

The construction *X mā X* can be translated as 'X and what is around X (what is
close to it)' or 'X and the like'.[78]

(11) [A6]
     nawāḥi həndəyyān mā   *həndəyyān, əl-yarāḥi,*
     regions Hendijan REL/NEG Hendijan DEF-Jarahi
     '(In) the surroundings of Hendijan, Hendijan and its surroundings, (and
     in) Jarahi, ...'

Holes suggests that the construction *X mā X* is related to echoic constructions
with *m-* as common in Turkish but also used in Gulf Arabic, in which *m-* sub-
stitutes the first letter of a repeated noun, e.g. (Bahraini Arabic) *kačra mačra*
'rubbish and such like' (Holes 2016: 102, fn. 24; cf. Lahdo 2009: 205 on such *m-*
doublets in the Arabic of Tillo in south-eastern Turkey). In my corpus there is
also one example of such a construction in KhA: *xarbaṭ marbaṭ* 'so-so, not that
well' [*xarbaṭ* lit. means 'he/it got confused'].

4.8.2.3   *lā* 'No; Not, Don't'
The most common use of *lā* in KhA as well as in all other dialects of Arabic is
to give a negative answer to a polar question, i.e. English 'No!' In this function,
and when the speaker wants to emphasize his/her negative answer, it is often
pronounced *laʔ*.

(12) [A4] and [A6]
     [A4] *mən   awwal-mā tṣīr*   *ətsammūn-ha*
          from first-REL become.IPFV.3SG.F call.IPFV.2PL.M-OBL.3SG.F
     ṭəlyān w   tˤaddā-l-ha   *farəd ṭəlt̟-təšhər,*
     lambs and pass.PFV.3SG.M-for-3SG.F INDEF three-months

---

78   Cf. Holes (2016: 102); and Bar-Moshe (2019: 69, fn. 4) on the same constructions with a
      similar meaning in Bahraini and in Jewish Baghdadi Arabic, respectively.

š-ətsammūn-a?   baʕad-hu ṭəlyān?
what-call.IPFV.2PL.M-OBL.3SG.M still-3SG.M lambs
[A6] *lā,* *ǝngǝl-l-a*   *yǝḍaʕ.*
        NEG say.IPFV.1PL-to-3SG.M yearling
'When they [i.e. the lambs] have just been born you call them *ṭǝlyān*
(lambs). But after some three months, what do you call them? Are they
still (called) *ṭǝlyān*?' 'No, we call it *yǝḍaʕ*.'[79]

Combined with an IPFV verb of the 2nd person, *lā* is used for prohibition, corresponding to a negated imperative (the imperative form itself cannot be negated
in Arabic).

(13) [A10]
    hāy *ǝd-dār*   *lā*   *thǝddīn-ha.*
    DEM DEF-room NEG open.IPFV.2SG.F-OBL.3SG.F
    'Don't open this room!'

In some cases, *lā* is also used to negate an IPFV verb in the indicative (instead
of the more frequent *mā*):

(14) [A1; talking about his school memories]
    lā   *naʕrǝf*   *ǝl-mǝʕalləm* *š-ygūl.*
    NEG know.IPFV.1PL DEF-teacher what-say.IPFV.3SG.M
    'We don't know what the teacher says.'

(15) [X3; lamenting how relationships have changed since she was young]
    baʕad ǝl-ǝxu   *lā*   *yʕarǝf*   *ǝxt-a.*
    DP   DEF-brother NEG know.IPFV.3SG.M sister-3SG.M
    'Nowadays the brother doesn't know his sister.'

KhA *lā* may also be used with the meaning 'lest' (cf. Holes 2016: 108 on the same
use of *lā* in Bahraini Arabic).

(16) [Ḥa1]
    gālō-l-i   *baʕad ǝnti* *tyōzīn*   *lā*
    say.PFV.3PL.M-to-1SG DP   2SG.F stop.IPFV.2SG.F NEG

---

79 Cf. Lane (1863: 39) on CA *ǧaḍaʕᵘⁿ* (applied to a sheep) 'a year old; and sometimes less than
    a year' [= 'yearling'].

MORPHOLOGY   221

yḥassnūn   *rās-əč*   *w*   *ydəbbūn-əč*
shave.IPFV.3PL.M head-2SG.F and throw.IPFV.3PL.M-OBL.2SG.F
b-əz-zəndān.[80]
in-DEF-jail
'They then said, "You (better) stop now lest they shave your head and put
you in jail."'

4.8.2.4   *mūš* 'Not'

This negation particle occurs in my corpus only in recordings of people from
Hoveyzeh, Ḥamīdīya, and Tustar (cf. 2.2.1). *muš* (with short *u*) is also used in
Negev Arabic (Shawarbah 2011: 325, sentences 1 and 2). In KhA, it is used only
for the negation of nouns.

(17) [Ḥ1]
      *hāḏa — yaʕni ham xafīf, **mūš** mətīn kəlləš.*
      DEM   DP   also thin NEG thick totally
      'This—it is also thin, not very thick.'

4.8.2.5   Serial Negation

When two or more items in a series are negated, often all components are
negated by *lā*. In case there are two negated items, *lā* ... *lā* corresponds to
English 'neither ... nor'.

(18) [A9]
      ən-naxla   *tṣīr*   *naḏīfa baʕad, **lā**   ʕazga, **lā***
      DEF-palm become.IPFV.3SG.F clean.F then NEG branch NEG
      *karba, **lā** saʕfa*   *yābsa, ən-naxla naḏīfa.*
      nodule NEG palm_frond.SGT dry.F DEF-palm clean.F
      'The palm tree is clean then, no branches, no nodules, no dry palm fronds,
      the palm tree is clean.'

(19) [Ḥ1]
      nəmši   *aḥəffāy, **lā**   lbāsāt **lā** nʕālāt.*
      go.IPFV.1PL barefoot NEG trousers NEG slippers
      'We (used to) go barefoot, (we had) neither trousers nor shoes.'

---

80   < P *zendān* 'jail' (Junker and Alawi 2002: 387), cf. LA (320).

The first item may, however, also be negated by *mā*, the second and—if there are any—following items by *lā* or *wa-lā* (cf. MSA *wa-lā* 'nor', e.g., *kayfa tuḥibbīna man lā ṭumūḥa lahu wa-lā raġbata fī l-ḥayāti?* 'How can you love someone who has no ambition nor any desire for life?', Badawi, Carter, and Gully 2016: 640).

(20) [A1]
  lā   *ʕəd-həm tannūr wa-lā*   *ʕəd-həm šī.*
  NEG at-3PL.M oven   and-NEG at-3PL.M thing
  'They had no oven nor anything.'

(21) [A1]
  mā bí   *ṭaʕəm wa-lā*   *šay.*
  NEG in.3SG.M taste   and-NEG thing
  'It has no taste nor anything.'

(22) [M1]
  mā rəḥət   *la-hāḏa w-lā*   *l-hāḏ.*
  NEG go.PFV.1SG to-DEM   and-NEG to-DEM
  'I didn't go to this one nor to that one.'

4.8.3 *Future*
The future marker *rāḥ* evolved by a grammaticalization process from *rāyəḥ* 'going', which is the AP of the verb *rāḥ* 'to go'.

(1) [A4]
  šlōn rāḥ yṣīr   *əš-šaṭṭ?*
  how FUT become.IPFV.3SG.M DEF-river
  'What will the river be like [once they open the dams]?'

Based on the fact that cognate forms of this future marker occur in Baghdadi Arabic (Muslim, Jewish, and Christian), as well as in Egypt, Damascus, and Beirut, Heikki Palva describes this future marker an old sedentary feature (Palva 2009: 21, 2006: 612; cf. Blanc 1964: 117–118 on this future marker in Jewish, Christian, and Muslim Baghdadi Arabic; for a good overview cf. Taine-Cheikh 2004: 219–220; 231).

In addition to KhA and MBA, the future marker *rāḥ* is further used in the *ɡələt*-type dialects of Basra (Mahdi 1985: 210–211, 225, 251) and al-Shirqat (cf. Leitner 2021: fn. 16 and the references and examples mentioned there).[81] Kwayriš and Šāwi Arabic have no future marker (cf. Leitner 2021).

---

81   According to a native speaker of Kerbala Arabic, in her dialects and some other dialects

MORPHOLOGY 223

Outside the *gələt* dialect group it is used—though not very frequently—in Bahraini Arabic (Holes 2016: 304, 2001: 216; Johnstone 1967: 152) and in Kuwaiti Arabic (here to express proximal intent 'to be about to', Holes 2016: 304).

If Palva's assumption that *rāḥ* is an old sedentary feature holds true, the KhA future marker *rāḥ* has probably been adopted by the Bedouin Arab tribes who inhabited Lower Iraq and some of which have later settled in Khuzestan (cf. 4.11.1.3.1 on the question whether the KhA prefix *də-* used for imperatives is also a sedentary-type feature). Regarding its current distribution, the use of this feature is definitely common to both the sedentary-type *qəltu* and Bedouin-type *gələt* dialects (like the indefinite article, cf. 4.9.6.2).

The AP form *rāyəḥ* F *rāyḥa* is also used to express future intent and occurs once in my corpus (*āna rāyḥa (a)sawwī-lak* 'I will make (for) you ...'). The form *rāḥ* occurs three times. More often, future reference is expressed merely with an IPFV verb (or an AP) without any future particle. In this case, future reference is usually indicated by a temporal adverb, as in the following example:

(2) [A6]
 ǧərīb təyīb   *tawlad.*
 soon give_birth.IPFV.3SG.F give_birth.IPFV.3SG.F
 'Soon she [the ewe] will give birth.'

4.8.4 *Presentative* hā

The presentative particle *hā* can be used as a (demonstrative) sentence/clause introducer or to emphasize the (pragmatic) importance of a fact or an event.[82] In this function of presentative introduction, *hā-* may be combined with an independent pronoun (cf. Fischer 1959: 159; 164), as in the next example.

(3) [M4, answering Abu ʕAdnān's question which city of Khuzestan he liked most]
 hā   *həwa, ʕAbbādān.*
 PRST 3SG.M Abadan
 'This is it, Abadan (of course).'

---

of central Iraq *ḥa* may also be used to mark future tense. This questions still needs further investigation.

82 Cf. Khan (2008: 704–705) for an overview of presentatives formed from demonstratives in Arabic dialects; cf. Fischer (1959: 48 and 163) on general remarks on the interjection *hā-* in various Arabic dialects; Johnstone (1967: 92) on the presentative *hā-* in Kuwaiti Arabic; and Holes (2001: 536; 2016: 89–92) on the presentative *hā-* in Bahraini Arabic; cf. 4.1.6.1.5 and fn. 12 on the hypothetical development of *hā* from a presentative to a demonstrative.

224   CHAPTER 4

As the following four examples show, the presentative *hā* often has a strong deictic character and can be translated as '(see,) there/here, see, look (here)':

(1) [Ḥ2]
     ʔāna yəbət   *bənt w-ḏəbaḥət-ha*   *w   hā*
     1SG   give_birth.PFV.1SG girl   and-kill.PFV.1SG-OBL.3SG.F and PRST
     damm-ha   bə-šīša.
     blood-3SG.F in-bottle
     'I bore a girl and killed her and (see), here is her blood in a bottle.'

(2) [Ḥa1]
     hā   šūf   əš-ḥalā-hən!
     PRST see.IMP.SG.M what-beauty-3PL.F
     'Look here how beautiful they are!'

(3) [Ḥ1]
     ət-talla   hēč hā   ṭōl-ha.
     DEF-brooch DEM PRST length-3SG.F
     'The brooch is like this, see, this big [lit. "this is its length"].'

(4) [Ḥ1, showing me her earlobe piercings]
     hāḏ hā   mamzūg.
     DEM PRST pierced
     'See, here I have holes [for earrings].'

4.8.5   *Discourse Particles and Interjections*

There are many different terms that deal with the parts of speech here called discourse particles (they are also called discourse markers, modal particles, etc.). In using the term discourse particle (DP), I generally follow the definition of Kerstin Fischer, who, with the employment of this term, suggests a focus on

> … small, uninflected words that are only loosely integrated into the sentence structure, if at all. The term particle is used in contrast to clitics, full words, and bound morphemes. Using the term discourse particle furthermore distinguishes discourse particles/markers from larger entities, such as phrasal idioms, that fulfil similar functions.
>
> FISCHER 2006: 4

MORPHOLOGY 225

In the following list of frequently used KhA DPs with examples illustrating some of their main functions, there are some items that may be inflected for gender but are still included as DPs based on their syntactical properties (e.g. sentence-peripheral position[83]) and pragmatic functions (e.g. focus, emphasis, etc.). Because DPs are usually polyfunctional and generally don't hold a meaning on their own (cf. Aijmer 2002: 22), for most of them no direct English translations are given. Their English translation, if there is any, may vary greatly according to the context in and function with which the respective DP is used. DPs are generally among the parts of speech hardest to translate from one language into another.

4.8.5.1   *yaʕni*

The discourse particle *yaʕni* appears 252 times in corpus. Its use often signals that an explanation or further qualification of what has been said will follow and is therefore often translated as 'so, that is, that means' (cf. Owens and Rockwood 2008: 85–86 on this discourse particle in various Arabic dialects).

(1)   [Ḥ1]
    *ənḥəṭṭ   hāḏanni əšǧābāt əhnā, ēh, **yaʕni** ḏahab.*
    put.IPFV.1PL DEM   earrings here yes DP   gold
    'We put these earrings here, yes, that is (eardrops made of) gold.'

(2)   [Ḥ1]
    *daššēna   **yaʕni** d-dīra,   ləgēnā-ha   šī   mgaffla*
    enter.PFV.1PL DP   DEF-village find.PFV.1PL-OBL.3SG.F some closed.F
    w   šī   baʕad-hi,   əd-dəkākīn əs-sūg.[84]
    and some not_yet-3SG.F DEF-shops DEF-market
    'So we entered the village—we found it. Some [stores] were (already) closed and some not yet—the shops of the market.'

---

83   DPs are very often sentence- or utterance-peripheral (cf. Aijmer 2002: 18).

84   The correct phrase would be *dəkākīn əs-sūg* 'the shops of the market'. The speaker, however, has also attached the definite article to the first word of this genitive construction, *dəkākīn* 'shops', which is unusual for KhA and Arabic in general. The speaker also makes a short pause before adding *əs-sūg* 'the market', which shows us that she originally only had the shops in mind and then added the market for further clarifying what she was talking about.

226 CHAPTER 4

(3) [M4]
yaʕni hāḏ əš-šaṭṭ   ənta   tšūf   čān
DP   DEM DEF-river 2SG.M see.IPFV.2SG.M be.PFV.3SG.M
əb-zamān-a   čān   yəḥkəm
at-time-3SG.M be.PFV.3SG.M rule.IPFV.3SG.M
'So, this river, you see, during its time it used to be very strong [lit. "rul-ing"].'

4.8.5.2 *baḷḷa*
This DP is generally used for polite requests, often connected with the meaning 'let's see' (etymologically derived from *b-allāh*, CA *bi-llāhi* 'by God').

(4) [F1]
ṣəbbī-l-i   baḷḷa čāy.
pour.IMP.SG.F-for-1SG DP   tea
'Please, pour me some more tea.'

(5) [A16, asking Maryam's aunt to sing a lullaby for us]
ēh baḷḷa tdabbrī-l-na   waḥda.
yes DP   find.IPFV.2SG.F-for-1PL one.F
'Yes, let's see if you can find one for us.'

(6) [A17, when I showed them pictures of agricultural equipment and asked them to give me their names in KhA]
hāḏa, baḷḷa ... ʔāna mā   ʔašūf-a ...
DEM DP   1SG NEG see.IPFV.1SG-OBL.3SG.M
'This (is a ...) let's see ... I can't see it ...'

4.8.5.3 *baʕad*
This DP often appears at the very end of an utterance and has a concluding cadence.

(7) [X3]
ʔəntəm hassa ham təḥčūn   ʕaǧam baʕad?
2PL.M now   also speak.IPFV.2PL.M Persian DP
'So, do you also speak Persian?'

(8) [A10, concluding her *sālfa* 'story']
ēh hāy hīya baʕad.
yes DEM 3SG.F DP
'So, this is it [the story].'

MORPHOLOGY

227

(9) [AB1]
hāḏa ləbəs-həm   baʕad.
DEM clothes-3PL.M DP
'So, these were their clothes'

4.8.5.4   *ča*

The use of the discourse particle *ča* (which occurs 69 times in my corpus) is considered one of the hallmarks of the KhA *ʕarab* dialects by speakers themselves (cf. 2.2.1). Outside Khuzestan, it is also used in Southern Iraq (Hassan 2016b: 47; 53). The origin of this discourse particle is likely rooted in the deictic element /k/ and possibly related to the presentatives used in the Gulf region, e.g. *ka* (+ pronoun) in (Bedouin-type) Bahraini Arabic, as in *"ka-hiyya yāya* 'here she comes now' … *ka yigūl ʕali!* 'now he's saying it was Ali (who stole the shoes)!'"* (Holes 2001: 447), which is also known for Kuwait (Johnstone 1967: 92) and Arabic dialects spoken in Bushehr, Southern Iran[85] (data from the FWF-funded research project "Arabic in Southern Iran", in which the author was employed 2020–2021).[86] It might also be related to the deictic copula *kū(we)* and the presentative *kwā* found in Northern and Western Syria and Anatolia (Procházka 2018c: 277–278; cf. Hanitsch 2019: 260–261 and the references mentioned there). Procházka (2018c: 278; 2021) also traces the etymology of these presentatives back to the deictic element *k* or the deictic particle /ka/ followed by a shortened form of the independent personal pronoun.

In KhA, the discourse particle *ča* often introduces questions or imperatives, can have a deictic function, and is used to express astonishment on part of the speaker. Cf. Leitner (2019) for further examples on the manifold functions of this discourse particle and fn. 74 above in this chapter on the use of *ča* for the introduction of the apodosis in conditional clauses.

(10) [A15]
ča əl-kūlər   mā yəštəġəl?
DP DEF-air_conditioner NEG work.IPFV.3SG.M
'Doesn't the air conditioner work?'

---

85   Cf. also the deictic element *ka-* + indirect object suffixes in Ṭuroyo (Neo-Aramaic): 3SG.M *kalé* 'There he is' 3SG.F *kalá* 'There she is' (Khan 2018: 242–243).

86   Cf. https://south-iranian-arabic.uni-graz.at/de/. In the dialect of the Šarqiyya region in Oamn, the verbal prefix *ka-* appears to have a different function, namely to emphasize perfect aspect (Eades and Watson 2013: 47).

(11) [Ḥ1]

xayya   taʕāli,   ča məšēna   yā   mōza!
sister.DIM come.IMP.SG.F DP go.PFV.1PL VOC Mōza
'Sister, come! We are already leaving, Mōza!'

(12) [A18] asks [Ḥa1] how they used to shop at the market when she was young

b-əflūs   təštərūn   yō taṭūn ...?   — hā ča
with-money buy.IPFV.2PL.M or give.IPFV.2PL.M — DP DP
š-nəṭī?
what-give.IPFV.1PL
'Did you buy with money or did you give ...?'—'Well [laughs] what (else) would we give (them but money)?'

4.8.5.5 *ham*

When used as a DP (cf. 4.3.2.5 on the homophonous adverb meaning 'also, too'), the meaning of *ham* seems to come closest to English 'just, simply', or '(not) even' (with negated clauses).

(13) [A4, telling me not to be shy about the picture we were taking with the shepherd]

***ham** məṯəl əbū-k   kān,*
DP   like   father-2SG.M be.PFV.3SG.M
'[Touch him on his shoulder] (just) as if he was your father.'

(14) [A19]

*rəğaʕət   l-əl-əkwēt   ḏallēt   **ham** farəd mədda,*
return.PFV.1SG to-DEF-Kuwait stay.PFV.1SG DP INDEF time_span
ən-nōb   baʕad, əyēt   baʕad   mā rəḥət.
DEF-time then   come.PFV.1SG anymore NEG go.PFV.1SG
'I came back to Kuwait, stayed (there) for some time, then came back and I didn't go (abroad) anymore.'

(15) [A4]

***ham** mā bī-č   wəḏrat laḥam.*
DP   NEG with-2SG.F piece.CS meat
'You don't have even a bit of meat on you [= you are gaunt]!'

4.8.5.6 *tara*

tara derives from the 2nd person SG.M IPFV of the CA verb *raʔā* 'to see', which is otherwise not used in KhA. Like most other DPs, KhA *tara* can fulfil different

MORPHOLOGY   229

functions and have various meanings (cf. Fischer 1959: 195). This particle is used
in many different dialects: for example, in Basra Arabic (Mahdi 1985: 188, who,
however, calls it a conjunction), Muslim Baghdadi Arabic (WB: 55), the dialect
of the Šukriyya in Eastern Sudan (Reichmuth 1983: 109–110), and in Bahraini
Arabic (Holes 2016: 281).[87] In my corpus, *tara* never occurs with a suffixed personal pronoun like it does in some other dialects (cf. Taine-Cheikh 2013: 146
and the references mentioned there).

One of its main functions is to emphasize or put stress on the predicate (cf.
Reichmuth 1983: 109–110 on the dialect of the Šukriyya; cf. Fischer 1959: 196 on
this particular function), as in the next example:

(16) [F1]
   dawwaxtī-na   ***tara, gəʕdi!***
   confuse.PFV.2SG.F-OBL.1PL DP   sit_down.IMP.SG.F
   'You have confused us—sit down!'

Another common function of *tara* is to introduce a subordinate clause with
an alternative meaning (similar to English 'otherwise ...'; cf. WB: 55 and Holes
2001: 195 on the same function of *tara* in Iraqi and Bahraini Arabic, respectively;
cf. also Taine-Cheikh 2013: 147; and Fischer 1959: 197). We also find *tara* in this
function in Basra-Arabic (Mahdi 1985: 188).

The following example is taken from a fairy tale in which a girl finds an
elderly couple hung up by a vulture from their eyelashes and who ask her to
help them get free. The phrase starting with *tara* directly follows the (SG.F)
imperative *nazzəlī-na* 'take us down!'

(17) [A10]
   nazzəlī-na,   ***tara ysawwī-č***
   take_down.IMP.SG.F-OBL.1PL DP   make.IPFV.3SG.M-OBL.2SG.F
   məṯəl-na.
   like-1PL
   '... take us down, because (otherwise) it [the vulture] will do to you as he
   did to us.'

4.8.5.7   *hēč ~ hēči*

The DP *hēč ~ hēči* is often used to confirm or emphasize a previous statement
(cf. Owens 1993: 201 on Nigerian Arabic). In this function it is often combined
with the DP *baʕad*.

---

87   Cf. Taine-Cheikh (2013: 145–149) for references to other dialects that use *tara* as a DP in
     many different functions.

230   CHAPTER 4

(18) [M1]
    *hāy Sāyša   ahnā b-əl-əmḥammra,   **hēči.***
    DEM live.AP.SG.F here in-DEF-Muḥammara DP
    'This one is living here, in Muḥammara; yes (that's the way it is).'

(19) [Ḥa1]
    baSad **hēči** *hāda l-farax   əl-məḏayyəg aftəhəm*
    DP   DP   DEM DEF-child DEF-uneasy understand.IPFV.1SG
    *əš-šənhu   mā šənhu,   * **hēči** *baSad.*
    DEF-what.SG.M REL what.SG.M DP   DP
    'So that's it; this child that is uneasy, I understand what is what [i.e. what
    his problem is]; that's how it is.'

Like *š-əsm-a* (lit.) 'What's its name?', *hēč* is also used as a filler while the speaker
is thinking of the right word or phrase and comes close to American English
'like', adding nothing to the truth value of a proposition.

(20) [A4]
    *w-ayyām əl   * **hēč** *əl-Sādīya   š-ətləbsan?*
    and-days REL DP   DEF-ordinary.F what-wear.2PL.F
    'And (on the) days, that are like—(on) the ordinary (days), what do you
    wear?'

(21) [A4]
    *əšgadd   mən naxīl-kəm   * **hēč** *b-əl-mīya   təmarraḏ*
    how_many of   palms-2PL.M DP in-DEF-hundred fall_sick.PFV.3SG.M
    mən ət-təlwīṯ?
    of   DEF-pollution
    'How many of your palms, like in per cent, fall sick because of the pollu-
    tion?'

(22) [Ḥa1, answering the question *čam yōm yəṭawwəl tannūr?* 'How long does
    (the construction of) a clay oven take?']
    maṯal āna w   nəḏərt-i   ʔāna, lō nāḏra   maṯal asawwi
    like   1SG and vow.CS-1SG 1SG if vow.AP.SG.F like   do.IPFV.1SG
    yōmēn,   lō maṯal **hēč** *mā-ni   nāḏra   ʔasawwi   ṯaləṯ*
    two_days if like   DP NEG-1SG vow.AP.SG.F do.IPFV.1SG three
    tayyām ha-š-šəkəl.
    days   DEM-DEF-kind
    'It depends on me and my vow: if I have vowed, I do (it) like in two days;
    if I, for example, have not vowed, it takes me three days—like that.'

MORPHOLOGY   231

4.8.5.8 *ʕūd*

This DP is often used when expressing wishes and guesses. It is also used in
Iraqi Arabic (WB: 327 "*ʕūd* (an interjection, approx.:) 'well, then'"; Mahdi 1985:
188 on Basra Arabic, who, however, calls it a conjunction).

(23) [A18]—[Ḥa1]
    hāḏa d-dǝgga   w   dāgga   ʕalē-k ...?— hāḏa ʕamma, hāḏa
    DEM DEF-tattoo and tattoo.AP.SG.F on-2SG.M   DEM aunt   DEM
    ʕamma madgūg   hāḏa ʕūd mǝ-tṣīr
    aunt   tattoo.AP.SG.M DEM DP when-become.IPFV.3SG.F
    ǝl-mara   tāxǝḏ   rayyǝl,   ǝthǝṭṭ   ǝhnā nǝyāšīn,
    DEF-woman take.IPFV.3SG.F husband put.IPFV.3SG.F here marks
    ʕūd ǝtṣīr   ḥǝlwa.
    DP   become.IPFV.3SG.F beautiful.F
    'And this tattoo, she tattooed you ...?'—'This, my dear, this (part) is tat-
    tooed, this shall be—when a woman is about to take a man [i.e. to marry],
    she puts here symbols [tattoes], (this way) she hopes to become (even
    more) beautiful.'

(24) [X3]
    hāy ġēr whayda   hēč nsawwi   ʕalḗ   ʕūd
    DEM only one.F.DIM DEM do.IPFV.1PL on.3SG.M DP
    yṣīr   ynām,   w-ǝngaṭṭḗ.
    become.IPFV.3SG.M sleep.IPFV.3SG.M and-cover.IPFV.1PL.OBL.3SG.M
    'This (is) another short one [lullaby] (that) I sing to him [the child] so he
    will sleep, and I cover him.'

According to my consultants, KhA *ʕūd* is also used to address someone who is
acting a bit arrogant, as in the following examples:

(25) [A14]
    ʕūd hassa ǝnta   wāyǝd ǝtʕarǝf!
    DP   now 2SG.M a_lot know.IPFV.2SG.M
    'You really think you know a lot!'

(26) [A14]
    ʕūd š-ǝtrīd?
    DP   what-want.IPFV.2SG.M
    'Who do you think you are! [lit. "What do you want?"]'

232   CHAPTER 4

4.8.5.9   *xō, xōš* 'Good, Okay'
The KhA discourse particles *xō* and *xōš* 'well; okay' derive from Pers. *xo, xob,
xoš*[88] (cf. WAD III: 527 and 529, map 394b, where, however, mainly adjectival
uses of *xōš* in various Eastern dialects are listed). On the KhA adverb *xōš* meaning 'well' cf. 4.3.2.20.

The DP *xō* (besides *xōb*) is also used in Iraqi Arabic (WB: 148; Mahdi 1985:
188 on Basra Arabic, who, however, calls it a conjunction); *xōb* is also used in
Bahraini Arabic (Holes 2016: 279–280).

KhA *xō* is often used when stating the obvious or something the hearer or
interlocutor is expected to know, because it has, for example, already been
explained previously (cf. Holes 2016: 279 on a similar function of *xōb* in Bahraini
Arabic).

(27) [A19]
    hassa hāy əl-ʔaraḍ   — xō gəlt-l-əč   tawwa — hāy
    now   DEM DEF-land   DP say.PFV.1SG-to-2SG.F just   DEM
    əl-ʔaraḍ   həna kāḍḍīn-ha   ʔāǧār.
    DEF-land here take.AP.PL.M-OBL.3SG.F rent
    'Now this field—well, I have just told you—this field here, we rent it.'

(28) [Ḥa1]
    ʔāna xō mənnā   gaṣīra w   mənnā   — yəǧall
    1SG   DP from_here short.F and from_here   respect.IPFV.3SG.M
    əl   yəsmaʕ,   yəǧall   əl   yəsmaʕ   —
    REL listen.IPFV.3SG.M respect.IPFV.3SG.M REL listen.IPFV.3SG.M
    əl-məṭi   ʕāli, ʔačalləb   bí.
    DEF-donkey tall hang_onto.IPFV.1SG with.3SG.M
    'So here me being short (as you can see) and there—pardon the expres-
    sion, pardon the expression—the donkey being tall, I hung onto it.'

In KhA, both *xō* and *xōš* and are often used phrase-initially as a filler.

---

88   In several spoken dialects of Persian, *xo* and *xob* are used as discourse particles and simple
    adjectives, whereas *xoš* is just used as an adjective (cf. Shabibi 2006: 160). Thus the Persian
    adjective *xoš* has been desemanticized in Khuzestani Arabic to function as a discourse
    particle with the meaning 'well, okay' (cf. Shabibi 2006: 160). According to my informants
    and data, the form *xōb* is not used in Khuzestani Arabic (contrast Matras & Shabibi 2007:
    143).

MORPHOLOGY   233

(29) KhA, Ahvaz (own data)
    xōš, š-ʕad-na,   taʕay   əhnā baba.
    DP   what-at-1PL come.IMP.SG.F here father
    'Alright, what (else) do we have. Come here, dear!'

Both DPs are often used in stories following the verb *gāl* 'to say' to introduce a
direct speech.

(30) [A10]
    lamman ġada   mən ʕad-həm, gāl-l-a   xō, hāy
    when   leave.PFV.3SG.M from at-3PL.M say-to-3SG.M DP DEM
    ər-rəmmānāt   š-asawwi   bī-hən?
    DEF-pomegranates what-do.IPFV.1SG with-3PL.F
    'When he left them, he said to him, "So what shall I do with these pome-
    granates?"'

4.8.5.10   *yalla* 'Let's Go! Come On!'

(31) [A12]
    yalla   ča nšūf   n-naʕayāt, ʕəlwīya!
    INTERJ DP see.IPFV.1PL DEF-sheep ʕəlwīya
    'Come on, let's see the sheep, *ʕəlwīya!*'[89]

4.8.5.11   *yəmma*
This interjection, homonymous with the address form *yəmma*, is a contraction
of the vocative particle *yā* and the noun *ʔəmm* 'mother' and used in both positive and negative situations: when the speaker wants to express that (s)he is
impressed by something or finds something appalling.

(32) [A15]
    yəmma, əšgadd   ḥalu yʕarfan.
    INTERJ how_much good know.IPFV.3PL.F
    'My God, how well they know (them)!'

---

89   This title denotes that her family's ancestors are said to go back to the prophet Muham-
    mad's family.

234 CHAPTER 4

4.8.5.12 *Ɂē ~ Ɂēh, Ɂay* 'Yes'

(33) [A12] and [A4]
Ġarība? Ɂēh Ġarība.
Ġarība yes Ġarība
'"Ġarība [a proper name]?" Yes, Ġarība.'

(34) [A10]
gāl-l-a hā, ənta tənsa? gāl-l-a Ɂē.
say-to-3SG.M DP 2SG.M forget.IPFV.2SG.M say-to-3SG.M yes
'He said, "What! So you (always) forget?" He said, "Yes".'

4.8.5.13 *wəl-*PRO
The particle *wəl* always appears with an enclitic pronoun and is mostly used for emphasis, focus, and the expression of astonishment. Ingham states that "*ča, wilak, wilič, wilkum, wilčan* ... are Mesopotamian and have no equivalent in Arabian dialects" and defines these particles as "expletives" (1982: 87).

(35) [A14]
wəl-ak štagēt-l-ak, wēn-ak?
DP-2SG.M miss.PFV.1SG-to-2SG.M where-2SG.M
'I really missed you. Where have you been (all the time)?'

(36) [A10]
gālat-l-a yəmma wəl-ak āna nāsya.
say.PFV.3SG.F-to-3SG.M mother DP-2SG.M 1SG forget.AP.SG.F
'She said to him, "My dear (son), I have (completely) forgotten".'

4.8.5.14 *Ɂagəl-l-ak* F *Ɂagəl-l-əč*
Ɂagəl-l-ak/Ɂagəl-l-əč lit. means 'I tell you (SG.M/F)' and is usually used for the introduction of questions to get the listener's attention.

(37) [A15]
Ɂagəl-l-əč əmm Sebastian ʕayūz? ḥəlwa?
say.IPFV.1SG-to-2SG.F mother Sebastian old_woman pretty.F
'I say, Sebastian's mother, is she old or (still) young?'

MORPHOLOGY   235

(38) [A18]

> *Ɂagəl-l-əč*   *b-əl-yōm*   *čənti*   *yāhəl,*
> say.IPFV.1SG-to-2SG.F at-DEF-day be.PFV.2SG.F child
> *šə-tḏakkrīn*   *ətsawwūn*   *ətlaʕbūn*
> what-remember.IPFV.2SG.F   do.IPFV.2PL.M   play.IPFV.2PL.M
> *maṯalan?*
> for_example
> 'I say, when you were a child, what do you remember of what you (PL)
> did—what you played, for example?'

4.8.6 *Jussive/Hortative Particle* xall

The jussive mode is expressed with the particle *xall* preceding an IPFV verb and corresponds to English 'let('s) ...'. It most frequently occurs with a verb in the 1PL. *xall* etymologically derives from *xalli*, the imperative of the verb *xalla* 'to allow, let; leave'. This particle is also used in the same function in other dialects of Arabic, e.g. in Iraqi Arabic (Erwin 1963: 142; Blanc 1964: 117; Mahdi 1985: 189), or in Bahraini Arabic (Holes 2016: 77). In rapid speech, the final geminate consonant *l* is often reduced to a single consonant [xal].

(1) [Ḥa1]

> *baḷḷa* **xall** *ənšərrb-a*   *māy* *fāyər*
> DP   HORT make_drink.IPFV.1PL-OBL.3SG.M water boiling
> *yəġsəl*   *ṣadr-a.*
> wash.IPFV.3SG.M chest-3SG.M
> 'Let's make him drink hot [lit. "boiling"] water: that makes him feel good
> [lit. "cleans his chest"].'

(2) [Ḥa1]

> *əgaʕdu*   **xall** *asōlf-əl-kəm.*
> sit.IMP.PL.M HORT tell.IPFV.1SG-to-2PL.M
> 'Sit down (and) let me tell you a story.'

(3) [A12]

> **xall** *yṭəggūn*   *ʕalē-ha* *ʕakəs.*
> HORT hit.IPFV.3PL.M on-3SG.F picture
> 'Let them take a picture of them [the sheep].'

(4) [A1]

> **xall** *aṣəbb-l-ak*   *čāy.*
> HORT pour.IPFV.1SG-to-2SG.M tea
> 'Let me pour you tea. ~ May I pour you some tea?'

236   CHAPTER 4

xall is always reduced to *xa-* in the following two phrases: *xa-yʕōn*-PRO, e.g. *xa-yʕōn-ak* lit. 'let him (God) help you, may he help you', which is said to someone envied for something; and *xa-ywalli* SG.F *xa-twalli* 'leave him/her alone'.

4.9 Nouns

In this chapter, the main KhA gender- and number-marking morphemes and/ or patterns, the construct state of nouns, diminutive patterns, and the elative pattern will be discussed.

4.9.1 *Gender*

Generally, there are two grammatical genders, masculine and feminine. Masculine nouns are by default unmarked. Feminine nouns are mostly marked by the feminine suffix *-a*, but there are also unmarked nouns which are treated grammatically as feminine because they denote biologically female beings. Finally, there exists a small closed class of unmarked feminine nouns which do not belong to the preceding class: these are mainly paired body parts and basic elements of nature. Biological gender is always stronger than grammatical gender—this is illustrated by nouns such as *zalma* 'man', which ends in *-a* but is still SG.M because it denotes a biologically masculine being. Nouns that end in *-a* that goes back to OA *ā?* are grammatically masculine, e.g. *ġada ~ ġada < ġadā?^{un}* 'lunch'.

i.   Feminine Suffix *-a*

Most feminine nouns end on the feminine marker *-a* (*-īya* after a *nisba*), e.g. *naxla* 'palm', *madarsa* 'school', *čabīra* 'big (SG.F)', *ḥalwa* 'beautiful (SG.F)', and *ʕarāġīya* 'Iraqi (SG.F)'. On status constructus forms cf. 4.9.3.

ii.   Grammatically Unmarked Feminines

These are (1) nouns that denote female beings—e.g. *ʔamm* 'mother', *ʕayūz* 'old woman', and *ʕarūs* 'bride'—and (2) nouns not marked by the feminine ending *-a* but grammatically feminine without biological reason. The latter include some paired body parts[90]—*ʔīd* 'hand, arm', *rīl* 'leg, foot', *ʕēn* 'eye', and *(ʔa)ḏān* 'ear' (cf. WAD I: 102–103 on accounts for this comparatively uncommon

---

90   Many other (smaller) body parts that come in pairs are masculine (as in most other dialects of Arabic: cf. Procházka 2004: 239), e.g. *ʕačas* 'elbow', *čāz (rayal)* 'heel', *xadd* 'cheek',

MORPHOLOGY

form for 'ear' in Basra Arabic and dialects of the Levant, and an etymological explanation)—and some words related to nature,[91] e.g. *gāʕ*[92] 'earth, ground, land', and *nār* 'fire'; and sharp items, e.g. *səččīn*[93] 'knife' (e.g. *səččīn bāšṭa* 'a sharp knife'). Further unmarked feminines in KhA are *baṭən* 'belly' (usually not feminine in CA and MSA, but feminine in other *gələt*, South Arabian, and North African dialects, cf. Procházka 2004: 241), *harəb* 'war' (also feminine in CA and MSA and some other, especially Central and Eastern Arabian dialects, cf. Procházka 2004: 246), and *dār* 'room'.[94]

4.9.2 *Number*
There are three numbers in KhA: singular, dual, and plural. In KhA, the use of the dual is still productive with most nouns. Whereas the singular is mostly unmarked, dual is marked by suffixes and plural by suffixes and/or via word-internal changes.

4.9.2.1 Collective Nouns
Collectives are nouns which semantically refer to a group or some sort of plurality, but morphologically are not plurals and cannot be quantified by a number (cf. Bettega and Leitner 2019: 16, fn. 11).

Verbs, pronouns, and adjectives that refer to a collective noun are usually grammatically SG.F or SG.M whenever this collective is perceived as one entity (cf. Bettega and Leitner 2019: 18–19 on the importance of the factor "individuation" in the choice of agreement patterns with collectives in KhA), e.g.

(1) [A10]
  əl-ġanam   yšarrəd.
  DEF-sheep.COLL run_away.IPFV.3SG.M
  'The sheep run away.'

---

  dēs '(female) breast', *čtāf* 'shoulder', and *ḥāyəb* 'eyebrow'. For a comparative view on this phenomenon cf. Procházka (2004: 238–241).

91 Cf. Procházka (2004: 241–243) on a comparative view on this phenomenon. In contrast with many other dialects (cf. Procházka 2004: 243), *māy* 'water' is not feminine in KhA.

92 On this noun, which is not feminine in OA, cf. Procházka (2004: 242).

93 On other Eastern and Western dialects of Arabic in which this noun is feminine, cf. Procházka (2004: 245).

94 Cf. WAD I: 68 on the not very widespread use of *dār* in the meaning of 'room' in some Western and Eastern Arabic dialects; in Iraq the main lexemes used for 'room' are *ġurfa*, *huġra*, and *gubba*.

238   CHAPTER 4

(2)   [A10]
       yat   *əl-ġanam,*   *ətrīd*   *tōrəd*
       come.PFV.3SG.F   DEF-sheep.COLL   want.IPFV.3SG.F   drink.IPFV.3SG.F
       mənn-a.
       from-3SG.M
       'The sheep came and wanted to drink [all verbs are SG.F] from it [the pol-
       luted water].'

In many cases, especially when the speaker wants to put the focus on the individuals of this collective, PL.F is used for referring to a collective (PL.M with a
human collective), e.g.:

(3)   [A1]
       lamman-mā ydəšš   *əb-ṭarma mālt*   *əd-dəwāb,*
       when-REL   enter.IPFV.3SG.M   in-stall   GL.SG.F   DEF-buffaloes
       rāʕī-hən,   *mən   yšūfann-a*   *yḥənnan*
       owner-3PL.F   when   see.IPFV.3PL.F-OBL.3SG.M   care.IPFV.3PL.F
       ʕalḗ.
       about.3SG.M
       'When he enters the buffaloes' stall, their owner/herder, when they [the
       buffaloes] see him, they care for him/feel compassion for him [verbs
       describing the buffaloes' actions are PL.F].'

4.9.2.2   Singular, Unit Nouns

As stated above, in the majority of cases there is no marker to indicate singular, e.g. *bāb* '(a) door', *səna* '(a) year'. The following singular or unit noun
morphemes are only used for singling out one individual from a collective item.
For many collective nouns, there is no separate unit noun and they may be sin-
gled out by using a so-called count noun, such as *rās* lit. 'head', which is used for
counting cattle and certain types of vegetables (similar to the English 'head'):
e.g. *rās bəṣal* 'an onion'; *rās ṯūm* 'a garlic bulb', lit. 'a head of garlic' (*ḥabba* would
denote one 'clove'); and:

(4)   [A6]
       xamsa w   təsʕīn rās   ṯēna   ᴾ*talafāt*ᴾ *əs-səna*
       five   and 90   head give.PFV.1PL   losses   DEF-year
       b-əš-šəta.
       in-DEF-winter
       'We lost 95 [head of sheep] this (past) year in winter.'

MORPHOLOGY   239

i.   Suffix -*a*

Due to its original function as a marker of the more specific in contrast to the
more general, the suffix -*a*, now generally used as a marker of the feminine,
also has the function of singling out an individual from a mass when suffixed
to a collective noun or describing the uniqueness of an action when attached
to a verbal noun (cf. Masliyah 1997: 70–71; 75). In KhA, this is the most common
morpheme for forming a unit noun from a collective noun. A unit noun with a
suffix -*a* is always grammatically feminine.

The suffixation of the marker -*a* often leads to structural changes due to the
vowel elision and the vowel raising rules (cf. 3.2.2.2), as in the first example
below. Sometimes a structurally different base is used for the unit noun, as in
the last two examples:

> *səmač* 'fish (COLL)' → *səmča* 'a fish'
> *tamər* 'dates (COLL)' → *tamra* 'a date'
> *hōš* 'cows (COLL)' → *hāyša* 'a cow'
> *naxīl* 'palm trees (COLL)' → *naxla* 'a palm'

ii.   Suffix -*āya*

Besides the suffix -*a*, KhA uses the suffix -*āya* to single out an individual of a collective. Cf. Blanc (1964: 73) on the use of this suffix in Muslim Baghdadi Arabic
and Holes (2016: 137) on its use in sedentary-type Bahraini Arabic.

> *šeker* 'sugar' → *šekrāya* 'one grain of sugar' ('sugar cube' is *fəṣṣ ġanəd*)
> *bəṣal* 'onions' → *baṣlāya* 'an onion' (also *rās bəṣal*)
> *xəbəz* 'bread' → *xəbzāya* 'one piece of (flat) bread'
> *čəšməš* 'raisins' → *čəšməšāya* 'a raisin'

4.9.2.3   Dual

In KhA, dual forms only exist for substantives (not for adjectives), but with
these they are commonly used. Often the word 'two', *ətnēn*, is additionally used
with the dual form of the noun. Adjectival attributes of dual heads are usually
in plural.

The dual is constructed with the dual suffix -*ēn* attached to a singular noun
in the construct state (cf. 4.9.3), e.g. *šahr-ēn* 'two months', *nōʕ-ēn* 'two types'.

Except for some nouns denoting body parts that come in pairs, the dual form
is not used with pronominal suffixes: instead, an analytical construction is used
consisting of the numeral 'two', *ətnēn*, and the noun in the plural, e.g.:

240   CHAPTER 4

(5) [A3]
   ətnēn banāt-i
   two   daughters-1SG
   'my two daughters'

This analytical way of expressing the dual is also often used without the presence of personal suffixes, e.g.:

(6) [M1]
   ʕand-i tnēn xawāt.
   at-1SG two sisters
   'I have two sisters.'

(7) [M1]
   ʕand-i wlēdāt   əẓġār   ətnēn.
   at-1SG boy.DIM.PL little.PL two
   'I have two little boys.'

(8) [Ḥ2]
   yyīb-l-a   tnēn xəbzāt.
   bring.IPFV.3SG.M-to-3SG.M two breads
   'He brings him two breads.'

Two nouns denoting body parts that come in pairs use their dual forms for both dual and plural (for this reason researchers often call such duals "pseudo-duals"): *ʔīd* 'hand, arm' DUAL/PL *ʔīdēn* '(two) hands, arms, handles (of a vessel)'; and *rīl* 'leg, foot' DUAL/PL *rīlēn* '(two) legs, feet'. Cf. 4.9.3 for the construction of their dual forms with pronominal suffixes. For other nouns denoting body parts that come in pairs dual forms can be used, but more frequently their respective plural forms with the numeral 'two' are used instead, e.g. *(ʔə)dān* 'ear' DUAL *dānēn* or *ətnēn dānāt* 'two ears', and *ʕēn* 'eye' DUAL *ʕēnēn* or *ətnēn əʕyūn* 'two eyes'. When in construct, these nouns always use the plural forms, e.g. *(ʔə)dānāt-i* 'my ears', and *əʕyūn-i* 'my eyes'.

4.9.2.4   External and Internal Plural
KhA has retained most OA internal plural patterns. Only for the pattern $*C_1uC_2uC_3$ have no examples been found (compare e.g. KhA *əktābāt* 'books' and OA $*kutub^{un}$). In addition, the OA plural patterns with prefixed *ʔa-* are only marginally retained, e.g. *ʔayyām* 'days', and *ʔaṣābīʕ* 'fingers'. In most cases, the plural patterns with prefixed *ʔa-* have been either replaced by external plural

MORPHOLOGY   241

forms, e.g. *nabīyīn* 'prophets' (cf. OA **ʔanbiyāʔ*[u95]), or the plural form is simply not in use anymore, e.g. *dəwa* 'medicine', which is used for both SG and PL (cf. OA **dawāʔ*[un] PL *ʔadwiya*[tun]). The external plural pattern *-āt* is remarkably productive and also replaces some OA internal plurals, e.g. *bəkānāt* 'places', *əktābāt* 'books', and *səʕālāt* 'questions'. Also remarkable is the high frequency of internal plurals of the patterns $\partial C_1 C_2 \bar{a} C_3(a)$ and $\partial C_1 C_2 \bar{u} C_3(a)$, which have also replaced some non-retained OA plural patterns, e.g. *sagəf* 'roof'—*əsgūf(a)* (cf. OA **suquf*[un] and **suqūf*[un]), and are used for loanwords (in addition to the external plural suffix *-āt*), e.g. *kərət* 'card'—*krūta* < Pers. *kārt*. Many loan words, among which Persian loanwords are of course most numerous, do not fit into the below outlined singular patterns, e.g. *nāmard* 'brute' < Pers. *nāmard* 'coward; brute'. For many of these Persian loans, however, Arabic internal plurals are constructed: e.g. *xətkār—xətākīr* 'ball-point pen' < Pers. *xod-kār*, and *bandar—banādər* 'port' < Pers. *bandar* (cf. Leitner 2020:127 for more examples on Persian lexical borrowings).

Both the additional PL morpheme suffixation to an internal plural (e.g. *əmlūkīya* 'kings') and the increased use of external plural morphemes (e.g. *ktābāt* 'books') may be considered peripheral phenomena because they are mainly documented for peripheral dialects (cf. Procházka 2002:119–120).

4.9.2.4.1   *External Masculine Plural Suffix* -īn
This suffix is the most productive external masculine plural morpheme and used to form the PL of:

i.   Masculine Nouns (Including Adjectives and Participles) Denoting Male Humans, e.g.:

> *gāʕəd* 'sitting (AP)' PL *gāʕdīn*
> *baṭṭāl* 'unemployed' PL *baṭṭālīn*
> *ʔaḥwāzi* 'Ahvazi' PL *ʔaḥwāzīyīn*
> *mḥammrāwi* 'person from Muḥammara'—*mḥammrāwīyīn*
> *nabi* 'prophet' PL *nabīyīn*

ii.   *səna* 'Year' PL *əsnīn* (This Exceptional Form Exists besides *sanawāt*, cf. 4.9.2.4.4)

This suffix is also used to form the decade of:

---

95   It could of course also be a retention of the OA plural *nabiyyīna* (see Quran 33:7).

242 CHAPTER 4

iii. Numbers from 3–9, e.g.

sətta 'six' → *səttīn* '60'

4.9.2.4.2 *External Masculine Plural Suffix* -īya
This external plural suffix is used to form the PL of:

i. Some Nouns Ending in -*i*[96] Which Denote Male Human Beings (Many Also Take the External PL Suffix -*īn*):

ḥarāmi 'thief'—*ḥarāmīya*

ii. Nouns Ending in -*či*

ġandarči 'shoemaker'—*ġandarčīya*
kəlāwči 'confidence man, thief'—*kəlāwčīya*
nəswānči 'womanizer'—*nəswānčīya*

4.9.2.4.3 *External Masculine Plural Suffix* -a
This external plural suffix is mainly used to form the plurals of nouns that have a singular pattern $C_1aC_2C_2\bar{a}C_3$ (mainly used for professions), e.g.:

ġannām 'shepherd'—*ġannāma*
dammām 'drummer'—*dammāma*

4.9.2.4.4 *External Feminine Plural Suffix* -āt
This plural suffix is used to form the PL of:

i. Most Feminine Nouns That End in the Feminine Marker -*a* (Including Adjectives and Participles), e.g.

sāʕa 'hour'—*sāʕāt*
marāǧəʕa 'origin'—*marāǧəʕāt*
ḥəlwa 'beautiful (SG.F)'—*ḥəlwāt*
dārsa 'having studied (AP.SG.F)'—*dārsāt*
mawǧūda 'present (originally PP.SG.F)'—*mawǧūdāt*

---

96 This concerns many nouns ending on the suffix -*či*, which derives from the Turkish suffix -*ci*. On this suffix in Syrian, Lebanese, and Iraqi Arabic cf. Procházka (2020: 96) and the references mentioned there.

MORPHOLOGY 243

ii. Some Grammatically Feminine Nouns That Do Not End in the Feminine
Marker -*a*, e.g.

(*ʔə*)*ḏān* 'ear'—*ḏānāt*

(9) [A14]
ḏānāt-i wāyəd bārdāt.
ears-1SG very cold.PL.F
'My ears are very cold.'

iii. Some Biologically Feminine Nouns That Do Not End in the Feminine Suffix -*a*, e.g.

bənt 'girl'—*banāt*
ʕarūs 'bride'—*ʕarūsāt*

Remarkable is the occurrence of *marāt* 'midwives' as a plural of *mara* 'woman'
('midwife' is usually *māma*) with a specialized meaning.[97]

iv. Many Masculine Nouns, Including Loanwords, e.g.

ktāb 'book'—*ktābāt*
čtāf 'shoulder'—*čtāfāt* (also *čtūf*, see 4.9.2.4.5: VIII)
ṭōf 'wall'—*ṭōfāt* (also *ṭīfān*)
drām 'container' < Engl. drum (container)—*drāmāt*
yəxčāla 'refrigerator' < Pers. *yaxčāl*—*yəxčālāt*

This morpheme is also used to form (1) diminutives of collectives and (2) plurals of some diminutive forms (cf. 4.9.4 for more examples), e.g.:
(1) *təmən* 'rice' → *təmən-āt* 'some rice'
(2) *wlēd* '(little) child/boy (DIM)' → *wlēd-āt* '(little) children/boys'
The external PL morpheme -*āt* has the allomorph -*yāt* when attached to a SG
form ending in -*i*, or -*a* (that does not derive from the feminine ending -*aᵗ*), e.g.
təknəlōžī-yāt 'technologies', *ḏəkrā-yāt* 'memories', and *maḥallī-yāt* 'local (PL.F)'.

---

97 Generally, the plural of KhA *mara* 'woman' is *nəswān*. The usually uncommon external
plural form *marāt* was used in only one sentence and might have been influenced by the
form *māmāt* 'midwives', which is also an external plural with the same meaning and was
used in the same sentence.

244 CHAPTER 4

The external PL morpheme -*āt* has the allomorph -*wāt* when attached to a SG form ending in -*u* (which is not an underlying -*w*) or -*ā*, e.g. *kīlu* 'kilo' PL *kīlūwāt*, and *ṣalā* 'prayer' PL *ṣalawāt*. The plural of *səna* 'year', *sanawāt*, is an archaism from OA and less common than its alternative plural form *əsnīn*.

As in most varieties of Arabic, the following kinship terms show irregular forms before the suffixation of the external PL morpheme -*āt*:

> *ʔəbu* 'father'—*ʔabbahāt* ~ *ʔəbbahāt*
> *ʔəmm* 'mother'—*ʔəmmahāt*
> *ʔəxt* 'sister'—*xawāt*

4.9.2.4.5 *Internal Plural (and Corresponding Singular) Patterns*

I. $C_1\bar{v}C_3$ (Used for PL.F Color Adjectives)

Singular $C_1aC_2C_3a$

> *sōda* 'black (F)'—*sūd*, *bēḍa* 'white (F)'—*bīḍ*

Singular $C_1\bar{a}C_3$

> *dār* 'room'—*dūr*

II. $C_1\bar{o}C_3a$

Singular $C_1vC_2C_2əC_3$

> *mayyət* 'dead'—*mōta* (also *mayytīn*)

III. $C_1əC_2C_3a$[98]

Singular C_1vC_2u

> *ʔəxu* 'brother'—*ʔəxwa* (also *ʔəxwān*)

Singular $C_1aC_2\bar{i}C_3$

> *faġīr* 'poor'—*fəġra*

---

98   Derived from diachronically different patterns: compare KhA *ʔəxwa* 'brothers' and *fəġra* 'poor (PL)' with OA **ʔixwa^{tun}* and **fuqarāʔ^u*.

MORPHOLOGY 245

IV. $C_1 \partial C_2 a C_3 \sim \partial C_1 C_2 v C_3$

The fact that there is morphological variation in the initial syllable of this and other internal plural patterns is partly due to phonological motivation (cf. 3.2.2.2) and partly reflects a speaker's choice between free variants.

Singular $C_1 v C_2 C_3 a$

> ġəṣṣa 'story'—ġəṣaṣ, ʔəbra 'injection, needle'—ʔəbar, dīra 'town'—ədyar ~ dəyar

V. $C_1 \partial C_2 \partial C_3$

Singular $C_1 v C_2 C_3 a$

> zəlma 'man'—zələm, ḥamra 'red (F)'—ḥəmər (M ḥamar—ḥəmrān)

VI. $C_1 v C_2 C_2 \bar{a} C_3$

Singular $C_1 \bar{a} C_2 \partial C_3$

> ḥārəs 'guard'—ḥərrās (also nāṭūr—nəwāṭīr, which is Aramaic)

VII. $\partial C_1 C_2 \bar{a} C_3 (a) \sim C_1 \partial C_2 \bar{a} C_3 (a)$

Singular $C_1 v C_2 v C_3$ (Concrete Nouns and Collectives)

> ʕərəs 'wedding'—əʕrās, čaʕab 'sheep's knee bones'—əččʕāb, balam 'boat' —əblām, walad 'boy, child'—əwlād ~ ūlad ~ ōlād, ḍəbəʕ 'hyena'—əḍbāʕa, rayəl 'husband'—əryāl (also əryūla)

Singular $C_1 \partial C_2 \bar{i} C_3 \sim \partial C_1 C_2 \bar{i} C_3$ (Mainly Adjectives)

> mətīn 'thick, fat—əmtān, ṯəġīl 'heavy'—əṯgāl, əčbīr 'big'—əkbār, əzġīr 'small'—əzġār

Singular $C_1 a C_2 C_3 a$ (Mainly Nouns With Feminine Ending -a; Unit Nouns)

> balda 'country'—əblād, dabba 'plastic barrel'—ədbāb, dalla 'steel bucket' —ədlāl

246　　　　　　　　　　　　　　　　　　　　　　　　　　　　　　　　　CHAPTER 4

Singular C₁āC₂əC₃

šāyəb 'old man'—*šəyāb*

Singular C₁v̄C₃ (Mainly Concrete Nouns and Collectives)

rūḥ 'soul'—*ərwāḥ, ṭōg* 'golden necklace'—*əṭwāga, dīs* 'big serving plate'—*ədyāsa*

Singular C₁v̄C₃a

lēla 'night'—*əlyāl, tāwa* 'frying pan'—*ətwāw* (also *tāwāt*)

Singular C₁əC₂i

məṭi—*məṭāya* 'donkeys'

VIII.　əC₁C₂ūC₃(a) ~ C₁əC₂ūC₃(a)

Plurals which belong to the OA pattern C₁uC₂ūC often add the suffix -*a*.

Singular C₁aC₂C₃(a) (C₁ēC₃ if C₂=*y*, C₁āC₃ if C₂=ʔ)

yadd—*ydūd* ~ *ydūda* (also *əğdād*) 'grandfathers; ancestors', *ḥabb* 'pill'—*əḥbūb(āt), dēs* '(female) breast'—*ədyūs, ʕēn* 'eye'—*ʕəyūn, rās* 'head'—*rūs, xēṭ* 'thread'—*əxyūṭ, baṭṭa* 'duck'—*əbṭūṭ* ~ *əbṭūṭa*

Singular C₁vC₂vC₃

hədəm 'piece of clothing'—*hədūm* ~ *əhdūm* 'clothes', *šəbəl* 'shovel'—*əšbūla, ṭəšət* 'vessel (washing bowl)'—*əṭšūta, bəšət* 'name of a kind of summer cloak'—*əbšūta, ṣaḥan* 'plate, dish'—*əṣḥūna, sagəf* 'roof'—*əsgūf(a)*

Singular əC₁C₂āC₃

əčtāf 'shoulder'—*əčtūf* (besides *əčtāfāt*, which is more common in Ahvaz, see 4.9.2.4.4)

MORPHOLOGY   247

IX. $C_1aC_2\bar{\imath}C_3$

Singular $C_1aC_2\partial C_3$

 ʕabəd '(male) slave'—ʕabīd

Singular $C_1\partial C_2\bar{a}C_3$

 ḥəmār 'donkey'—ḥamīr

X. $\text{ʔa}C_1C_2\bar{a}C_3$

Retained only in a very few words (otherwise the OA $\text{ʔa}C_1C_2\bar{a}C_3$ plural pattern is mostly replaced by the pattern $C_1aC_2\bar{a}C_3$—compare KhA xawāl and OA
*ʔaxwālᵘⁿ 'uncles'—or the pattern $\partial C_1C_2\bar{a}C_3$, compare, e.g. KhA əčtāf 'shoul-
der' and OA *ʔaktāfᵘⁿ 'shoulders').

Singular $C_1aC_2C_3$

 yōm 'day'—ʔayyām

XI. $\text{ʔa}C_1\bar{a}C_2\bar{\imath}C_3$

Singular $\text{ʔə}C_1C_2\partial C_3$

 ʔəṣbəʕ 'finger'—ʔaṣābīʕ, ʔəḏfər 'fingernail'—ʔaḏāfīr

XII. $\text{ʔa}C_1\bar{a}C_2i$

Singular $\text{ʔə}C_1\partial C_2$

 ʔəsəm 'name'—ʔasāmi

XIII. $C_1aC_2\bar{a}C_3$

Singular $C_1aC_2C_3$ ($C_1\bar{a}C_3$ if C_2=w)

 xāl '(maternal) uncle'—xawāl, ʕamm 'uncle (father's brother); PL also:
 ancestors, tribe'—ʕamām

248 CHAPTER 4

XIV. $C_1vC_2\bar{a}y\partial C_3$

Singular $C_1aC_2C_3a$

ḥāyša 'cow' (COLL *ḥōš*)—*hǝwāyǝš*

Singular $C_1\bar{a}C_2\partial C_3$

tāyǝr 'tire'—*tǝwāyǝr*

Singular $C_1\bar{a}C_2C_3a$

ʕāyla 'family'—*ʕawāyǝl*

Singular $C_1vC_2\bar{i}C_3(a)$

ḥabīb(a) 'beloved/dear one'—*ḥabāyǝb*, *makīna* 'machine'—*mǝkāyǝn*, *ḏǝbīḥa* 'sacrificial animal'—*ḏǝbāyǝḥ*, *waṣīfa* 'slave girl'—*wǝṣāyǝf*

Singular $C_1(a)C_2\bar{a}C_3a$

xarāba 'destruction'—*xarāyǝb*, *glāda* 'necklace'—*galāyǝd*

Singular $C_1aC_2\bar{u}C_3$

ʕayūz 'old woman'—*ʕayāyǝz*

XV. $C_1vC_2\bar{a}C_3i$

Singular $C_1aC_2\partial C_3$

ʔarǝḍ 'land'—*ʔarāḍi*

Singular $C_1aC_2C_3a$

ṭarfa 'tamarisk'—*ṭarāfi*

Singular $C_1\bar{v}C_3a$

nōʕa [noːħa] 'lamentation, chant (sung when someone has died)'— *naʕāwi* [naħaːwi]

MORPHOLOGY 249

Singular $C_1\bar{v}C_3i$

> *ġūri* 'tea pot'—*ġəwāri*

Singular $C_1\bar{v}C_3\bar{i}ya$, $C_1\partial C_2C_3\bar{i}ya$

> *ğūnīya* 'bag (of e.g. flour)'—*ğəwāni, hōlīya* 'female water buffalo'—*hawāli,*
> *tərčīya* 'earring'—*tarāči*

Singular $C_1aC_2C_3\bar{i}ya$

> *mazwīya* 'a kind of winter cloak'—*məzāwi*

XVI. $C_1\partial C_2C_2\bar{a}C_3$

Singular $C_1\bar{a}C_2i$

> *hāfi* 'barefoot'—*həffāy* (cf. OA **hāf^{in}* 'walking barefoot, without sandal
> and without boot' PL *hufāt^{un}*, Lane 1863: 605)

XVII. $C_1vC_2C_3\bar{a}n$ ($C_1\bar{i}C_2\bar{a}n$ When C_2=y/w)

Singular $C_1\bar{v}C_3$

> *hōš* 'house'—*hīšān, tōf* 'wall'—*tīfān, yār* 'neighbor'—*yīrān* (often pro-
> nounced *īrān*)

Singular C_1aC_2a

> *ʕama* 'blind'—*ʕamyān, mara* 'woman'—*nəswān* (suppletive PL derived
> from another root)

Singular $C_1aC_2aC_3$

> *xaras* 'dumb'—*xərsān, tarab* 'dust'—*tərbān, hamar* 'red (M)'—*həmrān* (F
> *hamra—həmər*)

Singular $ʔaC_2C_3aC_4$

> *ʔatraš* 'deaf'—*təršān, ʔaswad* 'black (M)'—*sūdān, ʔabyaḍ* 'white (M)'—
> *bīḍān*

Singular C₁vC₂i

C_1vC_2i

ṭəli 'lamb'—*ṭəlyān*

Singular C_1vC_2u

ʔəxu 'brother'—*ʔəxwān* (also *ʔəxwa*)

Singular $C_1aC_2\bar{u}C_3$

xarūf 'ram'—*xərfān*

Singular $C_1aC_2\bar{\imath}C_3$

zabīl 'basket made of palm-leaves'—*zəblān*, *ṣadīg* 'friend'—*ṣədǧān*

Singular $əC_1C_2\bar{e}C_3i$

əmʕēdi 'marshdweller'—*məʕdān*

XVIII. $C_1vC_2\bar{a}C_3əC_4 \sim əC_1C_2\bar{a}C_3əC_4$ **(Quadriliteral)**

Singular $C_1aC_2C_3aC_4$

markab—*marāčəb* ~ *əmrāčəb* ~ *əmrākəb* 'boat'

Singular $C_1\bar{a}C_3C_4a$

sālfa 'story'—*səwāləf*

Singular $C_1aC_2C_3\bar{u}C_4a$ (C_4=y)

daḥrūya 'egg'—*daḥāri*

XIX. $C_1vC_2\bar{a}C_3\bar{\imath}C_4 \sim əC_1C_2\bar{a}C_3\bar{\imath}C_4$ **(Quadriliteral)**

Singular $C_1vC_2C_3vC_4$ ($C_1\bar{e}C_3vC_4$ When C_2=y)

bēdar 'threshing ground'—*bəyādīr*

MORPHOLOGY

251

Singular $C_1vC_2C_3\bar{a}C_4(a)$ (Also When C_2 and C_3 Are Identical)

> *məknāsa* 'broom'—*məkānīs, dəšdāša* 'cloak'—*dəšādīš, ṭarrāda* 'long narrow boat'—*ṭarārīd, sayyāra* 'car'—*səyāyīr, ṭayyāra* 'airplane'—*ṭəyāyīr, dəkkān* 'shop, store'—*dəkākīn*

Singular $C_1aC_2C_3\bar{u}C_4$ (Also When C_2 and C_3 Are Identical)

> *tannūr* 'clay oven'—*tənānīr, ṣandūǵ* 'box'—*ṣanādīǵ, mašḥūf* 'type of boat'—*mašāḥīf*

Singular $C_1vC_2C_3\bar{\i}C_4$ (Also When C_2 and C_3 Are Identical)

> *ʕarrīs* 'groom'—*ʕarārīs* 'grooms; bridal couple', *səččīn* 'knife'—*səčāčīn, xanzīr* 'pig'—*xanāzīr*

Singular $C_1\bar{a}C_3\bar{u}C_4(a)$

> *kārūk* 'cradle'—*kəwārīk, māʕūn* 'dish'—*əmwāʕīn* [əm:a:ʕi:n], *xāšūga* 'spoon'—*xəwāšīg, fānūs* 'oil lamp'—*fəwānīs*

Singular $C_1\bar{o}C_3\bar{a}C_4$

> *yōxān* 'date storage'[99]—*yəwāxīn*

4.9.2.4.6 Mixed Patterns

As stated above (4.9.2.4), the combination of internal and external plural forms, may be considered a feature of peripheral dialects and is also known for other dialects (e.g. Procházka 2002: 120 on the dialect of the Çukurova in southern Turkey). Examples from KhA are:

> *ḥabb* 'pill'—*əḥbūb-āt*
> *ləʕbīya* 'toy'—*laʕābi* and *laʕābī-yāt*
> *malək* 'king'—*əmlūk-īya*
> *čtāf* 'shoulder'—*čtāf-āt*

---

99 Ḥassūnizadeh (2015:925): < *ǵōxān*, PL *yōwāxīn* 'place for collecting/storing dates [and other harvest yield]' < Pers. *ǵou* 'barley' + *xān* 'house'.

252   CHAPTER 4

The form *čtāf* was originally a plural but is used as a SG in KhA (compare *čitif* PL *čtāf*, *čtāfāt* in Iraqi Arabic, WB: 84). Thus, for forming the plural, the external plural morpheme *-āt* is added to the SG *čtāf* yielding *čtāfāt* (as also used in Iraqi Arabic).

4.9.3 *Construct State*

Nouns are in construct state in synthetic nominal attribution constructions (Arabic *ʔiḍāfa*) or when followed by a pronominal or dual suffix.

The basic syntagm for synthetic nominal attribution constructions is NOUN (in construct state) + NOUN/DEF-NOUN. The second noun is usually a (definite or indefinite) substantive, as in (1) and (2)(2), but may also be an adjective/participle (3) (note, however that the basic syntagm for adjectival attribution is DEF-NOUN + DEF-ADJECTIVE).[100]

(1)   [A9]
      ḥalīb əl-hōš
      milk DEF-cow.COLL
      'cow's milk'

(2)   [Ḥ1]
      ṭāsat   rōba
      bowl.CS yoghurt
      'a bowl (full) of yoghurt'

(3)   [A9]
      sənt   əl-yāya
      year.CS DEF-come.AP.SG.F
      'next year'

In the following, the changes that may occur when a noun is in construct state will be outlined (this only concerns nouns ending in *-a* or in the dual suffix *-ēn*).

i.   Feminine Nouns Ending in *-a*:

In construct state, feminine nouns ending in *-a* have the ending *-at*:

      səmča 'a fish'→ *səmčat əṣ-ṣəbūra* 'the ṣəbūra-fish'
      ṭāsa 'a bowl' → *ṭāsat rōba* 'a bowl (full) of yoghurt'

―――――――
100   Cf. Stokes (2020) for a recent discussion of the syntagm NOUN + DEF-ADJ in various

MORPHOLOGY 253

When the *-a* before the inserted *-t-* results in an open unstressed syllable, it is usually elided (and an epenthetic vowel is introduced after the first consonant if a three-consonant cluster resulted):

səmča 'a fish'→ *səməčt-ēn* 'two fish'
səna 'a year' → *səntēn* 'two years', *sənt əl-yāya* 'next year'
mara 'a woman; wife' → *mart əl-ḥağği* 'the Ḥağği's wife', *mart-i* 'my wife'

When the noun in construct state ends in *-īya* and a vowel-initial pronominal suffix or the dual suffix is added, the *-a* of *-īya* is dropped, yielding the construct state ending *-īt-*, e.g. *lūmīya* 'a lime' → *lūmītēn* 'two limes'; *ʔaṣlīya* 'origin' → *ʔaṣlīt-ak* 'your (SG.M) origin'; *ləʕbīya* 'a toy' → *ləʕbītēn* 'two toys' (but *ləʕbīyat əxt-i* 'my sister's toy'); *mazwīya* 'a kind of winter cloak' → *mazwīt-i* 'my winter cloak'. When a consonant-initial pronominal suffix is attached to the ending *-īya*, *-a-* is preserved, e.g. *ʔaṣlīya* 'origin' → *ʔaṣlīyat-na* 'our origin'.

Nouns of foreign origin that end in *-i* do not show any changes when in construct state, e.g.

ġūri 'a tea pot'→ *ġūrī-yi* 'my tea pot', *ġūrī-na* 'our tea pot'

ii.   Dual Suffix *-ēn*

In the two dual nouns that may be combined with a pronominal suffix (cf. 4.9.2.3)—*ʔīdēn* '(two) hands, arms; handles (of a vessel)', and *rīlēn* '(two) legs, feet'—the *-n* of the dual suffix *-ēn* is elided before the attachment of a pronominal suffix (diachronically seen a continuation of the OA construct state *-ay*). *-n* is not elided when the noun in construct state is in a synthetic nominal attribution construction, i.e. followed by another noun (or adjective). In the dual construct forms of *ʔīd-ēn* '(two) hands/arms' and *rīl-ēn* '(two) legs, feet', the *ē* of the dual suffix is often pronounced like *ī* before pronominal suffixes (other than 1 SG). The combination of the 1SG pronoun *-i* and the vowel *-ē-* of the dual suffix yields the suffix *-āy ~ -ayya*:

ʔīd-ēn '(two) hands/arms' → *ʔīd-āy ~ ʔīd-ayya* 'my (two) hands/arms',
ʔīd-ē-č 'your (SG.F) (two) hands/arms', *ʔīd-ḗ* 'his (two) hands/arms',
ʔīd-ēn əl-əbnayya 'the (two) hands/arms of the girl'.

---

dialects of Arabic; and Procházka (2018c: 267–269) on this syntagm in the Northern Fertile Crescent.

254   CHAPTER 4

When the dual noun *rīlēn* '(two) legs, feet' is in construct state, the base form of the noun *rīl-* is changed to *Pərl-* to which the dual suffix *-ē-* + pronoun might be attached or *-ēn* when followed by another noun (i.e. when in a synthetic nominal attribution construction):

> *rīl-ēn* '(two) legs, feet' → *Pərl-āy* ~ *Pərl-ayya* 'my (two) legs, feet', *Pərl-ē-ha* 'her (two) legs, feet', *Pərl-ḗ* 'his (two) legs, feet', *Pərl-ēn əl-əbnayya* 'the (two) legs/feet of the girl'.

iii.   *Pəbu* 'Father' and *Pəxu* 'Brother'

The words *Pəbu* PL *Pabbahāt* ~ *Pəbbahāt* 'father' and *Pəxu* PL *xəwān* ~*əxwān*, and *Pəxwa* 'brother' have the following construct forms: *(Pə)bū-* and *(Pə)xū-* (the PL *Pəxwa* has the construct form *xūt-*)—e.g. *(Pə)bū-y* 'my father', *(Pə)xū-y* 'my brother', *Pəxū xayt-a* 'his sister's brother',[101] *xūt-a* (or *əxwān-a*) 'his brothers', and *Pəbū bēhdaš*[P] 'caretaker'. See also:

(4)   [A10]
       *hāḏa **bū** drām,   hāḏa **bū** ṭāsa, hāḏa **bū** ğədər.*
       DEM GL container DEM GL bowl DEM GL pot
       'That one (came) with the container, that one with the bowl, the other one with a pot.'

KhA frequently makes use of the nouns *Pəmm* PL *Pəmmahāt* 'mother' and *Pəbu* PL *Pabbahāt* ~ *Pəbbahāt* 'father' to express possession (5) or innate qualities (6) (cf. Masliyah 1998: 120 on Iraqi Arabic). Such phrases are also used in conversations to describe a person by something he or she wears or by a characteristic feature or condition—often in a way making fun of him or her (cf. Masliyah 1998: 121–123). Further KhA examples from my corpus are:

(5)   [A1]
       Pəbū ḥalāl yʕarəf   ḥalāl-a.
       GL   cattle know.IPFV.3SG.M cattle-3SG.M
       'The owner of cattle knows his cattle.'

---

101   This term is used to describe an honorable, respectful man, described by my informants as one who: *ygūm ydāfəʕ ʕan-ha, mā yxalli wāḥəd yəḥči ʕala səmʕat-ha, ydāfəʕ ʕan šaraf-ha, ydāfəʕ ʕan ḥagg-ha* '(one who) gets up and defends her [i.e. his sister], he does not let anyone speak (badly) of her, he defends her honor, he defends her rights'. Also: *ənta xū xayt-ak* 'you are your sister's brother' is used in the same meaning.

MORPHOLOGY   255

(6) [A19]
rəšād ətnēn namūntēn, rəšād ʕad-na ʔəbū warǧat əl-ʕarīḍa,
cress two two_kinds cress at-1PL GL leave.CS DEF-broad
warǧat əl-ʕarīḍa yǧūlū-l-a   ʕayam, ʔəbū warǧat
leave.CS DEF-broad say.IPFV.3PL.M-to-3SG.M Persian GL leave.CS
əḍ-ḍaʕīfa rəšād ʕarab.
DEF-weak cress Arabic
'(Of the) cress (there are) two kinds: we have cress with broad leaves—
the one with the broad leaves they call "Persian"—and the one with the
small leaves (is called) Arabic cress.'

ʔəmm and *ʔəbu* may inflect for number in the above described function, when
referring to a plural head—as in (7), in which the PL *ʔəmmahāt* refers back to
the PL head *plāstīkāt* 'plastic bags'.

(7) [A9]
əl-plāstīkāt,   əzǧār   əzǧār   əmmāhāt kīlo
DEF-plastic.PL.F small.PL small.PL GL.PL.F kilo
'the plastic bags, (the) small (ones), of one kilo'

Such constructions are also used (among several other functions) for the description of prices and values, especially values of coins and bills (cf. Masliyah
1998: 119; Erwin 1963: 372):

(8) [Ḥ1]
ənwēṭ[102]   əbū xaməs tālāf
banknote.DIM GL five   thousand
'banknotes of five thousand'

4.9.4 *Diminutive*
In KhA, the diminutive is a productive category generally used by all speakers, men and women, but more frequently by women. As in most dialects (cf.
Masliyah 1997: 80 on Iraqi Arabic), diminutive forms are especially frequent
in certain text genres such as fairy tales, songs and riddles, in names of children's games, e.g. *ṭammt əxrēza* lit. 'concealment of a bead' (< *xəraz* 'beads')
(cf. Masliyah 1997: 82 on the name of this game in Iraqi Arabic). The main use
of the diminutive, determined by its context, is actually not smallness but the

---

102 Diminutive of *nōṭ* < Engl (*bank*)*note*.

256 CHAPTER 4

expression of affection, as a hypocorism, or, less commonly, to show contempt. In most cases, no English translation is given for the diminutive form because a literal translation for such forms would often sound odd.

The following is an example for the use of the diminutive to express affection:

(1) [A10]
    gālat-l-a   *yəmma rədd*   *əwlēd-i.*
    say.PFV.3SG.F-to-3SG.M mother go_back.IMP.SG.M son.DIM-1SG
    'She said to him: "Go back, my son."'

In the following, I will outline the different patterns and suffixes use to form the diminutive in KhA (cf. Leitner 2019).

i.   Internal Diminutive

The (internal) diminutive has the patterns $əC_1C_2\bar{e}C_3(a)$ ~ $C_1vC_2\bar{e}C_3(a)$ ~ $əC_1C_2ayC_3(a)$ ~ $C_1vC_2ayC_3(a)$, and $əC_1C_2ayyaC_3$. Examples from my data are:

> *laban* 'buttermilk' → *əlbēna*
> *ʔahəl* 'family' → *ʔahēla*
> *walad* 'boy, son' → *əwlēd*
> *ṣīnīya* 'tablet' → *əṣwēnīya*
> *ḥabība* 'beloved one (F)' → *əḥbayba*
> *šāyəb* 'old man' → *əšwayyab*
> *ṣaġīr* 'small' → *əzġayyar*

Diminutive patterns other than the above-mentioned are used with lexemes that have only two radicals or where C_2 is geminated:

> *mara* 'woman, wife' → *mrayya* (C_1C_2ayya)
> *ʔəmm* 'mother' → *ʔəmyēma* ($C_1əC_2y\bar{e}C_2$a)

The lexeme *ʔəxət* 'sister' has a DIM form *xayya*, which is often used for directly addressing a female person, as in the following example:

(2) [F1]
    ča mū mdawwər   *ʕalē-č*   **xayya?**
    DP NEG look_for.AP.SG.M for-2SG.F sister.DIM
    'Isn't he looking for you, sister?'

MORPHOLOGY   257

The plural of the internal diminutive is constructed with the external PL suffix -*āt* (cf. 4.9.2.4.4; cf. Holes 2016: 127 for similar forms in Bahraini Arabic), e.g.:

walad 'boy'	→ DIM *əwlēd* '(little) boy'	→ DIM PL *əwlēd-āt*
	'(little) boys, children'	
farax 'child'	→ DIM *əfrēx* '(little) child'	→ DIM PL *əfrēx-āt*
	'(little) children'	
ʕēn 'eye'	→ DIM *əʕwēn* 'eye'	→ DIM PL *əʕwēn-āt*
	'eyes'	
əflūs 'money'	→ DIM *əflēs* 'money'	→ DIM PL *əflēs-āt*
	'money'	
xōṣa 'ring'	→ DIM *əxwēṣ* '(little) ring'	→ DIM PL *əxwēṣ-āt*
	'(little) rings'	
ʕēš 'bread'	→ DIM *əʕwēš* '(small piece of) bread'	→ DIM PL *əʕwēš-āt*
	'(small pieces of) bread'	

The PL.F suffix -*āt* is also attached to non-diminutive nouns to add a diminutive meaning to a COLL, e.g. *təmən* 'rice' → *təmənāt* 'some rice'.

ii.   The Diminutive Suffix -*ūn*

Another diminutive construction used in KhA is the combination of internal diminutive patterns and the suffix -*ūn*, e.g. *šwayyūn* 'a little bit', *əgrayybūn* (< *ǵərīb*) 'very close, soon', and *zǵayyrūn* (< *zaǵīr*) 'tiny'. This diminutive formation is lexicalized and not productive. In Iraqi Arabic, we occasionally also find combinations of internal diminutive patterns and one of the diminutive suffixes -*ān* and -*ūn* (Masliyah 1997: 74). In Iraqi Arabic, as in KhA, the use of such combined diminutive patterns appears to be restricted to certain lexemes. The diminutive suffix -*ūn* is most likely of Aramaic origin (cf. Masliyah 1997: 72) and is elsewhere also found in Bahrain, all Baghdadi dialects, Kuwait, Oman (Holes 2016: 127, fn. 54), Syria and Lebanon (in the latter two only in fossilized forms, Procházka 2020: 93–94; cf. Fleisch 1961: 454, fn. 2), and even in Tunisia (cf. Procházka 2020: 93–94, fn. 22, who convincingly argues that this suffix must be a very old borrowing).

iii.   Combination of Pattern CēCəC and Suffix -*ūn*

There is another diminutive construction that combines yet another internal diminutive pattern, CēCəC ~ CayCəC, and the suffix -*ūn*: e.g. *hēləsūn* 'plucked'. The usage of this diminutive pattern appears to be restricted to certain contexts and genres like fairy tales.

258   CHAPTER 4

The development of the diminutive pattern CēCəC ~ CayCəC in KhA is unexplained. It might have developed as a diminutive CəwayCəC (*həwayləs*) from the AP form CāCəC (*hāləs*) and the subsequent deletion of /əw/. Its usage in the given example is clearly for minimization or expressing affection, since the example text is a fairy tale and it is animals who are speaking.

(3)   [A10]
      ... *gāl*   *əl-ġanam,*   *ḥāčat*   *əš-šaṭṭ,*
      say.PFV.3SG.M DEF-sheep.COLL speak.PFV.3SG.F DEF-river
      gālat-l-a: *hā šaṭṭ-na   xēbəṭūn?*
      say.PFV.3SG.F-to-3SG.M DP river-1PL polluted.DIM
      '... the sheep said, they talked to the river and asked it, "Our river, (why are you) polluted?"'

      gāl-ha: *šaṭṭ-na   xēbəṭūn   w   sədrat-na*
      say.PFV.3SG.M-OBL.3SG.F river-1PL polluted.DIM and lote_tree.CS-1PL
      ḥaytəṭūn   w   ṭwēr-na   hēləsūn   w   gmayla
      having_shed_leaves.DIM and bird.DIM-1PL plucked.DIM and Gmayla
      bēčəčūn,   ʕala brēġəš ṭāḥ   b-ət-tannūr ...
      crying.DIM about Brēġəš fall.PFV.3SG.M in-DEF-oven
      '—It [the river] answered, "Our river is polluted, and the lote tree has no leaves and our bird is plucked and Gmayla is crying because the *Brēġəš*[103] fell into the oven."'

iv.   Patterns CaCCūC(i) and CaCCūCa for the Diminutive of Proper Names

The pattern CaCCūC(i) is used to form the diminutive of feminine and masculine proper nouns and CaCCūCa to form the diminutive of feminine proper nouns. Cf. Procházka (2020: 94) on this pattern in Syrian and Lebanese dialects, and Masliyah (1997: 76; 86–87) on Iraqi Arabic, where this pattern is not restricted to proper names. Cf. Holes (2016: 128) on this pattern with the same function in Bahraini Arabic. Examples from KhA are:

      ʕĀyša → *ʕAyyūš*
      Māġəd, Maġīd, Amġad → *Maġġūd(i)*
      ʕAzīz → *ʕAzzūz*

---

103   Diminutive of *barġaš* 'small insect, midge' (cf. WB: 32 on Iraqi Arabic), the main character of this fairy-tale.

MORPHOLOGY   259

Amīna → *Ammūn*
Ḥasan, Ḥsēn → *Ḥassūn(i)*
Ḥasna → *Ḥassūna*
Marām → *Marrūma* (also *Marmar*)

i.   Suffix *-ō* for the Diminutive of Proper Names

Cf. Procházka (2020: 95–96) on this suffix and its possible origins in many Arabic dialects, and Holes (2016: 128, 464) on Bahraini Arabic.

ʕAbd (ər-Raḥmān) → *ʕAbdō*
ʕAdnān → *ʕAdnānō* (also *ʕAddūn(i)*)

4.9.5   *The Elative Form and Adjectives of the ʔaC₁C₂aC₃-Pattern*

The pattern $ʔaC_1C_2aC_3$ is used (a) to form the elative of adjectives and (b) for some (non-elative) adjectives that mostly denote colors or bodily deficiencies. Group (b) represents a closed class and are therefore listed separately from the productive elative forms (a).

(a)   Elative of Adjectives

Examples from my KhA data are: *ʔakbar* 'bigger, older' < *əčbīr* 'big', *ʔanḍaf* 'cleaner' < *naḍīf* 'clean', *ʔaḥsan* 'better' (suppletive form of the simplex *zēn* 'good'), and *ʔazġar* 'smaller, younger' < *əzġīr* 'small, young'.

Final gemination in $ʔaC_1aC_2C_2$-forms of geminated roots is reduced to a single consonant (cf. Ingham 1974: 248–250, fn. 2), e.g. *'ʔaxaf* 'lighter' < *xafīf* 'light', *'ʔaġal* 'less' < *ġalīl* 'little', and *'ʔaxas* 'worse' < *xasīs* 'bad (obsolete)'.

For comparison, the preposition *mən* is used, e.g.

(1)   [M4]
       ʔanḍaf mən hāya
       cleaner than DEM
       'cleaner than this'

The superlative is usually expressed by an adjective in the $ʔaC_1C_2aC_3$-pattern preceding a singular noun:

(2)   [M4]
       ʔakbar markab
       biggest ship
       'the biggest ship'

260   CHAPTER 4

For the absolute superlative, the adjective in the $?aC_1C_2aC_3$-pattern is definite: *əl-aǧall* 'the least, the smallest (amount)'.

(b)   Closed Class $?aC_1C_2aC_3$-Adjectives

Examples from KhA are: *?abraš* F *barša* 'sheep with a white body and a black face',[104] *?arʕan* 'stupid' F *raʕna* PL.M *rəʕnān* PL.F *raʕnāt* 'stupid' (cf. CA *?arʕan* 'foolish, stupid', Lane 1863: 1108), *ḥawal* F *ḥōla* PL *ḥōlān* 'cross-eyed', *ʕaray* F *ʕarya* PL.M *ʕaryān* 'have a lame leg' (cf. CA *?aʕraǧ*), *ʕama* F *ʕamya* PL.M *ʕamyān* 'blind', *ʕawar* F *ʕōra* PL.M *ʕōrān* 'blind with one eye', *xaras* F *xarsa* PL.M *xərsān* 'dumb' (< *?axras*, cf. 3.7.2 on the dropping of the initial syllable *?a-* in this form), *?aṭraš* F *ṭarša* PL.M *ṭəršān* 'deaf'.

4.9.6   *Definite and Indefinite Articles*
This chapter treats the KhA definite article *l-* and the indefinite article *farəd*.

4.9.6.1   Definite Article
The definite article has the basic form *l-*, e.g.

(1)   [Ḥa1]
      ?əḏa l-mara ...
      if   DEF-woman
      'If the woman ...'

In most contexts—i.e. whenever the preceding word does not end in a vowel—it begins with an anaptyctic vowel *ə*, e.g. *əl-ǧanam* 'the sheep'.

   The *l* of the definite article assimilates to a following (palato-)alveolar consonant (i.e. *t, ṭ, ṯ, d, ḏ, ḍ, s, ṣ, š, z, ẓ, ǧ, ž, č, l, n, r*); e.g. *əš-šaṭṭ* 'the river', and *əč-čaləb* 'the dog'.

   Whenever the noun begins with two consonants, an anaptyctic vowel *ə* is inserted before the consonant cluster (cf. 3.7.1; cf. Blanc 1964: 119–120 on Baghdad Arabic), or, when the first consonant of the noun is (palato-)alveolar, between the two consonants of the cluster, e.g.:

(2)   [Ḥa1]
      əl-əḥyār
      DEF-stones
      'the stones'

---

104   Cf. Edzard (1967: 308): "*barša* '(female) water buffalo with a white head'".

MORPHOLOGY 261

(3) [A1]
     əs-sənīn
     DEF-years
     'the years'

4.9.6.2 Indefinite Article

KhA makes use of an indefinite article *farəd*, which is, however, not the exact counterpart of the KhA definite article as its use is always optional and conditioned by pragmatic and semantic factors. An indefinite article *farəd* (or one of its cognate forms *fadd*, *fat*, etc.) is also used in Iraqi Arabic (Blanc 1964: 118–119; Erwin 1963: 355–358), Central Asian Arabic (Seeger 2013: 314), and Bandar Moqami Arabic (Leitner et al. 2021). Palva (2009: 23) describes the development of this indetermination marker as an originally sedentary feature found in the Mesopotamian dialect area. This would imply that this feature has spread very early to the regions in Iran and Central Asia where it is still used, because later on mainly Bedouin tribes settled in these areas. As suggested by Blanc (1964: 119) and Palva (2009: 23), the development of an indefinite article in these dialects was likely reinforced by the (very similar) use of indefinite articles in many other areal languages, such as Persian, Turkish, and Neo-Aramaic.

Its main functions are listed in the following:

i.   Introduction of the Main Agent of a Narration—Presentative

In KhA as well as in Iraqi and Central Asian Arabic, the indefinite article *farəd* is frequently used at the very beginning of a narrative to introduce the main agent.

(1) [Ḥ2]
     ḏāk əl-yōm əya   farəd ḏīf.
     DEM DEF-day come.PFV.3SG.M INDEF guest
     'One day a guest came.'

ii.   Marking of Further Specified Referents

In many cases, KhA *farəd* is used when the referent is further qualified (e.g. by an adjective or by a relative clause).

262   CHAPTER 4

(2) [A4]
farəd ġana ḥazīn
INDEF singing sad
'a sad (kind of) singing'

iii.   Intensifier (of Positive or Negative Qualities of a Referent)

KhA *farəd* is also used to emphasize the positive or negative qualities of a referent.

(3) [A14], Elicited
ʔəmm-i ṭəbxat akla čānat **farəd** ḥəlwa!
mother-1SG cook.PFV.3SG.F meal be.PFV.3SG.F INDEF good
'My mother cooked a meal that was really delicious!'

iv.   'Some', with Plural Referents

KhA *farəd* may also be used with plural referents. In such cases, it usually corresponds to English 'some'.

(4) [A10]
ybīʕ **farəd** laʕābīyāt.
sell.IPFV.3SG.M INDEF toys
'He sells some toys.'

v.   'Only', Scalar Adverb

The most common word for 'only' in KhA is *bass* (cf. 4.3.2.2). The use of *farəd* in this function is much less frequent and connected with contrast and emphasis.

(5) [A10]
ʕad-ha **fard** əwlēd.
at-3SG.F INDEF boy.DIM
'She has only one boy.'

vi.   Approximation (with Expressions of Time and Numbers)

With expressions of time and numbers, KhA *farəd* usually expresses an approximate quantity.

MORPHOLOGY 263

(6) [M4]
farəd ʕašər kīlowāt
INDEF ten kilos
'some 10 kilos'

vii. Politeness or Mitigation of an Imperative

KhA *farəd* may be used for mitigation of requests and commands (usually together with certain address forms such as *ʕēn-i* (lit.) 'my eye'), i.e. it makes a request appear more polite.

(7) [A14], Elicited
ğīb-l-i   *farəd glāṣ māy, ʕēn-i.*
bring.IMP.SG.M-to-1SG INDEF glass water dear-1SG
'Please, bring me a glass of water.'

4.10 Numerals

4.10.1 *Cardinal Numbers*
4.10.1.1   Cardinal numbers from 1–10

	Without a counted noun	With a counted noun
0	*ṣəfər*	— —
1	*wāḥəd* F *waḥda*	*wāḥəd* F *waḥda*
2	*ətnēn*	*tnēn*
3	*təlāta*	*tələt*
4	*ʔarbaʕa*	*ʔarbaʕ*
5	*xamsa*	*xaməs*
6	*sətta*	*sətt*
7	*sabʕa*	*sabəʕ*
8	*tamānya*	*təmən*
9	*təsʕa*	*təsaʕ*
10	*ʕašra*	*ʕašər*

The epenthetic vowels in the final syllables of the forms used with a counted noun may be deleted when the following noun starts with a vowel.

The counted noun after a cardinal number between three and ten comes in the PL, e.g. *ʔarbaʕ əsnīn* 'four years', *xaməs məšāḥīf* 'five boats', *xaməs xəwāšīg* 'five spoons', *sabʕ əwlād* 'seven boys/kids'. Also a counted noun after the number 'two' comes in the PL, if not a DUAL form is used instead (cf. 4.9.2.3), e.g. *tnēn xawāt* 'two sisters'.

Certain plural nouns which originally had *ʔa-* as the initial syllable, have a prefixed *t-* when following a cardinal number, e.g. *tələt tayyām* 'three days', *tələt təšhər* 'three months', *xaməs tālāf* '5,000'.

4.10.1.2   11–19

With and without counted noun

11	*ʔəhdaʕaš*
12	*ʔətnaʕaš*
13	*tələttaʕaš*
14	*ʔarbaʕtaʕaš*
15	*xaməstaʕaš*
16	*səttaʕaš*
17	*sabəʕtaʕaš*
18	*təməntaʕaš*
19	*təsaʕtaʕaš*

The counted noun comes after the cardinal number in the SG, e.g. *xaməstaʕaš səna* '15 years', *təməntaʕaš səna* '18 years'.

4.10.1.3   Tens, Hundreds, Thousands

20	*ʕašrīn*
30	*təlātīn*
40	*ʔarbaʕīn*
50	*xamsīn*
60	*səttīn*
70	*sabʕīn*
80	*təmānīn*
90	*təsʕīn*
100	*mīya*

MORPHOLOGY

(*cont.*)

200	*mītēn*
300	*t̲ələt̲-mīya*
400	*ʔarbaʕ-mīya*
500	*xaməs-mīya*
600	*sətt mīya*
700	*sabəʕ-mīya*
800	*t̲əmən-mīya*
900	*t̲əsəʕ-mīya*

1000	*ʔaləf*
2000	*ʔalfēn*
3000	*t̲ələt̲-tālāf*
4000	*ʔarbaʕ-tālāf*
5000	*xaməs-tālāf*
6000	*sətt-tālāf*
7000	*sabəʕ-tālāf*
8000	*t̲əmən-tālāf*
9000	*t̲əsəʕ-tālāf*
'million'	*məlyūn*

After tens, hundreds, and thousands the counted noun is SG and follows the number, e.g. *səttīn səna* '60 years', *xamsīn kīlu* '50 kilos', *səbʕa w sabʕīn marad̲* '77 illnesses', *mīyat kīlu* '100 kilos' (*mīya* ends in *-t* in the construct state, cf. 4.9.3), and *mīyat hala* 'a hundred welcomes', which is frequently used in the phrase *hala w mīyat hala* 'welcome and a hundred times welcome'.

4.10.2 *Ordinal Numbers*

The KhA ordinal numbers as listed below are not used by all speakers. Especially the younger generation and more educated persons tend to substitute these by their Persian equivalents. The loss of ordinal numbers seems to be typical for peripheral dialects and is also found in, for example, Cilician Arabic (Procházka 2000: 223). Especially the two forms *ʔawwalīya* and *sātt* 'sixth' are remarkable.

25.	M	F
1.	*ʔawwal*	*ʔawwalīya*
2.	*ṯāni*	*ṯānya*
3.	*ṯāləṯ*	*ṯālṯa*
4.	*rābəʕ*	*rābʕa*
5.	*xāməs*	*xāmsa*
6.	*sātt*	*sātta*
7.	*sābəʕ*	*sābʕa*
8.	*ṯāmən*	*ṯāmna*
9.	*tāsəʕ*	*tāsʕa*
10.	*ʕāšər*	*ʕāšra*

4.11   Verbal Morphology

Ingham (1974: 233–319) already provides an overview of all morphological forms of the verb in KhA and thus what follows is in many regards not new, though it differs from his descriptions in certain points regarding the systematization and presentation of the verbal patterns and inflectional types. In addition to the information on the verbal structure as already provided by Ingham, the morphology of participles and verbal nouns will be discussed and the complete paradigms of all verbal patterns and inflectional types will be provided. Furthermore, some comparative aspects will be included in the analysis.

The present analysis of the KhA verbal morphology is arranged primarily along the nine basic verbal patterns (also called forms, measures, or classes) used in KhA: Pattern I, II, III, [IV], V, VI, VII, VIII, X, as according to their traditional use in Arabic Studies. Pattern I verbs express the basic meaning of the verbal root from which all other patterns are derived. Both the basic and the derived patterns have certain morphological structures (templates) which will be described below.

Within each pattern, KhA like all other varieties of Arabic, has three main inflectional types of verbs: regular (also called sound or strong), geminated, and weak. Regular verbs are those verbs which end in a single consonant preceded by a short vowel and in which none of the root consonants is represented by a vowel in its PFV and IPFV structures. Geminated verbs have a final doubled consonant, i.e. $C_2=C_3$. In weak verbs one of the root consonants is *ʔ*, *y*, or *w*. In double weak verbs two root consonants are *ʔ*, *y*, or *w*. Triliteral weak verbs can

MORPHOLOGY 267

be initial (C₁=y, w), medial (C₂=y, w), or final weak (C₃=y, w). Verbs with C₁=ʔ form a subgroup of initial weak verbs; C₂=ʔ are like regular verbs but very rare and mostly loans from MSA; C₃=ʔ verbs have diachronically all transformed into final weak verbs. The former C₁=ʔ verbs 'eat' and 'take', as well as the verb 'come' will be treated as irregular verbs of Pattern I because their structures show characteristics of different verbal types. Wherever C₁ or C₂ is *y* < OA **ǧ*, the verb's structure follows that of regular verbs; if C₃ is *y* < OA **ǧ*, its structure is that of final weak verbs, e.g. *ʕawa—yaʕwi* 'bend' (cf. CA *ʕawiǧa*; Ḥassūnizadeh 2015: 2187).

The descriptions of the verbal patterns and their paradigms is preceded by some general notes on verbal inflection in KhA.

Within each chapter on a given verbal pattern, first the pattern's morpho-phonological structures as well as its semantic connotations are discussed, followed by a description of the inflection of the respective pattern. Each verbal pattern and type will be illustrated by an example providing the full paradigm in a table.

The description of the basic verbal structures of the triliteral and quadriliteral verb in KhA is followed by further subchapters on verbal nouns, pseudoverbs, verbs with object suffixes, and the continuation marker *gāʕad*.

Comparative Aspects

KhA has retained PL.F forms in all persons in both PFV and IPFV verbs. Apart from the plural of feminine humans, also the plural of inanimate items as well as animals tend to attract PL.F forms (cf. Bettega and Leitner 2019: 22–23; 34). All participles show four forms: SG.M, SG.F, PL.M, and PL.F, e.g. *nāyam, nāyma, nāymīn, nāymāt* 'sleeping (AP SG.M, SG.F, PL.M, PL.F)'. The retention of feminine plural forms, as stated above, 2.3, is a conservative feature typical of many Bedouin dialects.

As in other Mesopotamian as well as many non-Mesopotamian dialects, reflexes of the OA Pattern IV are no longer productive and only a few residual forms exist (cf. Ingham 1982a: 42–43; and Holes 2018: 152 on Bahraini Bedouin-type dialects). The OA Pattern IX is not attested in my data at all, nor was its use confirmed by any of my consultants (contrast Ingham 1974: 315–316, who does provide examples).

The KhA stem[105] vowel system of Pattern I does not provide information on the transitivity of a verb (contrast, for example, Najdi Arabic, which has pre-

---

105   Stem is defined here and in the following as the PFV or IPFV verbal base to which inflectional prefixes and suffixes are attached.

served the OA system, Ingham 1982a: 40). Its distribution rather depends on phonological rules with the 3SG.M PFV form CaCaC in the vicinity of gutturals and the form CəCaC in all other environments. This system is also shared with other (Mesopotamian and non-Mesopotamian) dialects of Arabic (cf. Ingham 1982a: 40; and Holes 2018: 138 on Bahraini Bedouin-type dialects).

4.11.1 *Inflection*

KhA verbs indicate tense/aspect (PAST-PRESENT/PFV-IPFV), mood (INDICATIVE, IMP for the 2nd persons of the IPFV), person (3rd, 2nd, 1st), number (SG, PL), and gender (F, M, concerns 2nd and 3rd persons).

The inflectional affixes are of the following three types: suffixes (PFV, except for 3SG.M, the suffix of which is Ø), prefixes (IPFV), or a combination of prefixes and suffixes (IPFV).

As the PFV is generally inflected via the attachment of suffixes, it is often labeled suffix-stem or s-stem and will therefore be presented with a hyphen after the stem in the discussion below of the morphological structure of the different verbal patterns and types. The IPFV, which is generally inflected via the attachment of prefixes (though in some persons verbs also carry a suffix), is often labeled prefix-stem or p-stem and will therefore be presented with a hyphen before the stem in the discussion below of the morphological structure of the verb.

IMP forms are also inflected via the attachment of suffixes, except for the 2SG.M, which is expressed by the mere IMP-stem.

In Arabic, the 3SG.M PFV verb, being the shortest and simplest of all verb forms, is used as the citation form of the verb, like the infinitive in English (cf. Erwin 1963: 86, fn. 2). For example, the 3SG.M PFV verb *rāḥ* has the actual meaning 'he went' but is also used as the citation form of the verb 'to go'.

Table 13 lists all prefixes and suffixes used for the inflection of KhA verbs.

4.11.1.1 Perfective

The basic PFV-suffix of both the 1SG and 2SG.M is -(ə)*t*. To avoid a final cluster -CC#, an anaptyctic ə is inserted, unless the verb is followed by a vowel-initial element. Compare *čənət nāyəm* 'I (M) was sleeping', and *čənt asōləf* 'I was telling'. There are, however, exceptions to this rule, especially in rapid speech. The suffixes of the 1PL, 1SG, 2PL.M, 2PL.F, 2SG.M, and 2SG.F are defined as consonant-initial suffixes. These forms often introduce a long vowel -*ē*- before the actual PFV-suffix, as shown in the table above. These forms will be mentioned below for each pattern and verbal type that uses them and is addressed in more detail and put in a wider linguistic context later in this chapter.

MORPHOLOGY   269

TABLE 13   Inflectional affixes

| | PFV | | IPFV | | IMP |
	Suffixes	Prefixes	Suffixes	Suffixes
SG 1 C	-(ə)t, -ēt	ʔa-	(-an)	
2 M	-(ə)t, -ēt	t(ə)-	-Ø	-Ø
2 F	-ti, -ēti	t(ə)-	-īn	-i
3 M	-Ø	y(ə)-	-Ø	
3 F	-at	t(ə)-	-Ø	
PL 1 C	-(ē)na	n(ə)-	-Ø	
2 M	-(ē)tu	t(ə)-	-ūn	-u
	Tustar: -(ē)tam			
2 F	-(ē)tan	t(ə)-	-an	-an
3 M	-aw	y(ə)-	-ūn	
	Tustar: -am			
3 F	-an	y(ə)-	-an	

The suffixes of the third persons, except for the zero-suffix-form 3SG.M, are all vowel-initial suffixes. This differentiation is important for morphological changes, as will be described below. The morphology of the stem remains unchanged before the consonant-initial suffixes. Before the vowel-initial suffixes of the 3SG.F, 3PL.M and 3PL.F, phonological changes often occur with regard to the last vowel of the stem.

The 2PL.M suffix -tu is typical for the *gələt*-dialect group (cf. Mahdi 1985: 91 on Basra; Salonen 1980: 80 on al-Shirqat; and Denz 1971: XLI on Kwayriš/Babylon Arabic); *qəltu*-dialects commonly have -tum (Palva 2009: 27). In some areas (according to consultants, mainly in villages on the banks of the Karkha river in western Khuzestan) -taw is used as the 2PL.M PFV suffix instead of -tu, e.g. *rəhtaw* 'you (PL.M) went' (cf. Ingham 1974: 138, fn. 1, who writes that while -tu is the default 2SG.M PFV suffix in Muhammara, it is -taw in Ahvaz). In all other areas, including Ahvaz, my consultants used -tu as the 2SG.M PFV suffix. In Tustar, the PL.M PFV suffixes are: 2PL.M -tam—e.g. *šəftam* 'you (PL.M) saw'—and 3PL.M -am, e.g. *əyam* 'they (PL.M) came', *ḍallam* 'they (PL.M) stayed' [T1]. According to my consultants, this is typical of the language of the Banū Kaʕab. Ingham states that this is a feature typical of the Central Najdi type of dialects (1982: 76, fn. 1).

-ē- PFV

KhA has an alternative formation of the PFV suffixes, inserting -ē- between the stem and any consonant-initial suffix (cf. Ingham 1974: 15–16). As in numerous other Arabic dialects, this form is regularly used with all final-weak and geminated verbs, e.g. *məšēt* 'I/you (SG.M) walked' verbs, *kaḍḍēt* 'I/you (SG.M) took hold of, grasped, caught'. In KhA, it is also frequently used with regular verbs of the various patterns as an alternative form to the PFV-patterns without -ē-: e.g. Pattern I *nəšdēt* ~ *nəšadət* 'I/you (SG.M) asked', Pattern II *fakkarēt* ~ *fakkarət* 'I/you (SG.M) thought', Pattern III *sōləfēna* ~ *sōlafna* 'we talked', Pattern V *təmarrəḍēt* ~ *təmarraḍət* 'I/you (SG.M) fell sick', Pattern VII *Pənməṭlēt* ~ *Pən-məṭalət* 'I/you (SG.M) lay down, made myself comfortable on the floor', and Pattern VIII *(Pə)štaġalēna* ~ *(Pə)štaġalna* 'we worked' [M1].

Diachronically seen, this pattern is a generalization of the paradigm of final-weak verbs like *ləga* 'to find' and *məša* 'to walk' (cf. Ingham 1982a: 39). This pattern first spread to geminate verbs like *kaḍḍ* 'to take (hold of), grasp', then to regular Pattern I and derived pattern verbs of all types (cf. Holes 2016: 193, fn. 128). In Khuzestan, according to my data, this feature is most common and the furthest developed among speakers from Hoveyzeh, Xafāǧīya, and Ḥamīdīya (cf. Meißner 1903: XLI; cf. Ingham 1973: 544), e.g. *tərsēna* 'we filled' (instead of *tarasna* as usually used in Ahvaz). Ingham notes that this feature was typical of the *ḥaḍar* dialects (1974: 16; 1973: 544). Outside Khuzestan, this feature is also common in Southern Iraq[106] as far north as Nasiriyya (Ingham 1974: 16, fn. 1; Jastrow 2007: 421). It also occurs in several Gulf Arabic dialects,[107] Bandar Moqami Arabic spoken in southern Iran (cf. Leitner et al. 2021), and even in some dialects in Sudan and North Africa (Holes 2016: 33–34). Holes (2016: 36; 185–187) suggests that this may be an old Gulf Arabic feature of an "original eastern Arabic coastal dialect" antedating the massive immigration of tribes from central Saudi-Arabia. He also suggests that this tendency towards consistent inflectional suffixes for all types of verbs might be a result of linguistic contact with non-Arabs (2016: 187). The existence of this feature in the geographically adjacent Gulf Arabic dialects, as well KhA's peripheral status, have probably supported the development of this innovation in KhA.

106　Including the city of Basra, cf. Mahdi (1985: 91 and 203, fn. 1), who adds that in Basra such forms do not occur with hollow, i.e. medial weak, verbs.

107　Cf. Holes (2016: 33–34); and Johnstone (1967: 92, 110) for Bahraini and N-Qaṭar. In Bahrain, it is mainly found in certain sub-dialects of Sunni Bahraini, i.e. Bedouin-type dialects of Bahrain. Holes states, however, that this feature is today disappearing from Bahraini Arabic, occurring more in (elderly) women's speech (2016: 185–187).

MORPHOLOGY 271

4.11.1.2   Imperfective

The IPFV-endings in *-n* in 2SG.F (*-īn*) and 2/3PL.M (*-ūn*) are typical of Bedouin-type dialects of the Arabian peninsular type as well as of all (*qəltu* and *gələt*) Iraqi dialects (Palva 2009: 29; 2006: 606), Anatolian Arabic (Jastrow 2006: 93–94), and Central Asian Arabic (Seeger 2013: 315).

As in all varieties of Arabic, including OA, the IPFV forms of the 2SG.M and 3SG.F are identical: both have a prefix *t-* and no suffix. The prefix *t-* can be affected by emphasis (cf. 3.4) or assimilate to the following consonant, if this is an alveolar or palatal stop, affricate, or fricative (cf. 3.1.3).

When the stem begins with two consonants, the IPFV-prefixes (except for that of the 1SG) consist of a consonant (*y*, *t*, or *n*) and a vowel *ə*—e.g. *yəktəb* 'he writes'. The prefix vowel can be *a*, especially if C_1 is a guttural, emphatic, or *r*— e.g. *yaʕzəm* 'he invites'. In some verbs, both *ə* and *a* are possible as prefix vowel, e.g. *yərkab ~ yarkab* 'he rides, mounts'.

Wherever the verbal stem begins with one single consonant, the IPFV-prefix has no vowel, e.g. *yḍayyəʕ* 'he loses', and *tgūlūn* 'you (PL.M) say'. Stems in which a vowel shift occurred that resulted in the structure -CvCC- (cf. 4.11.2.3 below), may be preceded or followed by a vowel—e.g. *təkətbīn ~ ətkətbīn* 'you (SG.F) write' (cf. Mahdi 1985: 100, and 103–105 on Basra Arabic)—even if the verb is uttered after a word ending in a vowel, e.g.:

(1)   [A14], Elicited
      ʔəhya təfakkr-a.
      3SG.F think.IPFV.3SG.F-OBL.3SG.M
      'She thinks it.'

The IPFV-prefix of the 1SG is *ʔa-*, except when the first root consonant of the verb is *ʔ*, *y*, or *w*, in which case the *a* of this IPFV-prefix combines with the consonant into a long vowel, yielding *-ā-*, *ē*, or *ō*.

-*an* after 1SG IPFV Verbs

A characteristic feature of KhA, also documented for the neighboring Iraqi dialects (cf. Ingham 1982a: 26), is the optional suffixation of *-an* after 1st person SG IPFV verbs of the medial weak and geminated type, e.g. *ʔarūhan* 'I go', *ʔaḍəllan* 'I stay' (cf. Ingham 2000: 127). Meißner described this feature for the dialect of Kwayriš/Babylon (1903: XXXVIII) as a remnant of the Arabic Energicus mode[108] and states that in Kwayriš it is mostly found in poetry. More

---

108   The Energicus mode, in Arabic called *an-nūn al-muʔakkida*, or *nūn at-tawkīd*, is an "optional ending of either single or geminate -*n*- which is occasionally suffixed to certain Semitic

272   CHAPTER 4

convincingly, Ingham explains this feature as a contraction of the postponed 1st person SG pronoun *ʔāna* (Ingham 2000: 127) and considers it a South-Mesopotamian feature. He further compares it to the suffixation of the 2SG.M pronoun *ant* after PFV verb forms in the dialect of the Āl Murrah of Southern and Eastern Arabia, as in *šifhant* 'did you see' < *šift ant* (Ingham 2000: 127, fn. 4). Similarly, Ori Shachmon notes that in Jewish dialects of northern Yemen 2nd person pronouns are suffixed to verbs, probably for the disambiguation of 1st and 2nd person SG PFV forms (2015: 261–263). Cf. Holes (2008: 483) for the frequent suffixation of independent pronouns to verbs or nouns in Omani Arabic. The explanation of this feature as a postponed 1st person SG pronoun therefore seems the most likely.

4.11.1.3   Imperative

The IPFV stem is also used for the imperative. The imperative forms will be provided in the paradigms of each verbal Pattern and type. The IMP prefix *ʔə-* occurs whenever a verbal stem of Pattern I begins with two consonants, e.g. *ʔəktəb* 'write (IMP.SG.M)'. For all other Patterns, when the verbal stem begins with two consonants, the IMP prefix *ʔə-* is optional but usually preferred and never stressed, e.g. *ʔəstaʕməli ~ staʕməli* 'use (IMP.SG.F)'. The prefix *ʔə-* can also be used optionally with "secondary" stems of the structure -CəCC- (cf. Mahdi 1985: 106 on Basra-Arabic), e.g. *ʔəkətbi ~ kətbi* 'write (IMP.SG.F)'. The IMP prefix *ʔ-* occurs whenever a verbal stem begins with a long vowel (concerns initial weak verbs), e.g. *ʔōzan* 'measure (IMP.SG.M)'. No IMP prefix occurs whenever a verbal stem begins with a single consonant, e.g. *nām* 'sleep (IMP.SG.M)'.

4.11.1.3.1   *Emphatic Imperative Prefix* də-

Imperatives with a prefix *də- ~ d-* (always *d-* before a vowel), express an emphatic, more energetic form of imperative. This prefix appears to be used in the same function in Baghdadi Arabic (Blanc 1964: 117), in the Arabic varieties of Basra (Mahdi 1985: 107) and Kwayriš (Meißner 1903: XXXIV), in Mardin

---

verb conjugations, particles, and prepositions. In Arabic, the energicus appears mostly in Classical Arabic" (Zewi 2007: 22). Its function in Arabic is generally described as strengthening or emphatic, or as adding "to the verb a nuance of subjective emotional involvement of the speaker" (Zewi 2007: 23). Zewi further states, that the energicus does not "exist in modern Arabic dialects" (2007: 23) and traces the evidence of insertion of *-n(n)-* between participles with verbal force and object pronouns, as found in several especially Gulf Arabic dialects but also elsewhere, back to pronominal elements and not to the energicus (Zewi 2007: 23–24); cf. Holes, (2011: 80–83) who discusses the origin of such participial constructions and their possible linkage to CA *tanwīn*, dialectal *tanwīn*, or the CA particle *ʔinna*.

MORPHOLOGY   273

and Harran-Urfa (Šāwi) Arabic in eastern Anatolia (Procházka 2018a: 169), in Christian-Maslawi Arabic (Hanitsch 2019: 61), and in some sedentary-type Bahraini Arabic village dialects (Holes 2016: 202). Colloquial Persian (esp. the northern varieties) also uses a prefix *d-* for strong or emphasized imperatives, e.g. *de-boro* 'Go (now)!' (pers. comm. Nawal Bahrani and Babak Nikzat, May 2021) and so does Kurmanjî Kurdish (cf. Procházka 2018a: 184 and the references cited there). The Mandaic imperative prefix *d-* (see Häberl 2019: 694–695) is probably also related.

Due to its occurrence in Jewish and Christian Baghdadi, Palva describes it as an old *qəltu* and with that as a sedentary feature (2009: 21–22; 2006: 612) (cf. 4.8.3 on the question of whether the KhA future marker *rāḥ* could also be a sedentary/*qəltu*-type feature). Grigore (2019: 114) proposes an Ottoman Turkish origin of this prefix (as an abbreviated form of *haydi/hayed/hadi* 'Come on!') and states that *de-* is also found in this function in contemporary varieties of Anatolian Turkish. Procházka (2018a: 183–184) questions this derivation arguing that "Turkish possesses a distinct suffix to intensify imperatives (*-sana/-sene*) and the use of *haydi* together with such forms is only optional" and instead points out that the particle might as well be of Arabic origin and a reflex of the OA demonstrative *dā/dī* (Procházka 2018a: 184). Whatever its ultimate source, its distribution allows us to consider it an old areal feature of the broader Mesopotamian linguistic area (possibly of Persian origin) that has been adopted by the incoming Bedouin tribes at a certain point in history.

(1) [Ḥa1]
     də-xall   asōləf   xayya!
     EMP-HORT tell.IPFV.1SG sister.DIM
     'Let me tell (my story), sister (and don't interrupt)!'

(2) [A14]
     d-əmšū-l-na!
     EMP-go.IMP.PL.M-for-1PL
     'Let's go! (addressed to 2PL)'

(3) [A14]
     də-fakk-ni   yalla, mā   təstəḥi?
     EMP-let_go.IMP.SG.M-OBL.1SG DP   NEG be_ashamed.IPFV.2SG.M
     'Let me go now! Aren't you ashamed!?'

274   CHAPTER 4

(4) [A14]
    də-xallī-ni   *ʔarūḥ!*
    EMP-let.IMP.SG-OBL.1SG   go.IPFV.1SG
    'Let me go please!'

Sometimes, *d-* is also used before interjections for additional emphasis, e.g.:

(5) [A14]
    d-yalla   ʔəməš!
    EMP-DP   go.IMP.SG.M
    'Come on, go now!'

4.11.1.4   Participles
All participles are inflected for gender and number, yielding four forms: SG.M,
SG.F, PL.M, and PL.F.

The SG.M form is unmarked. The SG.F, PL.M, and PL.F forms have the suffixes *-a*, *-īn*, and *-āt*, respectively. Before one of these three suffixes, the second
vowel *ə* of the SG.M AP pattern of Pattern I and the derived Patterns is elided,
e.g. (Pattern I) *nāyəm, nāyma, nāymīn, nāymāt* 'sleeping (AP SG.M, SG.F, PL.M,
PL.F)'.

We will here not discuss the syntactic (usually resultative) functions of the
AP[109] in KhA but only their morphological forms.

4.11.2   *Pattern I*
In contrast to all other patterns, Pattern I contains no formative elements and
can thus be described as derivationally basic (cf. Ingham 1974: 239).

4.11.2.1   Morphological Structure
Regular, medial ʔ roots

> PFV-stem: $C_1 \partial C_2 a C_3$-, $C_1 a C_2 a C_3$-
> IPFV-stem: -$C_1 C_2 \partial C_3$, -$C_1 C_2 a C_3$
> AP: $C_1 \bar{a} C_2 \partial C_3$
> PP: $ma C_1 C_2 \bar{u} C_3$

---

109   On the syntactic functions of participles in spoken Arabic, cf. Procházka and Batan (2016)
       for the Bedouin-type Šāwi-dialects; Hallman (2017) for Syrian Arabic; Holes (2016: 202–
       204) and Eades and Persson (2013: 350–365) for Gulf Arabic; and Erwin (1963: 219–220) for
       Muslim Baghdadi Arabic.

MORPHOLOGY   275

The first vowel of the PFV-stem is *ə* in non-guttural and non-emphatic environments; the second vowel is invariably *a*—e.g. *kətab* 'he wrote'. In the vicinity of emphatics, gutturals, or liquids, the first vowel of the PFV stem is usually *a*—e.g. *ṭabag* 'he covered', *laḥag* 'he lived to see', and *šarad* 'he fled' (cf. Ingham 1974: 239–240). In some cases and among some speakers, the first vowel of the PFV-stem is *a*, even when not in the vicinity of emphatics, gutturals, or liquids. The pronunciation of the first PFV stem-vowel of Pattern I verbs as *a* is, according to Ingham (1973: 540), typical of *ʕarab*-type KhA dialects, but he admits that some *ḥaḍar* speakers also have such forms. My data confirms the latter statement, because the forms with *a* are found among speakers from Ahvaz as well as Fəllāḥīya.

The basic IPFV stem vowel in non-guttural and non-emphatic environments is *ə*—e.g. *yəktəb* 'he writes', *yədrəs* 'he studies', and *yərkəḍ* 'he runs'. The stem vowel is often *a*, if C_2 or C_3 is a guttural or a liquid (cf. Mahdi 1985: 100–103 on Basra-Arabic)—e.g. *yədfaʕ* 'he pays', *yəṭḥan* 'he grinds', *našrab* 'we drink', and *yəbrad* 'he becomes cold'. Examples like *yəfrəg* 'he differs' and *yəġləb* 'he wins' show that the stem vowel is not necessarily *a* under these conditions. For many of these verbs, both vowels can be heard—e.g. *nəgʕəd ~ nəgʕad* 'we sit' (cf. Mahdi 1985: 105–106 on Basra Arabic). Further, there are some verbs with a stem vowel *a*, though they do not fulfill one of the aforementioned conditions (cf. Ingham 1974: 245–246), e.g. *yəlbas* 'he dresses' and *yəmtan* 'he gets fat'.

Geminated Roots ($C_2=C_3$)

> PFV-stem: $C_1aC_2C_2$-
> IPFV-stem: -$C_1əC_2C_2$, -$C_1aC_2C_2$
> AP: $C_1āC_2C_2$
> PP: ma$C_1C_2ūC_2$ (also often taken from Pattern V forms, e.g. *məṭḍarrar* 'damaged')

The stem vowel of the PFV of geminated roots is always *a*. The stem vowel of the IPFV is in most cases *ə*; only very few verbs have *a*, e.g. *ʕaḍḍ—yʕaḍḍ* 'to bite'.

Initial ʔ Roots

> PFV-stem: ʔəC_2aC_3-
> IPFV-stem: -āC_2əC_3
> AP: C_1āC_2əC_3
> PP: not attested

The PFV-patterns of initial *ʔ* verbs are the same as those of regular verbs. In the IPFV, the initial *ʔ* usually fuses with the prefix vowel, yielding *ā*. In the derived Patterns of initial *ʔ* verbs, especially Pattern II, V, and VII, *ʔ* has become *w* (cf. Meißner 1903: XLVI on the dialect of Kwayriš/Babylon), e.g. Pattern II *waččal—ywaččəl* 'to feed' (ʔ-k-l), Pattern V *twannas—yətwannas* 'to enjoy' (< ʔ-n-s), and Pattern VII *ʔənwačal—yənwačəl* 'to be eaten, be eatable' (ʔ-k-l).

Initial Weak Roots

> PFV-stem: waC_2aC_3-, yaC_2aC_3
> IPFV-stem: -$\bar{o}C_2aC_3$, -$\bar{e}C_2aC_3$
> AP: $C_1\bar{a}C_2aC_3$
> PP: not attested

The PFV-patterns of initially weak verbs are the same as those of regular verbs. The IPFV-patterns differ from those of regular verbs in that the weak initial consonant (*y* or *w*) is represented by a long vowel (*ō* or *ē*, respectively).

Medial Weak Roots

> PFV-stem: $C_1\bar{a}C_3$-
> IPFV-stem: -$C_1\bar{a}C_3$, -$C_1\bar{\imath}C_3$, -$C_1\bar{u}C_3$
> AP: $C_1\bar{a}yaC_3$
> PP: not attested

In medial weak verbs, C_2 historically represents either *y*, or *w*. In the PFV, the stem vowels combine with the consonant *y* or *w*, yielding *ā*. In the IPFV, the stem vowel *ə* combines with the consonant *y* or *w*, which yields *ī* or *ū*, respectively, or (less commonly) *ā*, which can derive from *y* or *w*.

Final Weak Roots

> PFV-stem: C_1aC_2a-, C_1aC_2a-
> IPFV-stem: -C_1C_2i, -C_1C_2a
> AP: $C_1\bar{a}C_2i$
> PP: maC_1C_2i

In the PFV of final weak roots, the second short vowel *a* combines with a final weak consonant (*y* or *w*), so that the stem ends in -*a* (when final). In the IPFV, the stem vowel *ə* combines with the final weak consonant, so that the stem

MORPHOLOGY   277

ends in *-i* or *-a* (when final). Verbs with an IPFV final vowel *-a* are less numerous than verbs with *-i*; the distribution of these two vowels is, however, not related to whether C_3 historically was *y* or *w*. Historically final *ʔ* roots synchronically have the same structure as final weak roots but always end in *-a* in the IPFV, e.g. *gara—yəgra* 'to read, study' (< *qaraʔ-a—yaqraʔ-u*).

Double Weak Roots

There are final weak roots with C_2=*y* or *w* (medial and final weak) that always show retention of the second root consonant, e.g. *šəwa* 'to roast' (medial and final weak) and are therefore not treated separately.

Initial and Final Weak Roots

> PFV-stem: wəC$_2$a-
> IPFV-stem: -ōC$_2$i, -ōC$_2$a
> AP: C$_1$āC$_2$i

PP: not attested
   The PFV-and IPFV structures are the same as the final weak verbs regarding the final vowels *-a* and *-i*. The structure of the initial syllable of the IPFV follows that of initial weak (C$_1$=w) verbs.

Irregular Verbs

> *kəla/ʔakal* 'to eat'
> PFV-stem: C$_1$əC$_2$a-, ʔaC$_2$aC$_3$
> IPFV-stem: -āC$_1$əC$_2$
> AP: māC$_1$əC$_2$
> PP: not attested
>
> *xada/ʔaxad* 'to take'
> PFV-stem: C$_1$aC$_2$a-, ʔaC$_2$aC$_3$
> IPFV-stem: -āC$_1$əC$_2$
> AP: māC$_1$əC$_2$
> PP: māC$_1$ūC$_2$

The structures of the KhA verbs for 'to eat' and 'to take' (both former C$_1$=ʔ) show characteristics of different verbal types. The full paradigms of these three verbs are given below (H). In the PFV, they usually have the same structure as

278   CHAPTER 4

final weak verbs (*kəla* 'to eat' and *xaḏa* 'to take'). Some speakers, mostly from
areas and towns such as Hoveyzeh, prefer forms in which C₁ is still *ʔ* (*ʔakal* and
ʔaxaḏ). In the IPFV of both forms, these two verbs still have the same structure as initially weak (C₁=ʔ) verbs with a long vowel *ā* in the first syllable due
to the underlying consonant *ʔ* (-*aʔ* > *ā*). As in other *gələt* dialects (cf. Meißner
1903: XLV on Kwayriš/Babylon; and Mahdi 1985: 115 on Basra), the KhA SG.M
imperative forms *ʔəkəl* and *ʔaxəḏ* have a prefixed *ʔə-* that has probably developed in analogy with the other Pattern I imperative forms such as *ʔəktəb* 'write
(IMP.SG.M)' (contrast, for example, the imperatives *xōd* and *kōl* in Syrian Arabic, Cowell 1964: 55–56).

> *ʔəya/ya* 'to come'
> PFV-stem: C₁əC₂a- ~ C₁a-
> IPFV-stem: -C₁C₂i ~ -C₁i
> AP: C₁āC₂

The PFV-as well as the IPFV-structure of the verb *ʔəya* ~ *ya* 'to come' is basically
that of final weak verbs.

The first syllable *ʔə-* in the PFV-forms is optional, yielding two alternative
base forms: *ʔəya* and *ya*. The forms with initial *ʔə-* are very common (in contrast to Muslim Baghdadi Arabic, cf. Erwin 1963: 101). The forms without initial
ʔə- tend to be preferred in the 3rd person forms which have vowel-initial suffixes, or when a vowel-initial object suffix is attached to the verb: e.g. *yēt-əč* 'I
came to you (SG.F)'. Synchronically, these alternatives appear to reflect different roots: (1) √ʔyy, which is of a regular final weak structure with a unique C₂=y
(historically < *ǧ*), and √yy, also a final weak root but with only two root consonants (cf. Ingham 1974: 278). Whereas in Basra Arabic the pronunciation of *ǧ*
in this verb varies between *ǧ* and *y* (Mahdi 1985: 127–128), in my KhA data only
a few instances have been found in which *ǧ* was retained (especially speakers
from Muḥammara). Speakers from Hoveyzeh and Xafaǧīya it was pronounced
with *ž*.

Examples:

> Regular, medial *ʔ*: *nəšad—yənšəd* 'to ask', *kətab—yəktəb* 'to write',
> *ləbas—yəlbas* 'to dress, put on (clothes)', *ʕaraf—yəʕrəf ~ yaʕrəf* 'to
> know', *saʔal—yəsʔal* 'to ask'
> Geminated: *šadd—yšədd* 'to tie up', *dagg—ydəgg* 'to hit; tattoo; knock;
> call (on the phone)', *radd—yrədd* 'to answer, return', *laff—yləff* 'to
> wrap', *ḥabb—yḥabb* 'to love; kiss', *ʕaḏḏ—yʕaḏḏ* 'to bite'.

MORPHOLOGY   279

Initial ʔ: *ʔāmar*[110]—*yāmər* 'to order',[111] *kəla—yākəl* 'to eat', *xaḏa—yāxəḏ*
'to take'

Initial weak: *wəyaʕ—yōyaʕ* 'to hurt', *wəṣal—yōṣal* 'to arrive', **wəlad—
yūlad* 'to give birth' (for this verb, M forms are, of course, not used),
wəgaf—yōgaf 'to stop', *yəʔas* (no IPFV) 'to despair, be disappointed',
yəbas—yēbas 'to dry (up)'

Medial weak: *nām—ynām* 'to sleep', *xāf—yxāf* 'to be afraid', *rād—yrīd*
'to want', *yāb—yyīb* 'to bring' (via *ǧ > y*), *čān—ykūn* 'to be', *rāḥ—yrūḥ*
'to go', *šāf—yšūf* 'to see', *ṣāṭ—yṣūṭ* 'to stir', *bāg—ybūg* 'to steal'

Final weak: *bana—yəbni* 'to build', *bəča—yəbči* 'to cry', *dara—yədri* 'to
know', *ḥəča—yəḥči* 'to talk, speak', *nəsa—yənsa* 'to forget', *ʕama—
yəʕma* 'to be blind', *gara—yəgra* 'to read, study', and *ləga—yəlga* 'to
find'

Initial and final weak: *waʕa—yōʕa* 'to wake up'.

4.11.2.2   Semantic Functions

Verbs of Pattern I can be transitive or intransitive and have no peculiar semantic functions because they simply express the basic meaning of the respective
verbal root.

4.11.2.3   Inflection

(A)   Regular Roots

kətab 'to write'	PFV	IPFV	IMP
SG 3 M	*kətab*	*yəktəb*	
3 F	*kətbat*	*təktəb*	
2 M	*kətabət*	*təktəb*	*ʔəktəb*
2 F	*kətabti*	*ətkətbīn*	*(ʔə)kətbi*
1 C	*kətabət*	*ʔaktəb*	
PL 3 M	*kətbaw*	*ykətbūn*	
3 F	*kətban*	*ykətban*	
2 M	*kətabtu*	*ətkətbūn*	*(ʔə)kətbu*

---

110 Meißner (1903: XLV) writes of the dialect of Kwayriš/Babylon, that in this and some other
     initial *ʔ* verbs the vowel *a* in the first syllable is lengthened so that they look like Pattern III
     verbs, but that their IPFV forms clearly showed that they belonged to Pattern I.

111 Mahdi (1985: 116) states that in Basra only elderly people use the IPFV form *yāmər*, other-
     wise *yuʔmur ~yiʔmur* is heard.

280   CHAPTER 4

(*cont.*)

kətab 'to write'	PFV	IPFV	IMP
2 F	*kətabtan*	*ətkətban*	*(ʔə)kətban*
1 C	*kətabna*	*nəktəb*	

Participles	AP	PP
SG M	*kātəb*	*maktūb*
F	*kātba*	*maktūba*
PL M	*kātbīn*	*maktūbīn*
F	*kātbāt*	*maktūbāt*

In forms where the vowel of the first syllable is in an unstressed position, i.e. before consonant-initial suffixes, it is often dropped. Then, the verb is usually preceded by an epenthetic vowel, e.g. *kətabət ~ əktabət* 'I/you (SG.M) wrote' (cf. Ingham 1974: 240–242). The first form, *kətabət*, appears to be the most common one in my data. The second variant occurs mainly in postvocalic environments, e.g. *ʔāna rkabət* 'I rode'. In postconsonantal environments, both forms may occur, e.g. *wēn šaradət? ~ wēn əšradət?* 'Where did you flee (to)?'. The second vowel of both the PFV-stem and the IPFV-stem vowel are elided when a vowel-initial inflectional or object suffix follows. Whereas the PFV-vowel *a* is elided without causing further changes (*kətab-* + *at* > *kətb-at* 'she wrote'), the elision of the IPFV-stem vowel results in the insertion of a new vowel after the first root consonant to avoid a three-consonant cluster (cf. Erwin 1963: 58–59 for Muslim Baghdadi Arabic). Subsequently, the prefix vowel in the resulting initial open syllable is also elided: *yəktəb-* + *ūn* > **yəktb-ūn* > **yəkətbūn* > *ykətb-ūn* 'they write'. The anaptyctic vowel inserted after the first root consonant is usually *ə*, but may also be *a*: e.g. *yhamsūn* 'they (PL.M) whisper'. The prefix *ʔə-* is optional in the IMP forms with suffixes (SG.F, PL.F, and PL.M), but obligatory in the IMP.SG.M. As noted in 4.11.1.1 above, regular Pattern I verbs also have alternative PFV forms with a long vowel *-ē-* inserted before consonant-initial suffixes (though not used by all speakers).

MORPHOLOGY

(B) Geminated Roots

dagg 'to hit, tattoo, knock'	PFV	IPFV	IMP
SG 3 M	*dagg*	*ydəgg*	
3 F	*daggat*	*tdəgg*	
2 M	*daggēt*	*tdəgg*	*dəgg*
2 F	*daggēti*	*tdəggīn*	*dəggi*
1 C	*daggēt*	*ʔadəgg*	
PL 3 M	*daggaw*	*ydəddūn*	
3 F	*daggan*	*ydəggan*	
2 M	*daggētu*	*tdəggūn*	*dəggu*
2 F	*daggētan*	*tdəggan*	*dəggan*
1 C	*daggēna*	*ndəgg*	

Participles	AP	PP
SG M	*dāgg*	*madgūg*
F	*dāgga*	*madgūga*
PL M	*dāggīn*	*madgūgīn*
F	*dāggāt*	*madgūgāt*

As in all Arabic dialects, the KhA PFV forms of the 1st and 2nd persons (i.e. forms with consonant-initial inflectional suffixes) of geminated roots are constructed via insertion of *-ē-*, which diachronically developed via analogy with the PFV conjugation of final weak verbs, cf. 4.11.1.1.

(C) Initial ʔ Roots

ʔāmar 'to order'	PFV	IPFV	IMP
SG 3 M	*ʔāmar*	*yāmər*	
3 F	*ʔāmərat*	*tāmər*	
2 M	*ʔāmarət*	*tāmər*	*ʔāmər*
2 F	*ʔāmarti*	*tāmrīn*	*ʔāmri*
1 C	*ʔāmarət*	*ʔāmər*	
PL 3 M	*ʔāməraw*	*yāmrūn*	

282   CHAPTER 4

(*cont.*)

ʔāmar 'to order'	PFV	IPFV	IMP
3 F	*ʔāməran*	*yāmran*	
2 M	*ʔāmartu*	*tāmrūn*	*ʔāmru*
2 F	*ʔāmartan*	*tāmran*	*ʔāmran*
1 C	*ʔāmarna*	*nāmər*	

Participles	AP	PP
SG M	*ʔāmər*	not attested

(D) Initial Weak Roots

wəṣal 'to arrive', *yəbas* 'to dry (up)'	PFV	IPFV	IMP
SG 3 M	*wəṣal, yəbas*	*yōṣal, yēbas*	
3 F	*wəṣlat, yəbsat*	*tōṣal, tēbas*	
2 M	*wəṣalət, yəbasət*	*tōṣal, tēbas*	*ʔōṣal*
2 F	*wəṣalti, yəbasti*	*tōṣlīn, tēbsīn*	*ʔōṣli*
1 C	*wəṣalət, yəbasət*	*ʔōṣal, ʔēbas*	
PL 3 M	*wəṣlaw, yəbsaw*	*yōṣlūn, yēbsūn*	
3 F	*wəṣlan, yəbsan*	*yōṣlan, yēbsan*	
2 M	*wəṣaltu, yəbastu*	*tōṣlūn, tēbsūn*	*ʔōṣlu*
2 F	*wəṣaltan, yəbasna*	*tōṣlan, tēbsan*	*ʔōṣlan*
1 C	*wəṣalna, yəbasna*	*nōṣal, nēbas*	

Participles	AP	PP
SG M	*wāṣəl* *yābəs*	not attested

Before inflectional suffixes, the vowel *ə* or *a* in the final syllable of the IPFV-stem is dropped.

MORPHOLOGY

(E) Medial Weak Roots

yāb 'to bring' PFV *nām* 'to sleep' *māt* 'to die'		IPFV	IMP
SG 3 M	*yāb, nām, māt*	*yyīb, ynām, ymūt*	
3 F	*yābat, nāmat, mātat*	*tyīb, tnām, tmūt*	
2 M	*yəbət, nəmət, mətət*	*tyīb, tnām, tmūt*	*yīb, nām, mūt*
2 F	*yəbti, nəmti, mətti*	*tyībīn, tnāmīn, tmūtīn*	*yībi, nāmi, mūti*
1 C	*yəbət, nəmət, mətət*	*ʔayīb, ʔanām, ʔamūt*	
PL 3 M	*yābaw, nāmaw, mātaw*	*yyībūn, ynāmūn, ymūtūn*	
3 F	*yāban, nāman, mātan*	*yyīban, ynāman, ymūtan*	
2 M	*yəbtu, nəmtu, məttu*	*tyībūn, tnāmūn, tmūtūn*	*yību, nāmu, mūtu*
2 F	*yəbtan, nəmtan, məttan*	*tyīban, tnāman, tmūtān*	*yīban, nāman, mūtan*
1 C	*yəbna, nəmna, mətna*	*nyīb, nnām, nmūt*	
Participles	AP	PP	
SG M	*yāyəb, nāyəm, māyət*	not attested	

The PFV-stem vowel is *ā* in forms with no or with vowel-initial suffixes (i.e. the 3rd person forms) and *ə*[112] in forms with consonant-initial inflectional suffixes (all other persons). In KhA, PFV-constructions via insertion of -*ē*- (cf. 4.11.1.1) are generally not common with Pattern I medial weak verbs. In my corpus such forms are also never used with the verb *šāf* (contrast Ingham 1974: 262–263, who does give examples, though noting that with medial weak verbs this structure is rarer than with regular verbs).

As Ingham (1974: 263) notes (for KhA and "as far north as al Kāḏimiyya, the Shīʕa district of Baghdād"), the verb *gāl* 'to say, tell' may be treated as a geminated verb in the PFV, yielding e.g. *gallēt* 'I/you (SG.M) said', and *gallēnā-lhəm* 'we told them (PL.M)' (cf. 4.1.3.1).

---

112   As Ingham (1974: 262) notes, KhA and Mesopotamian dialects do not maintain the vowel distinction *u* vs. *i* depending on whether C$_2$ is *w* (yielding *u*) or *y* (yielding *i*). The contrast *e/u*, as noted for some Muslim Baghdadi speakers and only for some verbs like *gumet* 'I/you (M.SG) got up' and *buget* 'I/you (M.SG) stole' (Blanc 1964: 195, fn. 119), is most likely phonetically conditioned: both examples provided by Blanc involve a labial and the velar

284   CHAPTER 4

The frequently-used verbs *rād—yrīd* 'to want' and *rāḥ—yrūḥ* 'to go' show
variant IPFV-stems in forms with suffixes—i.e. 2SG.F, 2/3PL.M, and 2/3PL.F—
which deletes the stem vowel, yielding -*rd*- and -*rḥ*-: e.g. *tərdīn* 'you (SG.F) want'
and *yərḥan* 'they (F) go'. The 1SG of *rād* 'to want' also shows this shortened IPFV-
stem when followed by another 1SG IPFV-verb: e.g. *ʔard ayīb* ... 'I want to get ...'.
These alternative forms exists next to the less common full forms, e.g. *trīdīn*
'you (SG.F) want' and *trūḥīn* 'you (SG.F) go' (cf. Blanc 1964: 106 and Erwin 1963:
128, fn. 1 and 129 on this feature in Muslim Baghdadi Arabic). The IMP forms
never have a prefix.

(F)   Final Weak

bəča 'to cry', *nəsa* 'to forget'	PFV	IPFV	IMP
SG 3 M	*bəča, nəsa*	*yəbči, yənsa*	
3 F	*bəčat, nəsat*	*təbči, tənsa*	
2 M	*bəčēt, nəsēt*	*təbči, tənsa*	*ʔəbči ~ ʔəbəč, ʔənsa*
2 F	*bəčēti, nəsēti*	*təbčīn, tənsīn*	*ʔəbči, ʔənsi*
1 C	*bəčēt, nəsēt*	*ʔəbči, ʔənsa*	
PL 3 M	*bəčaw, nəsaw*	*yəbčūn, yənsūn*	
3 F	*bəčan, nəsan*	*yəbčan, yənsan*	
2 M	*bəčētu, nəsētu*	*təbčūn, tənsūn*	*ʔəbču, ʔənsu*
2 F	*bəčētan, nəsētan*	*təbčan, tənsan*	*ʔəbčan, ʔənsan*
1 C	*bəčēna, nəsēna*	*nəbči, nənsa*	

Participles	AP	PP	
SG M	*bāči, nāsi*	*mansi*	

In the PFV, the stem vowel -*a* is elided and -*ē*- is introduced when a consonant-
initial inflectional suffix follows. The IPFV-stem vowel -*i* or -*a* is elided when
one of the vowel-initial inflectional suffixes is added. In the IMP SG.M of final
weak verbs with IPFV-stems ending in -*i* there are two variants, one with and

---

g in the immediate surroundings of the vowel; cf. 3.2.1.2. Under these phonetic conditions,
in KhA the stem vowel would also be pronounced [u]—e.g. KhA *gəmət* [gumɪt] 'I/you
(M.SG) got up'.

MORPHOLOGY

another without the final vowel: e.g. *ʔəmši ~ ʔəməš* 'go!' and *ʔəḥči ~ ʔəḥəč* 'speak!'
Basra Arabic, by contrast, appears to use only the forms with the final vowel
(Mahdi 1985: 125). In KhA, the forms lacking the final vowel introduce an anaptyctic vowel to separate the two final consonants. Ingham classifies the form
with the final vowel as *ḥaḍar-* and the one which lacks the final vowel as *ʕarab-*
type (2007: 577; 1973: 544). My consultants from Ahvaz (which is classified as
of *ʕarab-*type, according to Ingham's definition) confirmed, however, that they
used both forms equally.

(G)   Initial and Final Weak Roots

waʕa 'to wake up'	PFV	IPFV	IMP
SG 3 M	*waʕa*	*yōʕa*	
3 F	*waʕat*	*tōʕa*	
2 M	*waʕēt*	*tōʕa*	*ʔōʕa*
2 F	*waʕēti*	*tōʕīn*	*ʔōʕi*
1 C	*waʕēt*	*ʔōʕa*	
PL 3 M	*waʕaw*	*yōʕūn*	
3 F	*waʕan*	*yōʕan*	
2 M	*waʕētu*	*tōʕūn*	*ʔōʕu*
2 F	*waʕētan*	*tōʕan*	*ʔōʕan*
1 C	*waʕēna*	*nōʕa*	

Participles	AP	PP
SG M	*wāʕi*	not attested

The final vowels -*a* and -*i* of the PFV-and IPFV-stems, and their combination
with the respective inflectional suffixes, are the same as for the final weak verbs
(cf. above, (F)). The changes in the initial syllable of the IPFV-stem are the same
as in initial weak C_1=w verbs (cf. above, (D)).

286 CHAPTER 4

(H) The Irregular Verbs 'to Eat', 'to Take' (Both Former C_1=ʔ), and 'to Come'

kəla, ʔakal 'to eat'	PFV	IPFV	IMP
SG 3 M	*kəla, ʔakal*	*yākəl*	
3 F	*kəlat, ʔaklat*	*tākəl*	
2 M	*kəlēt, ʔakalət*	*tākəl*	*ʔəkəl*
2 F	*kəlēti, ʔakalti*	*tāklīn*	*ʔəkli*
1 C	*kəlēt, ʔakalət*	*ʔākəl*	
PL 3 M	*kəlaw, ʔaklaw*	*yāklūn*	
3 F	*kəlan, ʔaklan*	*yāklan*	
2 M	*kəlētu, ʔakaltu*	*tāklūn*	*ʔəklu*
2 F	*kəlētan, ʔakaltan*	*tāklan*	*ʔəklan*
1 C	*kəlēna, ʔakalna*	*nākəl*	

Participles	AP	PP	
SG M	*māčəl*	not attested	

xaḏa, ʔaxaḏ 'to take'	PFV		IPFV	IMP
SG 3 M	*xaḏa, ʔaxaḏ*		*yāxəḏ*	
3 F	*xaḏat* (less common: *xəḏat*), *ʔaxḏat*		*tāxəḏ*	
2 M	*xaḏēt, ʔaxaḏət*		*tāxəḏ*	*ʔəxəḏ*
2 F	*xaḏēti, ʔaxaḏti*		*tāxḏīn*	*ʔəxḏi*
1 C	*xaḏēt, ʔaxaḏət*		*ʔāxəḏ*	
PL 3 M	*xaḏaw* (less common: *xəḏaw*), *ʔaxḏaw*	*yāxḏūn*		
3 F	*xaḏan* (less common: *xəḏan*), *ʔaxḏan*	*yāxḏan*		
2 M	*xaḏētu, ʔaxaḏtu*		*tāxḏūn*	*ʔəxḏu*
2 F	*xaḏētan, ʔaxaḏtan*		*tāxḏan*	*ʔəxḏan*
1 C	*xaḏēna, ʔaxaḏna*		*nāxəḏ*	

Participles	AP	PP
SG M	*māxəḏ*	*māxūḏ*

MORPHOLOGY   287

The verbs *kəla* 'to eat' and *xaḍa* 'to take' are inflected in the PFV like final weak verbs. In the PFV of the verb *xaḍa*, the first stem vowel *a* may be raised to *ə* before vowel-initial consonant suffixes. In the IPFV, they have the same structure as initially weak (C_1=ʔ) verbs. The vowel *ə* in the final syllable of the IPFV-stem is dropped before suffixes. In the forms *ʔakal* 'to eat' and *ʔaxad* 'to take', the second vowel *a* of the PFV-stem is usually dropped before vowel-initial inflectional suffixes.

(ʔə)ya 'to come'	PFV	IPFV	IMP
SG 3 M	*(ʔə)ya*	*yyi* [ɪji] ~ *ʔəyyi* [ɪjːi]	
		Məʕdān: yəži	
3 F	*(ʔə)yat*	*təyi* ~ *təyyi*	
2 M	*(ʔə)yēt*	*təyi* ~ *təyyi*	*taʕāl*
2 F	*(ʔə)yēti*	*təyīn* ~ *təyyīn*	*taʕāy, taʕāli*
1 C	*(ʔə)yēt*	*ʔayi* ~ *ʔayyi*	
PL 3 M	*(ʔə)yaw*	*yyūn* [ɪjuːn]	
3 F	*(ʔə)yan* [jan ~ ɪjan]	*yyan* [ɪjan]	
2 M	*(ʔə)yētu*	*təyūn* ~ *təyyūn*	*taʕālaw*
2 F	*(ʔə)yētan*	*təyan* ~ *təyyan*	*taʕālan*
1 C	*(ʔə)yēna*	*nəyi* ~ *nəyyi*	

Participles	AP	PP
SG M	*yāy*	not attested
F	*yāya*	———————
PL M	*yāyīn*	———————
F	*yāyāt*	———————

In the IPFV-stem, the final vowel is always dropped before suffixes. In the PFV, -*ē*- is introduced before a consonant-initial inflectional suffix. As in many other dialects, this verb has a suppletive IMP (i.e. constructed from a different root).

4.11.3   *Pattern II*
As is characteristic for this Pattern in all varieties of Arabic, the second consonant is geminated.

4.11.3.1   Morphological Structure
Regular, Geminated ($C_2=C_3$), Initial/Medial Weak Roots

> PFV-stem: $C_1aC_2C_2aC_3$-
> IPFV-stem: -$C_1aC_2C_2əC_3$
> AP: m$C_1aC_2C_2əC_3$
> PP: m$C_1aC_2C_2aC_3$

Final Weak Roots

> PFV-stem: $C_1aC_2C_2a$-
> IPFV-stem: -$C_1aC_2C_2i$
> AP: m$C_1aC_2C_2i$
> PP: m$C_1aC_2C_2a$

Examples:

> Regular: *ḍayyaʕ—yḍayyəʕ* 'to lose'
> Geminated: *šaggag—yšaggəg* 'to tear (apart)', *ḥabbab—yḥabbəb* 'to kiss'
> Initial ʔ: *ʔaxxar—yʔaxxər* 'to postpone', *ʔamman—yʔammən* 'to trust',
> *ʔaǧǧar—yʔaǧǧər* 'to let, rent out'
> Initial weak: *waččəl—ywaččəl* 'to feed, nourish', *wallad—ywalləd* 'to give
> birth', and *yabbas—yyabbəs* 'to dry (trans.)'
> Medial weak: *bawwaʕ—ybawwəʕ* 'to see', *hawwas—yhawwəs* 'to dance,
> chant', and *yawwaz—yyawwəz* 'to marry (someone) to (someone
> else).'
> Final weak: *sawwa—ysawwi* 'to do, make', *samma—ysammi* 'to call sb.
> sth.', *bačča—ybačči* 'to make sb. cry', *ʕabba—yʕabbi* 'to fill', *rawwa—
> yrawwi* 'to form dough balls (for baking bread)'

4.11.3.2   Semantic Functions
This pattern is very productive and its verbs are usually transitive and often
causative or intensive—e.g. *xarrab* 'to destroy (sth.)', *gaʕʕad* 'to wake sb. up',
xaddar (*čāy*) 'to prepare (tea)', *lawwaʕ* 'to get on sb.'s nerves'—or denomina-
tive, e.g. *rawwab* 'to make yoghurt' < *rōba* 'yoghurt' ($C_2=w$). Foreign borrowings
are also often integrated as verbs in Pattern II: e.g. *gayyar* 'to get stuck' < Pers. *gīr*
šodan 'to get stuck', *ʕammar* 'to repair' < Pers. *taʕmīr kardan* 'to repair' (which
again goes back to the Arabic noun *taʕmīr* 'building, construction; repair'), and
čassab 'to glue' < Pers. *časb zadan* 'to glue'.

MORPHOLOGY

4.11.3.3   Inflection
(A)   Regular, Geminated, Initial/ Medial Weak Roots

ḍayyaʕ 'to lose'	PFV	IPFV	IMP
SG 3 M	*ḍayyaʕ*	*yḍayyəʕ*	
3 F	*ḍayyəʕat*	*tḍayyəʕ*	
2 M	*ḍayyaʕət, ḍayyaʕēt*	*tḍayyəʕ*	*ḍayyəʕ*
2 F	*ḍayyaʕti, ḍayyaʕēti*	*tḍayyəʕīn*	*ḍayyʕi*
1 C	*ḍayyaʕət, ḍayyaʕēt*	*ʔaḍayyəʕ*	
PL 3 M	*ḍayyəʕaw*	*yḍayyəʕūn*	
3 F	*ḍayyəʕan*	*yḍayyəʕan*	
2 M	*ḍayyaʕtu, ḍayyaʕētu*	*tḍayyəʕūn*	*ḍayyʕu*
2 F	*ḍayyaʕtan, ḍayyaʕētan*	*tḍayyəʕan*	*ḍayyʕan*
1 C	*ḍayyaʕna, ḍayyaʕēna*	*nḍayyəʕ*	

Participles	AP	PP
SG M	*mḍayyəʕ*	not attested
F	*mḍayyʕa*	—————
PL M	*mḍayyʕīn*	—————
F	*mḍayyʕāt*	—————

The second vowel *a* of the PFV-stem may be elided when a vowel-initial suffix follows. In this case the double consonant is reduced to a single consonant in pronunciation (cf. Blanc 1964: 54 on the reduction of geminate clusters to a single consonant in Baghdadi Arabic). PFV-constructions of Pattern II regular verbs via insertion of *-ē-* before consonant-initial suffixes (cf. 4.11.1.1) are a common alternative to the forms without *-ē-*. The second vowel *ə* of the IPFV-stem may also be elided when a vowel-initial suffix follows, which again leads to a reduction of the double to a single consonant. In geminated roots, the vowel and the double consonant are always retained. The IMP forms have no prefixes.

290   CHAPTER 4

(B)   Final Weak Roots

sawwa 'to make'	**PFV**	**IPFV**	**IMP**
SG 3 M	*sawwa*	*ysawwi*	
3 F	*sawwat*	*tsawwi*	
2 M	*sawwēt*	*tsawwi*	*sawwi*
2 F	*sawwēti*	*tsawwīn*	*sawwi*
1 C	*sawwēt*	*ʔasawwi*	
PL 3 M	*sawwaw*	*ysawwūn*	
3 F	*sawwan*	*ysawwan*	
2 M	*sawwētu*	*tsawwūn*	*sawwu*
2 F	*sawwētan*	*tsawwan*	*sawwan*
1 C	*sawwēna*	*nsawwi*	

Participles	AP	PP
SG M	*msawwi*	*msawwa*

Regarding the final PFV-stem vowel -*a*, the introduction of -*ē*-, and the final
IPFV-stem vowel -*i*, Pattern II final weak verbs follow the same rules as described above for Pattern I weak verbs.

4.11.4   *Pattern III*
4.11.4.1   Morphological Structure
Regular, medial weak, geminated roots ($C_2=C_3$)

> PFV-stem: $C_1\bar{a}C_2aC_3$-
> IPFV-stem: -$C_1\bar{a}C_2\partial C_3$
> AP: $mC_1\bar{a}C_2\partial C_3$
> PP: not attested

Final Weak Roots:

> PFV-stem: $C_1\bar{a}C_2a$-
> IPFV-stem: -$C_1\bar{a}C_2i$
> AP: $mC_1\bar{a}C_2i$
> PP: not attested

MORPHOLOGY

291

Pattern III is generally characterized by the presence of long vowel -ā-
between the first and the second root consonant. In Pattern III final weak verbs,
the PFV-stem ends in -a, and the IPFV-stem in -i.

Examples:

> Regular: *sāʕad—ysāʕəd* 'to help'
> Medial weak: *dāwəm—ydāwəm* 'to work', *ʕāyən—yʕāyən* 'to see'
> Final weak: *rāwa—yrāwi* 'to show', *ʕāfa—yʕāfi* 'to heal, cure', *ḥāča—*
> *yḥāči* 'to talk (to somebody)', *tāna—ytāni* 'to wait', *wāfa—ywāfi* 'to
> give back a loan'

4.11.4.2   Semantic Functions

Verbs belonging to this pattern can be both transitive and intransitive and are
of different semantic natures and cannot be grouped under one heading. This
pattern appears to be quite productive in KhA—as the verb *tāna—ytāni* 'to
wait' shows, which is only rarely expressed by a Pattern III verb.[113]

4.11.4.3   Inflection
(A)   Regular Roots

sāʕad 'to help'	PFV	IPFV	IMP
SG 3 M	*sāʕad*	*ysāʕəd*	
3 F	*sāʕədat*	*tsāʕəd*	
2 M	*sāʕadət ~ sāʕadēt*	*tsāʕəd*	*sāʕəd*
2 F	*sāʕadti ~ sāʕadēti*	*tsāʕdīn*	*sāʕdi*
1 C	*sāʕadət ~ sāʕadēt*	*ʔasāʕəd*	
PL 3 M	*sāʕədaw*	*ysāʕdūn*	
3 F	*sāʕədan*	*ysāʕdan*	
2 M	*sāʕadtu ~ sāʕadētu*	*tsāʕdūn*	*sāʕdu*
2 F	*sāʕadtan ~ sāʕadētan*	*tsāʕdan*	*sāʕdan*
1 C	*sāʕadna ~ sāʕadēna*	*nsāʕəd*	

Participles	AP	PP
SG M	*msāʕəd*	not attested

---

113   Elsewhere this form is attested for Saudi-Arabia/Naǧd, the east coast of the Arabian Penin-

The vowel *a* of the PFV-stem may be elided when a vowel-initial suffix follows. When it is retained, it is usually stressed and raised to *ə*. The vowel *ə* of the IPFV-stem is mostly elided before a vowel-initial suffix. Pattern III geminated verbs have the same structure as regular verbs of this pattern with the difference that the vowel *ə* of the IPFV-stem is never elided when a vowel-initial suffix follows. PFV-constructions of Pattern III regular verbs via insertion of -*ē*- before consonant-initial suffixes (cf. 4.11.1.1) are a common alternative to the forms without -*ē*-.

(B) Final Weak Roots

ḥāča 'to talk to'	PFV	IPFV	IMP
SG 3 M	*ḥāča*	*yḥāči*	
3 F	*ḥāčat*	*tḥāči*	
2 M	*ḥāčēt*	*tḥāči*	*ḥāči*
2 F	*ḥāčēti*	*tḥāčīn*	*ḥāči*
1 C	*ḥāčēt*	*ʔaḥāči*	
PL 3 M	*ḥāčaw*	*yḥāčūn*	
3 F	*ḥāčan*	*yḥāčan*	
2 M	*ḥāčētu*	*tḥāčūn*	*ḥāču*
2 F	*ḥāčētan*	*tḥāčan*	*ḥāčan*
1 C	*ḥāčēna*	*nḥāči*	

Participles	AP	PP
SG M	*mḥāči*	not attested

Regarding the final PFV-stem vowel -*a*, the introduction of -*ē*-, and the final IPFV-stem vowel -*i*, Pattern III final weak verbs follow the same rules as described above for Pattern I weak verbs.

---

sula, and Basra (WAD III: 380; contrast Mahdi 1985: 168, 177, 180 who gives *intiḍar* for Basra-Arabic); Muslim Baghdadi Arabic uses the (Pattern VIII of the root √nḍr) form *intiḍar* 'to wait' (WAD III: 379). Behnstedt and Woidich (WAD III: 380) derive the form *tāna* from *istāna* < *ista'nā (Pattern X of *ʔanā*). Meißner (1903: XLVI; XLIX) similarly derives the cognate Pattern I final weak form *tana—yitnā* from *taʔanna* (Pattern V of *ʔanā*).

MORPHOLOGY

4.11.5 *Pattern IV*

Pattern IV verbs, generally characterized by a prefix ʔa- in the PFV, are no longer productively used in KhA except for the verb ʔənṭa ~ ʔəṭṭa ~ (ʔə)ṭa[114]—yənṭi ~ yəṭṭi ~ yəṭi 'to give', which, however, has a prefix ʔə- instead of ʔa- in the PFV. Ingham (1982a: 92) gives the PFV form niṭa, which does not occur in my corpus. Behnstedt and Woidich (WAD III: 406, 408–409) explain the form ʔanṭa as a dissimilation from < *ʔaṭṭa < OA ʔaʕṭā. KhA ʔəṭṭa therefore may be an earlier but still used form of ʔənṭa, or the result of assimilation nṭ > ṭṭ. The KhA form ʔəṭa—yəṭi, which has probably developed from *ʔaṭṭa via elision of ṭ, is very frequent in my corpus, especially with imperatives.

Former Pattern IV verbs—if used—appear as Pattern I verbs, retaining the i/ī vowel of the original pattern in the IPFV-stem, e.g. nəkar—yənkər 'to deny', ṣarr—yṣərr 'to insist', ḏall—yḏəll 'to subjugate', and dār—ydīr 'to direct, administer'.

ʔənṭa, ʔəṭṭa ~ ʔəṭa 'to give'	PFV	IPFV	IMP
SG 3 M	ʔənṭa, ʔəṭṭa ~ ʔəṭa	yənṭi, yəṭṭi ~ yəṭi	
3 F	ʔənṭat, ʔəṭṭat ~ ʔəṭat	tənṭi, təṭṭi ~ təṭi	
2 M	ʔənṭēt, ʔəṭṭēt ~ ʔəṭēt	tənṭi, təṭṭi ~ təṭi	ʔənṭi, ʔəṭi
2 F	ʔənṭēti, ʔəṭṭēti ~ ʔəṭēti	tənṭīn, təṭṭīn ~ təṭīn	ʔənṭi, ʔəṭi
1 C	ʔənṭēt, ʔəṭṭēt ~ ʔəṭēt	ʔanṭi, ʔaṭṭi ~ ʔaṭi	
PL 3 M	ʔənṭaw, ʔəṭṭaw ~ ʔəṭaw	yənṭūn, yəṭṭūn ~ yəṭūn	
3 F	ʔənṭan, ʔəṭṭan ~ ʔəṭan	yənṭan, yəṭṭan ~ yəṭan	
2 M	ʔənṭētaw, ʔəṭṭētu ~ ʔəṭētu	tənṭūn, təṭṭūn ~ təṭūn	ʔənṭu, ʔəṭu
2 F	ʔənṭētan, ʔəṭṭētan ~ ʔəṭētan	tənṭan, təṭṭan ~ təṭan	ʔənṭan, ʔəṭan
1 C	ʔənṭēna, ʔəṭṭēna ~ ʔəṭēna	nənṭi, nəṭṭi ~ nəṭi	

Participles	AP	PP
SG M	mənṭi	not attested

As can be seen from the table, in the Pattern IV final weak verb ʔənṭa, ʔəṭṭa ~ ʔəṭa 'to give' the PFV-stem ends in -a, the IPFV-stem in -i. Regarding the final

---

114   The initial syllable ʔə- is usually dropped when an object suffix follows, e.g. ṭā-ni 'he gave me'.

294 CHAPTER 4

PFV-stem vowel -*a*, the introduction of -*ē*-, and the final IPFV-stem vowel -*i*, this verb follows the same rules as described above for Pattern I weak verbs.

4.11.6 *Pattern V*

4.11.6.1 Morphological Structure

Regular, Geminated (C_2=C_3), Initial/ Medial Weak Roots:

> PFV-stem: tC_1a$C_2$$C_2aC_3$-, ta$C_1aC_2$$C_2aC_3$-
> IPFV-stem: -tC_1a$C_2$$C_2aC_3$, -ta$C_1aC_2$$C_2aC_3$
> AP: mətC_1a$C_2$$C_2$ə$C_3$
> PP: mətC_1a$C_2$$C_2aC_3$

Final Weak Roots:

> PFV-stem: tC_1a$C_2$$C_2$a-, ta$C_1aC_2$$C_2$a-
> IPFV-stem: -tC_1a$C_2$$C_2$a, -ta$C_1aC_2$$C_2$a
> AP: mətC_1a$C_2$$C_2$i
> PP: not attested

The morphological template of this Pattern is similar to Pattern II in that the medial root consonant is doubled. Pattern V has a prefix *t*-, which can be affected by emphasis (cf. 3.4), or assimilate to the following consonant if this is an alveolar or palatal stop, affricate, or fricative (cf. 3.1.3).

The stem-vowels of Pattern V verbs are uniformly *a*, whereas Pattern II shows *ə* as second vowel in the IPFV-stem.

Examples:

> Regular: *tačabbaš—yətčabbaš* 'to learn'
> Geminated: *tmaddad—yətmaddad* 'to stretch out, lie down, take a rest'
> Initial weak: *twannas—yətwannas* 'to enjoy' (< ʔ-n-s), *tʔaxxar—
> yətʔaxxar* 'to be late'
> Medial weak: *tbawwaš—yətbawwaš* 'to cover the face with a *būšīya*'
> Final weak: *taʕadda—yətʕadda* 'to pass by (temporal 'time' or local)',
> *tḥanna—yətḥanna* 'to dye with henna'

4.11.6.2 Semantic Functions

Verbs of this Pattern are usually intransitive and thus normally do not have passive participles. They are often used to express a passive or reflexive meaning for which the active counterpart is mainly expressed by a corresponding Pattern II verb, e.g. *taḏabbaḥ* 'to be killed' (cf. Pattern II *ḏabbaḥ* 'to kill'), *takas-*

MORPHOLOGY

295

sar 'to be broken' (cf. Pattern II *kassar* 'to break sth.'), and *tyawwaz* 'to marry (someone)' (cf. Pattern II *yawwaz* 'to marry (someone) to (someone else), give in marriage').

4.11.6.3   Inflection
(A)   Regular, Geminated, Initial/ Medial Weak Roots

twannas 'to enjoy'	PFV	IPFV	IMP
SG 3 M	*twannas*	*yətwannas*	
3 F	*twannəsat*	*tətwannas*	
2 M	*twannasət, twannasēt*	*tətwannas*	*twannas*
2 F	*twannasti, twannsēti*	*tətwannsīn*	*twannəsi*
1 C	*twannasət, twannasēt*	*ʔatwannas*	
PL 3 M	*twannəsaw*	*yətwannsūn*	
3 F	*twannəsan*	*yətwannsan*	
2 M	*twannastu, twannasētu*	*tətwannsūn*	*tawannsu*
2 F	*twannastan, twannasētan*	*tətwannsan*	*twannəsan*
1 C	*twannasna, twannasēna*	*nətwannas*	

Participles	AP	PP	
SG M	*mətwannəs*	not attested for this verb	
F	*mətwannsa*	——————	
PL M	*mətwannsīn*	——————	
F	*mətwannsāt*	——————	

PFV-constructions of Pattern V regular verbs often insert -*ē*- before consonant-initial suffixes (cf. 4.11.1.1). The second vowel *a* of the IPFV-stem is usually elided when a vowel-initial suffix follows, which leads to a reduction of the double to a single consonant in pronunciation. But there are exceptions to this rule with retention of both the vowel and the double consonant, e.g. *yətwannəs-an* 'they (F) enjoy'. In geminated roots, the vowel and the double consonant are always retained.

296   CHAPTER 4

(B)   Final Weak Roots

ətʕadda ~ taʕadda 'to pass by'	PFV	IPFV	IMP
SG 3 M	*taʕadda*	*yətʕadda*	
3 F	*taʕaddat*	*tətʕadda*	
2 M	*taʕaddēt*	*tətʕadda*	*taʕadda*
2 F	*taʕaddēti*	*tətʕaddīn*	*ʔətʕaddi*
1 C	*taʕaddēt*	*ʔatʕadda*	
PL 3 M	*taʕaddaw*	*yətʕaddūn*	
3 F	*taʕaddan*	*yətʕaddan*	
2 M	*taʕaddētu*	*tətʕaddūn*	*ʔətʕaddu*
2 F	*taʕaddētan*	*tətʕaddan*	*ʔətʕaddan*
1 C	*taʕaddēna*	*nətʕadda*	

Participles	AP	PP
SG M	*mətʕaddi*	not attested

Regarding the final PFV-stem vowel *-a*, the introduction of *-ē-*, and the final IPFV-stem vowel *-a*, Pattern V weak verbs follow the same rules as described above for Pattern I weak verbs.

4.11.7   *Pattern VI*

4.11.7.1   Morphological Structure

Regular, Geminated ($C_2=C_3$), Initial/ Medial Weak Roots:

> PFV-stem: $tC_1\bar{a}C_2aC_3$-, $taC_1\bar{a}C_2aC_3$-
> IPFV-stem: $-tC_1\bar{a}C_2aC_3$, $-taC_1\bar{a}C_2aC_3$
> AP: $m\partial tC_1\bar{a}C_2aC_3$
> PP: not attested

Final Weak Roots:

> PFV-stem: $tC_1\bar{a}C_2a$-
> IPFV-stem: $-tC_1\bar{a}C_2a$
> AP: $m\partial tC_1\bar{a}C_2i$
> PP: not attested

MORPHOLOGY   297

The morphological template of this pattern differs from Pattern III in that it has a prefix *t-*, which can be affected by emphasis (cf. 3.4) or assimilate to the following consonant if this is an alveolar or palatal stop, affricate, or fricative (cf. 3.1.3). Also, the IPFV-stem of Pattern VI differs in its second vowel in both regular and final weak verbs from Pattern III.

Examples:

> Regular: *tbārak—yətbārak* 'to congratulate (sb.)'
> Geminated: *tḥābab—yətḥābab* 'to kiss each other'
> Initial weak: *taʔāmar—yətʔāmar ~ yətyāmar* 'to complot (against sb.); order (sb.) around'
> Medial weak: *tšāwaf—yətšāwaf* 'to see each other', *ṭṭāwab—yəṭṭāwab* 'to yawn' (< ṭ-ʔ-b)
> Final weak: *tsāwa—yətsāwa* 'to become equal'

4.11.7.2   Semantic Functions
Verbs of this Pattern usually imply mutual action.

4.11.7.3   Inflection
(A)   Regular, Geminated, Initial/ Medial Weak Roots

tbārak 'to bless sb.; congratulate sb.'	PFV	IPFV	IMP
SG 3 M	*tbārak*	*yətbārak*	
3 F	*tbārəkat*	*tətbārak*	
2 M	*tbārakət ~ tbārakēt*	*tətbārak*	*tbārak*
2 F	*tbārakti ~ tbārakēti*	*tətbārakīn*	*tbāraki*
1 C	*tbārakət ~ tbārakēt*	*ʔatbārak*	
PL 3 M	*tbārəkaw*	*yətbārakūn*	
3 F	*tbārəkan*	*yətbārakan*	
2 M	*tbāraktu ~ tbārakētu*	*tətbārakūn*	*tbāraku*
2 F	*tbāraktan ~ tbārakētan*	*tətbārakan*	*tbārakan*
1 C	*tbārakna ~ tbārakēna*	*nətbārak*	

Participles	AP	PP	
SG M	*mətbārak*	not attested	

298   CHAPTER 4

The final vowel of the PFV-stem and the IPFV-stem may be elided when a vowel-initial suffix follows. In geminated roots, the vowel is always retained, e.g. *yəṭḥābəb-ūn* 'they (M) kiss each other'. PFV-forms with consonant-initial suffixes may insert *-ē-* (cf. 4.11.1.1).

(B)   Final Weak Roots

tlāga 'to meet (accidentally)'	PFV	IPFV	IMP
SG 3 M	*tlāga*	*yətlāga*	
3 F	*tlāgat*	*tətlāga*	
2 M	*tlāgēt*	*tətlāga*	not attested
2 F	*tlāgēti*	*tətlāgīn*	not attested
1 C	*tlāgēt*	*ʔatlāga*	
PL 3 M	*tlāgaw*	*yətlāgūn*	
3 F	*tlāgan*	*yətlāgan*	
2 M	*tlāgētu*	*tətlāgūn*	not attested
2 F	*tlāgētan*	*tətlāgan*	not attested
1 C	*tlāgēna*	*nətlāga*	

Participles	AP	PP	
SG M	*mətlāgi*	not attested	

Regarding the final PFV-stem vowel *-a*, the introduction of *-ē-*, and the final IPFV-stem vowel *-a*, Pattern VI weak verbs follow the same rules as described above for Pattern I weak verbs.

4.11.8   *Pattern VII*
4.11.8.1   Morphological Structure
Regular and Initial Weak Roots:

> PFV-stem: $ʔənC_1əC_2aC_3$-
> IPFV-stem: $-nC_1vC_2əC_3$
> AP: $mənC_1əC_2əC_3$
> PP: not attested

MORPHOLOGY 299

Geminated Roots:

> PFV-stem: ʔənC$_1$aC$_2$C$_2$-
> IPFV-stem: -nC$_1$aC$_2$C$_2$
> AP: mənC$_1$aC$_2$C$_2$
> PP: not attested

Medial Weak Roots:

> PFV-stem: ʔənC$_1$āC$_3$-
> IPFV-stem: -nC$_1$āC$_3$
> AP: mənC$_1$āC$_3$
> PP: not attested

Final Weak Roots:

> PFV-stem: ʔənC$_1$əC$_2$a-
> IPFV-stem: -nC$_1$əC$_2$i
> AP: mənC$_1$əC$_2$i
> PP: not attested

The morphological template of this pattern is characterized by the prefix *ʔən-*. In both the PFV-stem and the IPFV-stem of medial weak verbs, the vowel is *ā*. In Pattern VII final weak verbs, the PFV-stem ends in *-a* and the IPFV-stem in *-i*.
  Examples:

> Regular: *ʔənfətaḥ—yənfətəḥ* 'to be opened', *ʔənməṭal—yənməṭəl* 'to lie down'
> Geminated: *ʔənḥall—yənḥall* 'to be opened', *ʔənḍarr—yənḍarr* 'to be hurt'
> Initial weak: *ʔənwəčal—yənwəčəl* 'to be eaten, be eatable'
> Medial weak: *ʔənṣād—yənṣād* 'to be fished'
> Final weak: *ʔənčəfa—yənčəfi* 'to fall over, tip over', *ʔənləga—yənləgi* 'to be found'

4.11.8.2   Semantic Functions
Pattern VII is usually—though not exclusively—used to express passive voice. Therefore, verbs of this pattern usually have no passive participles. This pattern is further used to express a "passive-potential" (Erwin 1963: 73), which in English could often be expressed with an adjective ending in '-able' or '-ible':

e.g. *ʔənwəčəl* 'to be eaten, be eatable' and *ʔənšāf* 'to be visible ~ can be seen'. In this sense they occur mainly negated as in the following example from my corpus:

(6) [X1]
     *mā   yənwəčəl,   əy waḷḷa,   hassa **hēč**.*
     NEG be_eaten.IPFV.3SG.M yes by_God now   DP
     '(The food nowadays) can't be eaten, by God; now it's like that [that bad]'

4.11.8.3   Inflection
(A)   Regular and Initial Weak Roots

ʔənməṭal 'to lie down'	PFV	IPFV	IMP
SG 3 M	*ʔənməṭal*	*yənməṭal*	
3 F	*ʔənməṭlat*	*tənməṭal*	
2 M	*ʔənməṭaләt*	*tənməṭal*	*ʔənməṭal*
2 F	*ʔənməṭalti*	*tənməṭlīn*	*ʔənməṭli*
1 C	*ʔənməṭaләt*	*ʔanməṭal*	
PL 3 M	*ʔənməṭlaw*	*yənməṭlūn*	
3 F	*ʔənməṭlan*	*yənməṭlan*	
2 M	*ʔənməṭaltu*	*tənməṭlūn*	*ʔənməṭlu*
2 F	*ʔənməṭaltan*	*tənməṭlan*	*ʔənməṭlan*
1 C	*ʔənməṭalna*	*nənməṭal*	

Participles	AP
SG M	*mənməṭal*

The PFV-stem vowel *a* is usually elided before vowel-initial suffixes. Some speakers insert -*ē*- before consonant-initial suffixes in verbs of this Pattern (cf. 4.11.1.1). In the IPFV-forms which have suffixes the stem is -nC_1aC_2C_3-, eliding the vowel *ə* of the final stem-syllable and showing *a*, not *ə*, after the first root consonant.

MORPHOLOGY

(B) Geminated Roots

Ɂənḍarr 'to be damaged'	**PFV**	**IPFV**	**IMP**
SG 3 M	*Ɂənḍarr*	*yənḍarr*	
3 F	*Ɂənḍarrat*	*tənḍarr*	
2 M	*Ɂənḍarrēt*	*tənḍarr*	not attested
2 F	*Ɂənḍarrēti*	*tənḍarr*	not attested
1 C	*Ɂənḍarrēt*	*Ɂanḍarr*	
PL 3 M	*Ɂənḍarraw*	*yənḍarrūn*	
3 F	*Ɂənḍarran*	*yənḍarran*	
2 M	*Ɂənḍarrētu*	*tənḍarrūn*	not attested
2 F	*Ɂənḍarrētan*	*tənḍarran*	not attested
1 C	*Ɂənḍarrēna*	*nənḍarr*	
Participles	**AP**		
SG M	*mənḍarr*		

As noted for geminated roots of Pattern I, those of Pattern VII insert of -*ē*- in PFV forms with consonant-initial inflectional suffixes; cf. 4.11.1.1.

(C) Medial Weak Roots

Ɂənšāf 'to be seen'	**PFV**	**IPFV**	**IMP**
SG 3 M	*Ɂənšāf*	*yənšāf*	
3 F	*Ɂənšāfat*	*tənšāf*	
2 M	*Ɂənšəfət*	*tənšāf*	not attested
2 F	*Ɂənšəfti*	*tənšāfīn*	not attested
1 C	*Ɂənšəfət*	*Ɂanšāf*	
PL 3 M	*Ɂənšāfaw*	*yənšāfūn*	
3 F	*Ɂənšāfan*	*yənšāfan*	
2 M	*Ɂənšəftu*	*tənšāfūn*	not attested
2 F	*Ɂənšəftan*	*tənšāfan*	not attested
1 C	*Ɂənšəfna*	*nənšāf*	

302   CHAPTER 4

(*cont.*)

Participles	AP
SG M	*mənšāf*

(D)   Final Weak Roots

ʔənčəfa 'to fall/tip over'	PFV	IPFV	IMP
SG 3 M	*ʔənčəfa*	*yənčəfi*	
3 F	*ʔənčəfat*	*tənčəfi*	
2 M	*ʔənčəfēt*	*tənčəfi*	not attested
2 F	*ʔənčəfēti*	*tənčəfīn*	not attested
1 C	*ʔənčəfēt*	*ʔančəfi*	
PL 3 M	*ʔənčəfaw*	*yənčəfūn*	
3 F	*ʔənčəfan*	*yənčəfan*	
2 M	*ʔənčəfētu*	*tənčəfūn*	not attested
2 F	*ʔənčəfētan*	*tənčəfan*	not attested
1 C	*ʔənčəfēna*	*nənčəfi*	

Participles	AP
SG M	*mənčəfi*

Regarding the final PFV-stem vowel *-a*, the introduction of *-ē-*, and the final IPFV-stem vowel *-i*, Pattern VII final weak verbs follow the same rules as described above for Pattern I weak verbs.

4.11.9   *Pattern VIII*
4.11.9.1   Morphological Structure
Regular and Initial Weak Roots:

> PFV-stem: $ʔəC_1təC_2aC_3$-, $ʔəC_1taC_2aC_3$
> IPFV-stem: -$C_1təC_2əC_3$
> AP: $məC_1təC_2əC_3$
> PP: not attested

MORPHOLOGY

Geminated Roots:

> PFV-stem: $\text{ʔəC}_1\text{taC}_2\text{C}_2\text{-}$
> IPFV-stem: $\text{-C}_1\text{taC}_2\text{C}_2$
> AP: $\text{məC}_1\text{taC}_2\text{C}_2$
> PP: not attested

Medial Weak Roots:

> PFV-stem: $\text{ʔəC}_1\text{tāC}_3\text{-}$
> IPFV-stem: $\text{-C}_1\text{tāC}_3$
> AP: $\text{məC}_1\text{tāC}_3$
> PP: not attested

Final Weak Roots:

> PFV-stem: $\text{ʔəC}_1\text{tvC}_2\text{a-}$
> IPFV-stem: $\text{-C}_1\text{təC}_2\text{i}$
> AP: $\text{məC}_1\text{təC}_2\text{i}$
> PP: not attested

Double (Initial and Final) Weak Roots:

> PFV-stem: $\text{ʔəttaC}_2\text{a}$
> IPFV-stem: $\text{-ttəC}_2\text{i}$
> AP: $\text{məttəC}_2\text{i}$
> PP: not attested

Pattern VIII verbs are characterized by the infix *-t-* after the first root consonant. Phonologically, this infix *t-* can be affected by emphasis (cf. 3.4), or might assimilate to the preceding consonant if this is an alveolar or palatal stop, affricate, or fricative (cf. 3.1.3). In initial weak Pattern VIII verbs, which are however not very common, C_1 assimilates to the following pattern consonant *-t-*. In Pattern VIII medial weak verbs, both the PFV-stem vowel and the IPFV-stem vowel is *ā*.

Examples:

> Regular: *ʔəštaġal*—*yəštaġəl* 'to work', *ʔəntəšal*—*yəntəšəl* 'to catch a cold', *ʔəftəkar*—*yəftəkər* 'to think, believe'
> Geminated: *ʔəftarr*—*yəftarr* 'to go around, wander'

304 CHAPTER 4

Medial weak: *ʔəḥtāǧ—yəḥtāǧ*[115] 'to need', *ʔəʕtāz* (ʕ-w-z)—*yəʕtāz* 'to need', *ʔərtāḥ—yərtāḥ* 'to relax', *ʔəštāg—yəštāg* 'to miss'
Final weak: *ʔəṣṭaba—yəṣṭəbi* 'to watch; pay attention (to)', *ʔəštaha—yəštəhi* 'to desire (food)'

Double (initial and final) weak: *ʔəttača—yəttəči* (ʕala) (cf. CA w-k-ʔ) 'to support one's weight (on), lean (against)'

4.11.9.2 Semantic Functions
Verbs in this pattern can be both transitive or intransitive and can have various meanings.

4.11.9.3 Inflection
(A) Regular roots

ʔəštaǧal 'to work'	PFV	IPFV	IMP
SG 3 M	*ʔəštaǧal*	*yəštəǧəl*	
3 F	*ʔəštəǧlat*	*təštəǧəl*	
2 M	*ʔəštaǧalət*	*təštəǧəl*	(*ʔə*)*štəǧəl*
2 F	*ʔəštaǧalti*	*təštaǧlīn*	(*ʔə*)*štaǧli*
1 C	*ʔəštaǧalət*	*ʔaštəǧəl*	
PL 3 M	*ʔəštəǧlaw*	*yəštaǧlūn*	
3 F	*ʔəštəǧlan*	*yəštaǧlan*	
2 M	*ʔəštaǧaltu*	*təštaǧlūn*	(*ʔə*)*štaǧlu*
2 F	*ʔəštaǧaltan*	*təštaǧlan*	(*ʔə*)*štaǧlan*
1 C	*ʔəštaǧalna*	*nəštəǧəl*	

Participles	AP	PP
SG M	*məštəbəh* (different word because there is no used AP of the verb *ʔəštaǧal*)	not attested
F	*məštəbha*	------
PL M	*məštəbhīn*	------
F	*məštəbhāt*	------

---

115 But *yəḥtāy* via *ǧ* > *y* in the phrase *mā yəḥtāy* 'it is not necessary that …'.

MORPHOLOGY   305

The vowel *a* in the final syllable of the PFV-stem is elided before vowel-initial
suffixes and the vowel in the preceding syllable raised to *ə*. Some speakers insert
-ē- in Pattern XIII (regular) PFV forms with consonant-initial suffixes (cf. 4.11.1.1).
In the IPFV-forms which have suffixes the stem is $-C_1taC_2C_3-$, i.e. the vowel *ə* of
the final syllable of the stem is elided and the first vowel is *a*.

(B)   Geminated Roots

ʔəftarr 'to go around'	PFV	IPFV	IMP
SG 3 M	*ʔəftarr*	*yəftarr*	
3 F	*ʔəftarrat*	*təftarr*	
2 M	*ʔəftarrēt*	*təftarr*	*ʔəftarr*
2 F	*ʔəftarrēti*	*təftarrīn*	*ʔəftarri*
1 C	*ʔəftarrēt*	*ʔaftarr*	
PL 3 M	*ʔəftarraw*	*yəftarrūn*	
3 F	*ʔəftarran*	*yəftarran*	
2 M	*ʔəftarrētu*	*təftarrūn*	*ʔəftarru*
2 F	*ʔəftarrētan*	*təftarran*	*ʔəftarran*
1 C	*ʔəftarrēna*	*nəftarr*	

Participles	AP	PP
SG M	*məftarr*	not attested

As noted for geminated roots of Pattern I, also Pattern VIII (geminated type)
PFV forms with consonant-initial inflectional suffixes insert *-ē-*, cf. 4.11.1.1.

(C)   Medial Weak Roots

ʔəʕtāz 'to need'	PFV	IPFV	IMP
SG 3 M	*ʔəʕtāz*	*yəʕtāz*	
3 F	*ʔəʕtāzat*	*təʕtāz*	
2 M	*ʔəʕtāzēt*	*təʕtāz*	not attested
2 F	*ʔəʕtāzēti*	*təʕtāzīn*	not attested
1 C	*ʔəʕtāzēt*	*ʔaʕtāz*	

306 CHAPTER 4

(*cont.*)

ʔəʕtāz 'to need'	PFV	IPFV	IMP
PL 3 M	*ʔəʕtāzaw*	*yəʕtāzūn*	
3 F	*ʔəʕtāzan*	*yəʕtāzan*	
2 M	*ʔəʕtāzētu*	*təʕtāzūn*	not attested
2 F	*ʔəʕtāzētan*	*təʕtāzan*	not attested
1 C	*ʔəʕtāzēna*	*nəʕtāz*	

Participles	AP	PP
SG M	*məʕtāz*	not attested

Unlike medial weak verbs of Pattern I, Pattern VIII medial weak verbs are generally constructed via insertion of -*ē*- before consonant-initial suffixes; cf. 4.11.1.1.

(D) Final Weak Roots

ʔəštaha 'to desire'	PFV	IPFV	IMP
SG 3 M	*ʔəštaha*	*yəštəhi*	
3 F	*ʔəštahat*	*təštəhi*	
2 M	*ʔəštahēt*	*təštəhi*	not attested
2 F	*ʔəštahēti*	*təštəhīn*	not attested
1 C	*ʔəštahēt*	*ʔaštəhi*	
PL 3 M	*ʔəštahaw*	*yəštəhūn*	
3 F	*ʔəštahan*	*yəštəhan*	
2 M	*ʔəštahētu*	*təštəhūn*	not attested
2 F	*ʔəštahētan*	*təštəhan*	not attested
1 C	*ʔəštahēna*	*nəštəhi*	

Participles	AP	PP
SG M	*məštəhi*	not attested

MORPHOLOGY 307

Regarding the final PFV-stem vowel -*a*, the introduction of -*ē*-, and the final IPFV-stem vowel -*i*, Pattern VIII final weak verbs follow the same rules as described above for Pattern I weak verbs.

(E) Double (Initial and Final) Weak Roots

ʔəttača (*ʕala*) 'to lean (against)'	PFV	IPFV	IMP
SG 3 M	*ʔəttača*	*yəttáči*	
3 F	*ʔəttačat*	*təttáči*	
2 M	*ʔəttačēt*	*təttáči*	not attested
2 F	*ʔəttačēti*	*təttáčīn*	not attested
1 C	*ʔəttačēt*	*ʔáttáči*	
PL 3 M	*ʔəttačaw*	*yəttačūn*	
3 F	*ʔəttačan*	*yəttáčan*	
2 M	*ʔəttačētu*	*təttačūn*	not attested
2 F	*ʔəttačētan*	*təttáčan*	not attested
1 C	*ʔəttačēna*	*nəttáči*	
Participles	AP	PP	
SG M	*məttáči*	not attested	

4.11.10 *Pattern IX*
This Pattern is no longer productively used in KhA.

4.11.11 *Pattern X*
4.11.11.1 Morphological Structure
Regular and Initial Weak Roots:

> PFV-stem: (ʔə)staC₁C₂aC₃-
> IPFV-stem: -staC₁C₂əC₃
> AP: məstaC₁C₂əC₃
> PP: not attested

308

Geminated Roots:

> PFV-stem: $(\text{ʔə})\text{staC}_1\text{aC}_2\text{C}_2$-
> IPFV-stem: $-\text{staC}_1\text{əC}_2\text{C}_2$
> AP: $\text{məstəC}_1\text{əC}_2\text{C}_2$
> PP: not attested

Initial Weak Roots:

> PFV-stem: $(\text{ʔə})\text{stāC}_2\text{aC}_3$-, $(\text{ʔə})\text{stōC}_2\text{aC}_3$-
> IPFV-stem: $-\text{stāC}_2\text{əC}_3$, $-\text{stōC}_2\text{əC}_3$
> AP: $\text{məstāC}_2\text{əC}_3$, $\text{məstōC}_2\text{əC}_3$
> PP: not attested

Medial Weak Roots:

> PFV-stem: $(\text{ʔə})\text{staC}_1\text{āC}_3$-
> IPFV-stem: $-\text{stəC}_1\text{īC}_3$, $-\text{stəC}_1\text{āC}_3$
> AP: $\text{məstəC}_1\text{āC}_2$, $\text{məstəC}_1\text{īC}_3$
> PP: not attested

Final Weak Roots:

> PFV-stem: $(\text{ʔə})\text{staC}_1\text{C}_2\text{a}$-
> IPFV-stem: $-\text{staC}_1\text{C}_2\text{i}$
> AP: $\text{məstaC}_1\text{C}_2\text{i}$
> PP: not attested

Medial and Final Weak Roots:

> PFV-stem: $(\text{ʔə})\text{staC}_2\text{a}$-
> IPFV-stem: $-\text{stəC}_2\text{i}$
> AP: $\text{məstəC}_2\text{i}$
> PP: not attested

Pattern x verbs are characterized by the prefix -ʔasta- or -ʔəstə- before the first root consonant. If C_1 is an emphatic, the consonants s and t are prone to assimilate to the emphatic consonant. The final vowel of this prefix is usually a, but a or ə in closed syllables, i.e. when followed by only a single consonant (cf. Ingham 1974: 309). In medial weak verbs the PFV-vowel is always ā,

MORPHOLOGY   309

while the IPFV-vowel is *ī* or *ā*. In final weak verbs, the PFV-stem ends in -*a*, the
IPFV-stem in -*i*.

Examples:

> Regular: *ʔəstaxbar—yəstaxbər* 'to seek news', *ʔastaʕdal—yastaʕdəl* 'to
> recover', *ʔəstaʕmal—yəstaʕməl* 'to use'
> Geminated: *ʔəstaʕazz—yəstəʕəzz* (*b*-) 'to care for sb./sth.'
> Initial weak: *ʔəstāhal—yəstāhəl* (ʔ-h-l) 'to deserve', *ʔəstōrah—yəstōrəh*
> 'to inhale'
> Medial weak: *ʔəstafād—yəstəfād* 'to derive benefit, use', and *ʔəstarāḥ—*
> *yəstərāḥ ~ yəstərīḥ* 'to relax'
> Final weak: *ʔəstabda—yəstabdi* 'to begin'
> Medial and final weak: *ʔəstaha—yəstəhi* 'to be ashamed'

4.11.11.2   Semantic Functions

Verbs in this pattern can be both transitive or intransitive. Some Pattern X verbs
are associated with adopting an attitude, asking for something, or with emotional states (cf. Ingham 1974: 309), but generally they have a variety of meanings.

4.11.11.3   Inflection
(A)   Regular Roots

ʔəstaʕmal 'to use'	PFV	IPFV	IMP
SG 3 M	*ʔəstaʕmal*	*yəstaʕməl*	
3 F	*ʔəstaʕmələt*	*təstaʕməl*	
2 M	*ʔəstaʕmələt*	*təstaʕməlīn*	*staʕməl*
2 F	*ʔəstaʕmalti*	*təstaʕməl*	*staʕməli*
1 C	*ʔəstaʕmalət*	*ʔastaʕməl*	
PL 3 M	*ʔəstaʕmələw*	*yəstaʕməlūn*	*staʕməlu*
3 F	*ʔəstaʕmələn*	*yəstaʕmələn*	*staʕmələn*
2 M	*ʔəstaʕmaltu*	*təstaʕməlūn*	
2 F	*ʔəstaʕmaltan*	*təstaʕmələn*	
1 C	*ʔəstaʕmalna*	*nəstaʕməl*	

Participles	AP	PP
SG M	*məstaʕməl*	not attested

310   CHAPTER 4

The vowel *a* in the final syllable of the PFV-stem is raised to *ə* before vowel-initial suffixes. PFV-constructions of Pattern X regular verbs may insert *-ē-* before consonant-initial suffixes (cf. 4.11.1.1).

(B)   Geminated Roots

ʔəstaʕazz 'to care (for sb.)'	PFV	IPFV	IMP
SG 3 M	*ʔəstaʕazz*	*yəstəʕəzz*	
3 F	*ʔəstaʕazzat*	*təstəʕəzz*	
2 M	*ʔəstaʕazzēt*	*təstəʕəzz*	*stəʕazz*
2 F	*ʔəstaʕazzēti*	*təstəʕəzzīn*	*stəʕazzi*
1 C	*ʔəstaʕazzēt*	*ʔastaʕəzz*	
PL 3 M	*ʔəstaʕazzaw*	*yəstəʕəzzūn*	
3 F	*ʔəstaʕazzan*	*yəstəʕəzzan*	
2 M	*ʔəstaʕazzētu*	*təstəʕəzzūn*	*stəʕazzu*
2 F	*ʔəstaʕazzētan*	*təstəʕəzzan*	*stəʕazzan*
1 C	*ʔəstaʕazzēna*	*nəstəʕəzz*	
Participles	AP	PP	
SG M	*məstəʕəzz*	not attested	

As noted for geminated roots of Pattern I, the PFV forms with consonant-initial inflectional suffixes of geminated roots of Pattern X are constructed via insertion of *-ē-*; cf. 4.11.1.1.

(C)   Initial Weak Roots

(ʔə)stāhal 'to deserve' *(ʔə)stōraḥ* 'to inhale'	PFV	IPFV	IMP
SG 3 M	*(ʔə)stāhal, (ʔə)stōraḥ*	*yəstāhəl, yəstōraḥ*	
3 F	*(ʔə)stāhəlat, (ʔə)stōrəhat*	*təstāhəl, təstōraḥ*	
2 M	*(ʔə)stāhalēt, (ʔə)stōraḥēt*	*təstāhəl, təstōraḥ*	*stōrəḥ*
2 F	*(ʔə)stāhalēti, (ʔə)stōraḥēti*	*təstāhlīn, təstōrḥīn*	*stōraḥi*
1 C	*(ʔə)stāhalēt, (ʔə)stōraḥēt*	*ʔastāhəl, ʔastōrəḥ*	
PL 3 M	*(ʔə)stāhalaw, (ʔə)stōrəḥaw*	*yəstāhlūn, yəstōrḥūn*	
3 F	*(ʔə)stāhəlan, (ʔə)stōrəhan*	*yəstāhlan, yəstōrḥan*	

MORPHOLOGY 311

(cont.)

(ʔə)stāhal 'to deserve' PFV		IPFV	IMP
(ʔə)stōraḥ 'to inhale'			
2 M	*(ʔə)stāhalētu, (ʔə)stōraḥētu*	*təstāhlūn, təstōrḥūn*	*stōraḥu*
2 F	*(ʔə)stāhalētan, (ʔə)stōraḥētan*	*təstāhlan, təstōrḥan*	*stōraḥan*
1 C	*(ʔə)stāhalēna, (ʔə)stōraḥēna*	*nəstāhəl, nəstōrəḥ*	

Participles	AP	PP
SG M	*məstāhəl*	not attested

The vowel *a* in the final syllable of the PFV-stem is either elided or raised to *ə* before vowel-initial suffixes. The insertion of *-ē-* in PFV forms with consonant-initial vowel suffixes is optional.

The vowel *ə* in the final syllable of the IPFV-stem is usually elided before vowel-initial suffixes.

(D)   Medial Weak Roots

ʔəstafād	PFV	IPFV	IMP
'to benefit, use'			
ʔəstarāḥ			
'to relax'			
SG 3 M	*ʔəstafād,*	*yəstəfād*	
	ʔəstarāḥ	*yəstərāḥ ~ yəstərīḥ*	
3 F	*ʔəstafādat*	*təstəfād*	
	ʔəstarāḥat	*təstərāḥ ~ təstərīḥ*	
2 M	*ʔəstafādēt*	*təstəfād*	*(ʔə)stərīḥ*, less common:
	ʔəstarāḥēt	*təstərāḥ ~ təstərīḥ*	*(ʔə)stərāḥ*
2 F	*ʔəstafādēti*	*təstəfādīn*	*(ʔə)stərīḥi ~ (ʔə)stərāḥi*
	ʔəstarāḥēti	*təstərāḥīn ~ təstərīḥīn*	
1 C	*ʔəstafādēt*	*ʔastəfād*	
	ʔəstarāḥēt	*ʔastərāḥ ~ ʔastərīḥ*	
PL 3 M	*ʔəstafādaw*	*yəstəfādūn*	
	ʔəstarāḥaw	*yəstərāḥūn ~ yəstərīḥūn*	

312 CHAPTER 4

(*cont.*)

Ɂəstafād 'to benefit, use' *Ɂəstarāḥ* 'to relax'	PFV	IPFV	IMP
3 F	*Ɂəstafādan* *Ɂəstarāḥan*	*yəstəfādan* *yəstərāḥan ~ yəstərīḥan*	
2 M	*Ɂəstafādētu* *Ɂəstarāḥētu*	*təstəfādūn* *təstərāḥūn ~ təstərīḥūn*	*(Ɂə)stərīḥu ~ (Ɂə)stərāḥu*
2 F	*Ɂəstafādētan* *Ɂəstarāḥētan*	*təstəfādan* *təstərāḥan ~ təstərīḥan*	*(Ɂə)stərīḥan ~ (Ɂə)stərāḥan*
1 C	*Ɂəstafādēna* *Ɂəstarāḥēna*	*nəstəfād* *nəstərāḥ ~ nəstərīḥ*	

Participles	AP	PP	
SG M	*məstəfād* *məstərīḥ ~* *məstərāḥ*	not attested	

Unlike in medial weak verbs of Pattern I, Pattern X medial weak verbs are generally constructed via insertion of *-ē-* before consonant-initial suffixes; cf. 4.11.1.1.

(E)   Final Weak Roots

Ɂəstabda 'to begin'	PFV	IPFV	IMP
SG 3 M	*Ɂəstabda*	*yəstabdi*	
3 F	*Ɂəstabdat*	*təstabdi*	
2 M	*Ɂəstabdēt*	*təstabdi*	*Ɂəstabdi*
2 F	*Ɂəstabdēti*	*təstabdīn*	*Ɂəstabdi*
1 C	*Ɂəstabdēt*	*Ɂastabdi*	
PL 3 M	*Ɂəstabdaw*	*yəstabdūn*	
3 F	*Ɂəstabdan*	*yəstabdan*	
2 M	*Ɂəstabdētu*	*təstabdūn*	*Ɂəstabdu*

MORPHOLOGY   313

(cont.)

ʔəstabda 'to begin'	PFV	IPFV	IMP
2 F	*ʔəstabdētan*	*təstabdan*	*ʔəstabdan*
1 C	*ʔəstabdēna*	*nəstabdi*	

Participles	AP	PP
SG M	*məstabdi*	not attested

As can be seen from the table, in Pattern X final weak verbs, the final PFV-stem vowel *-a* is elided when a consonant-initial inflectional suffix is added and *-ē-* is introduced before the suffix. The final IPFV-stem vowel *-i* is elided when one of the vowel-initial inflectional suffixes is added.

(F)   Medial and Final Weak

ʔəstaḥa (ḥ-y-y) 'to be ashamed'	PFV	IPFV	IMP
SG 3 M	*ʔəstaḥa*	*yəstəḥi*	
3 F	*ʔəstaḥat*	*təstəḥi*	
2 M	*ʔəstaḥēt*	*təstəḥi*	*ʔəstəḥi*
2 F	*ʔəstaḥēti*	*təstəḥīn*	*ʔəstəḥi*
1 C	*ʔəstaḥēt*	*ʔastəḥi*	
PL 3 M	*ʔəstaḥaw*	*yəstəḥūn*	
3 F	*ʔəstaḥan*	*yəstəḥan*	
2 M	*ʔəstaḥētu*	*təstəḥūn*	*ʔəstəḥu*
2 F	*ʔəstaḥētan*	*təstəḥan*	*ʔəstəḥan*
1 C	*ʔəstaḥēna*	*nəstəḥi*	

Participles	AP	PP
SG M	*məstəḥi*	not attested

314 CHAPTER 4

4.11.12 *Quadriliterals*
4.11.12.1 Morphological Structure
Basic Pattern

Regular Roots:

> PFV-stem: $C_1aC_2C_3aC_4$ -
> IPFV-stem: -$C_1aC_2C_3 \partial C_4$
> AP: $mC_1aC_2C_3 \partial C_4$
> PP: not attested

C_2=w/y Roots:

> PFV-stem: $C_1\bar{o}C_3vC_4$-, $C_1\bar{e}C_3vC_4$-
> IPFV-stem: -$C_1\bar{o}C_3 \partial C_4$, -$C_1\bar{e}C_3 \partial C_4$
> AP: $mC_1\bar{o}C_3 \partial C_4$, $mC_1\bar{e}C_3 \partial C_4$
> PP: not attested

C_2 and C_4=w/y Roots:

> PFV-stem: $C_1\bar{o}C_3a$-
> IPFV-stem: -$C_1\bar{o}C_3i$
> AP: not attested
> PP: not attested

Reduplicated Roots:

> PFV-stem: $C_1aC_2C_1aC_2$-
> IPFV-stem: -$C_1aC_2C_1 \partial C_2$
> AP: $mC_1aC_2C_1 \partial C_2$
> PP: not attested

Augmented pattern

Regular Roots:

> PFV-stem: $tC_1aC_2C_3aC_4$-
> IPFV-stem: -$tC_1aC_2C_3aC_4$
> AP: $m \partial tC_1aC_2C_3 \partial C_4$
> PP: not attested

MORPHOLOGY

C_2=w/y Roots:

> PFV-stem: $tC_1\bar{o}C_3aC_4$-, $tC_1\bar{e}C_3aC_4$-
> IPFV-stem: -$tC_1\bar{o}C_3\partial C_4$, -$tC_1\bar{e}C_3\partial C_4$
> AP: $m\partial tC_1\bar{o}C_3\partial C_4$, $m\partial tC_1\bar{e}C_3\partial C_4$
> PP: not attested

Reduplicated Roots:

> PFV-stem: $tC_1aC_2C_1aC_2$-
> IPFV-stem: -$tC_1aC_2C_1\partial C_2$
> AP: $m\partial tC_1aC_2C_1\partial C_2$
> PP: not attested

There are two patterns for quadriliteral verbs: a basic pattern and an augmented pattern marked by a prefix *t*-, which can assimilate to a following consonant as described above for the prefix *t*- of Pattern V.

In classifying the forms with a vowel -$\bar{o}$- or -$\bar{e}$- as quadriliterals with a weak second consonant, I follow the classifications of Bruce Ingham (1974: 317–318 on KhA), Haim Blanc (1964: 110 on Baghdadi Arabic), and Clive Holes (2016: 177–179 on Bahraini Arabic). Other scholars have classified these as extended forms of Pattern III with a vowel -$\bar{o}$- or -$\bar{e}$- instead of -$\bar{a}$- (e.g. Mansour 2006: 237 on Jewish Baghdad Arabic).

Examples:

Basic Pattern

> Regular: *xarmaš—yxarmǝš* 'to scratch', *dardaš—ydardǝš* 'to chat', *xarbaṭ—yxarbǝṭ* 'to mix (up)'
> C_2=w/y: *sōdan—ysōdǝn* 'to be crazy, become crazy', *sōlaf—ysōlǝf* 'to speak, tell, talk', *čēwar—yčēwǝr* 'to turn', *nēšan—ynēšǝn* 'to betroth'
> C_2 and C_4=w/y: *lōla—ylōli* 'to sing a lullaby', *ʕōʕa—yʕōʕi* 'to crow' (ono-matopoetic)
> Reduplicated: *galgal—ygalgǝl* 'to shake (intr., e.g. a tooth)', *lamlam* 'to pick up, collect, gather (the harvest)', *čabčab—yčabčǝb* 'to smoke marihuana', *čakčak—yčakčǝk* 'to smoke opium', *ṭagṭag—yṭagṭǝg* 'to drum on sth., make noise'

316   CHAPTER 4

Augmented Pattern

> Regular: *txarbaṭ—yətxarbaṭ* 'to be confused', *tǧašmar—yətǧašmar* 'to
> joke around'
> C₂=w/y: *tlōlaḥ—yətlōlaḥ* 'to swing', *tḥēwan—yətḥēwan* 'to be boorish,
> act like an animal, stupidly'.
> Reduplicated: *tgalgal—yətgalgəl* 'to shake (intr.; e.g. a tooth)'

4.11.12.2 Semantic Functions

Verbs in this pattern can be both transitive or intransitive. Many of the reduplicated verbs are related to triliteral Pattern I geminated verbs, e.g. *dagdag* 'to
drum' (cf. *dagg* 'to knock'). The quadriliteral verb usually describes a repetitive
or intensive performance of an action (cf. Procházka 1995b: 48–60 on a detailed
description of the semantic categories of reduplicated verbs in Arabic; and El
Zarka 2009: 63–66). Also, many are onomatopoetic (cf. El Zarka 2009: 66), e.g.
maʕmaʕ 'to bleat'.

Many derived pattern quadriliteral verbs are related to basic pattern quadriliteral verbs and often denote a passive meaning of the action indicated by the
verb in the basic pattern—e.g. *ttarǧam—yəttarǧəm* 'to be translated'—or are
derived from a noun: e.g. *tfalsaf* 'to speak learnedly' (cf. *faylasūf* 'philosopher').
In both patterns, verbs frequently derive from nouns, e.g. *sōlaf* 'to tell' < *sālfa*
'story; matter'. Because verbs in this pattern are mostly intransitive, they lack
passive participles.

4.11.12.3 Inflection
(A) Basic Pattern: Regular Roots

xarmaš 'to scratch'	PFV	IPFV	IMP
SG 3 M	*xarmaš*	*yxarməš*	
3 F	*xarməšat*	*txarməš*	
2 M	*xarməšət*	*txarməš*	*xarməš*
2 F	*xarmašti*	*txarməšīn*	*xarməši*
1 C	*xarməšət*	*ʔaxarməš*	
PL 3 M	*xarməšaw*	*yxarməšūn*	
3 F	*xarməšan*	*yxarməšan*	
2 M	*xarmaštu*	*txarməšūn*	*xarməšu*
2 F	*xarmaštan*	*txarməšan*	*xarməšan*
1 C	*xarmašna*	*nxarməš*	

MORPHOLOGY   317

(cont.)

Participles	AP	PP
SG M	*mxarməš*	not attested

The vowel *a* in the final syllable of the PFV-stem is raised before vowel-initial suffixes.

(B)   Basic Pattern: C$_2$=w/y Roots

sōlaf 'to speak, tell, talk' *čēwar* 'to turn'	PFV	IPFV	IMP
SG 3 M	*sōlaf* *čēwar*	*ysōləf, yčēwər*	
3 F	*sōləfat*	*tsōləf, tčēwər*	*sōləf, čēwər*
2 M	*sōləfət ~ sōləfēt* *čēwarət*	*tsōləf, tčēwər*	*sōlfi, čēwri*
2 F	*sōlafti ~ sōləfēti* *čēwarti*	*tsōlfīn, tčēwrīn*	
1 C	*sōləfət ~ sōləfēt* *čēwarət*	*ʔasōləf,* *ʔačēwər*	
PL 3 M	*sōləfaw* *čēwaraw*	*ysōlfūn,* *yčēwrūn*	
3 F	*sōləfan* *čēwaran*	*ysōlfan,* *yčēwran*	
2 M	*sōlaftu ~ sōləfētu* *čēwartu*	*tsōlfūn,* *tčēwrūn*	*sōlfu, čēwru*
2 F	*sōlaftu ~ sōləfētan* *čēwartan*	*tsōlfan,* *tčēwran*	*sōlfan,* *čēwran*
1 C	*sōlafna ~ sōləfēna* *čēwarna*	*nsōləf, nčēwər*	

Participles	AP	PP
SG M	*msōləf, mčēwər*	not attested

318   CHAPTER 4

(C)   Basic Pattern: C₂ and C₄=w/y Roots

lōla 'to sing a lullaby'	PFV	IPFV	IMP
SG 3 M	*lōla*	*ylōli*	
3 F	*lōlat*	*tlōli*	
2 M	*lōlēt*	*tlōli*	*lōli*
2 F	*lōlēti*	*tlōlīn*	*lōli*
1 C	*lōlēt*	*ʔalōli*	
PL 3 M	*lōlaw*	*ylōlūn*	
3 F	*lōlan*	*ylōlan*	
2 M	*lōlētu*	*tlōlūn*	*lōlu*
2 F	*lōlētan*	*tlōlan*	*lōlan*
1 C	*lōlēna*	*nlōli*	

Participles	AP	PP
SG M	not attested	not attested

Regarding the final PFV-stem vowel -*a*, the introduction of -*ē*-, and the final
IPFV-stem vowel -*i*, quadriliteral final weak verbs follow the same rules as
described above for Pattern I weak verbs.

(D)   Basic Pattern: Reduplicated Roots

lamlam 'to collect; harvest'	PFV	IPFV	IMP
SG 3 M	*lamlam*	*ylamləm*	
3 F	*laml̥mat*	*tlamləm*	
2 M	*lamlamət*	*tlamləm*	*lamləm*
2 F	*lamlamti*	*tlaml̥mīn*	*lamləmi*
1 C	*lamlamət*	*ʔalamləm*	
PL 3 M	*lamləmaw*	*ylaml̥mūn*	
3 F	*lamləman*	*ylamləman*	
2 M	*lamlamtu*	*tlaml̥mūn*	*lamləmu*
2 F	*lamlamtan*	*tlaml̥man*	*lamləman*
1 C	*lamlamna*	*nlamləm*	

MORPHOLOGY   319

(cont.)

Participles	AP	PP
SG M	*mlamləm*	not attested

The vowel in the last syllable of the PFV-stem is raised to ə before vowel-initial suffixes and *-ē-* is often inserted before consonant-initial PFV suffixes; cf. 4.11.1.1.

(A₁) Augmented Pattern: Regular Roots

txarbaṭ 'to be confused'	PFV	IPFV	IMP
SG 3 M	*txarbaṭ*	*yətxarbəṭ*	
3 F	*txarbəṭat*	*tətxarbəṭ*	
2 M	*txarbaṭət*	*tətxarbəṭ*	not used
2 F	*txarbaṭṭi*	*tətxarbəṭīn*	not used
1 C	*txarbaṭət*	*ʔatxarbəṭ*	
PL 3 M	*txarbəṭaw*	*yətxarbəṭūn*	
3 F	*txarbəṭan*	*yətxarbəṭan*	
2 M	*txarbaṭṭu*	*tətxarbəṭūn*	not used
2 F	*txarbaṭṭan*	*tətxarbəṭan*	not used
1 C	*txarbaṭna*	*nətxarbəṭ*	

Participles	AP
SG M	*mətxarbəṭ*

The vowel *a* in the final syllable of the PFV-stem is raised to ə before vowel-initial suffixes.

320 CHAPTER 4

(B₁) Augmented Pattern: C₂=w/y Roots

tsōdan 'to become crazy' *ṭḥēwan* 'to act like an animal'	PFV	IPFV	IMP
SG 3 M	*tsōdan, ṭḥēwan*	*yətsōdən, yəṭḥēwən*	
3 F	*tsōdənat, ṭḥēwənat*	*tətsōdən, təṭḥēwən*	
2 M	*tsōdanət, ṭḥēwanət*	*tətsōdən, təṭḥēwən*	not attested
2 F	*tsōdanti, ṭḥēwanti*	*tətsōdənīn, təṭḥēwənīn*	not attested
1 C	*tsōdanət, ṭḥēwanət*	*ʔatsōdən, ʔaṭḥēwən*	
PL 3 M	*tsōdənaw, ṭḥēwənaw*	*yətsōdənūn, yəṭḥēwənūn*	
3 F	*tsōdənan, ṭḥēwənan*	*yətsōdənan, yəṭḥēwənan*	
2 M	*tsōdantu, ṭḥēwantu*	*tətsōdənūn, təṭḥēwənūn*	not attested
2 F	*tsōdantan, ṭḥēwantan*	*tətsōdənan, təṭḥēwənan*	not attested
1 C	*tsōdanna, ṭḥēwanna*	*nətsōdən, nəṭḥēwən*	
Participles	AP		
SG M	*məṭḥēwən*		

The vowel *a* in the final syllable of the PFV-stem is raised to *ə* before vowel-initial suffixes.

(D₂) Augmented Pattern: Reduplicated Roots

tgalgal 'to shake (intr.)'	PFV	IPFV	IMP
SG 3 M	*tgalgal*	*yətgalgəl*	
3 F	*tgalgəlat*	*tətgalgəl*	
2 M	*tgalgalət*	*tətgalgəl*	not used
2 F	*tgalgalti*	*tətgalgəlīn*	not used
1 C	*tgalgalət*	*ʔatgalgəl*	
PL 3 M	*tgalgəlaw*	*yətgalgəlūn*	
3 F	*tgalgəlan*	*yətgalgəlan*	

MORPHOLOGY   321

(*cont.*)

tgalgal 'to shake (intr.)'	PFV	IPFV	IMP
2 M	*tgalgaltu*	*tətgalgəlūn*	not used
2 F	*tgalgaltan*	*tətgalgəlan*	not used
1 C	*tgalgalna*	*nətgalgəl*	

Participles	AP
SG M	*mətgalgəl*

The vowel *a* in the final syllable of the PFV-stem is raised to *ə* before vowel-initial suffixes and -*ē*- is frequently inserted in forms with consonant-initial PFV suffixes; cf. 4.11.1.1.

4.11.13   *Verbal Nouns*
A verbal noun (ar. *maṣdar* lit. 'source') is a fixed nominal form associated with a verb, that describes the event associated with that verb without temporal reference (cf. Rosenhouse 2009: 659).

Semantically, the verbal noun generally corresponds to the gerund in English.

Verbal nouns are also used in the so-called 'absolute object', ar. *mafʕūl muṭlaq* —as in *maḥyūč əḥyāča* 'woven', and *ydagg-na dagg* 'he hits us'. In general, spoken dialects of Arabic use verbal nouns less often than Modern Standard Arabic or Classical Arabic (cf. Rosenhouse 2009: 661). In my corpus there are very few instances of verbal nouns and they appear to be productively used for Pattern I and Pattern II verbs only; a few Pattern III and X verbal nouns are also attested, but they all seem to be loans from MSA (or Persian). As in OA and all contemporary dialects, there are various morphological patterns from which verbal nouns are derived from Pattern I verbs so that the pattern of the corresponding verbal noun cannot be predicted; common patterns are listed below:

Pattern I

CəCəC	*ləʕəb* 'playing'
CaCəC	*ġazəl* 'spinning', *ṭabəx* 'cooking', *ragəṣ* 'dancing', *ʔakəl* 'eating'
CaCCa	*gaʕda* 'sitting'
CaCāC	*karāb* 'plowing'

C(a)CāCa	*ṣabāḥa* 'swimming'
əCCāCa	*əktāba* 'writing'
CəCāC	*ǧəfāf* 'drying'
CəCūC	*sərūḥ* 'grazing'

Geminated Roots

CaCC	*gaṣṣ* 'cutting'
əCCāCa	*əsfāfa* 'braiding'

Initial Weak Roots

CəCāCa	*wənāsa* 'enjoying' (< the Pattern v verb *twannas* 'to enjoy')

Medial Weak Roots

CūC	*gūl* 'saying'
CōCa	*nōma* 'sleep, sleeping', *bōga* 'stealing'
CēC	*ṣēd* 'fishing'
CəyāCa	*ḥəyāča* 'weaving'

Final Weak Roots

CaCi	*ḥači* 'speaking, talking', *maši* 'walking'

Verbal Nouns Derived from Pattern II Verbs Seem to Be a Productive Category, Though Most Lexemes Are Likely Loans from MSA:

taCCīC	*taʕlīm* 'teaching', *tadrīb* 'training', *takrīb* 'trimming (of palm-trees)', *talwīṯ* 'pollution'

Final Week Roots

taCCīya	*tarbīya* 'breeding'

Other verbal nouns attested in the corpus are:

məṣādara 'exporting' (Pattern III), *ʔəxtəlāfa* 'difference; distinction' (Pattern VIII), *ʔəstəfāda* 'benefit' (Pattern X).

MORPHOLOGY

323

4.11.14 *Pseudoverbs*

The pseudoverbs, also called quasi-verbs, used in KhA are listed in the following and are all prepositions with pronominal suffixes. They are all negated with the particle *mā* (cf. 4.8.2.2).

4.11.14.1   *bī-*PRO 'to Be Able to', or 'There Is'

*bī-*PRO can express capability ('to be able to'), or, in impersonal statements, existence ('there is'; cf. 4.8.1.5). Syrian Arabic uses the preposition *fī* plus PRO to express the same meanings (Cowell 1964: 415).[116]

(7)   [M1]
      mā   bī-ya   ʔatrabbaʕ …
      NEG in-1SG sit_cross-legged.IPFV.1SG
      'I cannot sit cross-legged …'

(8)   [F1, describing how they used to prepare *māy həwa*, lit. "air water", a very simple dish of red sauce without meat]
      mā   bī   ṭamāṭa.
      NEG EXIST tomato
      'There were no tomatoes (in the past).'

4.11.14.2   *ʔəl-*PRO 'to Belong to'

(9)   [A1]
      ha-l-ġanam   əl   ʕad-ak   hāy ʔəl-i,   mā-hu   ʔəl-ak!
      DEM-DEF-sheep REL at-2SG.M DEM to-1SG NEG-3SG.M to-2SG.M
      'These sheep that you have, they belong to me, not to you!'

(10) [A6]
      hāy   əl-arəḍ   ʔəl-na.
      DEM DEF-land to-1PL
      'This property belongs to us ~ This property is ours.'

4.11.14.3   *ʕand-*PRO 'to Have'

As in the majority of all modern spoken dialects of Arabic (cf. Procházka 1993: 81–82), the preposition *ʕand ~ ʕənd* plus pronominal suffix is used for the expression of possession, equivalent to the English verb 'to have'.

---

116   Cf. Procházka (2018c: 285) on the possible Aramaic origin of this construction.

324   CHAPTER 4

(11) [M1]

> *ʕand-i wlēdāt   əẓġār   ətnēn.*
> at-1SG boy.DIM.PL little.PL two
> 'I have two little boys.'

4.11.15 *Verbs with Object Suffixes*

This chapter summarizes the morphophonological processes for pronominal suffixation on verbs.

i.   3PL.M ending *-aw* becomes *-ō-* when an object suffix (other than 3SG.M) is added, e.g.
      yāb-aw 'they (PL.M) brought' + 3SG.F suffix (*-hən*) → *yābō-hən* 'they (PL.M) brought them (PL.F)'

ii.   3PL.M ending *-aw* becomes *-ố* when a 3SG.M suffix is added, e.g.
      yāb-aw 'they (PL.M) brought' → *yāb-ố* 'they brought him'

iii.   The vowel in the final syllable of the PFV stem of Pattern I verbs is retained and stressed before vowel-initial object suffixes,[117] e.g.:
      kətab 'he wrote' → *kətáb-a* 'he wrote it (SG.M)'

iv.   In the IPFV of Pattern I verbs, the stem vowel is elided before vowel-initial object suffixes, and a new vowel is inserted after the first root consonant radical to avoid the otherwise resulting three-consonant cluster, e.g.:
      yəktəb 'he writes' → *ykətb-a* 'he writes it (SG.M)'

v.   When the 3SG.M suffix *-a* is added to a word that ends in a vowel, this vowel is lengthened and stressed, e.g.
      ġassal-nā 'we washed' → *ġassal-nā́* 'we washed it (SG.M)'

vi.   Final *-n* of IPFV verbs is elided before indirect object suffixes, e.g.:
      tġannīn 'you (SG.F) sing' → *tġannī-la* 'you (SG.F) sing for him'
      ywaddūn 'they (PL.M) send' → *ywaddū-lhən* 'they (PL.M) send (to) them (PL.F)'

vii. The 3SG.F PFV verbal suffix *-at* doubles the *-t* when a vowel-initial suffix is added, e.g.:
      ḥabbəb-at 'she kissed' → *ḥabbəb-att-a* 'she kissed him' (cf. 3.1.5 for further examples)

viii. The 3PL.F IPFV and PFV and (the optional) 1SG IPFV verbal suffix *-an* doubles the *-n* when a vowel-initial suffix is added, e.g.:
      ʔaḥaṭṭ-an 'I put' → *ʔaḥaṭṭ-ann-a* 'I put it (SG.M)' (cf. 3.1.5 for further examples)

---

117   Ingham (1973: 541) classifies the pattern CəCaC-a as *ḥaḍar* in contrast with the *ʕarab* pattern CCəC-a: e.g. *ḏbəḥ-a* 'he killed him'.

MORPHOLOGY   325

TABLE 14   *šāf* 'he saw' and *šāfat* 'she saw' with object suffixes

	šāf 'he saw' + object suffixes	*šāfat* 'she saw' + object suffixes
SG 1 C	*šāf-ni*	*šāfat-ni*
2 M	*šāf-ak*	*šāfatt-ak*
2 F	*šāf-əč*	*šāfatt-əč*
3 M	*šāf-a*	*šāfatt-a*
3 F	*šāf-ha*	*šāfat-ha*
PL 1 C	*šāf-na*	*šāfat-na*
2 M	*šāf-kəm*	*šāfat-kəm*
2 F	*šāf-čən*	*šāfat-čən*
3 M	*šāf-həm*	*šāfat-həm*
3 F	*šāf-hən*	*šāfat-hən*

ix. Geminated and medial weak SG.M PFV verbs optionally insert an anap-
     tyctic long vowel -*ā*- before consonant-initial suffixes (cf. 3.7.1), e.g.:
     ḥatt-ā-ha ~ *ḥatt-ha* 'he put it (F) down', *gāl-ā-lha* ~ *gāl-əlha* 'he told her'

x.   When an object suffix is added to a SG.F active participle of Pattern I verbs
     ($C_1\bar{a}C_2C_3a$), the AP ends in -*at*- as do feminine nouns ending in -*a* when
     in construct state (cf. 4.9.3). When the suffix is vowel-initial, one of the
     following two alternative changes occurs:

     (i)   Doubling of -*t*-: $C_1\bar{a}C_2C_3$att-, e.g.:
           šāyfa 'she had seen' (AP) + -*əč* (2SG.F pronominal suffix) → *šāyfatt-əč*
           'she saw you (SG.F)'

     (ii) Vowel shift: elision of final -*a* and insertion of an anaptyctic vowel *ə*
           after C_2: $C_1\bar{a}C_2\partial C_3$t-, e.g.:
           tārsa 'she had filled' (AP) + -*a* (3SG.M pronominal suffix) → *tārəst-a*
           'she had filled it (SG.M)'
           ḥātta 'she had put' (AP) + -*a* (3SG.M pronominal suffix) → *ḥāṭəṭṭ-a*
           [ḥaːtˤətˤˤːa] 'she had put it (SG.M)'

4.11.16   *Continuation Marker*

Present continuous is expressed with the particle *gāʕəd* ~ (less commonly)
ǧāʕəd lit. 'sitting', etymologically an AP of the verb *gaʕad* 'to sit', preceding a
verb in the IPFV. Palva describes the use of this marker as a sedentary feature
infrequently used in the *gələt*-dialects (2006: 612). This marker is used 11 times
in my corpus. Together with the use of the future marker *rāḥ* (cf. 4.8.3) and the
emphatic imperative prefix *də*- (cf. 4.11.1.3.1) this might be a sedentary or *qəltu*-
type feature of KhA.

326   CHAPTER 4

The KhA continuation marker can inflect for gender and number: *gāʕəd* (SG.M), *gāʕda* (SG.F), *gāʕdīn* (PL.M), *gāʕdāt* (PL.F), but often the SG.M-form is used for plural and female reference as well (cf. Ingham 1974: 33, who states that this form is most frequently used as indeclinable particle), e.g.:

(12) [M4]
    ʕAbbādān gāʕəd yəštəġlūn   *bī.*
    Abadan   CONT work.IPFV.3PL.M with.3SG.M
    'They are working on Abadan (cleaning it up).'

Some speakers use forms showing the historical sound shift *g* > *ǧ*, e.g. *ǧāʕəd*, or a shortened form *gāʕ*, which, however, occurs only once in my data.

This marker is also used in the *gələt*-dialect of Kwayriš/Babylon (Meißner 1903: VII), in Arabic dialects of the Syrian Desert (*ǧāʕid*), and in Ḥōrān (*gāʕid*) (Behnstedt 1997, Map 161, cf. Palva 2009: 28). It is also documented for Muslim Baghdadi Arabic, though not as a very common feature—usually, the continuation marker *da-*, which is typical of *qəltu*-dialects and not found in KhA (Palva 2009: 28), is used instead.

CHAPTER 5

Texts

This chapter provides a selection of seven texts from my corpus.[1] All texts are translated into English. My own Arabic utterances are also transcribed, but are, of course, not free of "mistakes" nor always fully consistent with the rules of KhA.

In the selected texts, speakers of different ages, both sexes, and diverse geographical origin are represented. The texts are also heterogeneous regarding genre, including descriptions and narratives as well as conversations. This selection of texts hopefully gives the reader a good impression of the rich culture and traditions of the Khuzestani Arabs.

Speaker A1 uses a somewhat more educated register, which can mainly be noticed by the MSA loans he uses such as the MSA preposition *fī* 'in' in preference to the KhA *bə-*: these MSA uses will be marked with the superscript MSA preceding and following the loan word or phrase.

5.1 Ahvaz, Abu Khazʕal [A1]

5.1.1 *Ahvaz [Here: the Province of Khuzestan]*

(1) *b-əl-aḥwāz   ṭabʕan   l-aḥwāz   manṭaǧa ḥārra*
    in-DEF-Ahvaz   of_course DEF-Ahvaz region   hot.F
    ət-ṣīr   ǧanūb ǧarb īrān wa   šarǧ ǧanūb šarǧ əl-ʕarāǧ
    3SG.F-become.IPFV south west Iran and east south east DEF-Iraq
    In Ahvaz—Ahvaz is of course a hot region, situated in the southwest of Iran and in the east-southeast of Iraq.

(2) *nās-ha   ᴹˢᴬmunḍuᴹˢᴬ lǧədam*
    people-3SG.F since   old_times
    Its people have been (here) from former times:

(3) *yaʕni mən zamān əsnīn əḥna sāknīn   əb-hāy*
    that_is from time year.PL 1PL live.AP.PL.M in-DEM.PROX.SG.F

---

[1] The complete corpus of texts containing 75,000 words will be published separately.

328   CHAPTER 5

l-manāṭəǧ   w-manṭaġa-t-na   ta-tġassəm   əla
DEF-region.PL and-region-F.CS-1PL 3SG.F-be_divided.IPFV into
I mean it has been a long time that we [Arabs] have been living in these
regions. Our province is divided into

(4) *manṭaġa-t   əš-šəmālīya   wa manṭaġa-t   ǧ-ǧənūbīya   manāṭəǧ*
region-F.CS DEF-northern.F and region-F.CS DEF-southern.F region.PL
əl-ǧənūbīya   ʔaktar-həm nās
DEF-southern.F most-3PL.M people
a northern region and a southern (one). In the southern regions, most
people

(5) *ʕāyšīn   ʕala ṣēd   əs-samač   w-ən-naxīl*
live.AP.PL.M on fishing DEF-fish.COLL and-DEF-palm.COLL
live from fishing, and palm (cultivation);

(6) *w-əl-hōr   əlli hōr   əl-fəllāḥīya   ʕəd-na ʔaw*
and-DEF-marshland REL marshland DEF-Fəllāḥīya at-1PL or
hōr   dōrag
marshland Dōrag
and the marshland, the marshland of Fəllāḥīya or [also called] the marshland of Dōrag[2] [which is a part of present-day Fəllāḥīya];

(7) *w   hāḏōl   ġəsma ʕāyšīn   w-ġasəm   mən əš-šaʕb*
and DEM.PROX.PL.M group live.AP.PL.M and-group of   DEF-people
əl-ʕarab əl-ahwāzi əlli ʕāyšīn   b-əl-ḥwēza
DEF-Arab DEF-Ahvazi REL live.AP.PL.M in-DEF-Hoveyzeh
and (in) these a part (of our people) lives. A group of the Arab people of
Ahvaz [by that he means the region of Khuzestan in general], who live in
Hoveyzeh

(8) *w-əl-xafaġīya   ṭabʕan   həmma ham ʕāyšīn   ʕəd-həm*
and-DEF-Xafaġīya of_course 3PL.M   also live.AP.PL.M at-3PL.M

---

2 Cf. (Lockhart 1965: 181) on the history of Dōrag and the fact that towards the close of the 16th
   century the Banū Tamīm and later the Banū Kaʕab occupied this city and the surrounding
   area. Under the latter, the city of Fəllāḥīya was built, five miles to the south of Dōrag, which
   thereafter fell into ruin. In 1933 the name of Fəllāḥīya was changed to Šādegān. The swampy
   area between Šādegān and the coast of the Persian Gulf is however still known as *hōr* ['swamp,
   marshland'] Dōrag.

TEXTS

329

> *tərbīya-t   əl-mawāši*
> breeding.F.CS DEF-cattle
>
> or in Xafaǧīya, they of course live by cattle-breeding.

(9) *Ɂa-ḥči   Ɂa-ḥči-l-ak   al-ġadīm yaʕni   walākən*
   1SG-speak.IPFV 1SG-speak.IPFV-to-2SG.M DEF-past that_is but
   ǧadīd ətǧayyar-at
   new   change.PFV-3SG.F
   I tell, I am telling you (how things were in) the past, but today it's different;

(10) *yaʕni   lyōm təknəlōžīyāt wa Ɂa-ḥči   ʕala š-šay   əlli*
    that_is today technologies and 1SG-speak.IPFV about DEF-thing REL
    kān   ġadīm ʕəd-həm
    be.PFV.3SG.M past   at-3PL.M
    today (there are) technologies, but I talk about the things that they had in
    the past.

(11) *wa lā yazāl al-ġasəm   mən ʕand-a   bāġi   ʕəd-həm*
    and yet   DEF-group of at-3SG.M remain.AP.SG.M at-3PL.M
    ḍall   matalan
    remain.PFV.3SG.M for_example
    And there is yet (another) group that still—for example

(12) *matalan   ʕəd-na tərbīya-t   əd-dəwāb*
    for_example at-1PL breeding-F.CS DEF-water_buffalo.COLL
    we have the breeding of water buffaloes;

(13) *tərbīya-t   əd-dəwāb   yaʕni ʕəd-na*
    breeding-F.CS DEF-water_buffalo.COLL that_is at-1PL
    b-əl-hōr
    in-DEF-marshland
    breeding of water buffaloes; in the marshlands we find (people who live
    by breeding water buffaloes).

(14) *ʕəd-na nās   y-gəl-ū-l-həm   al-məʕdān*
    at-1PL people 3-call.IPFV-PL.M-to-3PL.M DEF-marshdweller.PL
    There are some people among us, they are called the məʕdān [marshd-
    wellers].

(15) *hāḏōl* *məʕdān* *ʕəd-həm* *y-rabb-ūn*
DEM.PROX.PL.M marshdweller.PL at-3PL.M 3-breed.IPFV-PL.M
These *məʕdān*, they have, they breed,

(16) *šəǧla-t-həm* *y-rabb-ūn* *dəwāb*
job-F.CS-3PL.M 3-breed.IPFV-PL.M water_buffalo.COLL
their job is the breeding of water buffaloes.

(17) *əd-dəwāb* *yaʕni* *b-əṣ-ṣṭalāḥ* *b-əl-fəṣḥā*
DEF-water_buffalo.COLL that_is in-DEF-term in-DEF-Standard_Arabic
y-gəl-ū-l-ha *ǧāmūs*
3-call.IPFV-PL.M-to-3SG.F water_buffalo
(We use) the term *dəwāb* ['buffalo']; in Standard Arabic you say *ǧāmūs*.

(18) *y-rabb-ūn-ha* *fa* *yə-stafād-ūn* *mən* *ḥālīb-ha*
3-breed.IPFV-PL.M-3SG.F and 3-use.IPFV-PL.M of milk-3SG.F
They breed them and use their milk,

(19) *yə-stafād-ūn* *mən laḥam-ha*
3-use.IPFV-PL.M of meat-3SG.F
and they use their meat,

(20) *fa* *həma* *ʕāyšīn* *ʕala hāḏa* *š-šay*
and 3PL.M live.AP.PL.M on DEM.PROX.SG.M DEF-thing
and that's what they live on.

(21) *wa* *ʔaktar ən-nās* *əl-məʕdān* *ʕāyšīn* *yaʕni*
and most DEF-people DEF-marshdweller.PL live.AP.PL.M that_is
b-əl-hōr
in-DEF-marshland
And most people of the marshdwellers live in the marshlands,

(22) *yaʕni* *aktar ən-nās* *b-əl-hōr* *lākən*
that_is most DEF-people in-DEF-marshland but
most of the(ir) people (are) in the marshlands. But,

(23) *əb-sənīn* *əl-axīra* *lamman-mā* *əl-hōr* *ǧaff*
in-year.PL DEF-past.F when-REL DEF-marshland run_dry.PFV.3SG.M
in the past years the marshland ran dry,

TEXTS 331

(24) *yaʕni yəbas   əl-hōr   w-məṭar ġalīla fa*
that_is run_dry.PFV.3SG.M DEF-marshland and-rain little.F and
ṣār-at
become.PFV-3SG.F
the marshland ran dry, (as there was) little rain; drought made it become

(25) *maḥla b-əṣṭəlāḥ-na n-gəl-ha   maḥal*
dry.F   in-term-1PL 1PL-call.IPFV-3SG.F dry
dry: we call it *maḥal*.

(26) *yaʕni l-maḥal sən-t   əlli əd-dənya   mā tə-mṭər*
that_is DEF-dry year-F.CS REL DEF-world NEG 3SG.F-rain.IPFV
So *maḥal* is a year in which it doesn't rain.

(27) *y-gūl-ū(n)   səna mhal-at   səna mhal-at   ʕalē-na*
3-say.IPFV-PL.M year go_dry.PFV-3SG.F year go_dry.PFV-3SG.F on-1PL
You say the year is dry, the year has gone dry,

(28) *yaʕni   məṭar māku*
that_is rain   EXIST.NEG
meaning (that) there was no rain.

(29) *fa   kṯīr   mən ʕəd-həm əy-aw   l-əl-dīra*
and many of   at-3PL.M come.PFV-3PL.M to-DEF-town
And many of them came to the town—

(30) *əd-dīra   b-əṣṭəlāḥ-na yaʕni   l-madīna*
DEF-town in-term-1PL that_is DEF-town
we use the term *dīra* for *madīna* ['town']—

(31) *yaʕni y-aw   l-əl-dīra   w   səkn-aw   əd-dīra*
that_is come.PFV-3PL.M to-DEF-town and settle.PFV-3PL.M DEF-town
they came to the town and settled in the town,

(32) *fa   ḥatta dəwāb-həm   maʕ-həm*
and even water_buffalo.COLL-3PL.M with-3PL.M
and their water buffaloes (came) with them.

5.1.2 *Handicrafts*

(1) *ṭabʕan   mən əṣ-ṣanāyəʕ   əl   mawǧūda əlli   mawǧūda ʕəd-na*
of_course of   DEF-handicrafts REL existing.F REL existing.F at-1PL
Of course, to the existing handicrafts that we have

(2) *b-əl-aḥwāz   ᴹˢᴬkāfatanᴹˢᴬ hīya   ṣanʕ   əl-bārya*
in-DEF-Ahvaz sufficiently   3SG.F production DEF-reed_mat
in Ahvaz sufficiently belongs the production of reed mats.[3]

(3) *əl-bārya   y-ṣanʕ-ūn-hā   mən nōʕ gəṣab*
DEF-reed_mat 3-produce.IPFV-PL.M-3SG.F from kind reed
w-əl-gəṣab
and-DEF-reed
They make reed mats from a (certain) kind of reed.

(4) *ṭabʕan   əl-gəṣab ə-la   ʔasāmi ʔawwal-mā*
of_course DEF-reed to-3SG.M name.PL first-REL
y-xaḍḍər
3SG.M-turn_green.IPFV
The reed, of course, has (different) names. When it turns green for the
first time,

(5) *əsm-a   ʕangər əzġār   ʔawwal-mā y-xaḍḍər*
name-3SG.M ʕangər small.PL first-REL   3SG.M-turn_green.IPFV
it's called *ʕangər*: (it's still) small, when it greens up for the first time.

(6) *lamman-mā šwayy yə-ʕla   y-ṣīr   šahaf*
when-REL   a_little 3SG.M-grow.IPFV 3SG.M-become.IPFV šahaf
When it has grown a little bit bigger, it is called *šahaf*.

(7) *w-əḏa   ṣār   ʕāli kəlləš w-yəbas*
and-when become.PFV.3SG.M high   very   and-dry.PFV.3SG.M
y-ṣīr   gəṣab
3SG.M-become.IPFV reed
And when it's mature and dry, it's called gəṣab.

---

3 Cf. Holes on Bahraini Arabic (2016: 13): "*bari* pl *bawāri* 'reeds (used as a building material)' <
Aram *būriyā* 'reed mat', Akk *burû* 'reed mat'"; cf. Edzard (1967: 307), who writes that these big
reed mats were the industrial product of the *Məʕdān* par excellence.

TEXTS 333

(8) *fa hāḍa l-gaṣab b-aṣ-ṣṭalāḥ ǝlli yaʕni*
and DEM.PROX.SG.M DEF-reed in-DEF-term REL that_is
And this reed (is also known) under the term—

(9) *katīra mǝn ǝl hāḍa y-gūl-ū-l-ha papīrūs*
many.F of DEF DEM.PROX.SG.M 3-say.IPFV-PL.M-to-3SG.F papyrus
well, a lot of (people) call it papyrus;

(10) *fa yǝ-stǝfād-ūn mǝn ʕǝnd-a ḥatta mǝn gabǝl*
and 3-use.IPFV-PL.M of at-3SG.M even from past
and they used it already in former times.

(11) *y-ṭǝlʕ-ūn mǝn ʕǝnd-a wrāǧ y-saww-ūn mǝn*
3-take_out.IPFV-PL.M from at-3SG.M paper.PL 3-make.IPFV-PL.M of
lǝʔaǧl(?) ǝl-kǝtāba
for DEF-writing
They made paper from it and made (this) for writing.

(12) *fa hāḍa l-gǝṣab lamman-mā*
and DEM.PROX.SG.M DEF-reed when-REL
y-ṭǝlʕ-ūn-a
3-take_out.IPFV-PL.M-3SG.M
This reed, after they have pulled it out (of the soil),

(13) *w-ǝnnōb mǝn baʕǝd-mā yǝbas y-gǝṣṣ-ūn-a*
and-then when after-REL dry.PFV.3SG.M 3-cut.IPFV-PL.M-3SG.M
then, when it has dried, they cut it

(14) *w-ǝnnōba y-naḍḍf-ūn-a mǝn ǝl-warag w-ǝnnōb*
and-then 3-clean.IPFV-PL.M-3SG.M from DEF-leaf.COLL and-then
and then strip the leaves and then

(15) *y-fǝššg-ūn-a t-fǝššǝg yaʕni gāṣṣ*
3-split.IPFV-PL.M-3SG.M 2SG.M.split.IPFV that_is cut.AP.SG.M
b-ǝn-nǝṣṣ
in-DEF-half
they split it: you split it; it is cut in half.

(16) *mǝn baʕǝd-mā fǝššag-ō-(h)*
when after-REL split.PFV-3PL.M-3SG.M
After they have split it,

(17) *y-ṭīḥ-ūn   bī-(h)   y-səff-ūn-a   saff*[4]
3-begin.IPFV-PL.M with-3SG.M 3-weave.IPFV-PL.M-3SG.M weaving
they begin to weave it,

(18) *saff   yaʕni ḥālat nasīǧ   y-nəsǧ-ūn-a   nasəǧ*
weaving that_is like   weaving 3-weave.IPFV-PL.M-3SG.M weaving
weave. (The weaving of reed is) like weaving (cloth): like they weave a
textile,

(19) *yaʕni   šlōn y-nəsǧ-ūn   əl-xām   ʔaw əl-ṣūf*
that_is how 3-weave.IPFV-PL.M DEF-fabric or   DEF-wool
just like you weave fabric or wool.

(20) *fa   ha-l-gəṣab   ham y-nəsǧ-ūn-a*
and DEM-DEF-reed also 3-weave.IPFV-PL.M-3SG.M
And so they weave this reed

(21) *fa   ẏ-ṭəlʕ-ūn   mən ʕənd-a   l-bārya*
and 3-take_out.IPFV-PL.M from at-3SG.M DEF-reed_mat
and make reed mats from it.

(22) *əl-bārya   ṭabʕan   yə-stəfād-ūn   mən ʕəd-ha*
DEF-reed_mat of_course 3-use.IPFV-PL.M from at-3SG.F
The reed mats, they use it here, of course

(23) *əhnāka kawnan manṭaǧa-t-na   əhna manṭaǧa ḥārra*
there   since   region-F.CS-1PL 1PL region   hot.F
—considering that our region is a hot region—

(24) *yə-stəfād   mən ʕənd-ha l-əl-abnīya   ʔaktar w*
3SG.M-use.IPFV from at-3SG.F for-DEF-building most   and
l-əl-frāš
for-DEF-floor_mat.PL
they use it mainly for (house) building and for floor mats.

---

4 Cf. Holes on Bahraini Arabic (2001: 238–239): "*saff* ... 'plait, braid, weave (palm-fronds to make baskets, etc.)' ... *sifif* 'palm-matting'".

TEXTS 335

(25) *lan   əhya yābsa b-əsṭəlāḥ-na ǧāffa*
because 3SG.F dry.F in-term-1PL dry.F
Since it is dry—we say *ǧāffa* [instead of *yābsa*]—

(26) *w   mā t-ʕaddi   r-rəṭūba*
and NEG 3SG.F-pass_through.IPFV DEF-moisture
the moisture can't pass through.

(27) *yaʕni   ʔəda wāḥəd y-fərš-ūn-ha   b-əl-gāʕ*
that_is if one 3-cover.IPFV-PL.M-3SG.F on-DEF-floor
So, if one covers the floor with it,

(28) *fa   hīya ham bārda w   ham y-ṣīr   məṯəl ḥālat*
and 3SG.F also cold.F and also 3SG.M-become.IPFV like like
yaʕni
that_is
it is both cool and also

(29) *ʕāyəǧ mā bēn   əl-abnīya w   yə-stəfād-ūn   mən ʕənd-ha*
barrier REL between DEF-wall.PL and 3-use.IPFV-PL.M from at-3SG.F
a barrier between the walls and (therefore) they use it (for that).

(30) *l-əl-əsagəf yə-stəfād-ūn   w   l-əl-əfrāš   mən ʕənd-a*
for-DEF-roof 3-use.IPFV-PL.M and for-DEF-floor_mat.PL from at-3SG.M
They use it for the roof and for floor mats.

(31) *hāḏa   nōʕ mən əṣ-ṣanāyəʕ   əl-yadawīya   əl*
DEM.PROX.SG.M kind of DEF-handicrafts DEF-handmade.F REL
yə-stəfād-ūn-ha   b-əl-aḥwāz   hīya əl-bārya
3-use.IPFV-PL.M-3SG.F in-DEF-Ahvaz 3SG.F DEF-reed_mat
This is one of the handicrafts produced in Ahvaz, the reed mat.

(32) *ʕəd-na šay ṯāni   y-gəl-ū-l-a   l-ball*
at-1PL thing another 3-call.IPFV-PL.M-to-3SG.M DEF-palm_mat.COLL
We have another thing; they call it ball [palm mats].

(33) *əl-ball   həwwa nōʕ məṯl əl-bārya*
DEF-palm_mat.COLL 3SG.M kind like DEF-reed_mat
The palm mat is something like the reed mat,

(34) *bass y-səff-ūn-a*   *mən xūṣ[5]*   *ən-naxīl*
but 3-weave.IPFV-PL.M-3SG.M from palm_leaf.COLL DEF-palm.COLL
mən xūṣ   *ən-naxīl*
from palm_leaf.COLL DEF-palm.COLL
but you weave it with palm fronds, from palm fronds.

(35) *hāy*   *n-naxla*   *mətšakkəla mən əl-ǧədəʕ*   *māl-ha*   *ʔaw*
DEM.PROX.SG.F DEF-palm consisting.F of   DEF-trunk GL-3SG.F or
əl-yədəʕ
DEF-trunk
The palm consists of its trunk, [he repeats it with y because he wants to
show me that they usually pronounce *ǧ* as *y* in KhA];

(36) *w-ənnōb mən əl-yədəʕ*   *bī-ha*   *saʕaf*
and-then from DEF-trunk with-3SG.F palm_frond.COLL
and from the trunk it has fronds.

(37) *s-saʕfa*   *mālat-ha*   *saʕfa*
DEF-palm_frond.SGT GL.SG.F-3SG.F palm_frond.SGT
y-gəl-ū-l-ha   *yaʕni hāda*
3-call.IPFV-PL.M-to-3SG.F that_is DEM.PROX.SG.M
s-saʕaf
DEF-palm_frond.COLL
Its fronds, they call *saʕfa*, this, the fronds.

(38) *w-əs-saʕaf*   *bī-(h)*   *xūṣ*   *yaʕni*
and-DEF-palm_frond.COLL on-3SG.M palm_leaf.COLL that_is
l-warag   *māl-a*   *y-gəl-ū-l-a*   *xūṣ*
DEF-leaf.COLL GL-3SG.M 3-call.IPFV-PL.M-to-3SG.M palm_leaf.COLL
xūṣ
palm_leaf.COLL
And on the fronds are leaves; its leaves they call *xūṣ, xūṣ*.

(39) *fa*   *hāda*   *l-xūṣ*   *y-āxd-ūn-a*
and DEM.PROX.SG.M DEF-palm_leaf.COLL 3-take.IPFV-PL.M.3-SG.M
w-y-nəsǧ-ūn   *mən ʕənd-a*
and-3-weave.IPFV-PL.M from at-3SG.M
And they take these leaves and weave with them

---

5   Cf. Holes (2001: 164) on Bahraini Arabic: "*xūṣ* 'palm-fronds (used as a building material)'".

TEXTS

337

(40) *əh š-əsm-a*   *y-nəsǧ-ūn*   *mən ʕənd-a*
err what-name-3SG.M 3-weave.IPFV-PL.M from at-3SG.M
hāy   *əl al-bārya*
DEM.PROX.SG.F DEF DEF-reed_mat
- What's it called?[6]—they weave with them the ... reed mats ...

(41) *y-gūl*   *š-əsm-a*   *al-balla*   *al-balla*
3SG.M-say.IPFV what-name-3SG.M DEF-palm_mat DEF-palm_mat
Say, what's it called? Palm mats, they make palm mats from them.

(42) *y-saww-ūn*   *mən ʕəd-ha w-ṭabʕan*   *ḥatta* MSA*fī*MSA *ǧənūb*
3-make.IPFV-PL.M from at-3SG.F and-of_course even in   south
al-ʕərāǧ ham y-saww-ūn   *ʕəd-hən al-balla*
DEF-Iraq also 3-make.IPFV-PL.M at-3PL.F DEF-palm_mat
And of course also in southern Iraq they make palm mats.

(43) *w-mən*   *ən-naxla ṭabʕan*   *yə-stəfād-ūn*   MSA*kaṯīran*MSA *mən*
and-from DEF-palm of_course 3-use.IPFV-PL.M a_lot   from
ʕəd-hən maṯalan
at-3PL.F for_example
And they of course benefit a lot from the palm(s): For example,

(44) *y-saww-ūn*   *al-ḥasīr*   MSA*ʔay*MSA *al-balla*
3-make.IPFV-PL.M DEF-mat.PL that_is   DEF-palm_mat
they make mats, that is, the palm mats.

(45) *ʕəd-ak*   *y-saww-ūn*   *əz-zəblān*
at-2SG.M 3-make.IPFV-PL.M DEF-basket.PL
They make baskets [zabīl PL zəblān]

(46) MSA*ʔay*MSA *əs-salla*   *zəbīl*[7] *mən al-xūṣ*
that_is DEF-basket basket from DEF-palm_leaf.COLL
—that is, a (certain) basket, a basket made of palm leaves.

---

6   *š-əsm-a* lit. 'What is it's (M.SG) name?' is frequently used by speakers as a pause-filler, when (s)he is still thinking about a word or how to continue a phrase; cf. Bar-Moshe (2019: 73, fn. 9) on the same phrase with the same function in Jewish Baghdadi.

7   Cf. Holes on Bahraini Arabic (2001: 219): "*zabīl* 'basket made of palm-leaves'." Holes states that this word is related to Neo-Babylonian Akkadian *zabbīlu*, in Old Aramaic *zbīlā*, modern Iraqi Arabic *zbīl* (cf. also WB: 201) and Persian *zanbīl* (2016: 11).

338   CHAPTER 5

(47) *w-y-saww-ūn*   *mən əl-xūṣ*   *ṭabʕan*
and-3-make.IPFV-PL.M from DEF-palm_leaf.COLL of_course
y-saww-ūn   *mahaffa*
3-make.IPFV-PL.M fan
And they make—from the palm leaves, of course—they make fans,

(48) *yaʕni yə-thaff-ūn*   *bī-ha*   *hāḏa*   *mən ən-naxla*
that_is 3-fan.IPFV-PL.M with-3SG.F DEM.PROX.SG.M from DEF-palm
they fan with it, this (frond) of the palm;

(49) *w-ʕəd-ak*   *əl-məknāsa y-saww-ūn*   *mən ʕənd-ha*
and-at-2SG.M DEF-broom 3-make.IPFV-PL.M from at-3SG.F
and they (also) make brooms from it.

(50) *haḏanni*   *ṣ-ṣanāyəʕ*   *əlli mən ən-naxīl*
DEM.PROX.PL.F DEF-handicrafts REL from DEF-palm.COLL
yə-stəfād-ūn   *mən ʕəd-hən*
3-use.IPFV-PL.M from at-3PL.F
These (are) the handicrafts that they make from the palm tree.

(51) *ʕənd-ak yə-stəfād-ūn*   *nnōb y-yīb-ūn*   *čōlān*
at-2SG.M 3-use.IPFV-PL.M then 3-bring.IPFV-PL.M rushes
They use—then they take [lit. "bring"] the rushes[8]

(52) *ʔaw y-yīb-ūn*   *əl-ʕətəg*   *māl ən-naxla*
or 3-bring.IPFV-PL.M DEF-corymb GL DEF-palm
w-y-gaṣṣəṣ-ūn-a
and-3-cut.IPFV-PL.M-3SG.M
or the corymb [cluster of dates] of the palm and cut it,

(53) *w-ənnōb tāli y-ḥūč-ūn*   *ʕalē-(h)*   *yaʕni*
and-then then 3-weave.IPFV-PL.M on-3SG.M that_is
b-əl-xūṣ
with-DEF-palm_leaf.COLL
and then weave it (together) with the leaves.

---

8 Cf. Edzard (1967: 308), who states that *čōlān* is a rush-like weed growing at the edge of the *hōr* (scirpus brachyceras), 1–1.5 m. high, that is also used as animal fodder and for making sleeping mats.

TEXTS 339

(54) *fa y-saww-ūn   man Sand-a   gaffa*[9]
and 3-make.IPFV-PL.M from at-3SG.M basket
And they make a basket [*gaffa*] from it,

(55) *MSA?awMSA y-saww-ūn   man Sand-a   zabīl   ġawwi*
or   3-make.IPFV-PL.M from at-3SG.M basket strong
or a strong basket [*zbīl*];

(56) *fa ya-stafād-ūn   man Sand-a*
and 3-use.IPFV-PL.M from at-3SG.M
and thus they make use of it [the palm tree].

(57) *w tāni   šay alli mahamm hawwa al ya-stafād-ūn   man*
and another thing REL important 3SG.M REL 3-use.IPFV-PL.M from
l-at-tamar
for-DEF-date.COLL
And another thing that is important is (something) that they use for the
dates:

(58) *tabSan   artaylīya MSA?ayMSA hallāna*
of_course date_box that_is   date_box
the *rataylīya*,[10] that is (also called) *hallāna*.

(59) *bī-ha   nās   y-gal-ha   hallāna ?aw*
among-3SG.F people 3SG.M-call.IPFV-3SG.F date_box or
bī-ha   al-artaylīya
among-3SG.F DEF-date_box
Some people call it *hallāna* and some (call it) *artaylīya*:

(60) *tabSan   b-al-ahwāzi   y-gal-ū-l-ha   artaylīya*
of_course in-DEF-Ahvazi 3-call.IPFV-PL.M-to-3SG.F date_box
in the dialect of Ahvaz, they of course say *artaylīya*.

(61) *ar-rataylīya   yaSni   at-tamar   al y-žīb-ūn-a*
DEF-date_box that_is DEF-date.COLL REL 3-bring.IPFV-PL.M-3SG.M
The *rataylīya*—Well, they bring the dates,

---

9   Cf. Holes on Bahraini Arabic (2016: 13; cf. also 2001: 433): "*guffa* 'palm-leaf basket or pot' <
Akk *qappatu* (same meaning)"; used for the storage of dates.
10   Closable storing box for dates, often produced in Fallāhīya.

(62) əl   y-yīb-ūn-a   mn-ən-naxīl
REL 3-bring.IPFV-PL.M-3SG.M from-DEF-palm.COLL
w-y-ḥaṭṭ-ūn-a   b-əl-   b-əč-čərdāġ[11]
and-3-put.IPFV-PL.M-3SG.M in-DEF in-DEF-store_room
they bring them from the palms and they put them in the, in the store-
room.

(63) *əč-čərdāġ*   *əl-ambār*   *māl əl-tamər*
DEF-store_room DEF-store_room GL   DEF-date.COLL
y-gūl-ū-l-a   čərdāġ
3-say.IPFV-PL.M-to-3SG.M store_room
The *čərdāġ*—the store-room for the dates they call *čərdāġ*;

(64) *lākən əl-aḥwāzīy-īn*   *y-gūl-ū-l-a*   yōxān
but   DEF-Ahvazi-PL.M 3-say.IPFV-PL.M-to-3SG.M date_storage
yōxān
date_storage
but the people of Ahvaz call it *yōxān, yōxān*.[12]

(65) *əl-yōxān*   *mətšakkəl*   ənnu   ʔahl   ən-naxīl
DEF-date_storage consisting_of so_that people DEF-palm.COLL
The *yōxān* is made so ... the palm cultivators

(66) *y-ḥaṭṭ-ūn*   bī-(h)   əl-tamər
3-put.IPFV-PL.M in-3SG.M DEF-date.COLL
w-y-šərr-ūn-a
and-3-hang_up.IPFV-PL.M-3SG.M
store the dates in it, they hang them up (to dry).

(67) ənnōb baʕdēn b-əl-kəll   yōxān   tə-lg-īn   bī-(h)
then   then   in-DEF-every date_storage 2-find.IPFV-SG.F in-3SG.M
mədəbsīya
mədəbsīya
And then, in every date storage you (also) find a *mədəbsīya* [place for making *dəbəs* 'date syrup'].

---

11   LA (202): *čirdāġ* 'place for storing dates'; cf. WB (84) on Iraqi Arabic: "*čirdāġ* pl. *čarādīġ*
'summer cabin, a hut built on the river'". [Here and in the following the translations of the
Arabic originals given in Ḥassūnizadeh's KhA dictionary are my own.]
12   LA (925): < *ǧōxān*, PL *yəwāxīn*: 'place for storing dates' < Pers. *ǧaw* 'barley' + *xān(e)* 'house',
i.e. a storage place for barley and the like.

TEXTS   341

(68) *əl-mədəbsīya   gabəl   hassa dəbəs   y-ṭīḥ-ūn*
DEF-mədəbsīya formerly now   date_syrup 3-take.IPFV-PL.M
bī-(h)
with-3SG.M
The *mədəbsīya* in former times—today they take the *dəbəs*

(69) *y-fawwr-ūn   ət-fəwwar   lākən gabəl   laʔ*
3-cook.IPFV-PL.M 2SG.M-cook.IPFV but   formerly no
(and) cook (it), but in former times not.

(70) *y-ḥaṭṭ-ūn-a   b-əl-mədəbsa   yaʕni*
3-put.IPFV-PL.M-3SG.M in-DEF-mədəbsīya that_is
y-saww-ūn-l-a   farəd   maxzan
3-make.IPFV-PL.M-for-3SG.M INDEF store_room
They put it [the dates] in the *mədəbsa*. That is, they make a store-room
for them,

(71) *maxzan   mərabbaʕ mən ṭābūg   w-y-ḥaṭṭ-ūn   bī-(h)*
store_room square   of   clay_brick and-3-put.IPFV-PL.M in-3SG.M
tamər
date.COLL
which is square (and) made of clay brick, and they store the dates in it

(72) *w-əl-   y-xall-ūn-a   hnāka w-y-ḥaṭṭ-ūn*
and-DEF- 3-leave.IPFV-PL.M-3SG.M there   and-3-put.IPFV-PL.M
ḥadər   dalla
beneath bucket
and leave them there and put beneath (the dates) an (angular) bucket

(73) *ʔaw saṭəl   fa   hāḏa   mən əl-atar   al-ḥarāra malt*
or   bucket and DEM.PROX.SG.M from DEF-impact DEF-heat GL.SG.F
əš-šəməs əlli   ḥarr   ad-dənya
DEF-sun REL warm_up.PFV.3SG.M DEF-world
or a (round) bucket—and that (works thanks to) the heat of the sun that
warms up the earth.

(74) *y-ḍəll   y-ǧərr   y-yərr*
3SG.M-remain.IPFV 3SG.M-drip.IPFV 3SG.M-drip.IPFV
It [the date syrup, *dəbəs*] drips (and) drips—

(75) *yaʕni   y-ḏəll   y-naggəṭ   əd-dəbəs*
that_is 3SG.M-remain.IPFV 3SG.M-trickle_down.IPFV DEF-date_syrup
əl-xāləṣ
DEF-real
well, the real *dəbəs* keeps trickling down.

(76) *mū   hassa d-dəbəs   əlli y-šūf-ūn-a*
NEG now   DEF-date_syrup REL 3-see.IPFV-PL.M-3SG.M
b-əs-sūg   hāḏa   ṭabəx
in-DEF-market DEM.PROX.SG.M cooked
(This one is) not (like) the one that you can see nowadays on the market:
that one is cooked

(77) *hāḏa   mā   bī-(h)   ṭaʕəm walā šay*
DEM.PROX.SG.M NEG in-3SG.M taste   nor   thing
and has no taste nor anything.

(78) *lākən dāk   əd-dəbəs   ṭabīʕi*
but   DEM.DIST.SG.M DEF-date_syrup natural
But that *dəbəs* is natural,

(79) *mn-əṭ-ṭabīʕa   y-kədd-ūn-a   wa xāləṣ*
from-DEF-nature 3-take.IPFV-PL.M-3SG.M and real
they get it from nature [with natural ingredients]; that's (the) real (one).

(80) *dəbəs   y-kədd-ūn-a   fa   hāḏa*
date_syrup 3-take.IPFV-PL.M-3SG.M and DEM.PROX.SG.M
y-gəl-ū-l-a   dəbəs   əl-tamər
3-call.IPFV-PL.M-to-3SG.M date_syrup DEF-date.COLL
They make the *dəbəs* and call it date-*dəbəs*.

(81) *ʕəd-na dəbəs   ṭabʕan   ʕənab   ʕəd-na dəbəs   ʔašyā*
at-1PL date_syrup of_course grape.COLL at-1PL date_syrup thing.PL
ṯānīya
other.F
Of course, we have grape-*dəbəs*, we have *dəbəs* (made) of other things;

TEXTS 343

(82) *lākən əl-ahamm*   *əl-ši*   *b-əl-ahwāz*   *ʕad-na həwwa*
but   DEF-important.EL DEF-thing in-DEF-Ahvaz at-1PL 3SG.M
dəbs   *ət-tamər*
date_syrup DEF-date.COLL
but the most important thing in Ahvaz is the date-*dəbəs*.

(83) *ənnōba ʕad-ak*   *ən-naxīl*   *mənn-a*   *y-saww-ūn*   *mən*
then   at-2SG.M DEF-palm.COLL from-3SG.M 3-make.IPFV-PL.M from
ʕənd-a   *dəbəs*
at-3SG.M date_syrup
Then there is the palm tree, from which they make the *dəbəs*,

(84) *fa*   *ʕad-ak*   *ʕad-na ʔanwāʕ w-aġsām*   *ət-tamər*
and at-2SG.M at-1PL kind.PL and-type.PL DEF-date.COLL
and there is—we have different kinds of dates.

(85) *yaʕni*   *šūf*   *ʕad-ak*   *ət-tamər*   *əl-gəntār*
that_is see.IMP.SG.M at-2SG.M DEF-date.COLL DEF-Gəntār
See, there are (these kinds of) dates: the Gəntār [this and the following
are the names of varieties of dates],

(86) *ʕad-na tamər*   *əl-həllāwi*   *saʕamrān Saʕamr*   *ah əl-bərhi*
at-1PL date.COLL DEF-Həllāwi Saʕamrān Saʕamrān um DEF-Bərhi
we have the Həllāwi-date, Saʕamrān, Saʕamr um … the Bərhi,

(87) *əl-əbrēm*   *əl-əbrēm*   *ʔallad*   *əš-šay*   *əda*   *kān*
DEF-Brēm DEF-Brēm delicious.EL DEF-thing when be.PFV.3SG.M
xalāl
unripe_date.COLL
the Brēm—the Brēm is most delicious when it's not yet ripe [at this stage
dates are called *xalāl*],[13]

(88) *yaʕni*   *xalāl*   *əl-əbrēm*   *həwwa ladda-t-a*
that_is unripe_date.COLL DEF-Brēm 3SG.M taste-F.CS-3SG.M
so the unripe Brēm has (a delicious) taste.

---

13   Cf. WB (144) on Iraqi Arabic: *ˈxlāl* (coll.) dates, crisp and not yet ripe'.

(89) w *madīna-t ʕabbadān māšāʔaḷḷā kṯīr bī-ha brēm*
and town-F.CS Abadan God_willing many in-3SG.F Brēm
In the city of Abadan—God willing—there are many Brēm,

(90) *madīna-t ʕabbadān maʕrūfa b-əl-əbrēm ḥatta ʕəd-ha maḥalla*
town-F.CS Abadan famous.F with-DEF-Brēm even at-3SG.F place
the city of Abadan is famous for the Brēm; there is even a place

(91) *əsəm-ha maḥalla-t əl-əbrēm*
name-3SG.F place-F.CS DEF-Brēm
called the Place of the Brēm.

(92) *fa hāḏa yaʕni ənnu kṯīr ən-naxīl*
and DEM.PROX.SG.M that_is because many DEF-palm.COLL
And this, well, is (because) there are a lot of palm trees.

(93) *lākən maʕələsaf hāy əs-sənīn əl-axīra*
but unfortunately DEM.PROX.SG.F DEF-year.PL DEF-past.F
But, unfortunately, in the past few years,

(94) *bə-sabab ǧəfāf əl-məyyāh w amṭār ġalīla kān-at*
with-reason drought DEF-water.PL and rain.PL little.F be.PFV-3SG.F
due to the drying-up of the water, and (the fact that) there was little rain,

(95) *w-saww-aw əsdūd ʕala d-darəb fa hāḏa*
and-make.PFV-3PL.M dam.PL on DEF-road and DEM.PROX.SG.M
əl
DEF
and (that) they built dams in the river and this (led to) the (fact that) ...

(96) *māy-na ṣār əšwāyy mā kəṯīr ṣār*
water-1PL become.PFV.3SG.M a_little NEG much become.PFV.3SG.M
māləḥ w kəṯīra mən ən-naxal
salty and many.F of DEF-palm_trees
our water has decreased ... it has become very salty and many palm trees

TEXTS   345

(97) *maww-at   lan   əl-gāʕ   mallaḥ-at*
     die.PFV-3SG.F because DEF-soil become_saline.PFV-3SG.F
     ṣār-at   ṣabax b-əṣṭəlāḥ-na
     become.PFV-3SG.F saline in-term-1PL
     have died because the soil got salty [saline]: it became saline [*ṣəbax*], as
     we say.

(98) *ṣəbax yaʕni əl-gāʕ   əl-mālḥa*
     saline that_is DEF-soil DEF-saline.F
     ṣəbax denotes the saline soil,

(99) *yaʕni əl-gāʕ əl   bī-ha   mlūḥa ktīra   y-gūl-ha*
     that_is DEF-soil REL in-3SG.F salinity much.F 3SG.M-call.IPFV-3SG.F
     ṣabxāya
     saline
     and soil that has a high level of salinity they call ṣabxāya, saline:

(100) *yaʕni ṣabəx yaʕni ʔabyaḍ*
      that_is saline that_is white
      (it's) white.

(101) *fa   hāḏanni   n-naxīl   yaʕni ən-naxla ktīr*
      and DEM.PROX.PL.F DEF-palm.COLL that_is DEF-palm much
      tə-stəfād   mən ʕəd-ha
      2SG.M-benefit.IPFV from at-3SG.F
      And these palms: well, they benefit from the palm tree a lot,

(102) *mən tamər-ha   mən saʕaf-ha   mən*
      from date.COLL-3SG.F from palm_frond.COLL-3SG.F from
      karab-ha
      nodule.COLL-3SG.F
      with its dates, its fronds, its nodules (of the trunk)—

(103) *əḥna nə-stəfād   katīr mən ʕəd-ha*
      1PL 1PL-benefit.IPFV a_lot from at-3SG.F
      we benefit a lot from it.

346 CHAPTER 5

5.1.3 *Places, Tribes, Dialects*

(1) *ʕəd-na tarbīya-t ǝl šay ṯāni*
at-1PL breeding-F.CS REL thing another
We have another kind of breeding as well.

(2) *ʕəd-na manāṭǝǧ ramlīya b-ǝl-aḥwāz manāṭǝǧ ramlīya*
at-1PL region.PL sandy.F in-DEF-Ahvaz region.PL sandy.F
We have sandy regions, in Ahvaz, sandy regions,

(3) *wa ǝhnāka y-rabb-ūn bī-ha ǝl-īmāl* ^{MSA}*ʔay*^{MSA}
and there 3-breed.IPFV-PL.M in-3SG.F DEF-camel.PL that_is
ǝl-ǧamal ^{MSA}*ʔaw*^{MSA} *ǝl-ʔǝbǝl*
DEF-camel or DEF-camel.COLL
and there they breed camels [he uses three different terms, all denoting
'camel'],

(4) *y-rabb-ūn bī-ha maṭalan ṣōb ʕəd-ak*
3-breed.IPFV-PL.M with-3SG.F for_example towards at-2SG.M
rāmǝs ʕəd-na ǝhnāka īmāl ʕəd-na
Ramhormoz at-1PL there camel.PL at-1PL
they breed them. For example, towards Rāmǝs [Pers. Ramhormoz], there
we have camels,

(5) *ṣōb abu dǝbbǝs ṣōb lǝ-bsētīn w-ṣōb*
towards Abu_Dǝbbǝs towards DEF-Bostan and-towards
ǝl-ǝḥwēza
DEF-Hoveyzeh
towards Abu Dǝbbǝs [outskirts of Ahvaz], towards Bsētīn [Pers. Bostān;
north-west of Ahvaz], and towards Hoveyzeh,

(6) *ǝhnāka kǝṯīr ʕəd-na īmāl ʕəd-na*
there many at-1PL camel.PL at-1PL
there we have a lot (of) camels.

(7) *manṭaǧa y-gǝl-ū-l-ha daǧǧat ǝlʕabbās fōg ǝhnāka*
region 3-call.IPFV-PL.M-to-3SG.F Dasht-e_Abbas above there
We have a region they call Daǧǧat ǝl-ʕAbbās [Pers. Dasht-e Abbas]: above
there,

TEXTS   347

(8) *fōg   mūsəyān yamm   mūsəyān h(n)āk aktar nās   ʕəd-həm*
   above Musian   next_to Musian   there   most people at-3PL.M
   ġannām-a
   shepherd-PL.M
   above Musian, besides Musian, most of the people are shepherds.

(9) *ənnōb ʕəd-na manāṭəġ ṭānīya b-əl-ahwāz*
   then   at-1PL region.PL other.F in-DEF-Ahvaz
   Then we have other regions in Ahvaz

(10) *əlli   hīya ṣōb   təstar   w-ṣōb   əš-šaʕəbīya*
    REL 3SG.F towards Shushtar and-towards DEF-Šaʕbīya
    in the direction of Tustar [Persian Šuštar] or towards əš-Šaʕbīya,

(11) *əlli ʔāṯār   ʔəlām ham mawġūda bī-ha   w-nās-na*
    REL trace.PL Elam   also existing.F in-3SG.F and-people-1PL
    mawġūda əhnāka
    existing.F there
    which show traces of (the kingdom of) Elam, and our people (that) live
    there

(12) *wa   yə-ḥč-ūn   bə-lahǧa   yaʕni   māšāʔaḷḷā   yaʕni*
    and 3-speak.IPFV-PL.M with-dialect that_is God_willing that_is
    speak a dialect—God willing—

(13) *mən lahǧ-āt-na   al-ʕarabīya   əl-ahwāzīya   əṣ-ṣahīha*
    of   dialect-PL.F-1PL DEF-Arabic.F DEF-Ahvazi.F DEF-genuine.F
    əl-ġadīma
    DEF-old.F
    of our genuine and old Arabic dialects of Ahvaz.

(14) *ṭabʕan   hənāka ʔaktar həm   nās   sāknīn*
    of_course there   most 3PL.M people live.AP.PL.M
    Of course, most of the people living there

(15) *həm   čaʕab y-gəll-ū-l-həm   y-gəl-həm   čaʕab*
    3PL.M Kaab 3-call.IPFV-PL.M-to-3PL.M 3SG.M-call.IPFV-3PL.M Kaab
    they are called Čaʕab, they are called Čaʕab,

CHAPTER 5

(16) *əlli sāknīn   hnāka w-ʔāl kaṯīr   sāknīn*
REL live.AP.PL.M there and-Al_Kathir live.AP.PL.M
(those) who are living there; and the ʔĀl Kaṯīr (also) live (there),

(17) *tamīm sāknīn   hnāka fə-manāṭəǧ təstar   w   sūs*
Tamim live.AP.PL.M there in-region.PL Shushtar and Shush
the Tamīm live there in the region of Tustar and Sūs

(18) *əlḥadd əl-ǧənayṭara   ᴹˢᴬʔayᴹˢᴬ dəsfūl kəll-həm sāknīn   əhnāka*
to   DEF-Ġənayṭara that_is Dezful all-3PL.M live.AP.PL.M there
w-ʔarāḍi   kaṯīra w
and-land.PL many.F and
to əl-Ġənayṭara, that is, Dezful—they all live there; and there are many lands.

(19) *ḥālīyan ʔakṯar yaʕni   ʕəd-həm ʕāyšīn   ʕala z-zərāʕa*
now   most that_is at-3PL.M live.AP.PL.M on DEF-agriculture
And now the majority there live from agriculture.

(20) *ʕəd-na manāṭəǧ maṯalan   t-rūḥ-īn   maʕ əlʔasaf*
at-1PL region.PL for_example 2-go.IPFV-SG.F unfortunately
əl-əmḥammra
to-Muḥammara
We have places, when you go, for example—unfortunately—to Muḥammara [Persian Khorramshahr]

(21) *ʔaw ʕabbādān haḏanni   čān-an   aḥsan mədən-na   ʔaw*
or Abadan DEM.PROX.PL.F be.PFV-3PL.F better town.PL-1PL or
dəyār-na
town.PL-1PL
or Abadan, those were the best towns,

(22) *əlli   əb-zamān-hən kān-an   ʕāmr-āt*
REL in-time-3PL.F be.PFV.3SG.M-3PL.F built_up-PL.F
that were built up during their (good) times;

(23) *lākən bə-sabab   əl-ḥarəb ətdammar-an*
but with-reason DEF-war be_destroyed.PFV-3PL.F
but because of the war they were destroyed,

TEXTS   349

(24) *w-kəṯīr   rāḥ-an   mən ʕad-hən nās   tahaǧǧar-at*
and-many go.PFV-3PL.F of   at-3PL.F people be_displaced.PFV-3SG.F
w-məš-at   lə-manāṭəg əxrā
and-go.PFV-3SG.F to-place.PL other.F
and many people were displaced and went to other places.

(25) *w-ʕəd-na   nās   mən ʕarab l-ahwāz   hamma ʕāyšīn*
and-at-1PL people of   Arab DEF-Ahvaz also   live.AP.PL.M
ʕāyšīn   fə-l-mawāni   fə-l-mawāni
live.AP.PL.M in-DEF-port.PL in-DEF-port.PL
And we have people of the Arabs of Ahvaz who live, they live, at the ports,
at the ports.

(26) *əl-mawāni   ṭabʕan   b-əṣṭəlāḥ-na əl-banādər*
DEF-port.PL of_course in-term-1PL DEF-port.PL
The ports, of course, we call them *banādīr* [Arabic internal PL of Persian
bandar].

(27) *əhnāk ʕāyšīn   həmma əhnāka ʕarab sāknīn   məṯəl būšəhər*
there live.AP.PL.M 3PL.M   there   Arab live.AP.PL.M like Bushehr
They live there and they are Arabs: they live in Bushehr,

(28) *məṯəl ʕaslawīya ʕarab w-əhnāk   sāknīn*
like   Asalouyeh Arab and-there live.AP.PL.M
as in ʕAslawīya [Asalouyeh]. They are Arabs and they live there.

(29) *lākən yə-tkəlləm-ūn   b-əl-lahǧa   əl-xalīǧīya*
but   3-speak.IPFV-PL.M with-DEF-dialect DEF-Khaleeji.F
But they speak in the Gulf dialect,

(30) *mū b-əl-lahǧa   əl-ahwāzīya fa hāy*
NEG with-DEF-dialect DEF-Ahvazi.F and DEM.PROX.SG.F
lahǧa-t-həm   ʕan lahǧa-t-na   tə-xtələf
dialect-F.CS-3PL.M from dialect-F.CS-1PL 3SG.F-differ.IPFV
not the dialect of Ahvaz, so their dialect differs from our dialect.

350 CHAPTER 5

5.1.4 *War, Buffaloes, School—Memories of the Past*

(1) *ṭabʕan   ḏəkra-yāt   hənna kaṯīra w   w-bī-hən*
of_course memory-PL.F 3PL.F many.F and and-among-3PL.F
məʔələm-āt w-bī-hən   faraḥ
painful-PL.F and-among-3PL.F joy
Of course, there are a lot of memories, and among them are painful ones
and joyful ones,

(2) *w-bī-hən   yaʕni əṯʕadda   marāra*
and-among-3PL.F that_is pass.PFV.3SG.M bitterness
and some—well, (time) has passed bitterly.

(3) *w-ʔaḥad ḏəkra-yāt-i   ʔāna ʔa-ḏkər-hən*
and-one memory-PL.F-1SG 1SG 1SG-remember.IPFV-3PL.F
lamman-mā ṣār   ʕalī-na əl-ḥarəb
when-REL become.PFV.3SG.M on-1PL DEF-war
And one of the memories that I remember (is) when the war began [lit.
"on us"],

(4) *yaʕni lamman-mā bəd-at   əl-ḥarb*
that_is when-REL begin.PFV-3SG.F DEF-war
əl-ʔīrānīya-l-ʕərāgīya
DEF-Iranian.F-DEF-Iraqi.F
when the Iran-Iraq war began.

(5) *w   ʔāna kən-t   ʕəmr-i bḥawāli təsʕa əsnīn halḥədūd*
and 1SG be.PFV-1SG age-1SG about nine year.PL ca.
I was about 9 years old, about that age.

(6) *fa   gām-u   y-ḏ̣ərb-ūn   maḥalla-t-na*
and begin.PFV-3PL.M 3-hit.IPFV-PL.M place-F.CS-1PL
w-dagg-ō-ha   bə-ṣwārīx
and-hit.PFV-3PL.M-3SG.F with-rocket.PL
And they started destroying our site and hit it with rockets.

(7) *yaʕni kṯīr nās əṯkattal-at   kən-ət   xāyəf kəṯīr*
that_is many people be_killed.PFV-3SG.F be.PFV-1SG afraid much
Many people were killed; I was very afraid.

TEXTS   351

(8) *fa   šarad-na   ʔəhna ṣōb   al-fəllāḥīya   ṣōb   al-fəllāḥīya*
    and flee.PFV-1PL 1PL   towards DEF-Fəllāḥīya towards DEF-Fəllāḥīya
    And we fled to Fəllāḥīya [Persian Shadegan], to Fəllāḥīya,

(9) *ləʔan   al-fəllāḥīya   kān-at   bənəsbat   ʔāməna ʔaḥsan*
    because DEF-Fəllāḥīya be.PFV-3SG.F comparatively safe.F better
    mən al-ahwāz
    than DEF-Ahvaz
    because Fəllāḥīya was safe in comparison, better than Ahvaz.

(10) *fa   rəh-na   l-al-fəllāḥīya   əhnāka w-ətʕarraf-ət*
     and go.PFV-1PL to-DEF-Fəllāḥīya there   and-get_to_know.PFV-1SG
     ʕala   ṭaǧāf-t   al-fəllāḥīya
     about culture-F.CS DEF-Fəllāḥīya
     And we went there, to Fəllāḥīya, and I learned about the culture of Fəl-
     lāḥīya

(11) *ʔaktar al-ahwā(z)   mən al-ahwāz   hənāka*
     most DEF-Ahvaz of   DEF-Ahvaz there
     more than (about the culture of) Ahvaz.

(12) *fa   hnāka naxīl   kān-at   əlli   əl   ʔəsm-a*
     and there palm.COLL be.PFV-3SG.F REL REL name-3SG.M
     lə-tamər   w-ən-naxīl
     DEF-date.COLL and-DEF-palm.COLL
     And there were palm trees, that ... ¬ (what's) its name? ¬ dates, and palms

(13) *w-əd-dəwāb   w-əl-hōš   əlli   ʕəd-həm hənāka*
     and-DEF-water_buffalo.COLL and-DEF-cow.COLL REL at-3PL.M there
     and water buffaloes, and cows, which they have there.

(14) *ṭabʕan   al-hōš   yaʕni al-baǧar   b-əṣṭəlāḥ*
     of_course DEF-cow.COLL that_is DEF-cow.COLL in-term
     al-ahwāzīy-īn
     DEF-Ahvazi-PL.M
     Of course, *hōš* means *baǧar* ['cows'] in the dialect of the Ahvazis—

(15) *ʕāyšīn   ʕəd-na ʔanwāʕ əs-səmač   əs-səmač*
     live.AP.PL.M at-1PL kind.PL DEF-fish.COLL DEF-fish.COLL
     they live (there). We have different kinds of fish, fish,

352   CHAPTER 5

(16) *əs-səmač   anwāʕ   əs-səmač   ʕəd-na maṯalan*
     DEF-fish.COLL kind.PL DEF-fish.COLL at-1PL for_example
     əs-səmča   əlli ʕəd-na əḥna
     DEF-fish.SGT REL at-1PL 1PL
     (different) types of fish. We have for example—the (types of) fish that we
     have

(17) *yaʕni kṯīr ahl   al-aḥwāz   y-raġb-ūn-ha*
     that_is many people DEF-Ahvaz 3SG.M-want.IPFV-PL.M-3SG.F
     w-həwwa   ʔawwal šay   al-gaṭṭān w   al-bərzam
     and-3SG.M first thing DEF-Gaṭṭān and DEF-Bərzam
     (and) many of the people of Ahvaz like to eat, first of all, the Gaṭṭān, the
     Bərzam,

(18) *w-al-bənnīya   yaʕni haḏanni   as-səmč-āt   əlli*
     and-DEF-Bənnīya that_is DEM.PROX.PL.F DEF-fish-PL.F REL
     məmayyəz-āt
     special-PL.F
     and the Bənnīya.[14] These are the fish that are special(ly popular)

(19) *ʕəd al-aḥwāzīy-īn   w-bəlaxaṣṣ   b-əš-šəwi*
     at DEF-Ahvazi-PL.M and-particularly with-DEF-grilling
     haḏanni   yaʕni yə-šw-ūn-hən   w
     DEM.PROX.PL.F that_is 3-grill.IPFV-PL.M-3PL.F and
     among the people of Ahvaz, and particularly grilled; they grill them and
     so on.

(20) *w   šay lākən ʕəd-na səmča   məmayyəza bass al-ha   faṣəl*
     and thing but at-1PL fish.SGT special.F but to-3SG.F season
     xāṣṣ
     special
     We have a special fish (that), however, has a special season [in which you
     can catch it]:

(21) *yaʕni bass tə-yi   b-ər-rəbīʕ   w   hīya*
     that_is but 3SG.F-come.IPFV in-DEF-spring and 3SG.F

---

14   Cf. Edzard (1967: 308), who states that the *binni* is a 60–70 cm long edible fish from the *hōr*
     that belongs to the family of Cyprinidae (Barbus Bynni, Cyprinus Binny).

TEXTS   353

y-gəl-ū-l-ha   ṣabūra
3-call.IPFV-PL.M-to-3SG.F Ṣəbūra
it comes only in springtime, and it is called Ṣəbūra.

(22) hāy   səmča-t   aṣ-ṣabūra   tə-yi   mən
     DEM.PROX.SG.F fish.SGT-F.CS DEF-Ṣəbūra 3SG.F-come.IPFV from
     əl-baḥar
     DEF-sea
     This fish, the Ṣəbūra, comes from the sea

(23) lagal   ta-ḏabb   ṭərəb-ha   aṭ-ṭərəb   yaʕni
     because 3SG.F-throw.IPFV egg.COLL-3SG.F DEF-egg.COLL that_is
     because it lays its eggs [in the river]: the ṭərəb means

(24) əl-bēḏ   māl əs-səmač   yaʕni əd-dahāri   b-əṣṭəlāḥ-na
     DEF-egg GL DEF-fish.COLL that_is DEF-egg.PL in-term-1PL
     the eggs of the fish, the dahāri [eggs] as we call it.

(25) ʔət-ḏabb   ṭərəb   bə-šaṭṭ kārūn ʔaw ət-rūḥ
     3SG.F-throw.IPFV egg.COLL in-river Karun or 3SG.F-go.IPFV
     l-əl-ʕərāg   hamma
     to-DEF-Iraq also
     It lays its eggs in the river Karun. Or it goes to Iraq.

(26) fa   lākən maʕ əlʔasaf hāy   čam   səna əl-axīra
     and but unfortunately DEM.PROX.SG.F several year DEF-past.F
     But unfortunately, in these past years,

(27) w-əl-māy   ṣār   māləḥ w
     and-DEF-water become.PFV.3SG.M salty and
     with the water becoming salty and,

(28) w ǧafāf ham ṣār   w s-sədūd   əlli
     and drought also become.PFV.3SG.M and DEF-dam.PL REL
     bann-ō-hən
     build.PFV-3PL.M-3PL.F
     and the drought spreading and the dams that they built

(29) w-əl-māy   əlli xaḏ-ō-(h)
     and-DEF-water REL take.PFV-3PL.M-3SG.M
     and the water that they took,

(30) *maʕ əlʔasaf   əṣ-ṣəbūra   ġall-at   kəlləš əlli ḥatta*
unfortunately DEF-Ṣəbūra diminish.PFV-3SG.F totally REL even
yaʕni   ġalīla
that_is little.F
unfortunately, the Ṣəbūra has diminished totally. (Now) there are only few

(31) *mən nās-na   tə-ġdər   t-ākəl   tə-štəri*
of   people-1PL 3SG.F-be_able_to.IPFV 3SG.F-eat.IPFV 3SG.F-buy.IPFV
ṣbūra   bə-hāḏa   l-mənṭaġa
Ṣəbūra in-DEM.PROX.SG.M DEF-region
of our people that can eat and buy Ṣəbūra in this region.

(32) *š-a-tḏakkar   ʕala   l-ḥarəb   ʔē   ʔayyām əl-ḥarəb*
what-1SG-remember.IPFV about DEF-war yes day.PL   DEF-war
What do I remember of the war? The days of the war ...

(33) *ʔəḥna ʕəd-na kān   dəwāb   b-əl-bēt*
1PL   at-1PL be.PFV.3SG.M water_buffalo.COLL in-DEF-house
We had water buffaloes at home,

(34) *yaʕni   dəwāb-na   w-əktīr   ʕazāz   ʕəd-na*
that_is water_buffalo.COLL-1PL and-much dear.PL at-1PL
d-dəwāb
DEF-water_buffalo.COLL
our water buffaloes, we liked them a lot, the buffaloes.

(35) *w   d-dəwāb   əl-hən   asāmi   yaʕni   ʔəḥna*
and DEF-water_buffalo.COLL to-3PL.F name.PL that_is 1PL
n-sammī-hən   məṱəl mā   yaʕni
1PL-call.IPFV-3PL.F like   REL that_is
And the water buffaloes, they have names, we call them like, well—

(36) *hāḏa   l-maʕēdi   ʕand-a   dəwāb*
DEM.PROX.SG.M DEF-marshdweller at-3SG.M water_buffalo.COLL
ktīr   ʕazāz   ʕand-a   ʕazīz-āt yaʕni   məṱəl awlād-a
much dear.PL at-3SG.M dear-PL.F that_is like   child.PL-3SG.M
The marshdweller, he likes the buffaloes a lot, (they are) much-loved,
beloved like his kids;

TEXTS   355

(37) *məṭəl mā y-ḥəbb   awlād-a   y-ḥəbb*
      like   REL 3SG.M-love.IPFV child.PL-3SG.M 3SG.M-love.IPFV
      hāḏa   d-dəwāb
      DEM.PROX.SG.M DEF-water_buffalo.COLL at-3SG.M
      he loves these his buffaloes the way he loves his children.

(38) *w ʕəd-hən asāmi   məxtaləfa maṭalan   əl-garḥa*
      and at-3PL.F name.PL different.F for_example DEF-Garḥa
      And they have different names, for example the Garḥa,

(39) *əl-ḥōga   ən-nagda əḥlāla əl-yarba*
      DEF-Ḥōga DEF-Nagda Ḥlāla DEF-Yarba
      the Ḥōga,[15] the Nagda,[16] (the) Ḥlāla, the Yarba.

(40) *wa əl-a   əl-a   ʔasāmi kṯīra   wa y-samm-ūn-hən*
      and to-3SG.M to-3SG.M name.PL many.F and 3-call.IPFV-PL.M-3PL.F
      yaʕni
      that_is
      And they have, they have a lot of names, and they call them, like—

(41) *əšgadd-mā   mḥabbatan əl-hən   y-ḥəbb-ūn-hən*
      how_much-REL affection   to-3PL.F 3-love.IPFV-PL.M-3PL.F
      as much as they love them.

(42) *fa   əl-yāmūsa   ʔaw əl-ǧāmūsa   ʔaw*
      and DEF-water_buffalo.SGT or DEF-water_buffalo.SGT or
      əd-dəwāb   yaʕni ətə-ʕarraf   rāʕī-ha
      DEF-water_buffalo.COLL that_is 3SG.F-recognize.IPFV shepherd-3SG.F
      And the water buffalo [he gives three words all meaning 'water buffalo']
      knows its owner.

(43) *yaʕni b-hāy   latīfa ʔənnu əkṯīr ḥanīna*
      that_is with-DEM.PROX.SG.F nice.F so_that very compassionate.F
      ʕala rāʕī-ha
      about shepherd-3SG.F
      Well, it is really nice that it is very attached to its owner.

---

15   Cf. Edzard (1967: 310), who describes *ḥōga* as a female cross-eyed water buffalo.
16   Cf. Edzard (1967: 312), who describes *nagda* as a female water buffalo with white dots on
      her front; he further states that *garḥa* is just another name for *nagda*.

CHAPTER 5

(44) w   maʕrūf ənnu ḥatta yaʕni
and known that even that_is
And it's known that

(45) mā   wāḥəd yə-gdər   y-būg-ha
NEG one   3SG.M-be_able_to.IPFV 3SG.M-steal.IPFV-3SG.F
b-əsṭəlāḥ-na yaʕni   y-srəg-ha
in-term-1PL that_is 3SG.M-steal.IPFV-3SG.F
nobody could even steal it—in our dialect [we say *ybūg-ha*] that means
ysrəq-ha ['steal it']—

(46) lan   bass ət-ʕarraf   rāʕī-ha
because only 3SG.F-recognize.IPFV shepherd-3SG.F
because it only obeys its owner,

(47) mā   t-xalli   tə-mši   waya ʔaḥad fa   mən
NEG 3SG.F-leave.IPFV 3SG.F-go.IPFV with one   and of
hāḏa   yaʕni
DEM.PROX.SG.M that_is
it won't go with anybody else. And (because) of that,

(48) əl-ǧāmūsa   maʕrūfa ət-ḥənn   ʕala
DEF-water_buffalo.SGT known.F 3SG.F-feel_compassion.IPFV about
rāʕī-(h)   ʔaw rāʕī-ha
shepherd-3SG.M or shepherd-3SG.F
the buffalo is known for being attached to its owner.

(49) yə-ḥzən   ʕalī-ha   w   maʕrūf ənnu məṯəl
3SG.M-grieve.IPFV about-3SG.F and known that   like
y-gūl
3SG.M-say.IPFV
He [the owner] grieves for it; and it is known—one says, for example,

(50) ḥəzən məʕdān   yaʕni ʕəd-na maṯal əl-mʕēdi   ʔəda
grief marshdweller.PL that_is at-1PL saying DEF-marshdweller if
yə-ḥzən   ḥəzn-a   ġawwi
3SG.M-grieve.IPFV grief-3SG.M strong
'grief of the marshdwellers': that is, we have a saying, 'When the marshdweller grieves, his grief is strong'.

TEXTS   357

(51) *mən əd-ḏakra-yāt   əlli ʔa-tḏakkar-hən   ənnu əl-ḥarəb*
of   DEF-memory-PL.F REL 1SG-remember.IPFV-3PL.F that DEF-war
lamman-mā ṣār   ʕalī-na
when-REL   become.PFV.3SG.M on-1PL
Among the memories I have is that when the war came to us,

(52) *fa   kṯīr mən dəwāb-na   ʔaw ǧāmūs-āt-na*
and many of water_buffalo.COLL-1PL or water_buffalo-PL.F-1PL
māt-an   b-əl-ḥarəb
die.PFV-3PL.F in-DEF-war
many of our buffaloes died in the war,

(53) *bə-sabab   əl-ḥarəb fa hāy   kān-at   yaʕni kṯīr*
with-reason DEF-war and DEM.PROX.SG.F be.PFV-3SG.F that_is much
ətʔallam-na   bī-hən   əkṯīr
suffer.PFV-1PL with-3PL.F very
because of the war. And that was—well, we suffered a lot from this.

(54) *mawwat-an   lan   mā kān   ʕalaf w ḥarəb w*
die.PFV-3PL.F because NEG be.PFV.3SG.M fodder and war and
They died because there was no fodder and war and

(55) *w   čān   hāḏa   fa kṯīr yaʕni ʔattar-at*
and be.PFV.3SG.M DEM.PROX.SG.M and much that_is affect.PFV-3SG.F
ʕalī-na hāya   hāḏa   d-ḏakra-yāt   w
on-1PL DEM.PROX.SG.F DEM.PROX.SG.M DEF-memory-PL.F and
(there) was ... this, and these memories have shaped us immensely.

(56) *ṭabʕan   ḏakra-yāt   hənna kaṯīra*
of_course memory-PL.F 3PL.F many.F
Of course, there are a lot of memories

(57) *w   ḏakra-yāt   əl-mədərsa ṭabʕan madārəs-na əhna ā*
and memory-PL.F DEF-school of_course school.PL-1PL 1PL um
and memories of the school. Of course, our schools, er,

(58) *madārəs-na mā-haw   məṯəl madārəs-kəm   əntəm hnā*
school.PL-1PL NEG-3PL.M like school.PL-2PL.M 2PL.M here
our schools aren't like your schools here,

(59) əlli   t-šūf-ūn-hən   kəllši   mətwaffar l-əṭ-ṭāləb   w
REL 2-see.IPFV-PL.M-3PL.F everything provided for-DEF-pupil and
kəllši   ʕənd-a   w
everything at-3SG.M and
where you see that everything is provided for the pupils, and they have
everything and so.

(60) w   hāḏa   ʔəḥna məǧarrad zēn   mən ʕəd-na farəd
and DEM.PROX.SG.M 1PL   merely   good of at-1PL INDEF
galam
pencil
It was good if we had one pencil

(61) w   daftar   nə-ktəb   bī-(h)
and notebook 1PL-write.IPFV with-3SG.M
and a notebook to write in;

(62) w   ṣ-ṣabəḥ   əḏa mā n-rūḥ   harfi yaʕni harfi kūn
and DEF-morning if   NEG 1PL-go.IPFV early that_is early must
ən-rūḥ   bsaʕ
1PL-go.IPFV straightaway
and in the morning, if we didn't go early, well early, we had to come in
time.

(63) ʔəḏa mā rəḥ-na   harfi l-əl-mədərsa   t-šūf
if   NEG go.PFV-1PL early to-DEF-school 2SG.M-see.IPFV
əl-mədīr   b-əl-bāb   w-əl-ʕaṣa   b-īd-a
DEF-headmaster in-DEF-door and-DEF-stick in-hand-3SG.M
If we didn't get early to school, you saw the headmaster at the door, with
the stick in his hand,

(64) kān   həwwa y-rīd   yaʕni y-dəgg-na
be.PFV.3SG.M 3SG.M 3SG.M-want.IPFV that_is 3SG.M-hit.IPFV-1PL
dagg
hitting
wanting to hit us.

TEXTS 359

(65) *yaʕni əlḥadd yaʕni ʔəḥna nə-ġra   darəs w*
that_is until   that_is 1PL   1PL-read.IPFV lesson and
hāy
DEM.PROX.SG.F
Well until—We do study and so,

(66) *lākən əl-məškəla   əlli ʕəd-na ʔəḥna lə?an   ləġa-t-na*
but   DEF-problem REL at-1PL 1PL   because language-F.CS-1PL
ʔəḥna ləġa   ʕarabīya
1PL   language Arabic.F
but the problem we have (is) because our language is Arabic:

(67) *lākən mən   t-rūḥ   lə-mədərsa kūn   tə-ġra*
but   when 2SG.M-go.IPFV to-school   must 2SG.M-study.IPFV
b-əl-ləġa   l-fārəsīya   fa   kāraṭa kān-at   ʕalī-na
in-DEF-language DEF-Persian.F and disaster be.PFV-3SG.F on-1PL
when you go to school you have to study in the Persian language, and
(that) was a disaster for us.

(68) *mā   nə-ġdər   nə-ġra   lā   na-ʕrəf*
NEG 1PL-be_able_to.IPFV 1PL-read.IPFV NEG 1PL-know.IPFV
əl-məʕalləm š-y-gūl
DEF-teacher what-3SG.M-say.IPFV
We couldn't read; we didn't know what the teacher was saying,

(69) *wa   lā   wāḥəd kān   y-tarǧəm-na*
and NEG one   be.PFV.3SG.M 3SG.M-translate.IPFV-1PL
and there was nobody to translate for us.

(70) *fa   ʔəḥna maǧbūr-īn yaʕni əb-gəwwa-t   əs-sēf*
and 1PL   forced-PL.M that_is with-power-F.CS DEF-sword
And we had to, we were forced to—

(71) *wa   ʔahalīya-t-na   fōg   mən rūs-na   maǧbūr-īn*
and relatives-F.CS-1PL above of   head.PL-1PL forced-PL.M
nə-tʕallam
1PL-learn.IPFV
and (even) our families forced us to learn

(72) əl-ləǧa   l-fārəsīya   ǧarman Salī-na kān-at   fa
DEF-language DEF-Persian.F against on-1PL be.PFV-3SG.F and
hāy   kān-at   ahad əlli məSān-āt-na
DEM.PROX.SG.F be.PFV-3SG.F one   REL suffering-PL.F-1PL
the Persian language. It was against our will. And this was one of our suf-
ferings.

(73) w   ʔaktar šabāb-na əlhadd yaSni   xāməs ʔəbtədāʔi
and most youth-1PL to   that_is fifth   primary_school
And the majority of our young people, before the fifth stage of the primary
stage,

(74) ʔaw b-əl-mətwassəṭa   y-Sūf-ūn   əd-dərāsa
or   in-DEF-secondary_school 3-leave.IPFV-PL.M DEF-study
or at secondary school, they leave school

(75) wa yə-mš-ūn   əla sūg   əl-Samal bə-sabab   ham
and 3-go.IPFV-PL.M to   market DEF-job with-reason also
əl-faǧr   ṭabSan
DEF-poverty of_course
(and) they enter the job market: also because of the poverty, of course.

(76) yaSni šaSab-na   bīʔənna-hu   Səd-a   tarw-āt   katīra
that_is people-1PL although-3SG.M at-3SG.M resource-PL.F many.F
So our people, although they have many resources

(77) w   nās   yaSni ʔarəd-na ʔarəd tarya lākən šaSab-na   šaSab
and people that_is land-1PL land rich.F but   people-1PL people
faǧīr
poor
and people—I mean our land is a rich land—but our people are poor

(78) w-aktar   šabāb-na mā y-gədr-ūn   y-wassl-ūn
and-most youth-1PL NEG 3-be_able_to.IPFV-PL.M 3-reach.IPFV-PL.M
and the majority of our adolescents cannot reach

(79) əla marāhəl Sālya b-əd-dərāsa bə-sabab   əl-faǧr
to   degree.PL high.F in-DEF-study with-reason DEF-poverty
high degrees of education because of the poverty

TEXTS   361

(80) w-əl-ḥərmān   wa l-ašyāʔ   hāḏanni
and-DEF-exclusion and DEF-thing.PL DEM.PROX.PL.F
and the exclusion and such things.

5.2 Umm Saʕad [A10]

5.2.1 əl-Ḥamda [Girl's Name]

(1) gabəl   ən-nās   tə-gʕad   səwa   w-ət-sōləf
formerly DEF-people 3SG.F-sit.IPFV together and-3SG.F-tell.IPFV
māmən   təlfəzūn-āt
NEG.EXIST television-PL.F
Formerly people sat together and told stories; there were no televisions.

(2) ē   a-sōlf-əl-ha   ʕala   ḥamda
yes 1SG-tell.IPFV-to-3SG.F about Ḥamda
Yes. I will tell her about Ḥamda.

(3) ʕann-əč
from-2SG.F
Once upon [laughs]—

(4) ʕann-əč   w ʕan ḏīč   farəd əbnayya ʔəsəm-ha
from-2SG.F and from DEM.DIST.SG.F INDEF girl   name-3SG.F
ḥamda
Ḥamda
Once upon a time there was a little girl called Ḥamda.

(5) w   l-hāy   l-əbnayya bass əhəya tə-sraḥ
and DEF-DEM.PROX.SG.F DEF-girl   only 3SG.F 3SG.F-graze.IPFV
b-əl-ġanam   kəllšāy   mā ʕad-ha
with-DEF-sheep.COLL everything NEG at-3SG.F
And this girl was always just grazing the sheep, she had nothing (else).

(6) tə-sraḥ   b-əl-ġanam   hīya w   ṣaḥb-āt-ha
3SG.F-graze.IPFV with-DEF-sheep.COLL 3SG.F and friend-PL.F-3SG.F
She took out the sheep to graze, she and her girl friends.

362   CHAPTER 5

(7) *kəll   wahda ta-rği(ʕ)*   *ət-raǧǧaʕ*
each one.F   3SG.F-return.IPFV 3SG.F-bring_back.IPFV
əl-ǧanam   wa t-nām
DEF-sheep.COLL and 3SG.F-sleep.IPFV
Each one brought back the sheep and slept.

(8) *hāḏan   ṣahb-āt-ha   kəll wahda*
DEM.PROX.PL.F friend-PL.F-3SG.F each one.F
t-radd-əl-ha   radda   w   t-əyi
3SG.F-return.IPFV-to-3SG.F returning and 3SG.F-come.IPFV
t-nām
3SG.F-sleep.IPFV
These friends of hers, each one of them came back to her and went to
sleep.

(9) *y-gūl   ḏāk   əl-yōm*
3SG.M-say.IPFV DEM.DIST.SG.M DEF-day
They say that one day

(10) *hīya radd-at   radda-ha   ǧəddām w   nām-at*
3SG.F return.PFV-3SG.F returning-3SG.F early   and sleep.PFV-3SG.F
she came back earlier and slept.

(11) *ǧəf-at   əl-əbnayya nām-at   mā   dar-at*
fall_asleep.PFV-3SG.F DEF-girl sleep.PFV-3SG.F NEG know.PFV-3SG.F
šənhi   əs-sālfa
what.F DEF-story
The girl fell asleep. She slept and didn't realize what happened.

(12) *y-gūl   mən nām-at   ʔəhna hāḏan*
3SG.M-say.IPFV when sleep.PFV-3SG.F 3PL.F DEM.PROX.PL.F
radd-an   əya   sēkāri
return.PFV-3PL.F come.PFV.3SG.M peddler
While she slept, these (girls) came back. And a peddler came,

(13) *y-bīʕ   farəd laʕābə-yāt šəlʕ-an-l-a   ṣūf*
3SG.M-sell.IPFV INDEF toy.PL-PL.F take_out.PFV-3PL.F-for-3SG.M wool
naʕy-āt
ewe-PL.F
who sold some toys; they [her friends] gave him ewes' wool.

TEXTS   363

(14) *ġanam*   *ya-ṭ-an-l-a*   *šalʕ-an-l-a*
     sheep.COLL 3-give.IPFV-PL.F-to-3SG.M take_out.PFV-3PL.F-for-3SG.M
     ṣūf *ən-naʕya ya-ṭ-an-l-a*
     wool DEF-ewe 3-give.IPFV-PL.F-to-3SG.M
     They gave him the sheep (and) ewes' wool

(15) *w* *ya-ṭī-hən*   *š-əsm-a*   *ya-ṭī-hən*
     and 3SG.M-give.IPFV-3PL.F what-name-3SG.M 3SG.M-give.IPFV-3PL.F
     məgādəṣ   *maḥābəs*
     bracelet.PL ring.PL
     and he gave them—What's it called?—he gave them bracelets, rings.

(16) *əlḥāṣəl* *həya* *ḥamda* *nāyma*
     in_brief 3SG.F Ḥamda sleep.AP.SG.F
     And Ḥamda was sleeping.

(17) *gal-əl-ha*   *ḥamda ḥamda ḥəṣēn-əč*[17]   *ḥəṣēn-əč*
     say.PFV.3SG.M-to-3SG.F Ḥamda Ḥamda jealousy-2SG.F jealousy-2SG.F
     They said to her, 'Ḥamda, Ḥamda look what I have (and you don't);

(18) *ḥamda ḥamda ḥəṣēn-əč*   *ḥəṣēn-əč*
     Ḥamda Ḥamda jealousy-2SG.F jealousy-2SG.F
     Ḥamda, Ḥamda, look what I have.'

(19) *ʕēn-i*   *əmnēn*   *ʕēn-i*   *əmnēn*
     dear-1SG from_where dear-1SG from_where
     [Ḥamda responded,] 'My dear, where (did you get this), where?'

(20) *gāl-an-l-ha*   *mən* *d̲āk*   *əs-sēkāri*
     say.PFV-3PL.F-to-3SG.F from DEM.DIST.SG.M DEF-peddler
     They said: 'From this peddler'.

(21) *ʔəhya məš-at*   *gāl-at-l-a*   *yā* *sēkāri*
     3SG.F go.PFV-3SG.F say.PFV-3SG.F-to-3SG.M VOC peddler
     tānī-ni
     wait.IMP.SG-1SG
     She left, and said to him, 'Peddler, wait for me!'

---

17   According to my informants, the expression is usually *ḥənēṣ*-PRO (the form *ḥəṣēn*-PRO
     might be a slip of the tongue) and is used to make someone envy him/her for what s/he
     has; the origin of this term remains unclear.

364 CHAPTER 5

(22) *gāl-ha*   *yamm*   *ḏīč*   *əl-ġarbāya*[18]
say.PFV.3SG.M-3SG.F next_to DEM.DIST.SG.F DEF-poplar
He replied, '(I'll wait for you) next to that poplar.' [she laughs]

(23) *waṣal-ha*   *taʕaddā-ha*
reach.PFV.3SG.M-3SG.F pass_by.PFV.3SG.M-3SG.F
He reached it [the poplar] and (just) passed by it.

(24) *gāl-at-l-a*   *yā*   *sēkāri*   *tānī-ni*
say.PFV.3SG.F-to-3SG.M VOC peddler wait.IMP.SG-1SG
gāl-ha   *yamm*   *ḏīč*   *əṭ-ṭāḥmāya*
say.PFV.3SG.M-3SG.F next_to DEM.DIST.SG.F DEF-ṭāḥmāya_plant
waṣal-ha   *taʕaddā-ha*
reach.PFV.3SG.M-3SG.F pass_by.PFV.3SG.M-3SG.F
She said, 'Peddler, wait for me!' He replied, 'Next to that *ṭāḥmāya*[19] plant'.
He reached it [the *ṭāḥmāya* plant] and (just) passed by.

(25) *gāl-at-l-a*   *yā*   *sēkāri*   *tānī-ni*
say.PFV.3SG.F-to-3SG.M VOC peddler wait.IMP.SG-1SG
She said, 'Peddler, wait for me!'

(26) *gāl-ha*   *yamm*   *dāk*   *əl-bēt*   *əl-baʕīd*
say.PFV.3SG.M-3SG.F next_to DEM.DIST.SG.M DEF-house DEF-far
əl-ġaṣər
DEF-castle
He told her, 'Next to that far away house, the castle.'

(27) *lamma* *əltəft-at*   *mā*   *šāf-at*   *aḥad*   *ḥamda*
when turn.PFV.3SG.F NEG see.PFV.3SG.F anybody Ḥamda
As she turned (her head), Ḥamda didn't see anybody.

(28) *xaḏā-ha*   *ʔaṭāri*   *hāḏa*   *nəsər*
marry.PFV.3SG.M-3SG.F it_seems DEM.PROX.SG.M vulture
Maybe the vulture took her—

---

18   Likely related to the Proto-West-Semitic root **ġarab*, which probably referred to the 'Euphrates poplar' (Kogan 2011: 202); cf. CA *ġarabun* 'a species of trees (from which are made white drinking-cups …)' (Lane 1863: 2242).

19   Cf. CA *ṭaḥmāʔu* 'a species of plant growing in plain, or soft, land … not having wood fit for fuel nor such as is fit for carpentry, and eaten by the camels' (Lane 1863: 1831).

TEXTS   365

(29) *gabəl*   *ənsūra*   *y-gūl-ūn*   *ʕala zamān gabəl*
formerly vulture.PL 3-say.IPFV-PL.M on   time   former
in former times they said (there were) vultures.

(30) *y-gūl*   *waṣal*   *ha-l-ġaṣar*   *gāl-ha*
3SG.M-say.IPFV reach.PFV.3SG.M DEM-DEF-castle say.PFV.3SG.M-3SG.F
baʕad mā *ʕad-əč* *ṭalʕa*   *ət-ḍall-īn*   *əhnā*
still   NEG at-2SG.F permission_to_go_out 2-stay.IPFV-SG.F here
Well. And he reached that castle and said to her, 'From now on you won't
go anywhere, you stay here.'

(31) *gāl-ha*   *t-hadd-īn*   *hāḏ*   *al-bēt*   *w*
say.PFV.3SG.M-3SG.F 2-open.IPFV-SG.F DEM.PROX.SG.M DEF-house and
t-hadd-īn
2-open.IPFV-SG.F
He said, 'You (may) open this house, and you (may) open

(32) *hāy*   *əd-dār*   *w* *t-hadd-īn*   *hāy*
DEM.PROX.SG.F DEF-room and 2-open.IPFV-SG.F DEM.PROX.SG.F
əd-dār
DEF-room
this room and you (may) open this room,

(33) *bass hāy*   *əd-dār*   *lā* *t-hadd-īn-ha*
but DEM.PROX.SG.F DEF-room NEG 2-open.IPFV-SG.F-3SG.F
but don't open this room!'

(34) *ʔəhwa ʕāf-ha*   *w-məša*
3SG.M leave.PFV.3SG.M-3SG.F and-go.PFV.3SG.M
He left her and went away.

(35) *mən* *ʕāf-ha*   *w-məša*   *hīya* *ḍall-at*
when leave.PFV.3SG.M-3SG.F and-go.PFV.3SG.M 3SG.F stay.PFV.3SG.F
When he had left her and gone away, she was alone.

(36) *w-əl-*   *ḥall-at-əl-ha*   *hāy*   *əd-dār*
and-DEF open.PFV-3SG.F-for-3SG.F DEM.PROX.SG.F DEF-room
ləg-at   *bī-ha* *fars-āt*
find.PFV-3SG.F in-3SG.F mare-PL.F
And she opened this room and found in it mares.

(37) *ḥall-at*   *hāy*   *əd-dār*   *ləg-at*   *bī-ha*
open.PFV-3SG.F DEM.PROX.SG.F DEF-room find.PFV-3SG.F in-3SG.F
ʕayūz   *w*   *šāyəb*
old_woman and old_man
She opened that room, found in it an old woman and an old man,

(38) *mʕalləg-həm*   *mən*   *hədba*   *ʕəyūn-həm*
hang_up.AP.SG.M-3PL.M when eyelash eye.PL-3PL.M
hanging by their eyelashes.

(39) *y-gūl*   *hāy*   *ḥtār-at*
3SG.M-say.IPFV DEM.PROX.SG.F become_perplexed.PFV-3SG.F
gāl-ō-l-ha   *ʕēn-i*
say.PFV-3PL.M-to-3SG.F dear-1SG
She was perplexed. They begged her,

(40) *nəzzəlī-l-na*   *nəǧǧəḥī-n-na*
take_down.IMP.SG.F-to-1PL pass.IMP.SG.F-for-1PL
nəzzəlī-l-na
take_down.IMP.SG.F-to-1PL
'My dear, take us down, help us down, take us down.

(41) *tara y-sawwī-č*   *məṯəl-na*
DP 3SG.M-make.IPFV-2SG.F like-1PL
Otherwise it [the vulture] will hang you up [lit. 'make you'] like us.

(42) *w*   *ḥəllī-l-na*   *əl-bāb*   *ʔəḥna nə-šrəd*
and open.IMP.SG.F-for-1PL DEF-door 1PL 1PL-flee.IPFV
Open the door for us. We will flee

(43) *w*   *tə-šərd-īn*   *ləbsī-l-əč*   *yələd*   *wāwi*
and 2-flee.IPFV-SG.F wear.IMP.SG.F-for-2SG.F leather jackal
and you flee (too), wearing jackal leather.

(44) *ṣīri*   *məṯl əš-šāyəb*   *yələd*   *yə-ləbs-ūn*
become.IMP.SG.F like DEF-old_man leather 3-wear.IPFV-PL.M
You go like the old men who wear leather.'

(45) *gām-at*   *tə-ttača*   *ʕala ʕṣāya*
get_up.PFV-3SG.F 3SG.F-hold_onto.IPFV on stick
She got up, holding onto a stick

TEXTS

(46) w-məš-at   tayyəh-at-ha   w   lə məš-at
and-go.PFV-3SG.F leave.PFV-3SG.F-3SG.F and DEF go.PFV-3SG.F
and she left; she left[20] them [lit. 'her'] and went off.

(47) məš-at   gāʕ ət-šīl-ha   w   gāʕ
go.PFV-3SG.F land 3SG.F-carry.IPFV-3SG.F and land
ət-zəm-ha   w   gāʕ ət-ḥəṭṭ-ha
3SG.F-abandon.IPFV-3SG.F and land 3SG.F-put.IPFV-3SG.F
She went and came by a lot of lands and places [lit. she repeats twice 'land has carried her, land has abandoned her, and land has put her'],

(48) w   gāʕ ət-šīl-ha   w   gāʕ ət-zəmm-ha
and land 3SG.F-carry.IPFV-3SG.F and land 3SG.F-abandon.IPFV-3SG.F
w   gāʕ ət-ḥəṭṭ-ha
and land 3SG.F-put.IPFV-3SG.F
she went and came by a lot of lands and places

(49) waṣal-t   wəṣl-at-əl-ha   farəd   bəkān
reach.PFV-3SG.F reach.PFV-3SG.F-for-3SG.F INDEF Place
(until) she came to a (certain) place,

(50) wəṣl-at-əl-ha   farəd bəkān farəd ġaṣər māl malək
reach.PFV-3SG.F-for-3SG.F INDEF place INDEF castle GL   King
she came to a (certain) place, to a castle of a king.

(51) gāl-at   āna ʔa-ḍall-an   bə-hāḏa   ġaṣər māl
say.PFV-3SG.F 1SG 1SG-stay.IPFV-1SG in-DEM.PROX.SG.M castle GL
əl-malək
DEF-King
She said, 'I will stay in this, the king's castle.'

(52) y-gūl   mən ḍall-at   ʕənd-a gāl-ō-l-ha
3SG.M-say.IPFV when stay.PFV-3SG.F at-3SG.M say.PFV-3PL.M-to-3SG.F
As she stayed there. They said to her:

(53) ča ʔanti mā y-ṣīr   ət-ḍall-īn   əblāya šəġəl
DP 2SG.F NEG 3SG.M-become.IPFV 2-stay.IPFV-SG.F without work
'Hey you, you can't just stay here without working.'

---

20   Cf. Iraqi Arabi *tayyah* 'to lose, mislead, lead astray, confuse, confound' (WB: 61).

368 CHAPTER 5

(54) *mā   gāl-ō-l-ha*   *ḥasb-*[21] *āna*   *mū   šāyəb*
NEG say.PFV-3PL.M-to-3SG.F in_the_opinion_of-1SG NEG old_man
'No', she responded [lit. 'they said to her', probably mistakenly said by the
story-teller instead of 'she said to them'], 'Am I not an old man [i.e. too old
to work]?'

(55) *gāl-ō-l-ha*   *yā   šwayyəb*   *əl-xēr*
say.PFV-3PL.M-to-3SG.F VOC old_man.DIM DEF-good
na-ṭī-k   *hōš*   *tə-sraḥ*   *bī-hən*
1PL-give.IPFV-2SG.M COW.COLL 2SG.M-graze.IPFV with-3PL.F
They said to her: 'Dear old man, we give you cows to look after.'

(56) *gāl*   *āna əl-hōš*   *y-šarrəd*   *w   mā   bī-ya*
say.PFV-3SG.M 1SG DEF-cow.COLL 3SG.M-stray.IPFV and NEG in-1SG
She[22] replied, 'The cows, they stray; I'm not able (to do this job),

(57) *mā   ʔa-gdar*   *āna*
NEG 1SG-be_able.IPFV 1SG
I can't.'

(58) *gāl-ō-l-ha*   *ġanam*   *gāl-aw*   *l-əš-šāyəb*
say.PFV-3PL.M-to-3SG.F sheep.COLL say.PFV-3PL.M to-DEF-old_man
They told her, '(We give you) sheep'; they said to the old man

(59) *hīya   hīya   bnayya məṭəl ət-tərīg   ḥalā-t-ha*
3SG.F 3SG.F girl   like   DEF-light beauty-F.CS-3SG.F
—in fact (the old man) was the girl, whose beauty was like light,

(60) *bass mā   yə-dr-ūn*   *bī-ha   lābsa-t-əl-ha*
but   NEG 3-know.IPFV-PL.M in-3SG.F wear.AP.SG.F-F.CS-for-3SG.F
yələd
leather
but they didn't know that, because she was wearing a leather—

---

21   Meißner also mentions *ḥasbālah* 'he means' for Kwayriš/Babylon Arabic (1903: XXXVIII);
     cf. WB: 99 on "*ḥazbāl* (< *ḥasab bāl*) /with pronominal suffix/ in the opinion of" in Iraqi
     Arabic.

22   Actually the teller says 'he (said)' and she continues switching between M.SG and SG.F
     forms from here onwards when referring to the girl disguised as an old man. For the sake
     of a better understanding of the story, the author will always translate with SG.F forms
     wherever the agent is the disguised girl.

TEXTS   369

(61) na-ṭī-k   ġanam   gāl-həm
1PL-give.IPFV-2SG.M sheep.COLL say.PFV.3SG.M-3PL.M
'We give you sheep'. She responded to them,

(62) əl-ġanam   y-šarrəd   w   mā bī-ya   ʕalī-h
DEF-sheep.COLL 3SG.M-stray.IPFV and NEG in-1SG on-3SG.M
'Sheep run away; I am not able to do this.'

(63) gāl-ō-l-ha   ča na-ṭī-č   əbšūš   w
say.PFV-3PL.M-to-3SG.F DP 1PL-give.IPFV-2SG.F small_duck.PL and
bṭūṭa
duck.PL
They told her, 'So then we give you (small) ducks [əbšūš[23]] and ducks
[əbṭūṭ],

(64) t-sarḥ-īn   bī-(h)   tə-sraḥ   bī-han
2-graze.IPFV-SG.F with-3SG.M 2SG.M-graze.IPFV with-3PL.F
and you take care of them; you let them forage'.

(65) gal-l-a   xōš y-gūl   hīya bəʕd-at
say.PFV.3SG.M-to-3SG.M DP 3SG.M-say.IPFV 3SG.F go_away.PFV-3SG.F
ʕan ən-nazīl
from DEF-camp
And he [the girl disguised as an old man] said, 'Alright.' Well, then she
went away from the camp,

(66) tə-sraḥ   b-əl-əbšūš   w   b-əl-əbṭūṭ
3SG.F-graze.IPFV with-DEF-small_duck.PL and with-DEF-duck.PL
taking out the (small) ducks and the ducks to forage.

(67) y-gūl   šāf-at   əlwādəm maḥḥad nəzl-at
3SG.M-say.IPFV see.PFV-3SG.F people nobody take_off.PFV-3SG.F
yəld əl-wāwi
leather DEF-jackal
She saw no one there (so) she took off the jackal leather

---

23   Cf. WB (35) on Iraqi Arabic 'A variety of large, light colored domesticated duck'; however,
     according to LA (116) and my informants, the bašša is smaller than the baṭṭa, but both are
     domesticated ducks.

(68) w nəzl-at šaʕər rās-ha əš-šaʕr ha-l-ḥadd
and take_off.PFV-3SG.F hair head-3SG.F DEF-hair DEM-DEF-limit
y-gūm yə-gʕad
3SG.M-get_up.IPFV 3SG.M-sit_down.IPFV
and let her hair down [lit. 'head hair']—the hair was this long,

(69) ḥəlwa ḥēl tə-ktəl əmn-əl-ḥala
beautiful.F very 3SG.F-kill.IPFV from-DEF-beauty
very beautiful, killing with its beauty—

(70) nəzl-at šaʕər-ha
take_down.PFV-3SG.F hair-3SG.F
she let her hair down,

(71) ḏəbḥ-at-əl-ha baṭṭ šəw-att-a
kill.PFV-3SG.F-for-3SG.F duck grill.PFV-3SG.F-3SG.M
kəl-att-a
eat.PFV-3SG.F-3SG.M
killed a duck, grilled it, and ate it.

(72) xō rawwaḥ-an al-əbṭūṭ fəgd-ō-hən
DP come_back.PFV-3PL.F DEF-duck.PL count.PFV-3PL.M-3PL.F
The ducks came back[24] and they [the townspeople] counted[25] them.

(73) gāl-ō-l-ha ča baʕad waḥda
say.PFV-3PL.M-to-3SG.F DP still one.F
They said to her: 'Hey, one is missing!'

(74) gāl-at-əl-həm al-wāwi kəlā-ha
say.PFV-3SG.F-to-3PL.M DEF-jackal eat.PFV.3SG.M-3SG.F
She told them, 'The jackal ate it.'

(75) nōba nōbtēn ṯalāṯ ḏāk al-yōm əbn əl-malək
once twice three DEM.DIST.SG.M DEF-day son DEF-king
naṭar-ha
watch.PFV.3SG.M-3SG.F

---

24 LA (343): "*rawwaḥat əl-ġanam* '[the sheep] arrived at or came back to its lodging-place'".
25 *fəgad* 'to count' may be connected with CA *faqad* 'look for something lost' (Wahrmund 1877b: 424).

TEXTS   371

Once, twice, three times [she told them that same story]. (But) one day
the king's son watched her.

(76) *gāl   balla ?a-rd   a-šūf   šənhi l-ġaṣṣa*
     say.PFV.3SG.M DP   1SG-want.IPFV 1SG-see.IPFV what.F DEF-story
     He said [to himself], 'Let's see, I want to see what's the story

(77) *hāḏ   aš-šāyəb   yōmīya baṭṭ mā*
     DEM.PROX.SG.M DEF-old_man daily   duck NEG
     yə-lfī²⁶   ʕalē-na
     3SG.M-come_back.IPFV on-1PL
     of this old man, [and the reason] each day one duck doesn't come back
     to us.'

(78) *y-gūl   lamma šāf-ha   əbn al-malək*
     3SG.M-say.IPFV when see.PFV.3SG.M-3SG.F son DEF-king
     When the king's son saw her—

(79) *həlwa   ḥēl w-əš-šaʕr   ət-gūl   šərṭān ḏahab*
     beautiful.F very and-DEF-hair 2SG.M-say.IPFV cord   gold
     this beauty and the hair like golden cord—

(80) *šāf-ha   gal-l-a   ča*
     see.PFV.3SG.M-3SG.F say.PFV.3SG.M-to-3SG.M DP
     He saw her and said, 'Let's see.'

(81) *mā y-xāləf   y-gūl   gāl-ha   ča nti*
     NEG 3SG.M-matter.IPFV 3SG.M-say.IPFV say.PFV.3SG.M-3SG.F DP 2SG.F
     bayyna   ?ənti
     obvious.F 2SG.F
     Then he brought her (back)²⁷ and said to her 'It's obvious, you

(82) *lābsa-t-l-əč   yələd ənti mūhu   šāyəb   əbnayya*
     wear.AP.SG.F-F.CS-for-2SG.F leather 2SG.F NEG.SG.M old_man girl
     (just) wear a leather, you are not [lit. 'he is not'] an old man but a girl.'

---

26   LA (670): "*lifa yilfi* 'to come (back)'"; cf. Holes (2001: 481) and the references there on *lifa*
     (*ʕala*) 'to arrive at, visit' in Bahraini and Najdi Arabic.

27   Maybe she means that he brought her back to the castle.

372 CHAPTER 5

(83) *ḥatta əbn əl-malək gāl kūn ā-xəd-ha*
until son DEF-king say.PFV.3SG.M must 1SG-marry.IPFV-3SG.F
So the king's son said, 'I have to marry her'.

(84) *kaḍḍ w xaḏā-ha əbn əl-malək*
take.PFV.3SG.M and marry.PFV.3SG.M-3SG.F son DEF-king
šūfi-ha wēn
see.IMP.SG.F-3SG.F where
So he [lit. 'grasped and'] married her, the king's son. See what she has
become,

(85) *mən sāraḥa lē ṣəf-at əhya*
when grazing.F until remain.PFV-3SG.F 3SG.F
from herding (sheep) she has become—

(86) *māxəḏ-ha əbn əl-malək*
take.AP.SG.M-3SG.F son DEF-king
the king's son took her as his wife.

(87) *ē w baʕad waḥda tə-rd-īn a-sōləf-əč baʕad*
yes and still one.F 2-want.IPFV-SG.F 1SG-tell.IPFV-2SG.F still
waḥda
one.F
And do you want me to tell you yet another story?

5.3 ʕArab (ʕazīb) [A12], Semi-Nomads

5.3.1 *Conversations with Three Women*
Speakers: three women (A, B, C); Abu ʕAdnān (N); and Maryam Q. (M)

(1) A
ʔəbra n-dəgg ʔəbra w ṣxām-a
needle 1PL-hit.IPFV needle and soot-3SG.M
a-smallā ʕalē-kəm ṣxām əl-fānūs
1SG-say_the_name_of_God.IPFV on-2PL.M soot DEF-oil_lamp
We put a needle and (take) soot—the name of God upon you—soot of
the oil lamp.

TEXTS 373

(2) A

xō əl-fānūs ən-ṭēḥ mənnā məṭl as-səmād
DP DEF-oil_lamp 1PL-take.IPFV from_here like DEF-dung
Well, the oil lamp we take from it (some)like manure (?),

(3) A

w-ən-ḥaṭṭ-a ab-saḥan w waḥda
and-1PL-put.IPFV-3SG.M on-plate and one.F
ta-nǧaš-əl-na hāḏa hāḏa
3SG.F-tattoo.IPFV-for-1PL DEM.PROX.SG.M DEM.PROX.SG.M
hāḏa ʕayūn-na
DEM.PROX.SG.M eye.PL-1PL
and we put it on a plate, and one tattoos us this and this and this, our eyes.

(4) M

bə-ṣxām əl-fānūs y-dəgg-an
with-soot DEF-oil_lamp 3-tattoo.IPFV-PL.F
With soot of the oil lamp they made the tattoos.

(5) N

hāy əb-yōm banāt čən-tan
DEM.PROX.SG.F on-day girl.PL be.PFV-2PL.F
This was when you were girls.

(6) A

b-yōm čən-na ǧawān-īya
on-day be.PFV-1PL young-PL.M
When we were young.

(7) M

ʕad-kəm fānūs baḷḷa yībī-h a-rāwī-ha
at-2PL.M oil_lamp DP bring.IMP.SG.F-3SG.M 1SG-show.IPFV-3SG.F
Do you have an oil lamp? Please bring it so I can show it to her [she means me].

(8) N

ət-ḥall-an rāḥ-čan
2-make_pretty.IPFV-PL.F self-2PL.F
You made yourselves pretty.

(9)   A
 ē n-ḥalli   rāḥ(-na)
 yes 1PL-make_pretty.IPFV self(-1PL)
 Yes, we made (our)selves pretty.

(10) B
 fānūs ʕad-həm bass mā a-dri   wēn
 oil_lamp at-3PL.M but NEG 1SG-know.IPFV where
 They have an oil lamp, but I don't know where.

(11) N
 ta-ʕərəf   əl-fānūs rāwē-t-ha
 3SG.F-know.IPFV DEF-oil_lamp show.PFV-1SG-3SG.F
 She knows what a *fānūs* ('oil lamp') is, I showed it to her.

(12) A
 fānūs əbbaṭn əbbaṭn əl-kāntīna
 oil_lamp inside inside DEF-trailer
 The oil lamp is inside the trailer.

(13) B
 ḍaw y-šəʕl-ūn   bī-(h)
 light 3-ignite.IPFV-PL.M with-3SG.M
 This one, they make light with it.

(14) M
 hāḏi   y-šəʕl-ūn   bī-(h) ḍaw
 DEM.PROX.SG.F 3-ignite.IPFV-PL.M with-3SG.M light
 They make light with it.

(15) N
 l-ən-nūr b-əl-lēl
 for-DEF-light in-DEF-night
 For the light, at night.

(16) M
 fahəm-ti   y-ḥaṭṭ-ūn bī-(h) nafəṭ əšwayyūn
 understand.PFV-2SG.F 3-put.IPFV-PL.M in-3SG.M oil a_little_bit
 Do you know? They put oil in it, some.

TEXTS

(17) A
əftēma yību-h   il-yā   aku   b-əl-kāntīna   fānūs-na
Ftēma bring.IMP.SG.F-3SG.M to-1SG EXIST in-DEF-trailer oil_lamp-1PL
z-zaḡīr
DEF-small
Bring it to me. Ftēma, there is a small oil lamp in the trailer;

(18) A
yību-(h)   lō   č-čəbīr   əḡrəyyba yību
bring.IMP.SG.F-3SG.M or DEF-big Ġrayyba bring.IMP.SG.F
l-fānūs
DEF-oil_lamp
bring it (to me), or the big one. Ġrayyba, bring (me) the oil lamp!

(19) B
ʕārəf-t-a   šāyf-t-a   hīya
know.AP.SG-F.CS-3SG.M see.AP.SG-F.CS-3SG.M 3SG.F
ʕārəf-t-a   ʕārəf-t-a   šāyəf-t-a
know.AP.SG-F.CS-3SG.M know.AP.SG-F.CS-3SG.M see.AP.SG-F.CS-3SG.M
She knows it, she's seen it, she knows it, she knows it, she's seen it.

(20) N
šūfi   kēf[28] y-ṭabx-ūn   b-ən-nār   hāda
see.IMP.SG.F how 3-cook.IPFV-PL.M in-DEF-fire DEM.PROX.SG.M
Do you see how they cook? On the fire. This—

(21) M
mā   ʕad-kəm gās ča
NEG at-2PL.M gas DP
Say, don't you have gas?

(22) N
hassa əl-ǧədər ḥāṭṭ-īn   ʕala šənhi   hāy
now DEF-pot put.AP-PL.M on what.F DEM.PROX.SG.F
š-ət-samm-ūn   ən-nār
what-2-call.IPFV-PL.M DEF-fire
Now the pot you have put (there), how do you call the fire?

---

28   Generally, the KhA interrogative pronoun for 'how?' is *šlōn*; Abu ʕAdnān probably tries to
      use what he considers a more educated register.

(23) A
nār
Fire
Fire.

(24) N
la   šənhi   mən   nār   y-gəl-ū-l-a   hāy
NEG what.F of   fire 3-call.IPFV-PL.M-to-3SG.M DEM.PROX.SG.F
No, what kind of fire do you call this?

(25) A
karab
nodule.COLL
Nodules [of the palm tree used as firewood].

(26) N
karab
nodule.COLL
Nodules.

(27) N
čānūn
fireplace
Fireplace [*čānūn ~ kānūn*[29]]?

(28) A
kānūn
fireplace
(Yes,) *kānūn*.

(29) N
čānūn   hāḏa   ha
fireplace DEM.PROX.SG.M right
So this (is called) *čānūn*, right?

---

29   Cf. LA (196) on KhA: "*čānūn* 'burning fire' ... *al-kānūn mufradat al-ʕarabiyya wa-s-suryā-niyya ʔuxiḏat min al-ʔakadiyya* [*kānūn* is an Arabic and Syriac word taken from Akkadian]".

TEXTS   377

(30) A

ē   ē   ḥənna³⁰ nə-stələḏḏ   b-əṭ-ṭabəx   ʕala n-nār
yes yes 1PL   1PL-enjoy.IPFV with-DEF-cooking on DEF-fire
aḥsan mən əl-gās əl-gās mā y-fəčč   əṭ-ṭabxa
better than DEF-gas DEF-gas NEG 3SG.M-make_bad.IPFV DEF-food
Yes, yes. We like to cook on fire, that's better than gas. Gas doesn't—it
makes the food bad.

(31) Bettina Leitner

šlōn əl-kānūn
how DEF-fireplace
How (do you make) the fireplace [kānūn]?

(32) A

yalla lō š-əsm-a   hāḏ   karab   māl
dung or what-name-3SG.M DEM.PROX.SG.M nodule.COLL GL
naxal
palm.COLL
(With) dung. Or—What's it called?—(with) nodules of the palm trees.

(33) N

ḥağğīya tawa   a-hyəs-ha   gmayyla məṭəl
Ḥağğīya just_now 1SG-sense.IPFV-3SG.F Gmayyla like
ət-ġanni   tə-nʕi
3SG.F-sing.IPFV 3SG.F-lament.IPFV
Ḥağğīya, just now, I heard³¹ her, Gmayyla('s chanting), (she was) like
singing, lamenting [lit. 'announcing the death of someone']?

(34) A

ē   marīḏa tə-nʕi
yes sick.F 3SG.F-lament.IPFV
She is sick, she laments.

---

30 In all other places where I have made recordings, the speakers used ʔəḥna for the 1PL inde-
    pendent pronoun, not ḥənna.

31 Lit. 'felt' (see LA: 864), cf. Iraqi ḥayyas 'to feel, sense, be aware, cognizant' (WB: 486); the
    normal KhA verb for 'to hear' is səmaʕ—yəsmaʕ.

(35) N
tə-nʕi
3SG.F-lament.IPFV
She laments?

(36) A
ē
Yes
Yes.

(37) N
ham ət-ʕarf-īn   ət-ənʕ-īn   n-səǧǧəl
also 2-know.IPFV-SG.F 2-lament.IPFV-SG.F 1PL-record.IPFV
naʕāwi-č   hā
lament-2SG.F DP
Do you know how to lament (so) we (can) record your chant/lament?

(38) A
mā   (a)-ʕarəf³²   xarbaṭ marbaṭ
NEG 1SG-know.IPFV so_so
I don't know, not that well [lit. 'it got confused'].

(39) N
šwayyūn   bass hēči   n-rīd-a
a_little_bit only like_this 1PL-want.IPFV-3SG.M
Just a little bit, just like that we want it.

(40) A
la   mā   (a)-ʕarəf
NEG NEG 1SG-know.IPFV
No, I don't know.

(41) N
gmayyla mā   tə-nʕi
Gmayyla NEG 3SG.F-lament.IPFV
Gmayyla doesn't (know how to) lament?

---

32   < *mā ʔaʕarəf* 'I don't know'.

TEXTS   379

(42) A
  ġarība
  Ġarība
  Ġarība?

(43) N
  ēh ġarība
  yes Ġarība
  Yes, Ġarība.

(44) A
  lā   ġarība ġarība mā bī-ha   ʕayzāna
  NEG Ġarība Ġarība NEG in-3SG.F old.F
  No, Ġarība can't, she is old.

(45) N
  ʔənti mā   t-ʕarf-īn   ʔənti t-ʕarf-īn
  2SG.F NEG 2-know.IPFV-SG.F 2SG.F 2-know.IPFV-SG.F
  You don't know? You do know, right?

(46) B
  la   waḷḷā mā a-ʕaraf   āna mā a-ʕaraf   waḷḷā
  NEG by_god NEG 1SG-know.IPFV 1SG NEG 1SG-know.IPFV by_god
  By God I don't know, I don't know.

(47) M
  aku   əda   y-mūt   šaxəs aw ḥazīn   ē
  EXIST when 3SG.M-die.IPFV person or grieving yes
  This [kind of lamenting] is (used) when a person dies, or (for somebody)
  grieving.

(48) N
  ēh farəd ġana ḥazīn əl-ġana   māl-a   ḥazīn
  yes INDEF singing sad DEF-singing GL-3SG.M sad
  Yes, sad singing, its singing is sad.

(49) M
  tə-nʕi   məṭəl əl-ġana   bass ġana ḥazīn
  2SG.M-lament.IPFV like DEF-singing but singing sad
  Yes, lamenting is like singing, but sad singing,

(50) M

bass l-əl-šaxəṣ   əl   ḥazīn y-mūt
but for-DEF-person REL sad   3SG.M-die.IPFV
only for sad people (when someone) dies.

(51) Bettina Leitner

w   t-ʕarf-īn   farəd əġnīya l-əl-farəx
and 2-know.IPFV-SG.F INDEF song   for-DEF-child
And do you know any song for children?

(52) A

šlōn
How
How?

(53) N

l-əl-əfrūx   mən ʔənti ət-nowwm-īn-həm   hēč
for-DEF-child.PL when 2SG.F 2-lull.IPFV-SG.F-3PL.M like_this
ət-ġann-ī-l-a
2-sing.IPFV-SG.F-for-3SG.M
Like that, for the children. When you lull it, you sing for it,

(54) N

tə-nʕ-īn-l-a   t-lōl-ī(n)
2-chant.IPFV-SG.F-for-3SG.M 2-sing_a_lullaby.IPFV-SG.F
you chant for it, you sing for it a lullaby?

(55) A

ət-lōli   ʕalē-(h)
3SG.F-sing_a_lullaby.IPFV on-3SG.M
She sings a lullaby for it [the child].

(56) N

baḷḷa lōlī-l-na
DP   sing_a_lullaby.IMP.SG.F-for-1PL
Come on, sing us a lullaby!

TEXTS

(57) A

la la la la walad wayya l-walad yəmma nām   yā   mən
la la la la boy   with   DEF-boy dear   sleep.PFV.3SG.M VOC of
nōm   əl-ʕawāfi
sleep DEF-health.PL
Ah la la la la la ... boy, with the boy, dear, he slept a very good sleep,

(58) A

nōm   əl-əǵzayyəl   b-ət-ṭarāfi   gabəḷ   yə-nʕ-an   ʕala
sleep DEF-antelope in-DEF-void formerly 3-chant.IPFV-PL.F on
frūx-hən
child.PL-3PL.F
the sleep of the antelope in the void—in the past they sang for their
children—

(59) N

baʕad   baʕad   baʕad   baʕad
still   still   still   still
More, more, more.

(60) A

ēh   hnā   yā   l-walad   yəmma y-dəkkr-ūn-həm
yes here VOC DEF-boy dear   3-remember.IPFV-PL.M-3PL.M
šāl-aw   ḥaṭab   ēh   hnā   yəmma əhnā yəmma
carry.PFV-3PL.M firewood yes here dear   here dear
Yes here, the boy my dear, they remember them bringing the firewood,
yes, here my dear, here my dear.

(61) A

ēh   naʕ-an   ʕala frēx-āt-hən   gabəl   nəswān
yes chant.PFV-3PL.F on   child.DIM-PL.F-3PL.F formerly woman.PL
mū   məṯəl hassa
NEG like   now
Yes, in the past the women sang (lullabies) for their children, not like
today:

(62) A
hassa əl tə-nʕa w y-ḏaḥḥk-ūn ʕalē-(h)
now REL 3SG.F-chant.IPFV and 3-laugh_at-PL.M on-3SG.M
y-ʕāyb-ūn ʕalē-ha
3-make_fun_of.IPFV-PL.M on-3SG.F
today (if) a (woman) sings and so, they laugh at her, they make fun of her.

(63) N
la waḷḷāh baḷḷa ḥaǧǧīya t-ʕarf-īn
NEG by_god DP Ḥaǧǧīya 2-know.IPFV-SG.F
t-lōl-īn ʔənti
2-sing_a_lullaby.IPFV-SG.F 2SG.F
No, by God. Well Ḥaǧǧīya, can you sing a lullaby?

(64) B
əhya marīḏa
3SG.F sick.F
She is sick.

(65) C
marīḏa wēn āna
sick.F where 1SG
I am sick. How should I (sing a lullaby)?

(66) A
lō t-lōli t-wazzəz-ak
if 3SG.F-sing_a_lullaby.IPFV 3SG.F-irritate.IPFV-2SG.M
[laughs] If she sings a lullaby, she irritates you up. [Nāṣər laughs]

(67) B
ənta šrad-ət
2SG.M flee.PFV-2SG.M
(And) you flee.

References

Aijmer, Karin. 2002. *English Discourse Particles: Evidence from a Corpus*. Philadelphia: John Benjamins Pub. Co.

Akkuş, Faruk. 2017. 'Peripheral Arabic Dialects'. In *The Routledge Handbook of Arabic Linguistics*, edited by Elabbas Benmamoun and Reem Bassiouney, 454–471. Routledge Handbooks. London & New York: Routledge, Taylor & Francis Group.

Aksoy, Ömer Asım, ed. 1963. *Türkiyede halk ağzından derleme sözlüğü*. Vol. I–II. Ankara: Türk Tarih Kurumu Basımevi.

Aksoy, Ömer Asım, ed. 1974. *Türkiyede Halk Ağzından Derleme Sözlüğü*. Vol. VII. Ankara: Türk Tarih Kurumu Basımevi.

Al-Ani, Salman. 1976. 'The Development and Distribution of the the Arabic Sound "Qāf" in Iraq'. In *Essays on Islamic Civilization: Presented to Niyazi Berkes*, edited by Donald P. Little, 48–56. Leiden: Brill.

Al-Ani, Salman H. 2008. 'Phonetics'. In *Encyclopaedia of Arabic Language and Linguistics*, edited by Kees Versteegh, 3:593–603. Leiden—Boston: Brill.

Albarakat, Reyadh, Venkat Lakshmi, and Compton Tucker. 2018. 'Using Satellite Remote Sensing to Study the Impact of Climate and Anthropogenic Changes in the Mesopotamian Marshlands, Iraq'. *Remote Sensing* 10 (10): 1–22. https://doi.org/10.3390/rs1010 1524.

Al-Jallad, Ahmad. 2014. 'On the Genetic Background of the Rbbl Bn Hf'm Grave Inscription at Qaryat Al-Fāw'. *Bulletin of the School of Oriental and African Studies* 77 (3): 445–465. https://doi.org/10.1017/S0041977X14000524.

Al-Nassir, Abdulmunim Abdalamir. 1993. *Sibawaih the Phonologist: A Critical Study of the Phonetic and Phonological Theory of Sibawaih in His Treatise Al-Kitab*. London and New York: Kegan Paul International.

Anonby, Erik John, and Ashraf Asadi. 2018. *Bakhtiari Studies II: Orthography*. Acta Universitatis Upsaliensis. Studia Iranica Upsaliensia 34. Uppsala: Uppsala Universitet.

Badawi, El-Said M., M.G. Carter, and Adrian Gully. 2016. *Modern Written Arabic: A Comprehensive Grammar*. Second edition. Routledge Comprehensive Grammars. London; New York: Routledge.

Bahrani, Nawal, and Golnaz Modarresi Ghavami. 2019. 'Khuzestani Arabic'. *Journal of the International Phonetic Association*, 1–15. https://doi.org/10.1017/S00251003190002 03.

Bakalla, Muhammad Hasan. 2009. 'Tafxim'. In *Encyclopedia of Arabic Language and Linguistics*, 4:421–424. Leiden and Boston: Brill.

Banī Ṭuruf, Yūsuf ʿAzīzī, and Aḥmad Ǧābir. 1996. *Al-Qabāʔil Wa-l-ʕašāʔir al-ʕarabīya Fī Xūzistān: Maʕa Dirāsa Ḥawla l-Aʕrāf, Aš-Šiʕr, al-Fann Wa-t-Tārīx*. Beirut: Dār Kunūz al-Adabiyya.

384 REFERENCES

Bar-Moshe, Assaf. 2019. *The Arabic Dialect of the Jews of Baghdad: Phonology, Morphology, and Texts*. Semitica Viva 58. Wiesbaden: Harrassowitz.

Beeston, Alfred F.L., ed. 1982. *Dictionnaire sabéen: anglais-français-arabe*. Publication of the University of Sanaa, YAR. Louvain-la-Neuve: Peeters.

Behnstedt, Peter. 1993. 'Die demonstrativen Bildungen der syrisch-arabischen Dialekte'. *Zeitschrift für Arabische Linguistik*, no. 25: 76–94.

Behnstedt, Peter. 1994. *Der arabische Dialekt von Soukhne (Syrien). Teil 2: Phonologie, Morphologie, Syntax. Teil 3: Glossar*. Vol. 2. 2 vols. Wiesbaden: Harrassowitz.

Behnstedt, Peter. 1997. *Sprachatlas von Syrien. I: Kartenband*. Semitica Viva 17. Wiesbaden: Harrassowitz.

Behnstedt, Peter. 2000. *Sprachatlas von Syrien. II: Volkskundliche Texte*. Wiesbaden: Harrassowitz.

Behnstedt, Peter. 2016. *Dialect Atlas of North Yemen and Adjacent Areas*. Leiden: Brill.

Behnstedt, Peter, and Manfred Woidich. 2005. *Arabische Dialektgeographie*. Leiden.

WAD I = Behnstedt, Peter, and Manfred Woidich. 2011. *Wortatlas der arabischen Dialekte. I: Mensch, Natur, Fauna und Flora*. Leiden: Brill.

WAD II = Behnstedt, Peter, and Manfred Woidich. 2012. *Wortatlas der arabischen Dialekte. Band II: Materielle Kultur*. Leiden: Brill.

WAD III = Behnstedt, Peter, and Manfred Woidich. 2014. *Wortatlas der arabischen Dialekte III: Verben, Adjektive, Zeit und Zahlen*. Leiden: Brill.

WAD IV = Behnstedt, Peter, and Manfred Woidich. 2021. *Wortatlas der arabischen Dialekte IV: Funktionswörter, Adverbien, Phraseologisches: eine Auswahl*. Leiden: Brill.

Berlinches, Carmen. 2016. *El Dialecto Árabe de Damasco (Siria): Estudio Gramatical y Textos*. Colección Estudios de Dialectología Árabe 11. Zaragoza: Prensas de la Universidad de Zaragoza.

Bettega, Simone. 2019. 'Genitive Markers in Omani Arabic'. *Romano-Arabica* 19: 227–241.

Bettega, Simone, and Bettina Leitner. 2019. 'Agreement Patterns in Khuzestani Arabic'. *Wiener Zeitschrift für die Kunde des Morgenlandes* 109: 9–37.

Bettini, Lidia. 2006. *Contes Féminins de La Haute Jézireh Syrienne. Matériaux Ethno-Linguistiques d'un Parler Nomade Oriental*. Florence: Dipartimento di Linguistica.

Blanc, Haim. 1964. *Communal Dialects in Baghdad*. Cambridge (USA): Harvard Univ. Press.

Blanc, Haim. 1969. 'The Fronting of Semitic g and the Qāl-Gāl Dialect Split in Arabic'. In *Proceedings of the International Conference on Semitic Studies*, 7–37. Jerusalem: The Israel Academy of Sciences and Humanities.

Bloch, Ariel A. 1965. *Die Hypotaxe im Damaszenisch Arabischen, mit Vergleichen zur Hypotaxe im Klassisch-Arabischen*. Wiesbaden: Steiner.

Bouhania, Bachir. 2011. 'Le Touat Pluriglossique Ou Plurilingue'. *Cahiers de Linguistique et Didactique*, no. 4: 243–266.

Bravmann, Mëir Max. 1934. 'Vulgärarabisch *'ilā* "wenn"'. *Islamica (Leipzig)* 6: 338–340.

Brockett, A.A. 1985. *The Spoken Arabic of Khābūra on the Bāṭina of Oman.* Journal of Semitic Studies Monograph 7. Manchester.

Brustad, Kristen. 2000. *The Syntax of Spoken Arabic: A Comparative Study of Moroccan, Egyptian, Syrian, and Kuwaiti Dialects.* Washington: Georgetown University Press.

Cantineau, Jean. 1941. 'Les Parlers Arabes Des Territoires Du Sud'. *Revue Africaine* 85: 72–77.

Card, Elizabeth Anne. 1983. *A Phonetic and Phonological Study of Arabic Emphasis.* Ann Arbor: University Microfilms International.

Caubet, Dominique. 2007. 'Moroccan Arabic'. In *Encyclopedia of Arabic Language and Linguistics,* edited by Kees Versteegh, 3:273–287. Leiden: Brill.

Cowell, Mark W. 1964a. *A Reference Grammar of Syrian Arabic (Based on the Dialect of Damascus).* Washington D.C.: Georgetown University Press.

Dabir-Moghaddam, Mohammad. 2018. 'Academy of Persian Language and Literature'. In *The Oxford Handbook of Persian Linguistics,* edited by Anousha Sedighi and Pouneh Shabani-Jadidi, 318–329. Oxford: Oxford University Press.

Dahlgren, Sven-Olof. 2002. 'Arabs in Central and Eastern Iran'. *Orientalia Suecana* 148: 89–94.

De Jong, Rudolf. 2007. 'Gahawa-Syndrome'. In *Encyclopaedia of Arabic Language and Linguistics,* edited by Kees Versteegh, 2:151–153. Leiden—Boston: Brill.

De Planhol, X. 1986. 'Abadan, Ii. Modern Abadan'. In *Encyclopaedia Iranica. Vol. 2,* 53–57. London: Routledge & Kegan Paul.

Denz, Adolf. 1971. *Die Verbalsyntax des neuarabischen Dialektes von Kwayriš (Irak): Mit einer einleitenden allgemeinen Tempus- und Aspektlehre.* Wiesbaden: Steiner.

Devellioğlu, Ferit. 2006. *Osmanlıca-Türkçe Ansiklopedik Lûgat: Eski ve Yeni Harflerle.* 1. Ankara: Aydın Kitabevi.

Dixon, Robert M.W., and Alexandra Y. Aikhenvald, eds. 2002. *Word: A Cross-Linguistic Typology.* Cambridge; New York: Cambridge University Press.

Eades, Domenyk, and Maria Persson. 2013. 'Aktionsart, Word Form and Context: On the Use of the Active Participle in Gulf Arabic Dialects'. *Journal of Semitic Studies* 58: 343–367.

Eades, Domenyk, and Janet Watson. 2013. 'Tense and Aspect in Semitic: A Case Study Based on the Arabic of the Omani Šarqiyya and the Mehri of Dhofar'. In *Ingham of Arabia: A Collection of Articles Presented as a Tribute to the Career of Bruce Ingham,* edited by Rudolf de Jong and Clive Holes, 69:23–54. Studies in Semitic Languages and Linguistic. Leiden & Boston: Brill.

Edzard, Diez Otto. 1967. 'Zum Vokabular der Maʕdān-Araber im südlichen Iraq'. In *Festschrift für Wilhelm Eilers: Ein Dokument der internationalen Forschung zum 27. September 1966,* edited by Gernot Wiessner, 305–317. Wiesbaden: Harrassowitz.

Edzard, Lutz. 2009. 'Qāf'. In *Encyclopaedia of Arabic Language and Linguistics*, IV:1–3. Leiden: Brill.

Eid, Mushira, Alaa Elgibali, Kees Versteegh, Manfred Woidich, and Andrzej Zaborski. 2006. 'Introduction'. In *Encyclopaedia of Arabic Language and Linguistics*, I:v–x. Leiden—Boston: Brill.

Eksell Harning, Kerstin. 1980. *The Analytic Genitive in the Modern Arabic Dialects*. Göteborg: University of Goeteburg.

Eksell, Kerstin. 2006. 'Analytic Genitive'. In *Encyclopaedia of Arabic Language and Linguistics*, edited by Kees Versteegh, 1:82–85. Leiden: Brill.

El Zarka, Dina. 2009. 'Verbale Pluralität in Ägyptisch-Arabischen vierkonsonantigen Verben'. *Zeitschrift für Arabische Linguistik*, no. 50: 51–73.

Erwin, Wallace M. 1963. *A Short Reference Grammar of Iraqi Arabic*. Washington D.C.: Georgetown University Press.

Erwin, Wallace M. 1969. *A Basic Course in Iraqi Arabic*. Washington D.C.: Georgetown Univeristy Press.

Field, Henry. 1939. *Contributions to the Anthropology of Iran*. Chicago: Museum of Natural History.

Fischer, Wolfdietrich. 1959. *Die demonstrativen Bildungen der neuarabischen Dialekte*. 's-Gravenhage: Mouton.

Fischer, Wolfdietrich. 1961. 'Die Sprache der arabischen Sprachinsel in Uzbekistan'. *Der Islam* 36: 233–263.

Fischer, Wolfdietrich. 1972. *Grammatik des klassischen Arabisch*. Porta Linguarum Orientalium. Wiesbaden: Harrassowitz.

Fischer, Wolfdietrich, and Otto Jastrow. 1980. *Handbuch der Arabischen Dialekte*. Wiesbaden: Harrassowitz.

Fleisch, Henri. 1961. *Traité de Philologie Arabe: Préliminaires, Phonétique, Morphologie Nominale, Vol I*. Beirut: Imprimerie Catholique.

Gazsi, Dénes. 2011. 'Arabic-Persian Language Contact'. In *The Semitic Languages: An International Handbook*, edited by Stefan Weninger, Janet C.E. Watson, Michael Streck, and Geoffrey Khan, 1015–1021. Berlin, Boston: De Gruyter Mouton.

Gieling, Saskia M. 2006. 'Iraq Vii. Iran-Iraq War'. In *Encyclopaedia Iranica Online Edition*. https://iranicaonline.org/articles/iraq-vii-iran-iraq-war.

Gindin, Thamar E. 2009. 'Judeo-Persian Communities Viii. Judeo-Persian Language'. In *Encyclopædia Iranica*, XV/2:132–139. available online at http://www.iranicaonline.org/articles/judeo-persian-viii-judeo-persian-language.

Grigore, George. 2019. 'Deontic Modality in Baghdadi Arabic'. In *Studies on Arabic Dialectology and Sociolinguistics: Proceedings of the 12th International Conference of AIDA Held in Marseille from May 30th to June 2nd 2017*, edited by Catherine Miller, Alexandrine Barontini, Marie-Aimée Germanos, Jairo Guerrero, and Christophe Pereira. Livres de l'IREMAM. Aix-en-Provence: IREMAM. http://books.openeditio n.org/iremam/3878.

REFERENCES 387

Häberl, C.G. 2019. 'Mandaic'. In *The Semitic Languages.*, edited by John Huehnergard and Na'ama Pat-El, 679–710. Milton: Routledge.

Hallman, Peter. 2017. 'Participles in Syrian Arabic'. *Perspectives on Arabic Linguistics* 29: 153–179.

Hanitsch, Melanie. 2019. *Verbalmodifikatoren in den arabischen Dialekten: Untersuchungen zur Evolution von Aspektsystemen.* Porta Linguarum Orientalium 27. Wiesbaden: Harrassowitz.

Haspelmath, Martin. 1997. *Indefinite Pronouns.* Oxford Studies in Typology and Linguistic Theory. Oxford: New York: Clarendon Press; Oxford University Press.

Hassan, Qasim. 2016a. 'Concerning Some Negative Markers in South Iraqi Arabic'. In *Arabic Varieties: Far and Wide. Proceedings of the 11th International Conference of AIDA—Bucharest, 2015,* edited by George Grigore and Gabriel Biţună, 301–306. Bucharest: Editura Universităţii din Bucureşti.

Hassan, Qasim. 2016b. 'The Grammaticalization of the Modal Particles in South Iraqi Arabic'. *Romano-Arabica* 16: 45–55.

Hassan, Qasim. 2019. 'Reconsidering the Lexical Features of the South-Mesopotamian Dialects'. *Folia Orientalia* LVI: 205–218. https://doi.org/10.24425/FOR.2019.130710.

Hassooni Zadeh, Abd al-Amīr. 2015. *Mawsūʕat Al-Lahǧa al-ʔAhwāziyya [Encyclopedia of the Ahwazi Dialect].* Qom: Anwār al-Hudā.

Hinds, Martin. 1984. 'The First Arab Conquest in Fars'. *Iran* 22: 39–53.

Holes, Clive. 1991. 'Kashkasha and the Fronting and Affrication of the Velar Stops Revisited: A Contribution to the Historical Phonology of the Peninsular Arabic Dialects'. In *Semitic Studies in Honor of Wolf Leslau on the Occasion of His Eighty-Fifth Birthday, November 14th, 1991,* edited by Alan S. Kaye, 652–678. Wiesbaden: Harrassowitz.

Holes, Clive. 2001. *Dialect, Culture, and Society in Eastern Arabia. Vol. 1: Glossary.* Leiden: Brill.

Holes, Clive. 2006. 'Bahraini Arabic'. In *Encyclopedia of Arabic Language and Linguistics,* 1:241–255. Leiden: Brill.

Holes, Clive. 2007. 'Kuwaiti Arabic'. In *Encyclopedia of Arabic Language and Linguistics,* 2:608–620. Leiden: Brill.

Holes, Clive. 2008. 'Omani Arabic'. In *Encyclopedia of Arabic Language and Linguistics,* edited by Kees Versteegh, 3:478–491. Leiden: Brill.

Holes, Clive. 2011. 'A Participial Infix in the Eastern Arabian Dialects—An Ancient Pre-Conquest Feature?' *Jerusalem Studies in Arabic and Islam* 38: 75–98.

Holes, Clive. 2013. 'An Arabic Text from Ṣūr, Oman'. In *Ingham of Arabia: A Collection of Articles Presented as a Tribute to the Career of Bruce Ingham,* edited by Rudolf de Jong, Bruce Ingham, and Clive Holes, 87–107. Studies in Semitic Languages and Linguistics, Volume 69. Leiden; Boston: Brill.

Holes, Clive. 2016. *Dialect, Culture, and Society in Eastern Arabia. Vol. 3: Phonology, Morphology, Syntax, Style.* Leiden; Boston: Brill.

Holes, Clive, ed. 2018a. *Arabic Historical Dialectology: Linguistic and Sociolinguistic Approaches*. Oxford: Oxford University Press.

Holes, Clive. 2018b. 'The Arabic Dialects of the Gulf: Aspects of Their Historical and Sociolinguistic Development'. In *Arabic Historical Dialectology: Linguistic and Sociolinguistic Approaches*, edited by Clive Holes, 112–147. Oxford: Oxford University Press.

Hourcade, Bertrand, and et al., eds. 2012. *Irancarto*. Paris and Tehran: CNRS / University of Tehran. http://www.irancarto.cnrs.fr.

Huehnergard, John, and Na'ama Pat-El. 2018. 'The Origin of the Semitic Relative Marker'. *Bulletin of the School of Oriental and African Studies* 81 (2): 191–204.

Ingham, Bruce. 1973. 'Urban and Rural Arabic in Khūzistān'. *Bulletin of the School of Oriental and African Studies* 36: 523–553.

Ingham, Bruce. 1974. 'The Phonology and Morphology of the Verbal Piece in an Arabic Dialect of Khuzistan'. Unpublished dissertation, University of London.

Ingham, Bruce. 1976. 'Regional and Social Factors in the Dialect Geography of Southern Iraq and Khuzistan'. *Bulletin of the School of Oriental and African Studies* 39: 62–82.

Ingham, Bruce. 1982a. *North East Arabian Dialects*. London: Kegan Paul.

Ingham, Bruce. 1982b. 'Notes on the Dialect of the Dhafīr of North-Eastern Arabia'. *Bulletin of the School of Oriental and African Studies* 45: 245–259.

Ingham, Bruce. 1994. *Najdi Arabic: Central Arabian*. Amsterdam: Benjamins.

Ingham, Bruce. 1997. *Arabian Diversions: Studies on the Dialects of Arabia*. Reading: Ithaca Press.

Ingham, Bruce. 2000. 'The Dialect of the Miʕdān or "Marsh Arabs"'. In *Proceedings of the Third International Conference of AÏDA: Association Internationale de Dialectologie Arabe: Held at Malta, 29 March–2 April 1998*, edited by Manwel Mifsud, 125–130. Malta: Salesian Press.

Ingham, Bruce. 2005. 'Persian and Turkish Loans in the Arabic Dialects of North East Arabia'. In *Linguistic Convergence and Areal Diffusion: Case Studies from Iranian, Semitic and Turkic*, edited by Éva Ágnes Csató, 173–179. London; New York: Routledge Curzon.

Ingham, Bruce. 2006. 'Afghanistan Arabic'. In *Encyclopedia of Arabic Language and Linguistics*, edited by Kees Versteegh, 1:28–35. Leiden; Boston: Brill.

Ingham, Bruce. 2007. 'Khuzestan Arabic'. In *Encyclopedia of Arabic Language and Linguistics*, 2:571–578. Leiden: Brill.

Iványi, Tamás. 2006. 'Diphthongs'. In *Encyclopaedia of Arabic Language and Linguistics*, edited by Kees Versteegh, 1:640–643. Leiden—Boston: Brill.

Jastrow, Otto. 1973. *Daragözü—Eine Arabische Mundart Der Kozluk-Sason-Gruppe (SO-Anatolien)*. Nürnberg.

Jastrow, Otto. 1978. *Die mesopotamisch-arabischen qəltu-Dialekte. Band 1: Phonologie und Morphologie*. Wiesbaden: Steiner.

REFERENCES 389

Jastrow, Otto. 1981. *Die Mesopotamisch-Arabischen Qəltu-Dialekte. Band II: Volkskund-liche Texte in Elf Dialekten*. Wiesbaden: Steiner.

Jastrow, Otto. 2006. 'Anatolian Arabic'. In *Encyclopaedia of Arabic Language and Linguistics*, edited by Kees Versteegh, 1:87–96. Leiden: Brill.

Jastrow, Otto. 2007. 'Iraq'. In *Encyclopaedia of Arabic Language and Linguistics*, 2:414–424. Leiden: Brill.

Jastrow, Otto. 2018. 'Rescuing Iraqi Arabic Aku and Māku from the Hands of the Aramaicists'. *Zeitschrift für Arabische Linguistik* 67: 90–93.

Johnstone, Thomas M. 1963. 'The Affrication of "Kaf" and "Gaf", in the Arabic Dialects of the Arabian Peninsula'. *Journal of Semitic Studies* 8: 210–241.

Johnstone, Thomas M. 1967. *Eastern Arabian Dialect Studies*. London: Oxford University Press.

Junker, Heinrich F.J., and Bozorg Alawi. 2002. *Persisch-Deutsch: Wörterbuch*. 9., Unveränd. Aufl. Wiesbaden: Harrassowitz.

Kaye, Alan S., and Peter T. Daniels, eds. 1997. *Phonologies of Asia and Africa: Including the Caucasus*. Winona Lake, Ind: Eisenbrauns.

Khan, Geoffrey. 2008. 'Presentatives'. In *Encyclopaedia of Arabic Language and Linguistics*, edited by Kees Versteegh, 3:703–705. Leiden: Brill.

Khan, Geoffrey. 2018a. 'Remarks on the Historical Development and Syntax of the Copula in North-Eastern Neo-Aramaic Dialects'. *Aramaic Studies* 16 (2): 234–269. https://doi.org/10.1163/17455227-01602010.

Khan, Geoffrey. 2018b. 'Western Iran: Overview'. In *The Languages and Linguistics of Western Asia: An Areal Perspective*, edited by Geoffrey Haig and Geoffrey Khan, 385–397. London: Kegan Paul.

Klingler, Inge. 2017. 'Adverbien in den neuarabischen Dialekten Südarabiens (Jemen und Oman)'. *MA-Thesis University of Vienna*.

Kogan, Leonid. 2011. 'Proto-Semitic Lexicon'. In *The Semitic Languages: An International Handbook*, edited by Stefan Weninger, Khan Geoffrey, Michael Streck, and Janet C.E. Watson, 179–258. Berlin: De Gruyter Mouton.

Lahdo, Ablahad. 2009. *The Arabic Dialect of Tillo in the Region of Siirt (South-Eastern Turkey)*. Uppsala: Uppsala Universitet.

Lane, Edward William. 1863. *An Arabic-English Lexicon Derived from the Best and Most Copious Eastern Sources*. London: Williams and Norgate.

Leitner, Bettina. 2019. 'Khuzestan Arabic and the Discourse Particle Ča'. In *Studies on Arabic Dialectology and Sociolinguistics: Proceedings of the 12th International Conference of AIDA Held in Marseille from 30th May–2nd June 2017 [Online]*, edited by Catherine Miller, Alexandrine Barontini, and Marie-Aimée Germanos, Available on the Internet: http://books.openedition.org/iremam/3939. Livres de l'IREMAM. Aix-en-Provence: Institut de recherches et d'études sur les mondes arabes et musulmans.

Leitner, Bettina. 2020a. 'Khuzestan Arabic'. In *Arabic and Contact-Induced Change*, edited by Christopher Lucas and Stefano Manfredi, 115–134. Berlin: Language Science Press.

Leitner, Bettina. 2020b. 'The Arabic Dialect of Khuzestan (Southwest Iran): Phonology, Morphology and Texts'. PhD thesis. Vienna: University of Vienna.

Leitner, Bettina. 2021. 'New Perspectives on the Urban–Rural Dichotomy and Dialect Contact in the Arabic Gələt Dialects in Iraq and South-West Iran'. *Languages* 6 (4): 198. https://doi.org/10.3390/languages6040198.

Leitner, Bettina, Erik Anonby, Dina El-Zarka, and Mortaza Taheri-Ardali. 2021. 'A First Description of Arabic on the South Coast of Iran: The Arabic Dialect of Bandar Moqām, Hormozgan'. *Journal of Semitic Studies*.

Leitner, Bettina, and Abdul-Sahib Hasani. 2021. 'Arabic Proverbs and Idioms as a Mirror of Gender and Society: A Case Study from al-Guṣba (Southern Iran)'. *Wiener Zeitschift für die Kunde des Morgenlandes* 111: 99–120.

Leitner, Bettina, and Stephan Procházka. 2021. 'The Polyfunctional Lexeme /Fard/ in the Arabic Dialects of Iraq and Khuzestan: More than an Indefinite Article'. *Brill's Journal of Afroasiatic Languages and Linguistics* 13 (2): 1–44.

Leslau, Wolf. 1987. *Comparative Dictionary of Ge'ez (Classical Ethiopic): Ge'ez-English, English-Ge'ez, with an Index of the Semitic Roots*. Wiesbaden: Harrassowitz.

Lockhart, L. 1965. 'Dawraḳ'. In *Encyclopedia of Islam II*. Leiden, the Netherlands: Brill. http://dx-doi-org.uaccess.univie.ac.at/10.1163/1573-3912_islam_SIM_1752.

Macdonald, Michael C.A. 2008. 'Old Arabic (Epigraphic)'. In *Encyclopaedia of Arabic Language and Linguistics*, III:464–477. Leiden—Boston: Brill.

MacKenzie, D.N. 1968. 'An Early Jewish-Persian Argument'. *Bulletin of the School of Oriental and African Studies* 31 (2): 249–269.

MacKinnon, Colin. 2019. 'Dezfūlī and Šūštarī Dialects'. In *Encyclopædia Iranica, Online Edition*. http://www.iranicaonline.org/articles/dezful-03-dialect.

Mahdi, Qasim R. 1985. 'The Spoken Arabic of Baṣra, Iraq: A Descriptive Study of Phonology, Morphology and Syntax'. Dissertation, Exeter: Exeter University.

Maienborn, Claudia, and Martin Schäfer. 2019. 'Adverbs and Adverbials'. In *Semantics—Lexical Structures and Adjectives*, edited by Claudia Maienborn, Klaus von Heusinger, and Paul Portner, 477–514. Berlin, Boston: De Gruyter.

Majidi, Mohammad-Reza. 1986. *Strukturelle Grammatik des Neupersischen (Fārsi). Band I: Phonologie*. Hamburg: H. Buske.

Malaika, Nisar. 1963. *Grundzüge Der Grammatik Des Arabischen Dialektes von Bagdad*. Wiesbaden: Harrassowitz.

Mansour, Jacob. 2006. 'Baghdad Arabic Jewish'. In *Encyclopaedia of Arabic Language and Linguistics*, edited by K. Versteegh, I:231–241. Leiden—Boston: Brill.

Marçais, Philippe. 1944. 'Contribution à l' étude Du Parler Arabe de Bou-Saâda.' *Bulletin de l'Institut Français d'archéologie Orientale* 44: 21–88.

REFERENCES

Masliyah, Sadok. 1997. 'The Diminutive in Spoken Iraqi Arabic'. *Zeitschrift für Arabische Linguistik*, no. 33: 68–88.

Masliyah, Sadok. 1998. 'Abu and Umm in the Iraqi Dialect'. *Journal of Semitic Studies* 43 (i): 113–129.

Matras, Yaron, and Maryam Shabibi. 2007. 'Grammatical Borrowing in Khuzistani Arabic'. In *Grammatical Borrowing in Cross-Linguistic Perspective*, edited by Yaron Matras, Georg Bossong, and Bernard Comrie, 137–149. Berlin: Mouton de Gruyter.

Meißner, Bruno. 1903. 'Neuarabische Geschichten aus dem Iraq'. *Beiträge zur Assyrologie und Semitschen Sprachwissenschaft* 5 (1): 203.

Melcer, Ioram. 1995. 'The Analytical Genitive in the Jewish-Baghdadi Arabic Dialect'. *Zeitschrift für Arabische Linguistik*, no. 29: 59–76.

Modarresi Ghavami, Golnaz. 2018. 'Phonetics'. In *The Oxford Handbook of Persian Linguistics*, edited by Anousha Sedighi and Pouneh Shabani-Jadidi, 91–110. Oxford: Oxford University Press.

Müller-Kessler, Christa. 2003. 'Aramaic *ʔkʔ, lykʔ* and Iraqi Arabic *ʔaku, māku*: The Mesopotamian Particles of Existence'. *Journal of the American Oriental Society* 123 (iii): 641–646.

Mustafawi, Eiman. 2017. 'Arabic Phonology'. In *The Routledge Handbook of Arabic Linguistics*, edited by Elabbas Benmamoun and Reem Bassiouney, 11–31. Routledge Handbooks. London & New York: Routledge, Taylor & Francis Group.

Nadjmabadi, Shahnaz Razieh. 2005. '"Arabisert" oder "Iranisiert?" Siedlungsgeschichte in der iranischen Provinz Hormozgān am Persischen Golf'. *Die Welt des Islams* 45 (1): 108–150.

Nadjmabadi, Shahnaz Razieh. 2009. 'The Arab Presence on the Iranian Coast of the Persian Gulf'. In *The Persian Gulf in History*, edited by Lawrence G. Potter, 129–145. New York: Palgrave Macmillan US. https://doi.org/10.1057/9780230618459_7.

Nejatian, Mohammad Hossein. 2014. 'Ābādān Iii. Basic Population Data, 1956–2011'. In *Encyclopaedia Iranica Online Edition*. http://www.iranicaonline.org/articles/abadan-03-basic-population-data.

Nejatian, Mohammad Hossein. 2015a. 'Ahvaz Iv. Population, 1956–2011'. In *Encyclopaedia Iranica Online Edition*. http://www.iranicaonline.org/articles/ahvaz-04-population.

Nejatian, Mohammad Hossein. 2015b. 'Khorramshahr Ii. Population, 1956–2011'. In *Encyclopaedia Iranica Online Edition*. http://www.iranicaonline.org/articles/khorramshahr-02-population.

Niebuhr, Carsten. 1772. *Beschreibung von Arabien: Aus eigenen Beobachtungen und im Lande selbst gesammleten Nachrichten*. Kopenhagen. http://digi.ub.uni-heidelberg.de/diglit/niebuhr1772/0001/image.

Oberling, P. 1986. 'Arab Tribes of Iran'. In *Encyclopaedia Iranica. Vol. 2*, 215–219. 2. London: Routledge & Kegan Paul.

Owens, Jonathan. 1993. *A Grammar of Nigerian Arabic*. Semitica Viva 10. Wiesbaden: Harrassowitz.

Owens, Jonathan. 2006. *A Linguistic History of Arabic*. Oxford: Oxford University Press.

Owens, Jonathan, and Trent Rockwood. 2008. 'Yaʕni: What It (Really) Means'. In *Current Issues in Linguistic Theory*, edited by Dilworth B. Parkinson, 301:83–113. Amsterdam: John Benjamins Publishing Company. https://doi.org/10.1075/cilt.301.07owe.

Palva, Heikki. 2006. 'Dialects: Classification'. In *Encyclopedia of Arabic Language and Linguistics*, edited by Kees Versteegh, 1:604–613. Leiden: Brill.

Palva, Heikki. 2009. 'From Qəltu to Gilit: Diachronic Notes on Linguistic Adaptation in Muslim Baghdad Arabic'. In *Arabic Dialectology. In Honour of Clive Holes on the Occasion of His Sixtieth Birthday*, edited by Rudolf de Jong and Enam Al-Wer, 17–40. Leiden & Boston: Brill.

Parker, Philip M. 2008. *Webster's Turkish-English Thesaurus Dictionary*. San Diego, CA: ICON.

Paul, Ludwig. 2013. *A Grammar of Early Judaeo-Persian*. Wiesbaden: Reichert Verlag.

Paul, Ludwig. 2018. 'Persian'. In *The Languages and Linguistics of Western Asia: An Areal Perspective*, edited by Geoffrey Haig and Geoffrey Khan, 569–624. Berlin-Boston: De Gruyter Mouton.

Procházka, Stephan. 1993. *Die Präpositionen in den neuarabischen Dialekten*. Dissertationen der Universität Wien 238. Vienna: VWGÖ.

Procházka, Stephan. 1995a. 'Prepositions in Modern Arabic Dialects: Some Striking Changes Compared to Classical Arabic'. In *Actas XVI Congreso Union Européenne d'Arabisants et d'Islamisants (UEAI)*, edited by Concepción Vázquez de Benito and Miguel Ángel Manzano Rodríguez, 417–424. Salamanca: Agencia Española de Cooperación Internacional, Consejo Superior de Investigaciones Científicas, Union Européenne dArabisants et dIslamisants.

Procházka, Stephan. 1995b. 'Semantische Funktionen der reduplizierten Wurzeln im Arabischen'. *Archiv Orientalni*, no. 63: 39–70.

Procházka, Stephan. 2000. 'Some Morphological and Syntactical Characteristics of the Arabic Dialects Spoken in Cilicia (Southern Turkey)'. In *Proceedings of the Third International Conference of AÏDA: Association Internationale de Dialectologie Arabe: Held at Malta, 29 March–2 April 1998*, edited by Manwel Mifsud, 219–224. Valletta: Salesian Press.

Procházka, Stephan. 2002. *Die arabischen Dialekte der Çukurova (Südtürkei)*. Wiesbaden: Harrassowitz.

Procházka, Stephan. 2003. 'The Bedouin Arabic Dialects of Urfa'. In *AIDA: 5th Conference Proceedings, Association Internationale de Dialectologie Arabe (AIDA): Cádiz, September 2002*, edited by Ignacio Ferrando and Juan José Sánchez Sandoval, 75–88. Cadiz: Servicio de Publicaciones de la Universidad de Cádiz.

Procházka, Stephan. 2004. 'Unmarked Feminine Nouns in Modern Arabic Dialects'. In

REFERENCES 393

Approaches to Arabic Dialects. A Collection of Articles Presented to Manfred Woidich on the Occasion of His Sixtieth Birthday, edited by Martine Haak, Rudolf de Jong, and Kees Versteegh, 237–282. Leiden: Brill.

Procházka, Stephan. 2008. 'Prepositions'. In *Encyclopaedia of Arabic Language and Linguistics*, III:699–703. Leiden—Boston: Brill.

Procházka, Stephan. 2012. 'The Main Functions of Theophoric Formulae in Moroccan Arabic'. *Language Typology and Universals (STUF)* 65 (4): 383–397.

Procházka, Stephan. 2014. 'Feminine and Masculine Plural Pronouns in Modern Arabic Dialects'. In *From Tur Abdin to Hadramawt: Semitic Studies. Festschrift in Honour of Bo Isaksson on the Occasion of His Retirement*, edited by Tel Davidovich, Ablahad Lahdo, and Torkel Lindquist, 129–148. Wiesbaden: Harrassowitz.

Procházka, Stephan. 2018a. 'The Arabic Dialects of Eastern Anatolia'. In *The Languages and Linguistics of Western Asia*, edited by Geoffrey Haig and Geoffrey Khan, 159–189. Berlin-Boston: De Gruyter Mouton.

Procházka, Stephan. 2018b. 'The Arabic Dialects of Northern Iraq'. In *The Languages and Linguistics of Western Asia*, edited by Geoffrey Haig and Geoffrey Khan, 243–266. Berlin-Boston: De Gruyter Mouton.

Procházka, Stephan. 2018c. 'The Northern Fertile Crescent'. In *Arabic Historical Dialectology: Linguistic and Sociolinguistic Approaches*, edited by Clive Holes, 257–292. Oxford: Oxford University Press.

Procházka, Stephan. 2020. 'Arabic in Iraq, Syria, and Southern Turkey'. In *Arabic and Contact-Induced Change*, edited by Christopher Lucas and Stefano Manfredi, 83–114. Contact and Multilingualism 1. Berlin: Language Science Press.

Procházka, Stephan. 2021. 'Presentatives in Syrian and Lebanese Arabic'. In *Arabe, Sémitique, Berbère … Études Linguistiques et Littéraires*, edited by Nadia Comolli, Julien Dufour, and Marie-Aimée Germanos, 217–237. Paris: Geuthner.

Procházka, Stephan, and Ismail Batan. 2016. 'The Functions of Active Participles in Šāwi Bedouin Dialects'. In *Arabic Varieties: Far and Wide. Proceedings of the 11th International Conference of AIDA—Bucharest, 2015*, edited by George Grigore and Gabriel Bițună, 457–466. Bucharest: Editura Universității din București.

Procházka, Stephan, and Ines Dallaji. 2019. 'A Functional Analysis of the Particle Ṛā- in the Arabic Dialect of Tunis'. *Zeitschrift für Arabische Linguistik*, no. 70: 44. https://doi.org/10.13173/zeitarabling.70.0044.

Qafisheh, Haddi A. 1996. *A Glossary of Gulf Arabic: Gulf Arabic—English, English—Gulf Arabic*. Beirut: Libraire du Liban.

Reichmuth, Stefan. 1983. *Der arabische Dialekt der Šukriyya im Ostsudan*. Hildesheim: G. Olms.

Reinkowski, M. 1998. 'Türkische Lehnwörter im Bagdadisch-Arabischen: Morphologische Adaptation an die arabische Schemabildung und Bedeutungsveränderung'. In *Turkologie heute—Tradition und Perspektive: Materialien der dritten deutschen*

Turkologen-Konferenz, 239–253. Veröffentlichungen der Societas Uralo-Altaica 48. Wiesbaden: Harrassowitz.

Ritt-Benmimoun, Veronika. 2005. 'Witze und Anekdoten im arabischen Dialekt der Maṛāzīg (Südtunesien)'. *Wiener Zeitschrift für die Kunde des Morgenlandes* 95: 259–317.

Ritt-Benmimoun, Veronika. 2014. *Grammatik des arabischen Beduinendialekts der Region Douz (Südtunesien)*. Wiesbaden: Harrassowitz.

Rosenhouse, Judith. 1984a. 'Remarks on the Uses of Various Patterns of Demonstrative Pronouns in Modern Arabic Dialects'. *Zeitschrift der Deutschen Morgenländischen Gesellschaft* 134: 250–256.

Rosenhouse, Judith. 1984b. *The Bedouin Arabic Dialects. General Problems and a Close Analysis of North Israel Bedouin Dialects*. Wiesbaden: Harrassowitz.

Rosenhouse, Judith. 2006. 'Bedouin Arabic'. In *Encyclopaedia of Arabic Language and Linguistics*, edited by Kees Versteegh, 259–269. Leiden: Brill.

Rosenhouse, Judith. 2009. 'Verbal Noun'. In *Encyclopaedia of Arabic Language and Linguistics*, edited by Kees Versteegh, IV:659–665. Leiden—Boston: Brill.

Rubin, Aaron D. 2005. *Studies in Semitic Grammaticalization*. Winona Lake, Indiana: Eisenbrauns.

Salonen, Erkki. 1980. *On the Arabic Dialect Spoken in Širqāṭ (Assur)*. Helsinki: Suomalainen Tiedeakatemia.

Savory, R.M. 1986a. 'Khurramshahr'. In *Encyclopaedia of Islam, Second Edition*, V:65–66. Leiden: Brill.

Savory, R.M. 1986b. 'Khūzistān'. In *Encyclopaedia of Islam, Second Edition*, V:80–81. Leiden: Brill.

Seeger, Ulrich. 2002. 'Zwei Texte im Dialekt der Araber von Chorasan'. In *"Sprich doch mit deinen Knechten Aramäisch, wir verstehen es!" 60 Beiträge zur Semitistik. Festschrift für Otto Jastrow Zum 60. Geburtstag.*, edited by Werner Arnold and Hartmut Bobzin, 629–646. Wiesbaden: Harrassowitz.

Seeger, Ulrich. 2009. *Der Arabische Dialekt Der Dörfer Um Ramallah. 2: Glossar*. Wiesbaden: Harrassowitz.

Seeger, Ulrich. 2013. 'Zum Verhältnis der zentralasiatischen arabischen Dialekte'. In *Nicht nur mit Engelszungen. Beiträge zur Semitischen Dialektologie: Festschrift für Werner Arnold zum 60. Geburtstag*, edited by Renaud Kuty, Ulrich Seeger, and Shabo Talay, 313–322. Wiesbaden: Harrassowitz.

Shabibi, Maryam. 2006. 'Contact-Induced Grammatical Changes in Khuzestani Arabic'. Manchester: University of Manchester.

Shachmon, Ori. 2015. 'Agglutinated Verb Forms in the Northern Province of Yemen'. In *Arabic and Semitic Linguistics Contextualized: A Festschrift for Jan Retsö*, edited by Lutz Edzard, 260–273. Wiesbaden.

Shahnavaz, Shahbaz. 2005. *Britain and the Opening up of South-West Persia 1880–1914 a Study in Imperialism and Economic Dependence*. London: RoutledgeCurzon.

Shawarbah, Musa. 2011. *A Grammar of Negev Arabic: Comparative Studies, Texts and Glossary in the Bedouin Dialect of the 'Azāzmih Tribe*. Wiesbaden: Harrassowitz.

Statistical Center of Iran. 2016. 'Selected Findings of the 2016 National Population and Housing Census'. https://www.amar.org.ir/Portals/1/census/2016/Census_2016 _Selected_Findings.pdf.

Steingass, Francis Joseph. 2001. *A Comprehensive Persian-English Dictionary: Including the Arabic Words and Phrases to Be Met with in Persian Literature Being Johnson and Richardson's Persian, Arabic, and English Dictionary*. London: Routledge. https://dsal .uchicago.edu/dictionaries/steingass/.

Stokes, Phillip W. 2018. 'The Plural Demonstratives and Relatives Based on 'Vl in Arabic and the Origin of Dialectal Illī'. In *Re-Engaging Comparative Semitic and Arabic Studies*, edited by Daniel Birnstiel and Na'ama Pat-El, 127–150. Wiesbaden: Harrassowitz. https://doi.org/10.2307/j.ctvcm4fp0.

Stokes, Phillip W. 2020. '*Gahwat al-Murra*: The N + DEF-ADJ Syntagm and the * *at* > *Ah* Shift in Arabic'. *Bulletin of the School of Oriental and African Studies*, 1–19.

Taine-Cheikh, Catherine. 2004. 'Le(s) futur(s) en arabe. Réflexions pour une typologie'. Edited by Jordi Aguadé, Frederico Corriente, Ángeles Vicente, and Mohamed Meouak. *Estudios de Dialectología Norteafricana y Andalusí* 8: 215–238.

Taine-Cheikh, Catherine. 2013. 'Grammaticalized Uses of the Verb Ṛa(a) in Arabic: A Maghrebian Specificity?' In *African Arabic: Approaches to Dialectology*, edited by Mena Lafkioui, 121–160. Berlin: Mouton de Gruyter.

Talay, Shabo. 2008. 'Qabīlat Ṭayy—Der arabische Stamm der Ṭayy in Syrien und seine Sprache'. In *Between the Atlantic and Indian Oceans: Studies on Contemporary Arabic Dialects. Proceedings of the 7th AIDA Conference, Held in Vienna from 5–9 September 2006*, edited by Stephan Procházka and Veronika Ritt-Benmimoun, 437–446. Münster-Wien: LIT-Verlag.

Talay, Shabo. 2011. 'Arabic Dialects of Mesopotamia'. In *The Semitic Languages: An International Handbook*, edited by Stefan Weninger. Handbücher Zur Sprach- und Kommunikationswissenschaft 36. Berlin: De Gruyter.

Vicente, Ángeles. 2008. 'Personal Pronoun (Arabic Dialects)'. In *Encyclopaedia of Arabic Language and Linguistics*, III:584–588. Leiden—Boston: Brill.

Vocke, Sibylle, and Wolfram Waldner. 1982. *Der Wortschatz des anatolischen Arabisch*. Erlangen: Waldner.

Wahrmund, Adolf. 1877a. *Handwörterbuch der arabischen und deutschen Sprache. Band 1: Arabisch-deutscher Teil, 1. Abteilung*. Giessen: J. Ricker'sche Buchhandlung.

Wahrmund, Adolf. 1877b. *Handwörterbuch der arabischen und deutschen Sprache. Band 1: Arabisch-deutscher Teil, 2. Abteilung*. Giessen: J. Ricker'sche Buchhandlung.

Walstra, Jan, Vanessa Mary An Heyvaert, and Peter Verkinderen. 2010. 'Assessing Human Impact on Alluvial Fan Development: A Multidisciplinary Case-Study from Lower Khuzestan (SW Iran)'. *Geodinamica Acta* 23 (5–6): 267–285.

Waltisberg, Michael. 2006. 'Conjunctions'. In *Encyclopaedia of Arabic Language and Linguistics*, I:467–470. Leiden: Brill.

Watson, Janet. 2006. 'Adverbs'. In *Encyclopaedia of Arabic Language and Linguistics*, I:22–25. Leiden: Brill.

Watson, Janet C.E. 2007. *The Phonology and Morphology of Arabic*. The Phonology of the World's Languages. Oxford: Oxford Univ. Press.

Watson, Janet C.E. 1999. 'The Directionality of Emphasis Spread in Arabic'. *Linguistic Inquiry* 30 (ii): 289–300.

Watson, Janet C.E. 2011. 'Arabic Dialects (General Article)'. In *The Semitic Languages: An International Handbook*, edited by Stefan Weninger, 851–895. Berlin & Boston: De Gruyter Mouton.

Westphal-Hellbusch, Sigrid. 1962. *Die Maʿdan: Kultur und Geschichte der Marschenbewohner im Süd-Iraq*. Berlin: Duncker & Humblot.

Winford, Donald. 2003. *An Introduction to Contact Linguistics*. Oxford: Blackwell.

Woidich, Manfred. 2006. *Das Kairenisch-Arabische: Eine Grammatik*. Porta Linguarum Orientalium, N.S. 22. Wiesbaden: Harrassowitz.

WB = Woodhead, D.R., and Wayne Beene. 1967. *A Dictionary of Iraqi Arabic (Arabic-English)*. Washington D.C.: Georgetown University Press.

Yassin, Mahmoud Aziz F. 1977. 'Bi-Polar Terms of Address in Kuwaiti Arabic'. *Bulletin of the School of Oriental and African Studies* 40: 297–330.

Younes, Igor, and Bruno Herin. n.d. 'Šāwi Arabic'. In *Encyclopedia of Arabic Language and Linguistics, Online Edition*. Leiden: Brill.

Zagagi, Nimrod. 2016. 'Urban Area and Hinterland: The Case of Abadan (1910–1946)'. *The Journal of the Middle East and Africa* 7 (1): 61–83. https://doi.org/10.1080/2152084 4.2016.1148968.

Zarrinkūb, Abd Al-Husain. 1975. 'The Arab Conquest of Iran and Its Aftermath'. In *The Cambridge History of Iran: Volume 4: The Period from the Arab Invasion to the Saljuqs*, edited by R.N. Frye, 4:1–56. The Cambridge History of Iran. Cambridge: Cambridge University Press. https://www.cambridge.org/core/books/cambridge-history -of-iran/arab-conquest-of-iran-and-its-aftermath/6AB6C254CCD1E6D299449CD83 6500498.

Zenker, Julius Theodor. 1866. *Türkisch-Arabisch-Persisches Handwörterbuch*. Vol. 1. Leipzig: Verlag von Wilhelm Engelmann.

Zewi, Tamar. 2007. 'Energicus'. In *Encyclopedia of Arabic Language and Linguistics*, edited by C.H.M. Versteegh, II:22–25. Leiden: Brill.

Index of Subjects and Words

1st person pronoun   75
   see also Suffix *-an*
2nd person pronoun   75
3rd person pronoun   74

Absolute object   321
Active participles   274, 325
Adjectives   138, 232n, 237, 259–260
Adverbs   116–152
   Adversative   192, 208
   Interrogative   147–152
   Local   139–147
   Manner   128–139
   Temporal   118–128
Affrication   19, 21–22, 28, 44, 49, 51–52
Agreement   188–189, 237–238
Anaptyxis   64, 69–71, 159, 253, 260, 268, 280,
   285, 325
Apodosis   206n
Article   *see* Definite Article; Indefinite Arti-
   cle
Assimilation   43, 49, 53–56, 106, 159
Attribution   176–189, 252–255

Bedouin-type   15n, 17–19, 30, 44, 49, 51, 61,
   71, 73, 77, 267
Body parts   236–237, 240

Circumstantial clauses   194
Collective nouns   237–239, 243
Colors   244, 259
Comparative   175
Conditional conjunctions   205–207
Conjunctions   189
   Coordinating conjunctions   190–194
   Subordinating conjunctions   194–213
      Adversative conjunctions   208
      Causal conjunctions   202–204
      Concessive conjunctions   208
      Conditional conjunctions   205–207
      Final conjunctions   204–205
      Temporal conjunctions   197–201, 204,
         207, 209, 212
Consonant clusters   69–71
Consonants   43–57
Construct state   252–254, 325

Continuation Marker   325–326
Contrast   76–77
Contrast *u : i*   *see* Opposition *u : i*
Count nouns   238

De-affrication   56
Definite Article   106, 260
Deictic element /k/   214, 227
Demonstrative adverb   128–129
Demonstratives   86–98, 223–224
   Distal   95–98
   Proximal   87–95
Desonorization   55
Diminutive   177, 243, 255–259
Diphthongs   62, 64
Discourse particles   224–235
Dissimilation   55, 293
Double object constructions   84–86
Doubling   56–57, 82, 175, 256, 287,
   325
Dual   69, 239–240, 253, 254

Elative   259–260
Elision   30, 56, 63, 163, 293, 325
Emphasis   43, 65–67
Emphatic Imperative Prefix *də-*   272–274
Enclitic pronouns   77–81, 84–85, 112, 123–
   124, 174–176, 234, 324–325
Epenthesis   *see* Anaptyxis
Existential markers   104, 213–217
External plural suffixes   240–244, 251–252,
   257
əyyā-   *see* Double object constructions

Feminine Suffix *-a*   236, 239, 242, 252–253
Focus   178, 225, 234, 238
Future   28n, 222–223

g(a)hawa-syndrome   21, 22, 25–26, 71–72
gāl   81–82
Geminated roots   70, 259, 266, 270–271, 275,
   325
Gender   236–237
   Distinction   19, 22, 73–74
Genitive constructions   225n84
   see also Genitive exponent

398 INDEX OF SUBJECTS AND WORDS

Genitive exponent   113, 176–189
Grammaticalization   134, 176, 197, 222

ha-   92–93, 118, 223–224
ḥaḍar   *see* Urban
ham   131, 228
   ham … ham …   132
Have-constructions   323
hāy   89–91
hēč   129–130
Hortative   235
Hypothetical clauses   205
Hypothetical comparisons   209

Imāla   *see* Raising of final -*a*
Imperative   26, 263, 272–274, 278
   Negated imperative   220
Imperfective   271
Indefinite Article   99, 101, 102, 261–263
Indefinite pronouns   98–103
Independent *māl*-phrases   184–188
Independent pronouns   26n14, 73–77, 223, 377n30
Indetermination   *see* Indefinite article
Indirect object pronouns   79–82, 84–85
Inflectional affixes   63, 70, 75, 268–270
Intensifiers   128, 262
Interjections   224–235, 274
Internal plural patterns   240–241, 244–252
Interrogative adverbs   147–152
Interrogative pronouns   69, 109–114, 186, 187
Irreal clauses   207
Irregular verbs   277–278, 286–287

Jussive   235

Lengthening of vowels   53, 71, 77–78, 175, 279n110, 324
Loanwords   43, 44, 180, 241, 243
   From Persian   43, 47, 192
   From Standard Arabic   46, 53n18, 193, 204, 327

Mafʕūl muṭlaq   *see* Absolute object
māl   *see* Genitive exponent
Marshland features   27–28
Metathesis   57
Mixed plural patterns   251–252
Modal particles   *see* Discourse particles

Negation   27, 69, 82, 102, 217–222
Negative pronouns   82–84
Nomadic-type   23n13, 68, 75, 209
Numbers   242, 262, 263–266
   Cardinal   263–265
   Ordinal   265–266

Object pronouns   *see* Enclitic pronouns
Objects   79, 81, 84–85, 324–325
Onomatopoetic   315, 316
Opposition *u : i*   61–62, 283n

Participles   274
   see also Active Participle
Partitives   104–105
Passive   294–295, 299–300, 316
Perfective   268–270
Pharyngealization of *ʔ*   53, 207
Plural   *see* External plural suffixes; Internal plural patterns
Possession   79–80, 82, 160, 163, 178–179, 185, 254, 323–324
Possessive pronouns   *see* Enclitic pronouns
Prepositions   152–176, 323
Presentatives   223–224, 227
Prohibition   *see* Imperative, negated
Pronominal suffixes   *see* Enclitic pronouns
Pronouns   *see* Independent pronouns, Enclitic pronouns
Pseudoverbs   80, 82, 323

Quadriliteral roots   314–321
Quantifiers   114–116

Raising of **a*   30, 52n14, 63, 64, 64n25, 287, 292, 305, 310, 311, 317, 319, 320, 321
Raising of final -*a*   60
Reduplicated roots   314, 315, 316, 318, 320
Reflexive pronoun   108–109
Relative clause   106–108
Relative pronoun   106
Rhetorical questions   180n52, 217–218
Rural/*ʕarab*   17, 19–27, 66, 68, 70, 72, 98n, 117n27, 142, 143, 209, 227, 275, 285, 324n

šay ~ šī   101–102, 104
Secondary emphatic consonants   66–67

INDEX OF SUBJECTS AND WORDS

Sedentary-type 15n, 17–18, 28, 30, 67–68,
 222–223, 261, 273, 325
Shortening of vowels 59, 81–82
Singular 238–239
 Patterns 244–251
Singulative suffix 239
Sonorization 55
Stress 68–69, 217
Stress shift 57, 70, 71
Subordinate clause 195, 198–205, 209, 211,
 212, 229
Suffix -*an* 271–272
Suffixed pronouns *see* Enclitic pronouns
Superlative 259–260
Syllable structure 67–68
Syndetic relative clause 106–107

Topicalization 77

Unit nouns 238
Urban/*ḥaḍar* 17–27, 28n, 66, 68, 216, 270,
 285, 324n

Verbal inflection *see* Inflectional affixes
Verbal noun 321–322
Verbal patterns 274–321
Vowels 57
 Long 58–59, 62
 Short 59–64

Weak verbs 26, 266–267

ʕ*arab see* Rural